The Use and Abuse of Police Power in America

The Use and Abuse of Police Power in America

Historical Milestones and Current Controversies

GINA ROBERTIELLO, EDITOR

 ABC-CLIO™

An Imprint of ABC-CLIO, LLC
Santa Barbara, California • Denver, Colorado

Library of Congress Cataloging-in-Publication Data

Names: Robertiello, Gina, editor.
Title: The use and abuse of police power in America : historical milestones and current
    controversies / Gina Robertiello, editor.
Description: First edition. | Santa Barbara, California : ABC-CLIO, an Imprint of
    ABC-CLIO, LLC, [2017] | Includes index.
Identifiers: LCCN 2016052099 | ISBN 9781440843723 (acid-free paper) |
    ISBN 9781440843730 (ebook)
Subjects: LCSH: Law enforcement—United States—History. | Police—United States—
    History.
Classification: LCC HV7921 .U84 2017 | DDC 363.2/30973—dc23
LC record available at https://lccn.loc.gov/2016052099

ISBN: 978-1-4408-4372-3
EISBN: 978-1-4408-4373-0

21 20 19 18   4 5

This book is also available as an eBook.

ABC-CLIO
An Imprint of ABC-CLIO, LLC

ABC-CLIO, LLC
130 Cremona Drive, P.O. Box 1911
Santa Barbara, California 93116-1911
www.abc-clio.com

This book is printed on acid-free paper ∞

Manufactured in the United States of America

Contents

Preface

This reference book represents the culmination of centuries of events that have occurred in early America from the 17th century to the present. Since then, many critical incidents have occurred, leading to the need to address the police and the community. This encyclopedia was prepared to provide readers with an easy-to-use, accurate, up-to-date guide to the controversial past and current controversies facing our society in regard to relationships between the police and the public. It is presented as a quick reference to the chain of events, technological advances, changes in the law, and precedent-setting cases, confrontations, mandates, and debates that have affected perceptions of the police today.

The encyclopedia provides a unique approach to presenting the historical milestones that have affected police-community relationships. It allows the reader to develop a sense of the "climate" over time, in a clear, concise, and neutral manner—allowing them to increase their knowledge of previous and current events that have affected the way law enforcement carries out its public safety mandates. In addition, the focus on important and newsworthy situations allows undergraduates, graduate students, educators, and laypersons to better grasp the effects these incidents have had on the United States. By focusing on Blacks in conflict with the police, readers are able to evaluate the interactions between the police and the public, and the resulting influences that court cases, laws, encounters (often recorded), and the media have had on those perceptions. They are also able to more clearly identify why certain members of a community might have expectations that encounters with the police are going to end negatively. Those expectations might also affect their attitudes and reactions.

Each entry highlights the effects of historical events and social factors, as well as the influence of the media, in swaying public opinion and law-enforcement response. The value of the encyclopedia as a reference tool lies in the short essays that form the basis of more intensive investigations—a starting point for further research. The selection of topics was based on the most important and pressing issues that faced society in the past and that have shaped our views today. The people, cases, incidents, and events included in the encyclopedia are only a part of the many important factors that are worth examining in an effort to truly understand police-citizen relationships. The topics chosen for inclusion represent a diverse set of perspectives that affect the sentiment of minorities and non-minorities, law enforcement and citizens, as well as liberals and conservatives.

The task of researching these historical milestones is complicated by the conflicting opinions of members of law enforcement in comparison to the opinions of community members. There is a lack of a consensus on what constitutes fair and just treatment of minorities, and the subject generates debates, tensions, and numerous conflicts between the two groups, as well as within the community and among law enforcement officers. Each of the entries includes events and conflicts that shape our culture, perceptions, views, and actions. Attention to factual content and objectivity have been maintained, though it may be impossible to eliminate all unconfirmed information. The editor and authors apologize in advance for any unintentional inclusion of information gathered from sources that may not be reliable.

Topics include historical data on legal and societal limits to police power in early America—important amendments, policing of the past—to technological advances and the rise of organized crime. Specific cases are mentioned, as well as influential persons (Sir Robert Peel, Teddy Roosevelt, and William Bratton, to name a few). Next, law enforcement in the time of the political and social upheaval, and the reactions to that time, are covered (the Kerner Commission), and other important cases that set precedents for future cases (*Miranda v. Arizona*, *Terry v. Ohio*, *Mapp v. Ohio*) to give readers a perspective of the sentiment at the time. Readers will then learn of new mandates for exercising police power (Wilson and Kelling's Broken Windows Theory, the Rodney King beatings, Ruby Ridge). Finally, readers will be able to peruse essays on the intensifying debate about the American Police State,

Police officers are assigned to respond to calls for assistance by foot patrol and by motorized patrol, with the goal of protecting the public. They are contracted to enforce the law, make arrests, issue tickets, and reduce fear of crime. (Americanspirit/Dreamstime.com)

including information from the year 2000 to the present. Racial profiling, police mistreatment of the public, and certain well-known cases are discussed.

In particular, cases that have received recent media attention and those that have led the public to question police motives (Michael Brown, Trayvon Martin, Tamir Rice, Sandra Bland, Freddie Gray, and Eric Garner) are summarized. Additionally, variations in law enforcement attitudes about gun control, dash-cam videos, and body cameras, for example, are reviewed and examined. By looking at the different situations, readers can draw their own conclusions.

The process for choosing which material to include in the publication is a complex evolution of research and the application of the inclusion criteria. The groups included in this encyclopedia therefore represent only 80 of the major turning points, and many more could be examined in the future. The encyclopedia does contain a number of cases that, at the time of this writing, had still not been settled, had not gone to trial yet, and for which indictments had yet to be issued. However, as they met the criteria (controversial issues), they were included. These cases will need to be revisited and follow-up writings will be necessary.

The headings, events, and names include familiar, well-known contributors to the topic of police perceptions, either historically or more recently as news stories. Many of the people discussed in this encyclopedia are familiar names (presidents, leaders, governors, directors, mayors, victims, and offenders). Case law, amendments, acts, television shows, and current political events are also examined. They all deserve to be part of this comprehensive reference source. The 80 essays are arranged chronologically according to when the associated event occurred. They feature major turning points and events about the way law enforcement carries out its public safety and crime-fighting mandates. The goal has been to create an accessible and user-friendly resource for lay audiences.

This encyclopedia was compiled as a guide to review confrontations between the police and the public. Since the 17th century, negative sentiment among minorities in certain areas of the United States (Los Angeles, Baltimore, and Ferguson, for example) has grown. Each entry is about 2,000 words; as a whole, the collection will cover the major turning points from the 17th century to current times. Approximately one-half of the essays will include excerpts from important laws, speeches, reports, and studies pertaining to the subject matter.

The book also includes a summary of events, in order of occurrence, as a timeline. It is descriptive and will assist the reader with understanding the scope of the law enforcement issues that have existed, and why they continue to exist. It will also help set a frame of reference as to how some of the issues between the police and the public emerged and why we are where we are today regarding police-citizen relations. The goal of the book has been to inform people about historical milestones and events that have affected the United States, and to help shape current relationships and perceptions. By focusing on the history of policing, as well as previous cases, laws, and events, the reader will be informed about the context of perceptions of the police by the public. In addition, students and laypersons can critically analyze (with an educated perspective), what is presented to them in the media.

This book is geared toward undergraduate and graduate students who want to increase their knowledge of previous and current events that have affected the relationship between police and the public. However, laypersons would also benefit from the general knowledge they can gain about the way law enforcement carries out its public safety mandates.

Acknowledgments

When my first book was published in 2004, I had three very young children. My husband and parents had assisted me with child care and keeping sane while I completed my research. Now, almost 13 years later, my children are teenagers who don't need me as much anymore, so the burden has also been lifted from my husband and parents.

My parents, Russ and Angela Pisano, have always been my biggest supporters. I'm quite sure my husband, Peter Robertiello, perfected his golf game every day I said I was "busy working on the book" or too busy to go to lunch. I thank him for always telling me he knew I could do it—from writing my dissertation, to becoming a professor, to having children, to writing articles and books. He's never doubted my abilities, even when I doubted myself.

I'd especially like to extend my gratitude to my children: Brie, Gigi, and Joey. They are my motivation and my biggest accomplishment. They push me to be the best at everything I do, as a mom, and educator, and as a writer. I hope I did not take away too much time from them, and I also hope that watching me teach, read, and write has taught them that hard work does pay off.

I am grateful to my students at Felician University for being understanding if I was stressed out about meeting a deadline, and for the endless times they had to hear me talk about "the book." I also want to thank my colleagues at Felician, who have gone out of their way to support me.

I extend deep gratitude for the editors at ABC-CLIO—Kevin Hillstrom and Lori Hobkirk. Kevin originally approached me about the project, and Lori worked endlessly—we emailed too often! Her patience and support is much appreciated.

Finally, I thank my friends, the "Lunello Crew" and the "Aruba Crew," for putting up with me when I was tense and when I complained about how much work I had to do. I know I was sometimes referred to as the killjoy when the group proposed driving to Atlantic City at midnight or hopping on a plane to Florida with no bathing suits. But as we know, anything worth doing is worth the sacrifice. I am thankful to those who gave up quality time with me so I could complete this project.

Part 1: Legal and Societal Limits to Police Power in Early America (1600s–1800s)

FOURTH AMENDMENT

The Fourth Amendment is one of the most cited components of the Bill of Rights with regard to police powers and the rights of privacy to U.S. citizens. The right to be free from unreasonable searches and seizures is a foundation of American identity. The legal system has worked to find a balance between the right to privacy and the government's responsibility to protect the country. As law enforcement officers seek to obtain evidence to stop crime, this amendment has been used to prevent excessive use of search and seizure in this endeavor. This balance has been difficult to obtain and is an ever-present challenge as political, social, and terrorist activities continue to impact the United States.

The Fourth Amendment was included in the Bill of Rights to prevent "writs of assistance" from being used by government authorities. A writ is a court order, and a writ of assistance is an order issued by a court for law enforcement (i.e., police) to perform a certain task. Theses writs allowed the authorities to enter and search any house to seize property identified as being "prohibited or uncustomed." The writs were in effect from the time they were issued until six months after the life of the current sovereign in England. The colonists were greatly opposed to the searches and seizures associated with these writs. The Fourth Amendment established language that identified "reasonable" searches, which would be limited with regard to the area or person being searched, the timeframe for the search, and other procedure protections. The Fourth Amendment also indicated that there must be probable cause for a search to be conducted. The wording of the amendment clearly established the principles needed to limit the power of the police and other government officials and protect the rights of American citizens:

> The right of the people to be secure in their persons, houses, papers, and effects, against unreasonable searches and seizures, shall not be violated, and no warrants shall issue, but upon probable cause, supported by oath or affirmation, and particularly describing the place to be searched, and the persons or things to be seized. (National Archives)

Due to the wording of the Fourth Amendment, in most situations the police must have approval from a judicial representative to obtain a warrant. Exceptions to the

Former National Security Agency contractor Edward Snowden speaks via video conference to people in the Johns Hopkins University auditorium in Baltimore. The Intercept, an on-line news site whose founding editors were the first to publish documents leaked by Snowden, offered a behind-the-scenes glimpse into the NSA's work. (AP Photo/Juliet Linderman)

requirement for warrants have been established through a number of landmark cases, including *Weeks v. United States* (1914), *Katz v. Ohio* (1967), *Terry v. Ohio* (1968), and *New Jersey v. T.L.O.* (1985).

As a result of the court cases involving the Fourth Amendment, rules have been established that have limited the power of the police to conduct searches and seizures of private citizens and property. As the country has changed over the years, the application of this amendment has also changed due to near continuous challenges. Cases involving the arrest of suspects, the search of a person's body or property, searches in schools, drug testing of school athletes, blood and DNA samples of people in police custody, and many other topics have been questioned with regard to the legality of the issue based upon the principles established by the Fourth Amendment.

Three significant exceptions to the Fourth Amendment provisions are the "exclusionary rule," the "good faith exception," and the "inevitable discovery rule." The exclusionary rule was established in *Weeks v. United States* (1914). This rule prohibits the use of evidence collected during an illegal search. This was a landmark case, as it clearly indicated that the public had a right to privacy and unless there was probable cause for a search, evidence collected illegally could not be used in a court of law. This rule has been tested multiple times and there have been exceptions established by the courts.

The "good faith" exception to the exclusionary rule was established in *United States v. Leon* (1984). Evidence could be used in court if a police officer had acted in good faith and believed the search was legal. Another exception is the "inevitable discovery rule," which allows illegally obtained evidence to be used in court if it would have eventually been discovered during the course of the investigation, such as in *Nix v. Williams*, in 1984.

The Fourth Amendment continues to change as the United States experiences new challenges. Following the terrorist attacks of September 11, 2001, many changes related to police powers and searches were implemented in the United States. These changes have impacted the rights of privacy established by the Fourth Amendment. The U.S. PATRIOT Act provided additional powers to law enforcement and federal agencies in their quest to prevent future terrorist activities. These powers have caused significant debates regarding a person's privacy with regard to electronic communication and, in particular, cell phone privacy.

Advances in technology have caused the courts to determine if privacy rights apply to many devices. Wiretapping, the use of surveillance cameras, and eavesdropping were early procedures the courts had to address. New technology has also resulted in the re-examination of the Fourth Amendment with regard to the use of computers, cell phones, and GPS tracking technology by law enforcement agencies. The case of the *United States v. Jones* (2012) found that the use of GPS tracking technology is a search and must abide by the Fourth Amendment requirements.

While many amendments included in the Bill of Rights have needed little revision since written, the Fourth Amendment is not one of them. The Fourth Amendment will need to change as technology, social events, political actions, and public opinions change. The rights of American citizens to be safe in their homes from unreasonable search and seizure are an important part of the independence this country is based upon. The Fourth Amendment will be used to protect these rights, but it must be balanced against the responsibility of the government to protect the country and its citizens.

Paige H. Gordier

See also: Body Cameras; Community Policing Today; Fifth Amendment; Perceptions of Police Today; Sixth Amendment; *Terry v. Ohio*; Wiretapping

Further Reading

Cuddihy, William J. *The Fourth Amendment: Origins and Original Meaning 602–1791.* New York: Oxford University Press, 2009.

Editorial Board. "Another Hit to the Fourth Amendment." *The New York Times*, June 20, 2016. http://www.nytimes.com/2016/06/21/opinion/another-hit-to-the-fourth-amendment.html.

Gizzi, Michael C., and R. Craig Curtis. *The Fourth Amendment in Flux: The Roberts Court, Crime Control, and Digital Privacy.* Lawrence: University Press of Kansas, 2016.

Lee, Cynthia. *Searches and Seizures: The Fourth Amendment: Its Constitutional History and Contemporary Debate (Bill of Rights).* New York: Prometheus Books, 2011.

Schulhofer, Stephen J. *More Essential than Ever: The Fourth Amendment in the Twenty-First Century (Inalienable Rights)*. New York: Oxford University Press, 2012.

Zwerdling, Daniel. "Your Digital Trail: Does the Fourth Amendment Protect Us?" *All Things Considered*. October 2, 2013. http://www.npr.org/sections/alltechconsidered/2013/10/02/228134269/your-digital-trail-does-the-fourth-amendment-protect-us.

FIFTH AMENDMENT

The Fifth Amendment to the U.S. Constitution provides a number of important protections that limit the government's ability to investigate and prosecute individuals suspected of committing crimes. Related to investigation, the amendment is the source of the famous "right to remain silent," which protects individuals from being forced to testify against themselves. Related to prosecution, the amendment guarantees the right to grand juries in felony cases and prevents prosecutors from charging someone twice for the same crime. The Fifth Amendment also complements the Sixth Amendment by guaranteeing a fair hearing before anyone can be deprived of life, property, or freedom.

The text of the Fifth Amendment says the following:

> No person shall be held to answer for a capital, or otherwise infamous crime, unless on a presentment or indictment of a grand jury, except in cases arising in the land or naval forces, or in the militia, when in actual service in time of war or public danger; nor shall any person be subject for the same offense to be twice put in jeopardy of life or limb; nor shall be compelled in any criminal case to be a witness against himself, nor be deprived of life, liberty, or property, without due process of law; nor shall private property be taken for public use, without just compensation. (National Archives)

The first guarantee of the amendment involves the right to a grand jury in "infamous crimes." A grand jury is not the same thing as the jury used in a trial. Grand juries are empaneled for a period of time, rather than for one case, and they are part of the pre-trial process, rather than the trial process. Instead of determining guilt or innocence, a grand jury is a limit on overzealous prosecutors that dates back to medieval times. Essentially, a prosecutor needs to present the case to a grand jury for it to determine whether or not the case should actually go to trial, and if the grand jury determines there is enough evidence to justify bringing charges, it will issue a special legal document called an "indictment." By modern definitions, the Fifth Amendment guarantees this right to grand jury in all felony cases.

The second guarantee of the Fifth Amendment involves so-called "double jeopardy." Unlike in some countries, when the prosecution loses at trial, they cannot appeal the decision, and they cannot bring those charges against the defendant again. This substantial protection allows the jury to return an acquittal, even as a way of punishing what it believes to be severe misconduct by the police or prosecution—something that was famously accomplished in the O. J. Simpson murder trial in the 1990s. However, this rule is limited by the "same offense, same sovereign" principle. This means that double jeopardy does not protect a defendant from facing multiple charges for multiple crimes; although, if they are based on the same event, double jeopardy does prohibit being punished for each charge separately. Similarly, double jeopardy does not protect a defendant from facing the same charge by different levels of government. For instance, in the aftermath of the notorious Rodney King beating, several involved police officers were acquitted by California courts on assault charges, but they were convicted when charged at the federal level.

The third guarantee of the Fifth Amendment says that individuals cannot be forced to testify against themselves. In the early days of the United States up through the early 20th century, it was legally acceptable for the police to torture a confession out of a suspect; however, this practice was officially rejected in the 1930s, as the findings of the Wickersham Commission were released. This protection gained amplified importance in *Miranda v. Arizona*, in which the Supreme Court ruled the concern for preventing forced self-incrimination was so strong that police needed to inform people of their rights before interrogating them while in custody. Someone is considered "in custody" whenever it is reasonably clear that police have detained them and they are not free to leave. If the police question someone without giving them this important warning, any confession they make under questioning cannot be used against them at trial.

The right to remain silent is so important that it applies any time someone is in custody or being questioned in court, because it's impossible to know what the police or prosecutors might plan to do with the statements that are made. Furthermore, when in custody, the Fifth Amendment, like the Sixth, also guarantees the right to have an attorney present during questioning.

This does not mean that the right to remain silent is not subject to limitations, though. For one, it's possible to waive the right to remain silent, even implicitly, so long as the suspect has been properly made aware of it. Further, a person must clearly invoke the right before police are required to stop an interrogation. At the same time, this right does not extend to requirements to submit to procedures such as breathalyzers, drug screens, or blood tests. If prosecutors grant someone immunity from prosecution based on their testimony, the right no longer applies.

Finally, the Fifth Amendment guarantees two important broader rights that limit government action. Its guarantee of due process before the taking of life, liberty, or property is the basis of federal civil rights legislation that creates the ability to hold police accountable for things such as the use of excessive force through both civil suits and, potentially, criminal charges. However, the last guarantee protects people from the government seizing private property (for reasons other than law enforcement) without paying a fair price for it after a fair hearing.

Donald Roth

See also: Fourth Amendment; *Miranda v. Arizona*; Sixth Amendment; Wickersham Report on Soaring Crime during Prohibition

Further Reading

"The Bill of Rights: A Transcription." National Archives and Records Administration. http://www.archives.gov/exhibits/charters/bill_of_rights_transcript.html#6.

Dershowitz, Alan M. *Is There a Right to Remain Silent? Coercive Interrogation and the Fifth Amendment after 9/11*. New York: Oxford University Press, 2008.

Levy, Leonard W. *Origins of the Fifth Amendment: The Right Against Self-Incrimination*. Lanham, MD: Ivan R Dee, 1999.

Salky, Steven M., and Paul B. Hynes, Jr. *The Privilege of Silence: Fifth Amendment Protections Against Self-Incrimination*. Washington, DC: American Bar Association, 2015.

"What Are Your Miranda Rights?" MirandaWarning.org. http://www.mirandawarning.org/whatareyourmirandarights.html.

SIXTH AMENDMENT

The Sixth Amendment to the U.S. Constitution ensures several important rights for defendants facing criminal charges, especially that they will receive a fair trial. Its protections extend to the investigative phase of the pre-trial process, and they continue through any appeals filed. These protections include guarantees that a defendant doesn't have to wait too long for his or her day in court, that a defendant has a right to trial by jury for serious offenses, and that a defendant has a right to an attorney once he or she has been charged with a crime. The Sixth Amendment also influences the trial process by providing rights such as the right to have notice of the charges filed, to confront one's accusers, and to be able to compel witnesses to testify.

The text of the amendment says the following:

> In all criminal prosecutions, the accused shall enjoy the right to a speedy and public trial, by an impartial jury of the State and district wherein the crime shall have been committed, which district shall have been previously ascertained by law, and to be informed of the nature and cause of the accusation; to be confronted with the witnesses against him; to have compulsory process for obtaining witnesses in his favor, and to have the Assistance of Counsel for his defense. (National Archives)

The first guarantee is the right to a speedy and public trial. This right is considered important because people accused of crimes may end up waiting in jail for their trial date to come, particularly if they cannot post bail. Even with these guarantees, trial dates can be pushed back for a number of reasons, and exceptional cases can occur, such as that of Kalief Browder, who was held at Rikers Island for three years before charges were dropped in 2013 (Gonnerman 2014).

At the same time, the right to a public trial is less absolute than other parts of the Sixth Amendment because there are times for which publicity can be harmful to a defendant's rights or contrary to national security. Either side may petition the court for a closed trial, although the court is required to make sure that a non-public trial will still be fair to the defendant.

The second guarantee of the Sixth Amendment is the right to be heard by an impartial jury of one's peers. The "peers" in this case means that jurors are drawn from the general population living in the judicial district where the crime occurred;

In this artist's drawing, Ahmad Rahimi, center, listens to proceedings, November 17, 2016, as Federal Defender Peggy Cross-Goldenberg, standing, addresses the court during Rahimi's arraignment in New York. Rahimi was arraigned on charges that in September 2016, he set off bombs in New Jersey and New York that injured 30 people. (AP Photo/Elizabeth Williams)

although a trial can be moved to a new location if it will be impossible to find a fair jury in that location. In order for a jury to be able to give a fair verdict, they must be impartial, that is, not familiar with the case or biased to favor either the prosecution or the defendant. Additionally, the Supreme Court has held that there must be at least six jurors on a jury for it to be fair under the Sixth Amendment.

The overall right to be heard by a jury (instead of a judge) is not universal. Instead, it is only tied to "serious offenses," which the Supreme Court has taken to mean crimes carrying a sentence of more than six months. When a defendant's case is not heard by a jury, a judge acts as the person who both ensures that proper procedure is followed and who issues a verdict. This is called a bench trial, and a defendant may seek to waive his or her right to jury in preference of a bench trial. These waivers are more common when charges involve highly technical issues, an exceptionally gruesome crime, or the defendant has a long criminal record.

The Sixth Amendment also guarantees the right to hear and challenge the prosecution's case and the right to build an affirmative defense of your own. The right to hear the prosecution's case includes the right to notice of the nature and grounds of charges filed against you and the right to hear and challenge the prosecution's witnesses. In fact, the confrontation clause is why people giving testimony in court are called "witnesses." With narrow exceptions, the Constitution forbids the use of what is called "hearsay." Hearsay is offering second-hand information as evidence, such as having a friend to a witness of an assault testify as to what the witness saw. If the prosecution had the friend testify as a way to prove what the witness saw, without calling the witness to the stand, the defendant would not be able to challenge the accuracy of the witness' memory or any biases that person might have; that is, the defendant could not "confront" his or her accuser, and this type of evidence is not permitted at trial.

The right to build your own defense includes the right to call witnesses to testify on your behalf and the right to have an attorney represent you. The right to call witnesses includes the ability to compel people to testify when they do not want to through a special court order called a subpoena. This includes compelling access to things such as records or other physical evidence as part of the pre-trial process. As the pre-trial and trial process can be complex, the Constitution also guarantees a right to counsel, which can mean hiring your own attorney, or, when you cannot afford one, having an attorney, called a public defender, assigned to you at no cost.

The Sixth Amendment right to an attorney coordinates with a similar right under the Fifth Amendment, but it applies only in felony cases and begins once formal charges are filed through either an indictment or information. This means that you have a right to an attorney during the initial police investigation (because of the Fifth Amendment), but you must pay for that person yourself. However, the Sixth Amendment right, once triggered, grants your attorney broader authority to ensure the fairness of the investigation, such as being present to monitor police line-ups or other witness identification procedures.

Donald Roth

See also: Crime Control versus Due Process; Fifth Amendment; Fourth Amendment; *Mapp v. Ohio*

Further Reading

Duncan, David, Tommy E. Miller, Joelle Anne Moreno, and Paul Marcus. *The Rights of the Accused Under the Sixth Amendment: Trials, Presentation of Evidence, and Confrontation.* Washington, DC: The American Bar Association, 2013.

Gonnerman, Jennifer. "Before the Law." *The New Yorker,* October 6, 2014. http://www .newyorker.com/magazine/2014/10/06/before-the-law.

Levin, Mark R. *The Liberty Amendments: Restoring the American Republic.* New York: Threshold Editions, 2013.

Smith, Rick. *Sixth Amendment: The Right to a Fair Trial.* Edina, MN: Abdo Publishing, 2007.

Vile, John R. *A Companion to the United States Constitution and Its Amendments,* 6th ed. Santa Barbara, CA: Praeger, 2015.

SIR ROBERT PEEL AND PRINCIPLES OF MODERN POLICING

Sir Robert Peel (1788–1850) was prime minister of the United Kingdom twice— from 1834 to 1835 and from 1841 to 1846. Before this, he was chief secretary for

Ireland (1812–1818) and home secretary (1822–1827). When Prime Minister Lord Liverpool resigned in 1827, Peel stepped down as home secretary, but then he reclaimed the position in 1828 during Duke Wellington's new ministry. Though Peel presided over substantial changes in a variety of areas, his tenure as home secretary is most popular today because of his efforts in passing legislation that dealt with criminal law and, most notably, policing. For his work in this area, Peel is often credited with creating the Anglo-Peelian model of policing that survives to this day. Peel is credited with formulating nine foundational principles of policing, which continue to influence police thinking and practice today.

Peel's Legislative Accomplishments

Peel was responsible for the drafting, passing, and executing a number of important pieces of legislation. During his second tenure as prime minister, Peel helped to pass the Mines Act of 1842 and the Factory Act of 1844—laws that enhanced the working conditions of women and children. He fought to repeal the Corn Laws, to aid in Ireland's recovery from the potato famine—lowering the costs of imported grains, which Ireland desperately needed. Though he was eventually successful in doing so, his support of the repeal put him in opposition to the Conservative Party he had founded. The political capital he spent to repeal the laws cost him his position. He resigned thereafter, ending his public service career.

Peel's most impactful legislation, however, came in 1829 as then Home Secretary Peel drafted and passed the Metropolitan Police Act. The act was inspired by the need for a non-military, government body to protect public safety while simultaneously ensuring its professional administration protects individual liberty. In passing the act, Peel turned the previously haphazard system into the first systematic modern police department in London—the London Metropolitan Police Force (now, the Metropolitan Police Service, or, the Met). To this day, in honor of Peel's contributions to their founding, Metropolitan police officers are often referred to as Bobbies. Peel's police organization served as the model to be replicated throughout England. The organizational, structural, and functional roots of Anglo-Peelian policing continue to shape police departments throughout the United States and the United Kingdom.

Peelian Principles

The implementation of and later refinements to the Metropolitan Police Act gave rise to what are popularly known as Peel's Principles of Policing. These principles serve as a strategic guideline for police practice. Though there is good evidence to suggest Sir Robert Peel never actually outlined these principles himself, the policing system he created influenced police practice and thought enough to warrant his association with these principles.

Peel supported the Metropolitan Police Act (1829) in efforts to create an ethical and professional police force to replace the outdated constable-watch system that preceded it. Engrained in the Metropolitan Police Act were Peel's ideologies for how a police force should function. At the heart of his ideology was a focus on the role of the community in policing and the role of the police in the community. Due to the communal and organizational focus on policing, the Peelian principles made for a sensible transition into the crime-ridden, disorderly, and reform-minded 20th-century United States.

The principles discussed below laid the groundwork for preventive and control methods as well as organizational structure, authoritative limits, and public involvement. In 1938, the United States adapted the English policing style with the creation of the first American police—the Boston Police Department. Governments in Philadelphia and Milwaukee followed, creating their cities' first police departments, in the Anglo-Peelian vein. As recently as 2015, William Bratton, the police commissioner of the largest police department in the United States, cited Peel's principles in laying the groundwork for improving modern police service in the New York Police Department, in an environment in which police authority was again coming into question.

To further explain the impact of Peel's principles on today's policing strategies, the principles are presented in their totality below. According to Peel, to be a successful police force, all principles must be followed. Failing to implement all principles could lead to a more (rather than less) unethical police organization.

Peel's Principles of Policing

1. The basic mission for which police exist is to prevent crime and disorder as an alternative to the repression of crime and disorder by military force and severity of legal punishment.
2. The ability of the police to perform their duties is dependent upon public approval of police existence, actions, behavior and the ability of the police to secure and maintain public respect.
3. The police must secure the willing cooperation of the public in voluntary observance of the law to be able to secure and maintain public respect.
4. The degree of cooperation of the public that can be secured diminishes, proportionately, to the necessity for the use of physical force and compulsion in achieving police objectives.
5. The police seek and preserve public favor, not by catering to public opinion, but by constantly demonstrating absolutely impartial service to the law, in complete independence of policy, and without regard to the justice or injustice of the substance of individual laws; by ready offering of individual service and friendship to all members of society without regard to their race or social standing, by ready exercise of courtesy and friendly good humor; and by ready offering of individual sacrifice in protecting and preserving life.
6. The police should use physical force to the extent necessary to secure observance of the law or to restore order only when the exercise of persuasion, advice and warning is found to be insufficient to achieve police objectives; and police should use only the minimum degree of physical force, which is necessary on any particular occasion for achieving a police objective.

7. The police at all times should maintain a relationship with the public that gives reality to the historic tradition that the police are the public and the public are the police; the police are the only members of the public who are paid to give full-time attention to duties, which are incumbent on every citizen in the intent of the community welfare.

8. The police should always direct their actions toward their functions and never appear to usurp the powers of the judiciary by avenging individuals or the state, or authoritatively judging guilt or punishing the guilty.

9. The test of police efficiency is the absence of crime and disorder, not the visible evidence of police action in dealing with them (Mayhall 1985, 425–426).

Although no physical transcript of Peel formally addressing each principle exists, his ideals have been deduced and interpreted through scholarly writing as listed above.

Peel's Principles and Police Power

Many questions come up about the creation of a public police force: What are the actual responsibilities of the police? What is the police relationship with a military? And how much, if any, force will police be authorized to use to resolve citizen concerns? Peel's responses, as evidenced by the Metropolitan Police, suggest a view of police as preventing crime and disorder, a need to be clearly distinct from military operations, a use of physical force only as an absolute final option. Implied in his principles and in the practice of police under his leadership, and also as related to the questions above, Peel emphasized a close alliance with and reliance on citizens.

A vital part of navigating those relationships is how to properly use police discretion in day-to-day activities. The expansive nature of the police job and the relative autonomy of policing on the streets give rise to a wide amount of individual discretion on how to exercise power in myriad situations and in any number of ways. Ethical motives (i.e., Peelian principles) and a strict departmental protocol help to define for police officers the appropriate amount of discretion prescribed for any given situation. As Peel implies, a department's close ties to the community ensures they will have a strong understanding of what those goals are.

The fifth principle suggests a proscription of the police use of authority when managing those ties with citizens. It suggests, despite the inherently political nature of police-community relationships, that the law should ultimately guide these ties with citizens—regardless of an individual's race or social standing.

Police, as part of the citizenry themselves, should seek a productive relationship with their community and act with community interests in mind. The police are not external from the public. As such, displaying dominance and unjust authority is not a suitable way of interacting with a community because it damages public views of police authority of police and governmental actors and can lead to more serious uses of force by and toward police.

Peel's principles suggest public involvement with their police is instrumental for successful policing. In the police-citizen interaction, police are the ultimate source of authority. In dealing with offenders, Peel's eighth principle reminds police to fulfill their proper functions. Police are not to act as judges and adjudicators of wrongdoing.

According to Peel's second principle, the ability of police to perform their duties successfully depends on the respect they are granted by the public. In cases where the police disrespect the community they govern, the community will inevitably disrespect police authority, creating a cyclical pattern of mistrust. Similarly, the ideal police-citizen relationship places an obligation on citizens to cooperate with the lawful demands of police and to assist police in the execution of their duties, as they seek to co-produce orderly and safe neighborhoods.

Peel's sixth principle suggests police should use the least amount of physical force necessary to safely resolve a situation and that this force should be used only after persuasion, advice, and warnings have been exercised. In other words, the use of deadly force is limited to situations where no alternatives exist and when others' lives (or the officer's life) are in imminent danger.

An abuse of power undermines the foundation of policing a democratic society. A betrayal of these tenets will increase the danger faced by police and citizens and a diminution of the police reputation and respect of the community. Police success depends on cohesion between the community and its police. This is critical in stopping crime and disorder and ensuring safe interactions between officers and the public.

Peel's final principle focuses on what it means to be a successful police organization. He describes success not by the amount of police activity (i.e., arrest or citations) recorded, but by the lack of crime and disorder. In doing so, he argues that arresting individuals is a short-term solution for a long-term problem. Arrests are not the resolution to a problem but rather a displacement of a problem. Crime exists in a community where relationships are broken. Police should focus on fixing the broken community bonds and regaining the respect and trust necessary for society to thrive. Again, proving a strong police-community relationship is the cornerstone for a successful crime-free area. Correspondingly, it is our responsibility as citizens to pursue the respect of our governing body by obeying laws and discussing the needs and desires of community with our police officers.

Peel's Death and Legacy

Peel died July 2, 1850, following a fall from his horse. His remains lay in a vault in St. Peter's church in Drayton Bassett, England. He and his wife, Julia Floyd, had seven children, many who had successful careers of their own in government and military positions.

With the potential for abuse of power with every negative police encounter, it is crucial for police and members of society to be further educated on their role in society. The work of Sir Robert Peel and his policing principles are an important starting point for understanding and properly applying police power.

Kyle Conklin and Michael J. Jenkins

See also: Bow Street Runners; Community Policing Today; William Bratton (1947–), Police Commissioner; Wilson and Kelling's Broken Windows Theory

Further Reading

Brown, J. *The Future of Policing.* New York: Routledge, 2013.

Gash, N. *Sir Robert Peel: The Life of Sir Robert Peel to 1830*, 2nd edition. London: Faber and Faber, 1985.

Mayhall, P. *Police-Community Relations and the Administration of Justice.* New York: Wiley, 1985.

Steverson, L. *Policing in America: A Reference Handbook.* Santa Barbara, CA: ABC-CLIO, 2008.

BOW STREET RUNNERS

The Bow Street Runners were a type of proto-police force, operating under the authority of a magistrate's court in London, founded in Georgian-era England, in the mid-18th century. Historically, they represent the basis of the Metropolitan Police, connecting to the concept of a "modern" police force.

Prior to the formation of the Runners, law enforcement in Britain was largely in private hands. Here, relatively wealthy people who were the victims of crimes could pay others to track down thieves. Poorer people were reliant upon the goodwill of others to detain a suspected criminal. (Incentives were sometimes offered for volunteers through rewards for the apprehension of criminals associated with more serious crimes.) Any person so captured was required to be taken to a parish constable or a night watchman to be arrested and incarcerated. Trial was by a magistrate.

Because of rising crime levels in London and associated concerns voiced by the burgeoning middle class, the idea of forming a body of men who could go onto the streets to catch thieves and other wrong-doers came into being. The Runners were founded in 1749 by magistrate and novelist Henry Fielding (1707–1754)—whose works included the satirical novel *Tom Jones*—together with his half-brother Sir John Fielding (1721–1780). For this reason, the Runners were first referred to as "Mr. Fielding's People." Henry Fielding was the second magistrate at Bow Street, which opened in 1740, again reflecting the rising crime rate in London.

The original Bow Street Runners consisted of six men. (Six remained the typical number, with the exception of occasional assistants, until 1765 when the numbers steadily grew.) The founding of the Runners by a senior magistrate conferred upon them legal status, and they operated out of the magistrate's office. A basic set of rules was put in place that provided for their regulation.

"Bow Street Runners" was never an official name; it arose by virtue of the group being attached to Bow Street magistrates' office. Although the group referred to themselves as "Runners," it was generally felt by the members that the moniker "Bow Street Runner," when used by the public at large, was derogatory.

The duties of the Runners included some functions recognizable with police forces today, although there were also some exceptions. The Runners, for example, were authorized to serve writs and arrest offenders, provided authority was given

John Townsend, a Bow Street Runner. The Runners were forerunners of the modern police force and policed the streets in conjunction with nightwatchmen, but were more efficient. Nicknamed "Robin Redbreasts" because of the red waistcoats they wore. (Hulton Archive/Getty Images)

by a magistrate in relation to a reported crime. Crimes were not only reviewed, but there was also an attempt at analysis, and the communication system put in place by Fielding represented an early form of intelligence gathering.

A key difference with today's police forces was that the Runners did not, at first, patrol the streets (although they later engaged in touring key areas), nor did they engage in any crime detection activities.

Additionally, in the early years, being a Runner was not considered a "profession" and, given the lack of state support, they were not initially paid. Instead, they earned money through rewards issued for the apprehension of a suspected criminal. This variable payments system led to some occasional corrupt practices with individual Runners (although the general perception of the Runners was that of a hard-working and committed team).

This reward process for thief-catching led to varying levels with the Runners' activities, including a period in 1753 when the government pulled back from offering rewards, leading to temporary cessation of the service. The service was restored when a sum of money was given to the chief magistrate at Bow Street, from which payments could be given to the Runners as a wage. This semi-professionalization of the Runners required clerks to support the payment process, providing an early basis of civil administration to support police activities. The clerks also collected information on crimes and criminals, creating an early type of criminal database. Over time, the public was encouraged to report crimes to the court, with the expectation that a Runner would be dispatched.

As the number of Runners grew, associated services were also formed. One such example was the Bow Street Horse Patrol, formed in 1805. These law enforcement officials rode through the streets of London on horseback and were the first law enforcement officials to wear a uniform. This group was followed by the Dismounted Horse Patrol, formed in 1821, to oversee the suburbs of London. The success of the core Runners also led similar offices modeled on Bow Street being established throughout London's boroughs.

In later years, from 1815 onward, the government, which had sanctioned an extension of patrolmen on London's streets, made greater use of the Runners for crime investigation, and the Runners consequently became less associated with apprehending targeted criminals. This was coincidental with the day-to-day activities of the Runners falling under the government Home Office, with the offices of Bow Street performing a basic administrative function. The Runners were also being called upon more frequently to investigate criminal acts outside of London, a situation made possible by a decline in the crime rate in London.

Overlapping with the activities of the Runners in later years was the formation of the Metropolitan Police Service in 1829 by Robert Peel. Although the Runners continued for a further 10 years, it was the success of the first professional police service in the city that led to the disbandment of the Runners in 1839. Some of the Runners were absorbed into the police force, and others were retired.

The legacy of the Runners was to provide a building block for the professionalization of the police service and the codification of law enforcement, through rules and regulations. By offering evidence in court, the Runners also shaped the way criminal trials were held. Perhaps, most importantly, the activities and evolution of the Runners led to a significant extension of state control into the private sphere.

Tim Sandle

See also: Community Policing Today; Police Authority to Detain; Sir Robert Peel and Principles of Modern Policing

Further Reading

Beattie, J. M. *The First English Detective: The Bow Street Runners and the Policing of London, 1750–1840.* Oxford: Oxford University Press, 2012.

Senior, H. *Constabulary: The Rise of Police Institutions in Britain, the Commonwealth, and the United States.* Toronto: Dundurn Press, 1997.

SOUTHERN SLAVE PATROLS

Slave patrols were teams of White men who enforced discipline upon Black slaves in southern states prior to the American Civil War. Their main tasks were to ensure slaves were compliant in the undertaking of their duties and to catch runaway slaves.

Slavery was common in the Southern United States, from the early colonies until the post–Civil War era. The slave system was so entrenched that it represented the foundation of the social and economic system of the U.S. South.

The origins of the slave patrols dates to South Carolina in 1704. The patrols were constituted due to the perceived fear, and in some cases the reality, of slave revolts. These concerns matched the significant increase in slavery needed to work the plantations, with slaves shipped in to support the exponential increase of cotton farming and processing. Both activities required high volumes of manual labor, and expansion was made possible through the invention of the cotton gin (a device for removing the seeds from cotton fiber). By 1860, slave numbers stood at more than 4 million (Berlin 1999).

The use of patrols picked up during 1739, after the bloody suppression of the Stono Rebellion in the South Carolina Colony. There were fears among plantation owners of further rebellion. In recognition of the tougher tactics required, the government agreed to compensate plantation owners of any damage caused by patrols in exercising their duty.

The first "patrols" (or "paddyrollers") were ad-hoc gatherings of men, semi-volunteered to patrol in return for rewards of alcohol, small sums of money, or tobacco. When these incentives proved insufficient for the necessary numbers of patrols, and the commitment to timekeeping, a more formal structure of slave patrols developed. The term "Southern" in front of "slave patrol" came into use once the Northern states formally abolished slavery in 1804.

The formal structure established a set of rules (or "slave codes"), for both the White men who signed and for the slaves. The slave codes varied state-by-state, such as different curfew times; however, the codes justified racial power. One commonality was that all slave codes made slave ownership "legal"; for example, the code for South Carolina stated, "All negros, mulattoes, mestizo's or Indians, which at any time heretofore have been sold, or now are held or taken to be, or hereafter shall be bought and sold for slaves, are hereby declared slaves; and they, and their children, are hereby made and declared slaves" (Hurd 2009, 299).

For most slaves, this included carrying identification cards and papers. For a slave to wander freely, she or he had to have authorized papers (passes stating their owner's name, where the slave was from, when the slave was allowed to be away from the plantation, and for how long). Without such proof, the slave was detained, possibly beaten, and returned to the owner. If no owner could be traced, the slave was sent for auction.

For the slave patrols, the slave codes provided the basis of legitimizing authority. However, beyond the concept of slave ownership, the rules and authority varied state by state. The common tasks included surveillance as well as controlling the Black slave population with force and coercion.

The slave patrols were also allowed to carry weapons and instruments to enforce control. Here, many patrols were equipped with guns and whips, and some acted essentially as local militia. Slave patrols were authorized to question, beat, whip, and segregate suspected runaway slaves. This included patrolling roads and capturing any slave found wandering; searching slave residences for weapons and books, enforcing curfews, and breaking up any gatherings of slaves. Another function was more symbolic: to encourage slave obedience through the threat of force, thereby controlling, to an extent, through terror.

As to the make-up of the typical member of a slave patrol, these were almost exclusively White men, often drawn from the working classes. Slave patrols were typically constituted in small groups of fewer than 10 men. They ordinarily rode horses and operated during daylight hours. Each patrol was given a "beat" to patrol, typically made up of areas of 10 square miles. The largest recorded slave patrol was in Charleston, South Carolina, where, in 1837, one patrol was made up of more than 100 men (Walker 1999).

In some regions, the patrols were formed from volunteers who were keen to earn employment; whereas in other areas, it was an expectation—a civic duty—that men of adult age took turns in going out on patrol.

Leading up to the American Civil War, the activities of the slave patrols became shaped by the Fugitive Slave Act of 1850. These laws were established to ease tensions between Northern and Southern states, which meant that slaves who crossed borders into the North would be returned and conferred further legitimacy to the patrols. This returning of men to bondage was later revoked during the war, and the fear of crossing the border curtailed the power of the slave patrols to pursue their quarry.

The Black population was not completely subjugated by the patrols, and there are documented examples of slaves fighting back. Cases, sometimes successful, of resistance increased during the Civil War years.

The slave patrols finally came to end following the victory of the Union over the Confederacy in 1865 as the American Civil War reached its end. While this was the end of the patrols as formal units, some of the ideas of racial control and White superiority became manifest into the ideology of post-war organizations that sought to pursue the continuance of "racial" segregation. A prominent example is the Ku Klux Klan, which was formed during the post-war Reconstruction era.

The legacy of the slave patrols had an influence upon modern policing. This included the concept of paying people to enforce rules and giving them regulations to follow. Furthermore, the terms "patrol" and "beat" became entered into common usage. To add to this, the use of profiling, based on the brief of stopping "trouble" before it started and the use of identification cards, as a means to assess the "legal" status of an individual, became methods absorbed by U.S. police law enforcement.

Tim Sandle

See also: Colonial Night Watches; Police Brutality; Racial Profiling; Trayvon Martin Shooting

Further Reading

Berlin, I. *Many Thousands Gone: The First Two Centuries of Slavery in North America.* Cambridge, MA: Harvard University Press, 168–170, 1999.

Hadden, S. *Slave Patrols: Law and Violence in Virginia and the Carolinas.* Cambridge, MA: Harvard University Press, 2001.

Hurd, J. *The Law of Freedom and Bondage in the United States.* New York: Applewood Books, 2009.

Meltzer, M. *Slavery: A World History.* New York: Da Capo Press, 225–227, 1971.

Walker, S. A. *The Police in America*, 3rd ed. Boston, MA: McGraw-Hill College, 1999.

COLONIAL NIGHT WATCHES

Based on practices used in England, the colonial night watch system was developed in Boston, Massachusetts, in 1631 during Colonial times. The system was composed of a group of townspeople who volunteered to assist in maintaining order throughout the night. Policing, in general, followed the British system, and the night watch system was easily adapted to the colonies. It is widely considered to be a part of the very first law enforcement system in America.

Night watchmen were primarily adult male residents whose duties included a variety of tasks. Despite being a volunteer service, many of these men were actually meeting other colonial obligatory requirements, such as being required to report to service when summoned or being forced to patrol as a form of punishment. Or they may have volunteered simply to avoid military service.

Initially, the colonial night watch system was designed to maintain order in the streets of Boston during the night. Eventually, the system expanded to include New York and Philadelphia. Maintaining order included any number of functions, including reporting fires, warning others of impending dangers or riots, and raising the hue and cry system. The hue and cry system required the night watchman to pursue suspected criminals while, at the same time, seek assistance through loud cries for help, if necessary. Theoretically, townspeople would come to the aid of the night watchman and assist him in capturing suspected robbers and burglars.

Colonial night watchmen initially patrolled the city on foot, using gas lamps as their guide. Because of the immense darkness of the cities at night, the gas lamps were used not only to help the night watchmen see, but also to help deter criminal and deviant behavior. As the system developed over time, bells, dogs, and rattles were introduced to help them throughout the night.

In 1652, the Dutch city of Nieuw Amsterdam (later renamed New York, in 1664, when it was taken over by the British) implemented its own version of the night watch system when a rattle watch system was established. Under the rattle watch system, the night watchmen were given a small, wooden, handheld rattle that was to be used as a sound-generating alarm, much like the use of standard-issue whistles in modern policing.

A few years later, in 1658, Nieuw Amsterdam became the first city to compensate the night watchmen by hiring eight men to patrol the city at night. The city of Philadelphia implemented its own colonial night watch system in 1700 to help patrol the city, and a few years later, in 1749, it passed a law that allowed for a local tax to compensate the night watchman. Wardens were given authority to hire watchmen as needed. Townsmen were no longer required to volunteer when summoned. Only men interested in the paid job were encouraged to apply.

The night watchmen responded to criminal behavior but only when requested by victims or witnesses. Public health violations, such as natural disasters or fires, were the only types of activity that required watchmen to be proactive and not rely on the victims or witnesses to call them to action.

Unfortunately, the night watch system in colonial times was not a particularly effective crime reduction strategy, as many of the night watchmen routinely drank on duty, were often completely intoxicated, or slept throughout the night. As the watch system became more time consuming and difficult, fewer men volunteered. With the monetary incentive of tax collection in certain areas, apprehending law violators was a not seen as a priority.

Even when a watchman was willing to be sober and alert throughout the night, often he would not be able to find help when it was needed. The night watchman was habitually ridiculed and harassed by the local townspeople when he was seeking assistance from them. Instead of assisting in the pursuit of the suspected outlaw, the townspeople would routinely help the fleeing felon escape from apprehension.

By the mid-1700s the night watch system was found to be completely ineffective. In most cases, the system became more favorable to those who were committing the crimes than to those who were solving them. However, in 1749, a new law passed in Philadelphia that would restructure the watch system in an attempt to address some of the negative problems that were being produced by these professional criminals.

Industrialization produced a drastic change in the development of American policing. In 1833, Philadelphia became the first American city to implement a day watch system, making it the first city with a 24-hour watch. When Boston established the first police force in America in 1838, it was developed with a day and night watch system that worked independently of each other. In New York, as the population increased, a day watch system was implemented in 1844, as a direct precursor to the establishment of its police force in 1845.

Despite the presence of law enforcement in the colonies, law enforcement responsibilities still rested primarily in the hands of individual citizens, as it had in England. But as a result, when immediate action was needed, citizens would take matters into their own hands, which resulted in an American style of vigilantism. The night watch system eventually proved ineffective and alternative solutions were needed to help fight crime.

Georgen Guerrero and Doshie Piper

See also: Bow Street Runners; Law Enforcement in the Wild West; Sir Robert Peel and Principles of Modern Policing; Southern Slave Patrols

Further Reading

Conser, James A., Rebecca Paynich, and Terry E. Gingerich. *Law Enforcement in the United States*, 3rd ed. Boston, MA: Jones & Bartlett Learning, 2011.

Dempsey, John S., and Linda S. Forst. *An Introduction to Policing*, 8th ed. Independence, KY: Delmar Cengage Learning, 2015.

Johnson, David R. "The Early Days of American Law Enforcement." *American Law Enforcement: A History*. Wheeling, IL: Forum Press, 1981.

Potter, Gary. "The History of Policing in the United States, Part 1." Eastern Kentucky University, Police Studies Online, 2013. http://plsonline.eku.edu/insidelook.

PINKERTON DETECTIVE AGENCY AND PRIVATE POLICING

The Pinkerton Detective Agency and private policing trace their origins and growth to the industrialization of the United States in the 1850s and 1860s. The growth of private security also paralleled the development of uniformed, public policing agencies, and penitentiaries, and the expansion of the criminal code and court system. Industrialization, urbanization, and rapid population growth from immigration accompanied an increase in crime in urban areas. With formal policing agencies fragmented and limited by jurisdictional boundaries, private policing organizations such as the Pinkerton Detective Agency would transcend these boundaries and become the protective as well as the enforcement agents of the industrialists, particularly in its ability to protect private industry and the expansion of infrastructure, most notably, the railroad.

In 1851, Allan Pinkerton established the first private security and investigation agency in the United States. The Pinkerton's Protective Patrol began as an agency that augmented the Chicago metropolitan police. During the U.S. Civil War, Pinkerton's agency conducted espionage for the Union Army. After the Civil War, the Pinkerton Detective Agency became the primary protective agency for the growing railroad industry and also functioned as an expanded police force to protect the property of railroad and coal mining executives. Prior to the development and expansion of public law enforcement, the security industry was an effective mechanism to protect private-sector assets from risks and ensure continuity of business operations.

Allan Pinkerton was born on August 25, 1819, in Scotland. He learned the cooper (barrel maker) trade. Also as a young man, he became involved in a political movement in Great Britain that resulted in a king's warrant being issued for his arrest. Before he could be apprehended on the warrant, Pinkerton boarded a ship with his wife and sailed to Nova Scotia. Then he traveled to Chicago, where he opened a cooper business.

The beginning of Pinkerton's work as a detective occurred in 1847. While visiting a nearby island to obtain lumber, Pinkerton observed suspicious activity. He informed the sheriff, who had returned to the island with Pinkerton and a group of deputies. What Pinkerton uncovered was a gang of counterfeiters. The arrest of the counterfeiters gave publicity to Pinkerton, who was later asked by local shopkeepers to assist with apprehending counterfeiters in town.

After completing successful undercover work that resulted in the arrest of a suspected counterfeiter, Pinkerton worked as a deputy sheriff of Kane County, Illinois. After one year, he left the sheriff's office, and shortly thereafter the U.S. Postal Service appointed him as a Special United States Mail Agent to investigate postal thefts and robberies in Chicago. Working as a postal agent, Pinkerton solved a case involving a postal employee who stole a large amount of banknotes, money orders, and checks.

Pinkerton started his own detective agency around 1850, along with partner Edward A. Rucker, who was a Chicago lawyer. The agency was originally named the North-Western Detective Agency, and the logo featured the slogan "We Never Sleep" along with a human eye. This became associated with the term "private eye."

The Pinkerton Detective Agency and the private policing industry were instrumental in crime prevention because of the vacuum created by jurisdictional boundaries that limited public law enforcement. No federal agencies focused on enforcement and crime prevention the way that the Pinkerton Detective Agency did. However, the U.S. Marshals Service was established in 1789, and throughout the 1800s, the marshals were tasked with many non–law enforcement responsibilities and court administration. Sheriffs could enforce laws only within their own counties. Police departments in large cities were often understaffed, politically influenced, and corrupt. The city police departments were also limited by jurisdictions. In rural areas, law enforcement consisted mostly of sheriffs, rural marshals, bounty hunters, and the occasional deputy. With an absence of centralized law enforcement and closely held political bound-

William A. Pinkerton with railroad special agents Pat Connell (left) and Sam Finley (right), ca. 1880. Allan J. Pinkerton, William's father, founded the private security guard and detective agency. The agents were responsible for employment screening, protective services, security, and crisis management. (Library of Congress)

aries, the expansive railroad industry became a lucrative target for robbers. In the mid-1800s, the major railroads contracted with Pinkerton, paying the agency a yearly retainer of $10,000 to provide protective services.

During the Civil War, Pinkerton offered his services to the Union as an intelligence analyst and investigator of Confederate spy rings. His agents were involved in interrogating and pursuing suspected Confederate informants, and Pinkerton himself conducting military espionage for the Union Army. Pinkerton advised President Abraham Lincoln about safety concerns while traveling outside of Washington. He provided Lincoln with a security detail for a journey to Washington, and it would be 40 years before the Secret Service would provide full-time security for the president. At the end of hostilities, Pinkerton's additional responsibilities within the War Department included the investigation of contractors who were accused of overcharging the government for supplies.

After the Civil War, the Pinkerton Detective Agency was the main agency tasked with protecting the property of industrialists in the coal mining industry. The

Pinkerton Detective Agency served as an expanded police force to infiltrate coal mine strikes. Franklin B. Gowen, president of the Philadelphia & Reading Railroad, called upon the Pinkerton Detective Agency and his own Coal and Iron Police to infiltrate and stop labor organization and discontent among his workers. By the late 1800s, private policing was the key industry tasked with protecting private-sector assets from risks and ensuring continuity of business operations.

The Pinkerton Detective Agency was instrumental in protecting property, profit, and crime prevention in regions that had no established law enforcement. Pinkerton was also a pioneer in gathering and sharing intelligence and even photographs about suspects and criminals in the days before the establishment of a Federal Bureau of Investigation. The extent to which the policing function should be privatized is a controversy that will likely continue.

Jonathan Kremser

See also: Corruption; Crime Prevention Techniques; Law Enforcement in the Wild West; Secret Service

Further Reading

Hess, K. M. *Introduction to Private Security*, 5th ed. Belmont, CA: Wadsworth, 2009.

Horan, J. *The Pinkertons: The Detective Dynasty that Made History*. New York: Bonanza Books, 1967.

Maggio, E. *Private Security in the 21st Century: Concepts and Applications*. Boston: Jones and Bartlett, 2009.

Nemeth, C. P. *Private Security and the Law*, 3rd ed. Burlington, MA: Elsevier Butterworth-Heinemann, 2004.

Spitzer, S., and A. T. Scull. "Privatization and Capitalist Development: The Case of the Private Police." *Social Problems* 25, no. 1 (1977): 18.

Weiss, R. "The Emergence and Transformation of Private Detective Industrial Policing in the United States, 1850–1940." *Crime and Social Justice* 9 (1978): 35–48.

LAW ENFORCEMENT IN THE WILD WEST

The term "Wild West" conjures up some of the most colorful myths and legends. From James Butler "Wild Bill" Hickok to Billy the Kid, Wyatt Earp, and Jesse James, the Wild West is remembered as a time of badges versus bandits, where high noon would see the lawman—tall, slender, and steely eyed—meeting outside the saloon for a duel against the outlaw. Each would gaze across the distance with a hand steadily positioned above his pistol. With the sun gleaming off the star of his vest and the sweat trickling down the outlaw's face, the tension would build until—bang!

The expanding frontiers of the American West (1800–1900) was often without law and order, and therefore the lawman, gunfighter, and outlaw were central to the role of the creation of the *legend* of a "wild" West. The peace officer was inseparably linked to the image of the gunfighter, and so the image of justice equally requires the image of crime. There is a certain romanticism that comes with Hollywood tales of yesteryear. The good versus evil motif is played out by those wearing white or black cowboy hats. They have, throughout the years, created a nostalgic sense of contemplating how people in the Wild West found honor and greatness through real-life Western heroes who roamed the plains under cloudy skies and through muddy waters, not only among the lands that they worked and protected, but also among the lawlessness and injustice that arose from them.

The spread of law enforcement during this time was a considerable accomplishment for a democratic nation, and understanding the role of Western peace officers first requires understanding the scope and characteristics of crime and violence in the West. As with any law enforcement perspective, crimes are legal wrongs codified through legislative bodies and enforced through the executive branch of government. With expansion through railroads and cattle drives, crime accompanied increased populations where cultures clashed through varied value systems, economic status, occupations, and simple geographies. Most pioneers, however, were busy building new lives for themselves rather than fending off constant assaults from robbers and strangers passing by in the constant, hostile environment often portrayed in movies, television, and radio. State and territorial laws in addition to town ordinances often controlled the carrying of weapons and, generally, rules of society were not much different from today, where public intoxication, disorderly conduct, theft, and sex crimes plague a nation. Much of the lawlessness—from cattle and horse rustling to organized crime and mail frauds—were attributed to downward curves both before and after the Civil War (Langum 1985).

Law enforcement officers must protect property and life, prevent crime, and command order within a social framework. Lawmen of the American West were not labeled as cops, police, or even law enforcement officers, but rather peace officers, "law dogs," sheriffs, marshals, rangers, and "badges." Those who were called upon to accept the tin star were often ranchers, cattlemen, buffalo hunters, and homesteaders—many of whom came home or wandered the Great Plains after Civil War. They worked on railroads, mines, or even part of the cattleman's association (Horan 1980). They were often elected by local citizens who were terrorized by rustlers and horse thieves. Some of them were buried shortly after being elected while the town searched for a new, foolish hero to emerge. Those who survived had to be fast and accurate with a gun, able to track killers and bands of outlaws for days, and possess the physical strength to handle drunken cowboys and mobs (and the intelligence to know when not to). They had to have moral integrity and be able to resist bribes and corruption among mounting pressures from local politicians who were often themselves corrupt.

The roles and responsibilities of Western peace officers varied with their jurisdiction and position, from town marshals, city peacemakers, and county sheriffs to state agents such as the Texas Rangers or federal law enforcement such as Deputy U.S. Marshals. Other roles included a legally organized posse or casual deputy, private detectives, and agencies such as Wells Fargo and Pinkerton. Finally, there were vigilantes who lived by the compass of their own morality, using extra-legal

Pat Garrett (1850–1908), Sheriff of Lincoln County, New Mexico, captured Billy the Kid on December 20, 1880. After his trial and death sentence, the Kid escaped in April 1881. Garrett tracked him down in Fort Sumner, New Mexico. He ambushed and killed the Kid in a hotel room on July 14, 1881. (Everett Collection Historical/Alamy Stock Photo)

measures to exact their own brand of justice. And bounty killers, as the proverbial "good" bad guy, were oft-reformed outlaws or mysterious gunfighters who cooperated with the law in an effort to achieve selfish wealth, even if it meant helping people along the way.

Whether public or private law dogs, various circumstances in the Wild West hampered the American law enforcement officer. Distance, primitive transportation, hostile ranchers, public disturbances, serving legal writs, outlaw sympathizers, an apathetic public, and city or county councils looking for booming towns and then leaving when it didn't work out often left the Western officer with a mess to clean up and very little manpower to help. On certain trails, a horse and gun were their best friends, and if they failed in the eyes of their community, they were replaced.

Contrary to popular culture, the job of the Western peacekeeper was not glamorous. Much like today's law enforcement officer, it was routine yet dangerous. Jurisdictional issues among other officers led to infighting and negligence toward their oath of office. There were gunfights on the run or ambushes and, in the case of a law enforcement death, the body would be returned wrapped in a blanket or slicker and tied across the saddle of a horse or back of a wagon. The widow would receive his gun or horse, and there were no pensions for families.

Families of the Western lawman accepted death as a natural part of a violent and unpredictable territory. They were killed by runaway steer, stampeding cattle, bites from rabid vermin, or drunks acting foolishly in a saloon. Natural elements such as lightning, flash floods, quicksand, and even ice were challenges among their many other responsibilities. Despite such difficulties, law enforcement was not without advantages in the Wild West. Many officers owned businesses on the side, such as saloons and their concessions (gambling and alcohol). They also had ready access to stables and hotels and some even received a percentage of taxes in larger, mining towns.

Although some would consider those perks such as a discounted meal or free coffee by contemporary standards, extra-curricular activities led others to operate outside the boundaries of the law. In one case, a band of brothers (while wearing badges) stole horses and killed a man who was interested in of their girlfriends (Weis 1985). In another case, Henry Brown (1857–1884), town marshal in Caldwell, Kansas, robbed a bank, killed the bank's employees, and was later hanged by a lynch mob. As was the case in the Wild West, whether you wore a black hat or white hat was sometimes a matter of who you asked and what territory you were in.

The following is a list of notable lawmen and law agencies of the Wild West: James Butler "Wild Bill" Hickok, Wyatt Earp, Bill Tilghman, Tom "Bear River" Smith, Doc Holliday, Bat Masterson, William Wallace, Fred Dodge, David Cook, Charles Neiman, L. B. Blair, Henry Morse, Chauncey Whitney, John Slaughter, Jim Courtright, the Texas Rangers, William and Robert Pinkerton, Pinkerton Detective Agency, and Wells Fargo.

The Western police establishment from 1800 to 1900 can be viewed from two distinct vantage points. The first is the popular image of the Wild West lawman, although heavily influenced by novels, film, and television, who yet had showmanship qualities and a personal flavor that helped to define the mystique of law and order. The other is the more dogmatic and realistic view where, for the most part, battles against crime were less than dramatic and unsung, carrying out administrative duties, paperwork, and routine tasks. Either way, they were labeled as fearless and professional white-hat heroes.

Brian Kinnaird

See also: Colonial Night Watches; Crime Control versus Due Process; Crime Prevention Techniques; Pinkerton Detective Agency and Private Policing; Southern Slave Patrols

Further Reading

DiLorenzo, Thomas J. "The Culture of Violence in the American West: Myth versus Reality." *The Independent Review* (Fall 2010). http://www.independent.org/publications/tir/article.asp?a=803.

Horan, James. *The Authentic Wild West: The Lawmen.* New York: Crown Publishers, 1980.

Langum, David, ed. "Law in the West." *Journal of the West.* Manhattan, KS: Sunflower University Press, 1985.

Weis, Harold. "Western Lawmen: Image and Reality." David Langum, ed. *Law in the West.* Manhattan, KS: Sunflower University Press, 1985.

Weiser, Kathy. "Old West Legends: U.S. Marshals—Two Centuries of Bravery." *Legends of America.* 2014. http://www.legendsofamerica.com/law-usmarshals.html.

INTERNATIONAL ASSOCIATION OF CHIEFS OF POLICE

The International Association of Chiefs of Police (IACP), often referred to as the most important police organization, is a professional association for law enforcement worldwide. Established in 1893, IACP aims to promote law enforcement assistance and cooperation within society, as with community and problem-orienting policing, and among international policing agencies. Policies on professional ethics, behavior, and public interactions have been constructed and endorsed by the organization. IACP advocates for technological advancements in policing, as with the use of nonlethal weapons, global positioning systems, and crime mapping. The recruitment of competent and distinguished cadets into the profession is also of significant importance.

The organization's history commenced prior to 1893. Its inception dates back to 1871, when James McDonough, the police chief of St. Louis, Missouri, coordinated the National Police Convention (NCP). Many topics were discussed at that convention, such as juvenile delinquency, alcoholism, prostitution, uniform crime reports, and the impact of the Civil War on increased crime. The continuance of the NCP was brief.

In 1893, the police chief of Omaha, Nebraska, discussed with numerous police departments the importance of cooperation between law enforcement agencies, in order to decrease crime and apprehend criminals. He advocated for a voluntary association of police executives, which would meet to discuss law enforcement concerns with the intention to promote cooperation between departments. The initial meeting, establishing the National Chiefs of Police, was held in Chicago, Illinois, during the World's Fair, with 51 chiefs present.

By 1897, there was a demand for a central clearinghouse of criminal behavior in Washington, D.C. At the 1901 meeting in New York City, the organization's name was changed from the Police Union to the International Association of Chiefs of Police, with Major Richard H. Sylvester, who was then chief of the police department in Washington, D.C., elected as the first president of IACP. Sylvester is known for the development of many paramilitary aspects of policing.

One distinguished IACP president (1921–1922) was August Vollmer. He was chief of police in Berkeley, California. Vollmer is widely considered to be the father of modern policing, a campaigner of police reform, and an advocate for technological advancements in law enforcement. IACP has established an honorary award in recognition of Vollmer, which is bestowed annually to a recipient within law enforcement involved in the utilization of novel forensic technology.

Over the years, many other awards have been added to that list. There are awards for excellence in victim services, law enforcement volunteering, civil rights, criminal investigation, police aviation, community policing, and terrorism, to name a few. The IACP also sponsors different campaigns, such as the Air Bag Safety Campaign, Safe and Sober, and the IACP Tribute to Slain Officers.

IACP, with headquarters located in Alexandria, Virginia, has promoted, or developed, a number of advancements in law enforcement throughout the years, which are still used today. These innovations include national fingerprinting identification, annual nationwide data on criminal arrests (e.g., the Uniform Crime Report), community policing, facial recognition, and license plate readers (LPRs). In the 1970s, the IACP was granted Consultative Status by the United Nations (UN) in recognition of IACP's endeavors in UN countries. The 1970s are notable for IACP's

The president of one of the largest police organizations in the United States apologized for mistreatment of minorities, calling it a "dark side of our shared history" that must be acknowledged and overcome. Terrence Cunningham, president of the International Association of Chiefs of Police, said at the group's annual conference in 2016 that police have historically been a face of oppression, enforcing laws that ensured legalized discrimination and denial of basic rights. (AP Photo/Elliot Spagat)

construction of a national repository for collecting data on bombs and other explosives. Presently, the Federal Bureau of Investigation (FBI) oversees this data center. The organization has also been active in promoting summits on violence, homicide, and youth violence. With more than 100 members, IACP's Psychological Services Section issues guidelines for many types of police psychological services.

Membership in the IACP can be combined with Section membership, depending on one's area of expertise. Examples include the Drug Recognition Expert Section, the Capitol Police Section, the Indian Country Law Enforcement Section, the Legal Officers Section, the Police Psychological Services Section, the Public Transit Police Section, the Railroad Police Section, and the University/College Police section. Membership in these sections is limited to those who work in those particular fields.

IACP publishes a monthly magazine, *The Police Chief*. Diverse topics impacting law enforcement are analyzed, such as community-police relations, cybercrime, victim services, global policing, terrorism, traffic safety, mental health, human and civil rights, and officer safety and wellness.

In 2015, the IACP partnered with the National Association for the Advancement of Colored People (NAACP) and Yale University and received a $7 million award from the Department of Justice (DOJ) to address community healing and to reduce harm in communities. The agencies will also examine the impact of trauma and community harm by assisting law enforcement agencies with developing comprehensive, evidence-based response strategies, and developing interventions to promote community engagement in light of all of the recent incidents of violence between the police and the public. The goal is to create a collaborative partnership to help increase understanding between the community and the police, and to help develop skills and practices that will improve relationships and guide law enforcement in carrying out their duties.

IACP was originally created for the intent of promoting cooperation and communication between law enforcement agencies within the United States. Since its inception, it is now composed of not only U.S. law enforcement agencies, but has expanded to international police. IACP has provided valuable examinations into a variety of topics impacting not only law enforcement agents, but also the public, as with victims of crime. It has also developed and/or promoted a number of technological advancements in the field of law enforcement. Today, the IACP is considered a leader in forming strategic partnerships with the NAAP, the DOJ, and Rapid Response Teams (RRT), which include victim assistance, mental health, law enforcement, and community leaders.

Stephanie L. Albertson

See also: Community Policing Today; Secret Service; Uniform Crime Reports; Wickersham Report on Soaring Crime during Prohibition

Further Reading

Collier, B. "International World Police." *Journal of Criminal Law and Criminology* (1931–1951) 23, no. 3 (1932): 545–548.

International Association of Chiefs of Police (IACP). http://www.theiacp.org.

Police Chief Magazine. http://www.policechiefmagazine.org.

Upson, L. D. "The International Association of Chiefs of Police and Other American Police Organizations." *Annals of the American Academy of Political and Social Science* 146 (1929): 121–127.

CRIME CONTROL VERSUS DUE PROCESS

Based on media portrayals and public opinion, it appears that the police and the community may believe in different methods to keep everyone safe and free from exposure to crime and the risk of victimization. Yet, the goals really should be the same for all parties—the public wants to be free to walk around their communities, day or night, without worrying about their safety, the security of their families, and their possessions. The police should take pride in their responsibility to keep the streets crime-free, and they should want the community to feel safe.

Crime Control Model

Does freedom really mean something different for police and for the general public? Because freedom is so important, every effort must be made to prevent crime from occurring and to control crime when it does occur. This focus is called the Crime Control Model. It was constructed by Herbert Packer to represent one of the two competing systems of values that exist and operate in society today. What it means is that the government (and police departments) carry the responsibility of deterring and controlling crime. To deter crime, there is a responsibility on the part of the police as well as on lawmakers. There is also pressure on the court system to punish wrongdoers. In order for deterrence to work, a criminal must believe that the likelihood of getting caught is high. Logically, this would deter or prevent that criminal from committing the crime that was being considered. However if deterrence theory really works, why do people still commit crimes?

An explanation is that there is possibly not a significant chance of the criminal getting caught in the first place, and therefore the certainty of being discovered decreases, which in turn increases the likelihood the criminal will continue with committing the crime. For example, if a child is told not to eat the candy in the pantry, but he knows that no one will notice or catch him, he will be more inclined to do it, without regard for the repercussions.

Another factor to consider is that the less likely one is to get caught and the less likely any punishment will be handed down, the more likely the crime will be committed. So, even if a crime is committed, there are no consequences for that behavior. Most criminals learn these crime-versus-punishment rules rather quickly. The chance of getting caught committing a crime is low in certain areas where officers are overworked, spread too thin, or overcrowded conditions exist in a particular geographic location. Thus, one can commit a crime with a low risk of detection. Therefore, there is no deterrence—criminals steal, and they get something for free, and that only reinforces their chance of doing the act again. It is simple positive reinforcement at work. Even if a punishment for criminality is severe (a lengthy sentence, or even a death sentence), if the chance of getting caught (certainty) is low, criminals may be willing to take the risk.

The last factor to consider in regard to deterrence is the swiftness of the response by law enforcement and the court system. For example, if someone smokes cigarettes for a number of years, the chance of developing lung cancer rises. But if that smoker knew that smoking today would definitely lead to lung cancer and would lead to that cancer tomorrow, he would be much more likely to reconsider smoking. So, if a would-be offender thinks before he acts, and he realizes that the chance of getting caught is high, that the punishment for that crime is strict, and that the punishment will take effect immediately, he might be deterred, and crime may be controlled.

Does Deterrence Work?

Law enforcement officers have been trained to control crime. Their goal is to achieve a high rate of apprehension of offenders, which should lead to a high rate of conviction and disposition of cases. In this way, criminals would be caught, processed, incarcerated, and off the streets. Then, the community would be safer. The emphasis is on efficiency and speed, as well as deterrence and repression of crime.

This seems like a positive goal that the community would support. However, there are a few problems with the model of law enforcement. First, it is based on the assumption that deterrence works (i.e., swift, certain, and severe action and punishment will repress crime). Yet, research shows that many offenders do not think about the consequences of their actions before they commit a crime. In fact, the Positivist School of thought states that those who commit crime may do so due to factors beyond their control. Biological, psychological, and sociological explanations have been used as reasons to move the blame off of the individual and onto genetics, mental illness, low IQ, environmental factors, and so on. If this is the case, then it would not matter how likely one is to be caught, how quickly one is punished, or how severe that punishment is.

Further, based on the number of criminals incarcerated, it seems clear that most people do not care what the consequences are for an act; they do not think they are going to be caught. According to the Classical School of thought, criminals are rational and reasoning. Hence, they weigh the pros and cons of their actions. Most people are going to realize that criminals are not likely to be caught. Therefore, they cannot be processed through the system at all.

The biggest problem with the Crime Control Model has more to do with legal issues than those other factors. The government might see deterrence theory and the Crime Control Model as a panacea. Law enforcement might enforce the law with this model in mind. But in revisiting the goals of the Crime Control Model, we see some discrepancies with the Constitution and the notions of fairness and accuracy.

If the Crime Control Model focuses on getting the bad guys off the street as quickly as possible, we may have a justice system that is too quick to judge and may judge in a way that is unfair to minorities, low income residents, and males. While all citizens wish to be safe, they do not want their safety to come at the expense of their rights. If our criminal justice system is to survive, confidence in the outcome of a case is necessary. The community cannot believe that citizens are treated unfairly or that the wrong individuals are being convicted. Yet, the Crime Control Model is focused on safety. Asking people to give up some freedom, time, and privacy for the sake of controlling crime is a hard sell for some, but it may be worth the "deprivation" for others.

Example

One example of the Crime Control Model is the airport security rules and regulations established after September 11, 2001. People are checked, prodded, x-rayed, frisked, and forced to remove shoes and other garments in order to board a plane. Lots of time is wasted in the name of security. Is this considered giving up freedoms? Is safety important enough to allow any and all action to be taken by the government to control crime? Who gets hurt the most in this predicament? Many citizens understand that they are giving up some liberties but would rather give up time than be a on a plane with a terrorist or a bomb. Others (who may have nothing to hide and are law-abiding as well) say that the government should not be as controlling.

Due Process Model

The competing model with Crime Control has been the Due Process Model, which was labeled by Herbert Packer, a law professor and criminologist. Although its focus is on freedom, too, it states that freedom is so important that every effort must be taken to ensure that criminal justice decisions are based on accurate, fair, and reliable information. Rather than supporting the goal of a high rate of apprehension, the Due Process Model is more focused on protecting citizens from unlawful intrusion into their private lives, apprehending while protecting individual rights, and emphasizing a formal decision-making process that is fair and balanced.

There is a belief within the criminal justice system that is it better to let ten guilty men be released than to convict one innocent man. This means that arrests, convictions, and sentences must be correct and based on accurate and reliable information. This should be true for the circumstances surrounding the approach of an officer, to the arrest phase, to the line-up, fingerprinting, trial, and release of a suspect. The Due Process Model stresses the importance of improved interrogation tactics, which include better representation by counsel in the courtroom and protection from illegal detention, cruel punishment, and unreasonable search and seizure. This model clearly shows a lack of faith in the criminal justice system and in the police in general.

Accuracy and fairness are intertwined in the Due Process Model because of the need for evidence that the decision-making process is correct. The government is interested in quickly arresting and processing (and getting dangerous offenders off the street). However, the public is interested in making sure the correct person is taken off the street while his or her individual rights are protected. In addition, the community wants to make sure that in the process of attempting to identify who the offender may be, innocent parties' rights are not violated for the sake of controlling crime. There is less of a focus on the resolution and more on rights, and how evidence is gathered. The model is used to limit police power, emphasizing liberty over order.

It is a difficult balancing act in that the goal of protecting the community often has to come at a cost. Law-abiding citizens might need to be inconvenienced (stopped, questioned, arrested) in order to determine who the responsible party actually is. Yet, many members of the community do not support the Crime Control Model because they feel it is applied in a biased or discriminatory manner.

This leads to conflict within the community as well as to conflict between the police and the community. The direction of the sentiment of the community seems to be moving toward support for the Due Process Model. The Black Lives Matter movement is a good example of this view, where groups of mostly well-meaning citizens (not just minorities) have come together to gain respect and justice for those they think the police have victimized. These groups feel as though the police accuse, arrest, and shoot (and ask questions later), and that they act this way with minorities more so than with non-minorities.

Goals

The ultimate goal is for the government, law enforcement, and citizens to agree. The aim is to try to stress the importance of taking on the role of the other—so law enforcement and citizens can consider how it might feel to be treated in a way that appears unfair by the opposition. Interestingly, some research has shown that offenders might be more law-abiding if they perceive that they are being treated fairly. Hence, a commitment to professionalism and respect is the most critical objective. Both Crime Control and Due Process are necessary. We need both order and liberty. The approach might be different, but the goal of both models is still to eliminate and deter crime and punish offenders.

Gina Robertiello

See also: Crime Prevention Techniques; Fourth Amendment; Fifth Amendment; Police Accountability; Sixth Amendment

Further Reading

Cabral, A. I. P., C. H. D. P. L. Cabral, and M. L. Q. Soares. "Brazil and the Inter-American System for the Protection of Human Rights: Conventionality Control on the Criminal Lawsuit no. 470." *Towards a Universal Justice? Putting International Courts and Jurisdictions into Perspective*, 222–243. Leiden: Brill, 2016.

Crawford, K., and J. Schultz. "Big Data and Due Process: Toward a Framework to Redress Predictive Privacy Harms." *Boston College Law Review* 55, no. 93 (January 2014). http://lawdigitalcommons.bc.edu/cgi/viewcontent.cgi?article=3351&context=bclr.

Lerman, A. E., and V. M. Weaver. *Arresting Citizenship: The Democratic Consequences of American Crime Control*. Chicago, IL: University of Chicago Press. 2014.

Levi, M. *Regulating Fraud (Routledge Revivals): White-Collar Crime and the Criminal Process*. New York: Routledge, 2013.

Loader, Ian, and Richard Sparks. "Ideologies and Crime: Political Ideas and the Dynamics of Crime Control." *Global Crime* 17, no. 3–4 (2016): 314–330.

Neubauer, David W., and Henry F. Fradella. *America's Courts and the Criminal Justice System*. Belmont, CA: Wadsworth Publishing, 2013.

Singh, Anne-Marie. *Policing and Crime Control in Post-Apartheid South Africa*. New York: Routledge. 2016.

Part 2: Technological Advances and the Rise of Organized Crime (1900–1950)

CHARLES BECKER (1870–1915)

Gambling, betrayal, corruption, and murder led to the execution of Charles Becker, a former lieutenant on the New York police force. Becker quickly became part of the corruption that was common in New York City politics during this time. He supplemented his income through financial kickbacks associated with overlooking illegal gambling operations. Herman Rosenthal, a Manhattan gambler, filed a complaint against Becker after he failed to protect Rosenthal's illegal casino despite earning a financial kickback. Becker was accused and convicted of arranging the murder of Rosenthal to prevent the man from testifying against him. Becker was the first person to be executed for murder that occurred during official law enforcement duties. After two trials, he was executed on July 30, 1915.

Charles Becker was the sixth child born to German immigrants on July 26, 1870, in Calicoon Center, New York. He traveled to New York City when he was 20 to seek employment, working at a variety of odd jobs, one of which was as a bouncer at the Atlantic Gardens, which was a German beer garden. He became interested in law enforcement after meeting Big Tim Sullivan. Sullivan led the Democratic political machine known as Tammany Hall, which was an organization best known for taking care of the city's poor and immigrant population. However, as time progressed, the organization became known for political corruption. Becker paid a fee of $250 to Tammany Hall in 1893 to become an officer for the New York police force.

Becker's first appointment as an officer was in the Fulton Street area, followed by an assignment to the Tenderloin district. This district—located within an area that included 3rd Avenue on the east, 7th Avenue on the west, 23rd Street on the south, and 44th Street on the north—was home to a broad range of illicit business practices including prostitution brothels, gambling casinos, and other vice operations. The term "vice" refers to those activities that are considered immoral. Placement in this district provided Becker with ample opportunities to supplement his income through corruption affiliated with these business activities.

By 1907, Becker was officially promoted to sergeant; however he was unofficially promoted to the position of bagman for Captain Max Schmittberger. In his role as bagman, Becker collected and distributed proceeds from the extortion of those who operated the brothels and casinos. Becker was later promoted to lieutenant, after

Police Lieutenant Charles Becker (shown in 1914), was a lieutenant for the New York City Police Department. Notoriously corrupt, Becker was sentenced to death after being convicted of murder. (Library of Congress)

Schmittberger was terminated for charges of corruption. By 1911, Becker controlled the Tenderloin district, overseeing illegal operations in the area.

Several men, including gangster Jacob "Big Jack" Zelig, worked alongside Becker to silence any threats to their illicit business operations such as causing severe physical harm, or even death, to those perceived as interfering in their money-making establishment. One of these threats was 38-year-old Herman "Beansy" Rosenthal, who privately paid Becker to protect his illegal gambling establishment, the Hesper Club, from police interference. After being open for only one month, Becker raided Rosenthal's casino, which resulted in extensive damage to the establishment. Becker was acting under the orders of the new police commissioner Rhinelander Waldo. Waldo was a progressive politician who was eager to end political and police corruption throughout the city. Despite the reason for the raid, Rosenthal felt betrayed and filed a complaint against Becker.

Learning of the complaint filed against him, Becker told Zelig that Rosenthal needed to be dealt with immediately. Two gamblers—"Bald Jack" Rose and Harry Vallon—informed Zelig where Rosenthal could be found in the early hours of July 16, 1912. Zelig sent four men to the Metropole Hotel at 147 43rd Street, located just east of Broadway near Times Square, where they waited outside for Rosenthal. The men approached Rosenthal as he left the hotel restaurant, shooting him in cold blood. Rosenthal died in the street outside the hotel after being struck multiple times at close range.

Many New York citizens were in the area of the Metropole Hotel when the shooting occurred and were able to identify the killers, who included "Dago" Frank Cirofici, Louis "Lefty Louie" Rosenberg, Harry "Gyp the Blood" Horowitz, and Jacob "Whitey Lewis" Seidenschmer. All four men were taken into custody, tried, and convicted for the murder of Rosenthal. On April 14, 1913, at Sing Sing Prison, in Ossining, New York, they were executed by electric chair. These four were not the only men to face consequences for Rosenthal's murder. Zelig was killed earlier by a gangster who had been hired to silence him about Becker's role in the situation. Unfortunately for Becker, this was not enough to protect him for his part in Rosenthal's murder.

Becker was tried in the fall of 1912 for first degree murder. This trial was prosecuted by Charles Whitman and his assistant prosecutor, Frank Moss, and presided over by Judge John Goff, who had the reputation of having no tolerance for political and police corruption. Becker was found guilty for Rosenthal's murder, in large part due to testimony by gamblers Rose and Vallon, but that conviction was later overturned based on grounds that Judge Goff did not provide the defense with a fair trial. A second trial was held in the spring of 1914, prosecuted by Whitman and presided over by Judge Samuel Seabury. Again, Becker was found guilty and was sentenced to execution in the electric chair.

Becker attempted to appeal the second conviction, and while not successful, he did manage to postpone the execution for more than one year. On July 20, 1915, at Sing Sing Prison, time ran out and Becker was executed in the electric chair. Up to the time of his execution, he had pleaded his innocence, stating that he had ordered Zelig to get Rosenthal out of town rather than to have him murdered. Lieutenant Becker is likely the only officer executed for crimes that were connected to his official duties as a police officer.

Tamara J. Lynn

See also: Corruption; Gangsters of the 1900s; Teddy Roosevelt's Fight against Police Corruption; Wickersham Report on Soaring Crime during Prohibition

Further Reading

Cohen, S. *The Execution of Officer Becker: The Murder of a Gambler, the Trial of a Cop, and the Birth of Organized Crime.* New York, NY: Carroll & Graf Publishers, 2006.

Dash, M. *Satan's Circus: Murder, Vice, Police Corruption and New York's Trial of the Century.* New York, NY: Three Rivers Press, 2007.

Lardner, James, and Thomas Reppetto. *NYPD: A City and Its Police.* New York: Holt Paperbacks, 2001.

Roberts, S. "100 Years after a Murder, Questions about a Police Officer's Guilt," *City Room: Blogging from the Five Boroughs,* posted on July 15, 2012. http://cityroom.blogs.nytimes.com/2012/07/15/100-years-after-a-murder-questions-about-a-police-officers-guilt/?_r=0.

Welch, Richard F. *King of the Bowery: Big Tim Sullivan, Tammany Hall, and New York City from the Gilded Age to the Progressive Era.* Albany: State University of New York Press, 2009.

Whalen, Bernard, Jon Whalen, and William J. Bratton. *The NYPD's First Fifty Years: Politicians, Police Commissioners, and Patrolmen.* Lincoln, NE: Potomac Books, 2015.

GANGSTERS OF THE 1900s

A gangster can be defined as a member of a gang of violent criminals. Some gangs are part of organized crime, which provides resources to support large criminal activities such as racketeering and gambling rings. Gangsters have played an interesting role in American history and have become a part of popular culture. Early gangsters were often viewed with reverence and given respect by the public. Several of the mafia families that were well established in the early 20th century in the United States continued to operate through the end of the century.

There are many famous gangsters, including: Al Capone, Lucky Luciano, Bonnie and Clyde, Vito Genovese, and John Gotti. Their impact on the development of organized crime was substantial and is still felt today. Many law enforcement agencies have focused a lot of their resources on ending the illegal activity of the gangsters, but most have had limited success in that endeavor.

Gangsters brought excitement and presented a flashy image to a country experiencing Prohibition in the 1920s and suffering through the Depression in the 1930s. The image of an early American gangster often involves silk suits, expensive jewelry, and nightclubs.

The number of Italian immigrants who came to the United States in the late 19th and early 20th centuries was staggering. In New York City alone, historian Thomas Repetto reported that there were more than 500,000 Italian immigrants. During this period, the Italian Fascist dictator Benito Mussolini was attacking the Sicilian mafia in Italy. This was a good time for the mafia to escape to the United States.

New York and Chicago were the early homes of the American Mafia. The sale of illicit liquor in the 1920s provided the Italian American organized crime network with an opportunity to rise to power. At the end of Prohibition, it was a simple process to move into other organized crime activities. Soon, the Mafia was actively involved in numerous other criminal enterprises, including money laundering, bribing police and public officials, smuggling, illegal gambling, loan-sharking, and contract killings. The gangsters were also involved in legal businesses such as garbage collection, construction, and nightclubs. Like their counterparts in Italy, the Mafia maintained a strict code of conduct that prohibited any cooperation with government authorities and demanded secrecy.

Vito Genovese (1897–1969) was an Italian American mobster who rose to power during Prohibition in the American Mafia and would later become leader of the Genovese crime family. He died of a heart attack and is buried in New York. (Library of Congress)

Because many Mafia families were involved in the same criminal enterprises, conflicts quickly arose. Bloodshed was common, and when two of the biggest Italian American gangs fought for control of New York City, it was called the Castellammarese War. Following the war, Salvatore Marazano (1886–1931) believed he was the new boss. This was short lived though, as Lucky Luciano (1897–1962) had him killed the same year.

Luciano then founded the Commission, which was a board of directors that had the responsibility of setting policies and mediating problems between Mafia families. There were five main Mafia families in New York, and other cities had one family each. The five most powerful families in New York City were the Genovese family, the Luciano family, the Bonanno family, the Gambino family, and the Lucchese family.

Al Capone (1899–1947) is one of the most well-known gangsters of the 1900s. Capone became involved in a street gang in Brooklyn after quitting school after the sixth grade. In 1920, Capone was invited to Chicago to join the Colosimo mob. By 1952, Capone became the boss of that organization. He was known for being ruthless and demonstrated that on February 14, 1929, when his mob committed the St. Valentine's Day Massacre. Capone's mob killed seven members of a rival gang who had posed as police officers. The victims were lined up against a wall and killed with machine guns.

Another powerful gangster was Vito Genovese (1897–1969). Genovese started as a street gang member, but became a professional killer. He was a member of the Genovese family and helped expand their operations to reach nationwide. When United States law enforcement started pursuing Genovese for a murder he had contracted, he fled to Italy. Genovese was an advisor to Mussolini during World War II, but later was arrested and sent back to the United States. The only witness to the murder that Genovese was charged with had died, so Genovese was acquitted and took control again of the family. Genovese was one of the few Mafia leaders who was heavily involved in the drug trade. He rose to a position of power over several mafia families, but it did not last long because he was arrested on narcotics charges and sent to prison. He died there in 1969.

The Italians were not the only ethnic group with gangsters. Jack Diamond (1897–1931) was an Irish American gangster who worked out of Philadelphia. He was also known as Gentleman Jack. In addition to his work in Philadelphia, Diamond oversaw alcohol sales in Manhattan. Diamond had conflicts with several gangs in New York and was shot by his enemies. Another Irish American gangster is James Coonan (1946–). Coonan operated in New York and set up his own gang to get revenge for his father's murder. Coonan's father was kidnapped by another famous gangster in the 1960s: Mickey Spillane. Spillane had Coonan's father beaten and killed. Coonan was sentenced to prison for murder.

There were other American gangsters who were not part of the Mafia. John Dillinger, Pretty Boy Floyd, Bonnie and Clyde, and Ma Barker were a few gangsters who were active during the 1930s. Dillinger was a famous gangster who was most active in the 1930s. Dillinger (1903–1934) spent a significant amount of time in prison for an attempted robbery he committed when he was 21. While in prison, Dillinger became very bitter and angry because his codefendant had received only a 2-year sentence in comparison to his 10- to 20-year sentence. Upon release from prison, Dillinger immediately became a vicious leader of a violent gang. In less than a year, his gang killed 10 men and wounded 7, killed a sheriff, robbed police arsenals and banks, and staged three jailbreaks. Dillinger was killed by FBI agents in 1934.

American bank robber Pretty Boy Floyd (1904–1934) was active at the same time as Dillinger. The public viewed Floyd positively because he often shared the money he stole, and because of that, he was known as "the Robin Hood of the Cookson Hills." Floyd was known for his use of a machine gun in his crimes and he worked with a group of accomplices. After Dillinger was killed, Floyd became "Public Enemy No. 1," but he was able to avoid capture for another year. When the FBI caught up with Floyd, a gun fight occurred and he was shot. Floyd died of those wounds a few minutes after he was shot.

Although history is full of male gangsters, there were also a few women who gained notoriety for this criminal activity. Ma Barker (1873–1935) was a mother who formed the Barker-Karpis Gang in 1931. Barker had four sons who were always getting in trouble with the law. Barker refused to discipline her sons and would always defend them. When the boys started getting more involved in more serious crime, Barker provided them with a hideout and lived vicariously through them. The Barker-Karpis Gang became known for excessive violence and meaningless killings. They robbed banks, and in one of their final heists, took more than $250,000. Barker was killed in a shootout with FBI agents in 1935.

Bonnie Parker (1910–1934) and Clyde Barrow (1909–1934) have been the subject of many movies and books on gangsters of the 1900s. This pair was known for numerous killings, robbery and kidnapping. The FBI launched one of the largest manhunts of the time in an effort to catch them. Bonnie and Clyde killed several police officers and embarrassed other criminal justice agents when they successfully broke into a maximum security prison in Texas to free a friend of theirs. On May 23, 1934, a posse waited for Bonnie and Clyde to return Sailes, Louisiana, based on a tip they had received about Bonnie and Clyde's whereabouts. When their car appeared, the officers opened fire and killed both Bonnie and Clyde.

Members of criminal gangs are also considered gangsters. Early gangs developed in the 1920s and 1930s, and usually were made up of friends and family members trying to project a "tough guy" image. Few of the early gangs were involved in serious criminal activity. Black gangs began to grow in numbers in the 1940s and became involved in theft, prostitution, forgery, extortion, and gambling. Street gangs continued to develop in the 1950s. These criminal groups' memberships were often based upon race and location within a city. Street gangs were involved in many of the same activities as the Mafia, and in some cases, the gangs would work with the Mafia.

One gang leader from the 1950s helped form an alliance between his street gang and the Mafia. The founder of the Cobras street gang in Chicago was Henry (Mickey the Cobra) Cogwell (1946–1977), who was a liaison to the Italian Mafia, but was later killed by another gang they were aligned with: the P-Stone Nation. Members of the P-Stone Nation may have killed Cogwell for getting too close to the Mafia.

In the 1960s, a new, violent African American gang called the Crips emerged. Raymond Washington (1953–1979) and Stanley Tookie Williams (1953–2005) utilized the Crips in Los Angeles to protect themselves and their neighborhood from other gangs. Other African American gangs formed to protect themselves from the Crips. Their biggest rival gang is the Bloods, which was founded by Sylvester Scott (1951–2010) and Vincent Owens (1952–2008). The Crips and the Bloods have thousands of members who engage in many criminal enterprises.

Toward the end of the 20th century, there were still many gangsters actively working in the United States. The Mafia and other organized crime groups continued to operate protection rackets and engage in extortion, smuggling, and drug dealing. Police agencies were still trying to bring down the large Mafia families with varying levels of success.

John Gotti (1940–2002) started working for the Gambino family in New York in the 1960s. Gotti had an extensive arrest record and had already served time in jail by his 21st birthday. He spent three years in prison, and he was released in 1971. Gotti then returned to the Gambino family, and soon afterward committed his first murder. Although there were several eyewitnesses who identified Gotti as the killer, he made a deal with the court for a lesser charge and served only four more years in prison.

Gotti was promoted within the family and grew in power. Paul Castellano, the family boss, did not approve of Gotti's behavior, which included gambling and drug dealing. Castellano was soon killed and Gotti took over as the head of the family. Although it took several attempts, law enforcement was finally able to convict Gotti in 1992 and keep him in prison. Gotti died in federal prison in 2002.

Paige H. Gordier

See also: J. Edgar Hoover (1895–1972), Director of the FBI; Law Enforcement in the Wild West; Wickersham Report on Soaring Crime during Prohibition

Further Reading

Bonanno, Bill, and Gary B. Abromovitz. *The Last Testament of Bill Bonanno: The Final Secrets of a Life in the Mafia.* New York: William Morrow Paperbacks, 2011.

Lupo, Salvatore. *History of the Mafia.* New York: Columbia University Press, 2009.

Raab, Selwyn. *Five Families: The Rise, Decline, and Resurgence of America's Most Powerful Mafia Empires.* New York: Thomas Dunne Books, 2006.

SECRET SERVICE

The United States Secret Service grew from only a small number of special agents and operatives into a fully functioning state-of-the-art law enforcement agency. In 2016, there were nearly 7,000 U.S. Secret Service employees throughout the world. The agency started its humble beginning on July 5, 1885, and was formed under the Department of the Treasury. The first director of the agency, William P. Wood, was sworn into office to take the leadership role of the newly formed agency in 1965. The origin of the Secret Service dates back to the American Civil War, when the Secret Service investigated the Ku Klux Klan in the 1860s. It also conducted detailed counter-espionage missions during the World Wars; this allowed the agency to provide a better service to the American people.

In 1870, the headquarters for the Secret Service moved from Washington, D.C., to New York City. However, the agency would move back to Washington, D.C., only four years later. In 1877, when the U.S. Congress passed legislation outlawing the counterfeiting of gold and silver coins, the Secret Service was tasked as the only law enforcement agency to combat counterfeiting, which was a part of its original mission. In 1894, the Secret Service had a part-time assignment of providing protection to the president of the United States while still maintaining its primary objectives, which were counterfeit currency and other financial-related crimes. The main focus of the Secret Service was to locate the individuals who made the counterfeit currency before the money would go into circulation throughout the country. The agency protection activities were often less active than they are today; they would protect the president, vice president, their family members, or other individuals based on the needs of the agency. Even during this time, the agency was still involved in other activities outside their standard protocol of financial crimes.

In 1901, the agency began to shift its focus to more of a protection agency. The Secret Service was asked to serve as the central agency to protect the president, which came after the assassination of President William McKinley. President McKinley was the third active U.S. president to be assassinated while in office. Because of the high level of assassination rates that had occurred in the United States, the focus had to partly shift to that of a protection agency. In 1907, the Sundry Civil Expense Act allocated funding to allow the Secret Service to protect the president of the United States, and in 1908 the Secret Service started to provide protection for the president. It was not until 1913 that Congress authorized the permanent protection of the president, and it was decided that the Secret Service would be the agency tasked with this permanent protection role.

The permanent protection duty was part of the Treasury Department Appropriations Act of 1913, which allowed the Secret Service, in part, to shift the missions of the agency. In 1915, a significant shift of focus was undertaken; President Wilson had tasked the Secretary of the Treasury to recruit the Secret Service to investigate any foreign espionage that was being committed in the United States. Two years later, Congress enacted legislation making it a federal crime to threaten the president of the United States, by any means. This refers to mail or any other means that could have been utilized to cause a threatening act against the president.

In 1922, the Secret Service became an even larger federal agency with the absorption of the White House Police Force. This is now known as the Uniformed Division of the agency. The new division was created at the request of President Harding, who stated the security of the White House was to be conducted by specially trained law enforcement officers. However, it was not until 1930 when President Hoover directed the White House Police Force to be under the supervision of the U.S. Secret Service. In 1936, the agency shifted the title of its law enforcement officers from operatives to special agents, and it was not until nearly 20 years later that a formal training academy for special agents was in full operation. The specialized training was a three-week investigative course that covered different areas of investigations conducted by the Secret Service. In 1971, nearly 60 acres of land was purchased by the U.S. government where a state-of-the-art academy would be built for training Secret Service special agents. This training academy was designed to conduct training specific to the mission statement of the Secret Service.

The September 11, 2001, terrorist attacks against the United States changed the dynamic of the federal government and the world as we knew it. The Homeland Security Act of November 2002 (HSA) formed the U.S. Department of Homeland Security, and 22 federal law enforcement agencies were transferred under its command. The HSA created the cabinet position of the Secretary of Homeland Security. The main purposes of the HSA are to avert terrorist attacks within the United States and to have an improved network of shared information among all law enforcement agencies. Thus, in 2002, the Secret Service was to be detached from the Department of Treasury, and it was absorbed as one of the 22 agencies that formed the U.S. Department of Homeland Security.

Under the Department of Homeland Security, the U.S. Secret Service is not only responsible for the protection of the presidential detail, but it is also responsible for the protection of any foreign dignitaries that visit the United States. For example, when world leaders arrive in New York City for events such as the United Nations General Assembly, it is the mission of the Secret Service to protect the world leaders and their spouses. The special agents must work with the security details from other nations—even those the United States might consider enemies—to provide overall safety to the entire event and all personnel. As a result, Secret Service special agents undergo extensive training at the James J. Rowley Training facility as well as the Federal Law Enforcement Training Centers (FLETC) outside Washington, D.C. While at FLETC, the Secret Service special agents receive instruction in conducting criminal investigations, sometimes alongside other special agents from various federal agencies. Upon completing the criminal investigations training program, the special agents are required to complete an additional four-and-a-half month training program at the training facility outside of Washington, D.C., where they undergo training specific to the duties of a special agent with the Secret Service. Some of these training programs include dignitary protection services, the investigation of counterfeit money, and extensive training in the handling and shooting of firearms.

The U.S. Secret Service Uniformed Division also provides security for the president and his or her family at the White House, security for the vice presidential living quarters at the Naval Observatory, and security for other locations in Washington, D.C., such as the Treasury Building, which they are mandated by law to protect.

Even with such great responsibility, the Secret Service has been plagued by controversy and scandal, especially in the early 2000s. One scandal that occurred was in 2012 when eight special agents were relieved of their duties for soliciting prostitutes in Colombia, while they were in an official capacity. The special agents were a part of the presidential detail and brought prostitutes back to their hotel rooms. This incident brought negative media attention to the agency, and it weakened the public's trust. Within a short period after the prostitution scandal, the Secret Service was inundated with more scandals, including several breaches to the White House by intruders with weapons and individuals with questionable backgrounds coming into close contact with President Barack Obama. Specifically, on December 10, 2013, President Obama was in very close proximity to a person who claimed to be a sign language interpreter at the Nelson Mandela memorial service in South Africa. However, the person was not a sign language interpreter, which caused fear about the credentials of the individual. Although the South African government admitted it had not conducted a full background check on the individual, it is the Secret Service's responsibility for the protection of the president and, therefore, it should have identified the interpreter prior to the event. The interpreter had a violent, criminal background, which was later discovered after the breach. Months later, there was a breach to the White House when a vehicle followed the motorcade of one of President Obama's daughters onto the White House grounds. Within the same timeframe, an armed individual was able to gain access to the White House by leaping over the security fence and running into the East Room of the White House, which demonstrated the lack of security that was provided to the president by the Secret Service.

These are just a few examples where the Secret Service negated its responsibility to carry out its duties outlined within its mission statement and to protect the president of the United States. The Secret Service's budget was drastically cut in 2011, which led to the lowest staffing levels in its history. The low staffing levels may have contributed to the breaches in security; however, it would be difficult to prove this was the sole reason behind these troubling times for the men and women of the Secret Service.

Anthony Aceste and Marco Aliano

See also: Gangsters of the 1900s; J. Edgar Hoover (1895–1972), Director of the FBI; Teddy Roosevelt's Fight against Police Corruption

Further Reading

Ambinder, M. "Inside the Secret Service." *The Atlantic* 307, no. 2 (March 2011): 70–78.

Katz, Eric. "Embattled Secret Service Spent Just 25 Minutes Training the Average Officer in 2013." *Government Executive.* February 12, 2015. http://www.govexec.com/management/2015/02/embattled-secret-service-spent-just-25-minutes-training-average-officer-2013/105270/.

"The U.S. Secret Service: Protecting Presidents Throughout History." National Law Enforcement Museum. January 2012. http://www.nleomf.org/museum/news/newsletters/online-insider/january-2012/us-secret-service-protecting-the-presidents.html.

"United States Secret Service: An Agency in Crisis." Report by the Committee on Oversight and Government Reform, December 3 2015. https://oversight.house.gov/report/united-states-secret-service-an-agency-in-crisis.

"USSS History." United States Secret Service Web Site. http://www.secretservice.gov/about/history/events.

TEDDY ROOSEVELT'S FIGHT AGAINST POLICE CORRUPTION

Approximately six years before he became the 26th president of the United States (1901–1908), Theodore "Teddy" Roosevelt served a short stint as a New York City police commissioner. The city's Republican mayor, William Strong, appointed Roosevelt to serve as a commissioner on May 6, 1895. At that time, the office of police commissioners consisted of a bipartisan board of four: two from the Democratic Party and two from the Republican Party. Mayor Strong appointed Roosevelt with the understanding that he was to put an end to the political corruption within the police department and "clean up the streets" of New York. Strong was particularly frustrated with the corrupt influence of the Democratic political organization, Tammany Hall (also known as the Sons of St. Tammany, Society of St. Tammany, or the Columbian Order). Roosevelt's ambitious police reform and city "clean up" agenda focused on several main factors: honesty, harsh punishment, strict vice control, and ending political corruption.

Roosevelt's Fight

Policing in the late 19th century took place during a period referred to as the Political Era, which spanned the mid-19th century to about 1920. It was termed the Political Era because local politicians influenced nearly every aspect of police work, including police management. Local politicians had tremendous influence on hiring decisions, specifically, who was hired or appointed, who was promoted, and who was fired. Roosevelt wanted to end the current patronage system (sometimes referred to as a spoils system) in hiring. Politicians often rewarded supporters, friends, and relatives with government jobs, including jobs within the police department, after winning the election. Some positions were granted in exchange for money, for example, one could be hired as a patrol officer for $200 to $300 or be promoted to police captain for approximately $15,000. His belief was that one's political ties or wealth should not determine hiring and promoting decisions.

Roosevelt shared Mayor Strong's distaste for political corruption—a view that developed while he served for six years as Civil Service Commissioner of New York (1889–1895). Roosevelt's tenure as Civil Service Commissioner shaped his vision and subsequent handling of the New York City Police Department. He found politics to be disreputable and rejected any intention of becoming another political hack while serving as a police commissioner. He recognized the police department had a cultural problem that accepted moral and political corruption as the status quo.

One of his first orders of business was to remove the corrupt police chief and Tammany Hall member Thomas Burns. Burns's dismissal led to senior patrol officers retiring, as they supported the status quo. This allowed Roosevelt to fill those positions with officers he saw fit by using the merit system. He believed that officers should earn their position by their own record, merit, and fitness for the role. Roosevelt also believed that valor should be a component used for promotions, as it increased the morale of the police force when brave and courageous officers were recognized.

Roosevelt's second order of business was to verify whether the patrol officers were actually performing their duties and obeying police codes of conduct. He warned that he would be personally ensuring that police were performing their patrol duties. Policing duties during this period were neighborhood-orientated and performed via foot-patrol of assigned posts (beats), which allowed officers to participate in the neighborhood social life. Initially, police did not take the order to enforce all laws and codes of conduct seriously. They believed doing so would be nearly impossible, as enforcing all laws could consume the police force for months, and the codes-of-conduct manual consisted of more than 100 pages of detailed instructions. To their dismay, the officers soon realized that Roosevelt was quite serious.

Roosevelt befriended Jacob Riis, a long-time New York resident and journalist for the *Tribune* and *Evening Sun*. To his promise, Roosevelt walked with Riis along the streets at night, equipped with a precinct map so they could see if patrol officers were performing their duties. As predicted, they caught officers sleeping, drinking inside taverns, conversing with prostitutes, and missing from their posts. Roosevelt would wake a sleeping patrol officer or approach an officer conversing with a prostitute and ask him in a stern voice if that was how he patrolled his post. If Roosevelt and Riis noticed officers missing from their assigned posts, they would search nearby taverns to track them down. Once confronted, the patrol officers would yell back at Roosevelt to mind his business (not recognizing him, as he was commissioner only for a few weeks). An officer caught conversing with a prostitute threatened to beat Roosevelt with his nightstick, and a missing patrol officer located outside a tavern cursed at Roosevelt and threatened to "pull him in." Roosevelt calmly introduced himself and ordered the officers back to their posts. Roosevelt required all derelict officers to report to headquarters at 9:30 a.m. the following morning, where he reprimanded them for a half an hour and promised to fine them if they were caught repeating such behavior.

With the assistance of the press, the news traveled quickly that Roosevelt was following through on his promise to personally ensure that officers were performing their patrol duties. Riis had promised Roosevelt that he would not write about their "night adventures," but Riis was allowed to share their stories with his colleagues. Local newspapers began writing articles about Roosevelt's escapades, including the incident where one officer threatened to beat the commissioner with his nightstick. Roosevelt's "night adventures" made for humorous political cartoons. Newspapers published one of Roosevelt dressed as a cowboy "lassoing" sleeping police officers and another of him dressed in a police uniform, wielding a nightstick about to strike a sleeping officer on the bottom of his shoes to wake him. In due time, officers heeded the message and began performing their patrol duties and obeying codes of conduct. Local newspapers then began running headlines that noted police officers were no longer lounging on the streets or emerging from taverns.

Roosevelt's third order of business was to raise the moral standards within the police department. In the 1890s, New York City was commonly referred to as the "vice capital of the United States" due to the large amount of prostitution, gambling, and alcohol consumption among the city's residents and visitors. Vice crimes had a significant impact on policing, both with regard to the moral behavior of the patrol officers and opportunities for corruption. The center of police corruption was the non-enforcement of the Sunday Excise Laws, otherwise known as "blue laws." Such laws originated during the Colonial Period and prohibited gambling and alcohol consumption on Sundays in order to enforce morality. In the 19th century, the laws expanded to prohibit attendance of baseball games, horse races, and the theater, and forbade the sale of nearly everything except food and medicine. Such blue laws had been on the books in New York since 1857 but were rarely observed. In enforcing the blue laws, Roosevelt's focus was mainly on the sale of alcohol, and he believed that taverns had too strong an influence in political life. Irish Catholic Tammany Hall members dominated the police force at the time. As such, Tammany Hall and police captains were able to extort hundreds of dollars per tavern to "look the other way." Consequently, many Tammany Hall members were current or former tavern owners. Therefore, the non-enforcement of the blue laws was a profitable means of political corruption.

Avery Andrews, another commissioner on the board and Roosevelt's closest ally, assisted in enforcing the blue laws. Similar to Roosevelt, Andrews walked the streets at night to observe whether or not taverns were serving alcohol and if patrol officers were performing their duties and enforcing the laws. While patrolling, Andrews noted patrol officers standing outside of taverns "looking the other way" while patrons were drinking alcohol inside. Andrews reported his findings back to Roosevelt, who grew angry that the officers were not performing their policing duties. He summoned a meeting with police captains and lectured them about enforcing *all* laws. He believed that no law should be placed on the books if it were not meant to be enforced, and no social class was protected from the law.

Police received a lot of opposition from residents—including the wealthy and the politically well-connected, who often frequented taverns on Sundays—on their enforcement of the blue laws. Sunday was the only day off for most workers, and they enjoyed spending their day inside taverns. Sunday was also the most profitable day of the week for tavern owners, and enforcing the laws meant that taverns would be forced to close and eventually would have to close permanently. Although unpopular among police as well, Roosevelt stressed that one's personal opinion of the law had little to do with enforcing it. Enforcing the blue laws would prove to be difficult, as it required a police force of about 3,800 to verify whether nearly 8,000 taverns were serving alcohol. Roosevelt stood his ground, and in June 1895 he had more than 2,000 officers scattered throughout the streets on Sundays. Some tavern owners surrendered by closing their establishments and raising their window shades, allowing police unobstructed views inside. Other taverns went out of business or moved to other jurisdictions, whereas others disobeyed the blue laws and the vice and corruption continued.

Roosevelt set ambitious goals as police commissioner and by his own admission was a foolish optimist. During his brief and tumultuous tenure, he became a reformer in dealing with political corruption and additional problems of an urbanized society in order to make the police department more honest and efficient. The position of police commissioner was demanding from the start, both physically and emotionally. In a June 16, 1895, letter he wrote to Anna Roosevelt—his brother Elliot's wife—he stated how corrupt the New York Police Department was and described how he had been patrolling the streets at night, sometimes going 40 hours at a stretch without any sleep (Brands 2006). After less than two years as a police commissioner, the position became unbearable and Roosevelt considered stepping down. Roosevelt was appointed assistant secretary of the Navy on April 6, 1897, by President William McKinley, and the Senate later confirmed. Roosevelt was overjoyed by the opportunity and stepped down as a New York City police commissioner on April 19, 1897.

During his brief tenure as a commissioner, Roosevelt was unable to achieve all of his goals. Because of this, his legacy as a police commissioner is sometimes viewed as a failure—vice crime and political corruption continued after his departure. Others, however, argue that his tenure was groundbreaking, and the city's problems never returned to the level they were before the Roosevelt era. His influence and reform efforts marked the beginning of the transition to the Reform Era of policing, where political influence gave way to the professionalism of police. Although such reform took place decades after Roosevelt's tenure, his efforts brought greater awareness to the political and moral corruption within New York City's police department, which made a lasting impression (no matter how slight) for years to come. Roosevelt tried his best to fight vice crime and corruption, but he was not successful in ending it. Although vice and corruption in the police department continued for decades, his vision and efforts to improve the lives of New Yorkers has not been forgotten.

Melanie Clark Mogavero

See also: Corruption; Gangsters of the 1900s; Law Enforcement in the Wild West; Secret Service

Further Reading

Roosevelt, Theodore. *Autobiography*. Edited by W. Andrews. New York: Charles Scribner's Sons, 1958.

Brands, H. W. *The Selected Letters of Theodore Roosevelt*. Lanham, MD: Rowman & Littlefield, 2006.

Grantham, Dewey W. *Theodore Roosevelt: Great Lives Observed*. Englewood Cliffs, NJ: Prentice-Hall, 1971.

Jeffers, H. Paul. *Commissioner Roosevelt: The Story of Theodore Roosevelt and the New York City Police, 1895–1897*. Hoboken, NJ: John Wiley & Sons, 1996.

Zacks, Richard. "The Police Commish." *Time,* June 25, 2006.

Zacks, Richard. *Island of Vice: Theodore Roosevelt's Quest to Clean Up Sin-Loving New York*. New York: Anchor, 2012.

ACLU

The American Civil Liberties Union (ACLU) is a private, nonprofit entity that aims to protect the rights of individuals, groups, and organizations that are guaranteed to them under the laws of the United States and the U.S. Constitution. The purpose of the ACLU is to serve as the nation's guardian of liberty. Although ACLU representatives are often involved in or intentionally insert themselves into discussions surrounding controversial issues across America, their focus is really to defend and preserve speech, expression, and other individual rights and freedoms afforded to people under the Bill of Rights. The Bill of Rights is the first 10 amendments to the U.S. Constitution, which collectively outlines specific prohibitions on governmental power, including police authority. The ACLU engages closely with American communities, courts, and lawmaking bodies to ensure that civil rights and other liberties are not violated by law enforcement.

Liberties such as due process, privacy, and freedom of speech are provided to every U.S. citizen by the Bill of Rights and the Constitution. However, these rights are not always protected and may be infringed upon, making organizations such as the ACLU relevant and useful to American society. The ACLU is often labeled as the frontrunner of individual rights contests in the United States, as it has involved itself in many Supreme Court decisions and many other federal and state cases. Beyond involvement in cases specifically concerning civil rights violations, the ACLU tries to stay ahead of rights infringements and remain relevant to contemporary legal issues, such as those impacting women, inmates, national security, and interactions between police officers and citizens. Media statements aimed at specific groups are frequently utilized by the ACLU to weigh in on new or ongoing liberty issues.

The ACLU was established in 1920 by Roger Baldwin and Crystal Eastman as a product of the National Civil Liberties Union. The primary reason for the creation of the ACLU was to focus on civil rights violations and amnesty cases following World War I. Throughout the 1920s and 1930s, amnesty and censorship cases that violated individual and group rights under the Constitution represented the primary efforts of the ACLU. In addition, political and labor rights were a strong concern of the organization during this time.

However, as World War II commenced, the ACLU shifted its focus toward the issues of freedom of speech and conscientious objection. A major argument that the ACLU inserted itself into was the debate over the internment of Japanese Americans in the shadow of World War II. The internment took place in 1942, was authorized by President Franklin D. Roosevelt after Japan attacked Pearl Harbor, and involved the forced relocation and imprisonment of roughly 120,000 people.

A majority of these individuals were American citizens. The ACLU spoke out against the internment early on, calling it racial discrimination and an attack on civil liberties.

In the 1950s, the ACLU challenged the widespread anticommunist efforts and sentiments in America that were fueled by Senator Joseph McCarthy of Wisconsin, which often led to erroneous and unfair accusations against Americans for allegedly being communists or communist sympathizers, as well as aggressive and invasive investigations of them. As opponents of McCarthyism—the practice of making accusations of treason against persons to restrict their political criticism without proper regard for evidence—the ACLU asserted that individuals cannot and should not be punished for their beliefs (as indicated by the First Amendment). The fight against anticommunism became a much larger issue, however, as the federal government began to partner with the Federal Bureau of Investigation (FBI) to conduct questionable surveillance of suspected communists, which the ACLU saw as an obvious violation of the Fourth Amendment.

The ACLU expanded its focus in the 1960s to include issues beyond the First Amendment, such as privacy rights, criminal procedure violations, and equal protection considerations. Such expansion was largely influenced by the civil rights movement and resulting racial segregation issues. In the late 1970s, the ACLU defended a neo-Nazi group that sought to march through a large Holocaust survivor settlement in Skokie, Illinois. This action by the ACLU to stand for free speech led thousands of its members to resign from the organization. Interestingly, many of the laws that the ACLU utilized to protect the American Nazis' right to free speech were the same laws it used during the 1960s when jurisdictions in the South tried to stop civil rights protests.

The ACLU has played an influential role in United States Supreme Court cases related to the use and misuse of police power through direct legal support and indirect legal briefs. *Mapp v. Ohio* (1961) was a landmark case that dealt directly with illegally collected evidence by law enforcement. In this case, Cleveland police were tipped off that Dollree Mapp may have been housing a man who was wanted for questioning in the bombing of a rival racketeer's home. Three police officers approached Mapp's residence, asked to search her home, and were subsequently denied by Mapp. Mapp stated that she would not allow the search without a warrant. Later that evening, multiple officers stormed Mapp's home, stating they had a search warrant. Mapp was shown a piece of paper, but she was not allowed to read or review the document. Mapp and her attorney were never provided a copy of the warrant. The search yielded illegal pornographic material, betting paraphernalia, and Virgil Ogletree (i.e., the man wanted for questioning in the bombing case). Mapp was later found guilty under Ohio law for possession of lewd and lascivious materials from the pornographic material found during the search. The Supreme Court reviewed Mapp's appeal and ruled in a 6–3 decision that her Fourth Amendment search and seizure rights had been violated. The ruling was made following an influential brief filed by ACLU attorney Bernard Berkman, who successfully argued on Mapp's behalf that the search of her home was unconstitutional. This decision ultimately bound all states to exclude evidence illegally obtained by violation of the Fourth Amendment, thereby requiring law enforcement to follow constitutionality when attempting to search suspects and their property.

Another case that the ACLU was involved in was *Miranda v. Arizona* (1966). The Phoenix Police Department arrested Ernesto Miranda based on circumstantial evidence that 10 days earlier he had been involved in the kidnapping and rape of an 18-year-old woman. Miranda was interrogated by police for two hours before confessing in a written statement to the rape charge. His statement included an admission that his confession was voluntary and free of police pressure. At no time during the interrogation, however, was Miranda informed of his right to remain silent or his right to counsel. Miranda was found guilty and sentenced for the crimes. Miranda's court-appointed attorney appealed the case, and it went to the Supreme Court, citing that Miranda was convicted solely based on the confession. The appeal, which was prepared by ACLU representatives and one of Phoenix's largest law firms, asserted that the confession was inadmissible because Miranda was unaware of his rights under the Constitution. The Supreme Court agreed, granting another victory for an ACLU-supported case and requiring law enforcement to verbally inform individuals of their rights (to have an attorney and to remain silent) prior to any interviews or interrogations. Without the aid of ACLU representation, many observers believe that Miranda's fate would have been quite different.

More recently, in *Safford Unified School District v. Redding* (2009), the Supreme Court ruled in favor of Savana Redding, a middle school student who was backed by the ACLU. School officials at Safford Middle School received a report that Redding had given a classmate pain medications and subsequently conducted a strip search. They did not find any medications and failed to contact Redding's parents throughout the investigation. The ACLU provided legal representation by submitting a legal brief to the U.S. Supreme Court, which raised two questions of Constitutional privacy. The first issue concerned whether or not it was reasonable to strip-search a 13-year-old girl because of unreliable accusations that she held legal drugs. The second issue concerned whether or not it was the duty of school officials to know not to order such a search of a child based on unreliable accusations. The Supreme Court voted 7–2 that the strip search violated Redding's Fourth Amendment rights, but the court did not hold the school or its employees directly responsible.

Since 9/11, the ACLU has fought for individual privacy and other civil rights with respect to national security. With numerous legal briefs, active petitions, and lawsuits filed against government agencies and leaders, the ACLU has challenged the United States regarding warrantless wiretapping by the National Security Agency (NSA) and the reduction of freedoms under the USA PATRIOT Act and USA FREEDOM Act. Some say that recent United States antiterrorism laws have restricted individual rights and freedoms and allowed many law enforcement agencies to infringe upon liberties. In response, the ACLU and its ongoing "Keep America Safe and Free" campaign has attempted to provide oversight of federal, state, and local law enforcement agencies and other government entities. Through legal representation and public petitioning, the ACLU has been a leading force in not only making potentially questionable policing and government activity known to the public, but also in limiting the power of many agencies and laws to restrict individual rights and freedoms.

Many experts in the legal field believe that the ACLU is not only important to preserving American civil liberties, but it may also be critical to the further development of policy to aid in controlling authority in government, including police power. The landmark Supreme Court cases that feature ACLU involvement highlight how the organization may effectively help with keeping law enforcement and other powerful individuals in check. It is likely that the ACLU will continue to monitor the interactions between police and citizens as it seeks to ensure and protect the rights and freedoms afforded to individuals in the United States.

David Patrick Connor and Raymond Elliot Doyle Cowles

See also: Fifth Amendment; Fourth Amendment; *Mapp v. Ohio*; *Miranda v. Arizona*; Wiretapping

Further Reading

Cottrell, Robert C. *Roger Nash Baldwin and the American Civil Liberties Union*. New York: Columbia University Press, 2001.

Donohue, W. A. *Twilight of Liberty: The Legacy of the ACLU*. Piscataway, NJ: Transaction Publishers, 2001.

Gora, Joel M., David Goldberger, Gary M. Stern, and Moron H. Halperin. *The Right to Protest: The Basic ACLU Guide to Free Expression*. Carbondale, IL: Southern Illinois University Press, 1991.

Mapp v. Ohio, 367 U.S. 643. (1961).

Miranda v. Arizona, 384 U.S. 436. (1966).

Safford Unified School District v. Redding, 531 F. 3d 1071. (2009).

Uniting and Strengthening America by Fulfilling Rights and Ensuring Effective Discipline over Monitoring (USA Freedom) Act of 2015. Public L. No. 114–123, 129 Stat. 268 (2015).

Uniting and Strengthening America by Providing Appropriate Tools Required to Intercept and Obstruct Terrorism (USA Patriot) Act of 2001. Public L. No. 107–156, 115 Stat. 272 (2001).

Walker, Samuel. *In Defense of American Liberties*. Carbondale, IL: Southern Illinois University Press, 1999.

J. EDGAR HOOVER (1895–1972), DIRECTOR OF THE FBI

The rise of the Federal Bureau of Investigations (FBI) in the United States as the foremost law enforcement agency in the world can be traced to the influence and impact of a single individual, J. Edgar Hoover. Hoover ruled over the FBI and its predecessor agencies from 1926 until his death in 1972. Remarkably, his involvement with the FBI came at the end of a national scandal that rocked the United States, the Teapot Dome, and his separation from the agency ended as another national scandal began gathering momentum, Watergate. However, it was the years between that would greatly shape our nation's strong belief in, as well as our underlying mistrust of, federal law enforcement.

In order to better appreciate Hoover's influence on our collective view of federal law enforcement, we must start at the beginning. Hoover was born January 1, 1895, in Washington, D.C. His parents were civil servants who worked for the government. Yet, it was his mother, Anna Marie Scheitlin Hoover, who had the greatest influence on the individual he was to become. By all accounts, she was an authoritarian figure who strictly instilled her own views of morality and patriotism into a young Hoover, which would shape his worldly view and inspired him to become a politician. Hoover would later credit his mother with instilling these qualities, and he lived with her into his early forties. Although he never truly reached his goal of being a politician, Hoover did graduate from Georgetown University School of law with both a bachelor's and master's degree in law.

Upon graduation from law school, Hoover followed his parents' example and became a civil servant. Specifically, at the start of World War I, Hoover took a position working for the Justice Department, reviewing alien enemy internment and deportation cases. This position allowed him to secure draft exemption status due to his work. During his time at the Justice Department, he was known for his staunch conservatism, patriotism, and efficiency in his job. These qualities led to his appointment by U.S. Attorney General Mitchell Palmer to head the newly constructed General Intelligence Division (GID) of the Bureau of Investigations (BOI) for the Justice Department. The GID was tasked with gathering information on radical leftist groups in the United States as well as anyone engaged in insurrectionary activities. Many attribute Hoover's rapid advancement in the BOI to his investigative performance of alien enemies during World War I.

Hoover's work with the GID culminated in a massive sting operation later known as the Palmer Raids, ascribed to the

John Edgar Hoover (1895–1972) was the first director of the Federal Bureau of Investigation (FBI) of the United States. Hoover is credited with instituting centralized fingerprint files and forensic labs. (Library of Congress)

bombing of Palmer's home. On January 2, 1920, agents under Hoover's instruction arrested more than 500 people in three different cities who were believed to be engaging in insurrectionary and leftist activities. Most of these arrests were conducted without evidence or without legally obtained search warrants. Many of the people arrested were innocent bystanders who were caught up in Hoover's ambition. In all, the raids lasted several more weeks with several thousand arrests. In the end, approximately 500 individuals were deported due to their perceived radical activities. Eventually, the legality of the raids was questioned, which led to the ouster of Palmer. Hoover, however, emerged from the events having gained a solid reputation as an individual who could get the job done. This was the first known time where Hoover engaged in questionable tactics of legality to do what he believed was right for the country.

Despite the disgrace of the Palmer Raids, Hoover was appointed director of the BOI by President Calvin Coolidge to help restore the agency's reputation. Hoover took the position under the terms that the bureau head was to report directly to the U.S. attorney general and was to have no influence from political entities. Once settled into his position, Hoover began to mold the agency's mission to reflect his own morality and conservatism.

By the early 1930s the United States was facing a real threat from organized crime. Throughout the Midwest, in small towns and large cities, gangsters were engaging in illegal activities, creating problems in communities. The local law enforcement at this time was underequipped, shorthanded, and underfunded to deal with the problems caused by these gangsters. In addition, the image of the gangster had been romanticized by those in the media to the point that gangsters had become the princes of pop culture.

Hoover's main charge at this time was to restore order throughout the Midwest. To do this, Hoover began recruiting new agents to the BOI (later changed to the FBI in 1935). In particular, Hoover began recruiting White, college-educated males and instilled in them his own sense of values, patriotism, and conservatism. The new recruits were expected to adhere to a strict moral code, including abstinence from alcohol as well as the comforts of the opposite sex. These new recruits would become synonymous with the term G-Men, or Government Men.

In early 1933, several federal agents were escorting noted gangster and bank robber Frank Nash back to federal prison in Kansas City when they were gunned down by several other gangsters trying to free Nash. Four agents lost their lives along with Nash in what would be known as the KC Massacre. Many historians point to this event as a turning point in Hoover's assault on gangsters. An investigation ensued, looking for those responsible. The BOI claimed to find evidence that implicated several gangsters in contributing to the shootout. However, many at the time and in later years believed much of the evidence may have been falsified. Following the KC Massacre in mid-1934, Hoover pushed congress for authority to make arrests under the Interstate Commerce Act. This was a new power given to agents of the BOI, as they had not had the authority to make arrests prior to this. Once given authority, Hoover's agents raged a brutal war on many gangsters, leading to several deaths and many arrests, including those of George "Machine Gun" Kelly and John Dillinger.

These raids instilled the FBI as an important part of the national law enforcement movement and gave rise to the authority of the FBI in pop culture. In particular, the FBI G-Men were viewed as tech-savvy government agents who upheld the national moral code of conservatism.

After World War II (1939–1945), the Cold War came about mainly because of the economic and political conflicts between the communist Soviet Union and the democratic United States. The rivalry resulted in concerns of Communist and leftist sympathizers and Soviet spies in the United States, creating a threat to U.S. security. These concerns were not completely unfounded. The Union of Soviet Socialist Republics (USSR) had an extensive history of espionage activities within the United States, as the result of assistance from U.S. citizens during World War II. This was a time referred to as the Red Scare, due to intense anticommunist hysteria. Communists were associated with their allegiance to the red Soviet flag; thus, they were referred to as "Reds."

The Red Scare resulted in many government actions that greatly affected U.S. society and government. During this time, the government took a draconian approach in ascertaining whether a person was deemed a government loyalist or communist. The creation of the House Un-American Activities Committee provided its members with the authority to research and scrutinize the loyalty of federal employees. The Red Scare culminated with the interrogation and examination of many employees within not only the government, but also Hollywood, which was perceived as sympathetic to communist ideals. In Hollywood, those perceived as un-American were blacklisted, unable to acquire employment within the film industry. Dossiers were created from these investigations, often obscured from public knowledge, on thousands of U.S. citizens through orders by Senator Joseph R. McCarthy. Many people were required to testify and respond to a battery of questioning before the government regarding their political ideology. By the late 1950s, the investigations and apprehension toward communist sympathizers had lost steam.

J. Edgar Hoover was associated with the facilitation of these controversial and aggressive investigations, which maintained the objective of ascertaining communist sympathizers within the United States. Under Hoover's supervision, not only were dossiers created on alleged communists, but also telephones were wiretapped and stringent surveillance conducted by FBI agents toward communist sympathizers. It was well known that Hoover was vehemently opposed to communism. World War I and the communist ideology of Vladimir Lenin were significantly influential factors governing Hoover's communist animosity.

The FBI assisted in gathering pertinent information against arguably the most high-profile and controversial case concerning accusations of communist sentiment: Julius Rosenberg (1918–1953) and his wife, Ethel Rosenberg (1915–1953). In 1951, both were found guilty of espionage. They were each sentenced to death by electrocution and died nearly two years later in Sing Sing Prison, in Ossining, New York. Prior to the Rosenbergs' trial, in a 1949 case, FBI agents were successful in producing sufficient evidence and establishing the guilt of 12 leaders associated with the American Communist Party, who were convicted of a plot to overthrow the U.S. government.

Regardless of the intentions associated with any protest, riot, or demonstration, Hoover ascribed communist sentiment as its motivation. Hoover believed Martin Luther King, Jr., to be a supporter of communism, in addition to the National Association for the Advancement of Colored People (NAACP) members perceived as radicals. Hoover's disdain for Martin Luther King, Jr., was the rationale for ordering FBI agents to conduct surveillance on both King and the NAACP. Yet, no proof was discovered to support his theory. He used the riots during the 1960s to his advantage, by establishing concerns of a Black rebellion within the public. This strategy worked to Hoover's advantage, by expanding the role of the FBI's domestic intelligence, and Hoover was permitted to extend his service as the director of the FBI beyond the age of mandatory retirement.

The unstable, violent, and rebellious times during the late 1920s and early 1930s were instrumental is establishing Hoover's authority and control within the United States. There was an urgency for authority, and Hoover was yearning to fill this void. However, by the end of Hoover's tenure at the FBI, the need for security and belief in authority had been replaced by the country's need for transparency and openness. Hoover never adapted to this need and was greatly damaged by his clandestine operations, encroachment on personal freedom, and obscurity in security. Ultimately, while his rise was timely, his methods negatively influenced the view of the FBI for many years following his death. It has been only since the early 2000s that the FBI has regained much of the national trust that was lost during World War II.

During his prolonged tenure as FBI director, Hoover confronted gangsters, Nazis, and Communists. Although his abuse of power associated with the illegal surveillance of government officials, civil rights activists, the NAACP, and Hollywood elite made Hoover a controversial figure, he is attributed with elevating the FBI to an internationally recognized and respected criminal justice agency. He incorporated a number of technological advancements into the agency, reinforcing its reputation as an elite crime-fighting agency. Hoover was the first director of the FBI; he maintained this title until the age of 77, when he succumbed to a heart attack in his Washington, D.C. home on May 2, 1972.

John Raacke and Stephanie L. Albertson

See also: Gangsters of the 1900s; Secret Service; Wickersham Report on Soaring Crime during Prohibition; Wiretapping

Further Reading

Cecil, M. "Coming on Like Gang Busters: J. Edgar Hoover's FBI and the Battle to Control Radio Portrayals of the Bureau, 1936–1958." *Journalism History* 40, no. 4 (2015): 252–261.

Cohen, S. "J. Edgar Hoover." *Journal of Social History* 34, no. 3 (2001): 703–706.

Ellis, M. "J. Edgar Hoover and the 'Red Summer' of 1919." *Journal of American Studies* 28, no. 1 (1994): 39–59.

Farnsworth, S. J. "Seeing Red: The FBI and Edgar Snow." *Journalism History* 28, no. 3 (2002): 137–145.

Gentry, C. J. *Edgar Hoover: The Man and the Secrets*. New York: W. W. Norton, 1991.

Hack, R. *Puppetmaster: The Secret Life of J. Edgar Hoover*. Beverly Hills, CA: Phoenix Books, 2007.

O'Reilly, K. "The FBI and the Politics of the Riots, 1964–1968." *Journal of American History* 75, no. 1 (1988): 91–114.

Washburn, P. "J. Edgar Hoover and the Black Press in World War II." *Journalism History* 13, no. 1 (1986): 26–33.

WICKERSHAM REPORT ON SOARING CRIME DURING PROHIBITION

The era of Prohibition in the United States began with the ratification of the Eighteenth Amendment and the subsequent enactment of the Volstead Act. Going into effect in 1920, Prohibition—the nationwide ban on the manufacture, sale, and distribution of alcohol—lasted until the Twenty-First Amendment repealed the Eighteenth Amendment in 1933. For more than a decade, severe restrictions were placed on alcohol at the federal level. One of the primary byproducts of this illegalization was the formation and promulgation of criminal enterprises and organized crime. The nation was already dealing with increasingly high levels of violent crime, and additional illegal acts created by the passing of these pieces of legislation only exacerbated these issues. During the period of Prohibition (1920–1933), both prison admissions and homicide rates increased dramatically, reaching levels that would not be seen again until the 1970s. As a result, President Herbert Hoover charged the National Commission on Law Observance and Enforcement (NCLOE) to examine the effects of alcohol prohibition and other crime-related matters. The result involved a series of reports produced and disseminated by the Wickersham Commission. The Commission was known as such because it was chaired by George W. Wickersham, a lawyer who ascended the ranks of domestic and foreign policy, highlighted by this leadership position.

Wickersham had previously served, under President William Taft, as the U.S. attorney general from 1909–1913. In the interim, he continued to practice law and served on various committees, boards, and cabinets. In addition to his domestic service, he represented the United States in several positions, advocating for justice and helping to improve international relations. He accepted multiple appointments, such as Special Commissioner of the War Trade Board to Cuba by President Woodrow Wilson and in 1923 he was invited by the French government to visit the French territories of Algiers and Morocco to study their colonial administration. He also took up additional appointments and nominations such as vice president of the Council of the International Union of League of Nation Societies (a precursor to the United Nations), president of the Japan Society—which was created to promote friendly relationships between the countries—president of the

Council on Foreign Relations, and one of his last positions before his death was service on the Committee on Progressive Codification of International Law.

As a result of Wickersham's extensive knowledge and ability, President Hoover appointed him the chair of the National Commission on Law Observance and Enforcement. Due in part to Wickersham's previous experience in the political arena, but also due to his experiences in investigation, evaluation, and policy—which notably led him to the presidency of the American Law Institute—Wickersham was deemed the perfect leader in identifying a solution to issues surrounding Prohibition and crime of the late 1920s.

The Commission was charged with several tasks, one of which—as their report states—related specifically to the "problem of the enforcement of prohibition under the provisions of the Eighteenth Amendment of the Constitution and laws enacted in pursuance thereof. . . ." The Commission released a series of reports, or volumes, discussing topics that spanned the related areas of alcohol prohibition, crime, laws, courts, criminal procedure, prisons, immigration, and law enforcement—just to name a few. In each volume, the Commission outlined the issue(s) at hand, provided analysis and critique, and, where possible, provided suggestions for public policy and future considerations.

For example, one of the more contentious topics examined in the Wickersham Commission's reports was the issue of recording and reporting criminal statistics. At the time, there was no national database or collection procedure in place. The International Association of Chiefs of Police (IACP) was establishing the Uniform Crime Report (UCR) with the help of the Bureau of Investigation (later to be renamed the Federal Bureau of Investigation, or FBI). The Commission produced *The Report on Criminal Statistics* (volume 3), which was negatively critical of the proposed national database system, at least insofar as its coordination and management. A result of fate—and scheduling—the UCR was implemented before this volume could be published. Despite agreeing with the idea that the country should have an accurate method to collect national crime data, the Commission did not believe the Bureau of Investigation was the most appropriate agency to do so—a criticism that was supported.

Moreover, the *Report on Penal Institutions, Probation, and Parole* (volume 9) coincided with, and many argue influenced, a change of perspective in the field of corrections. At the time of this report's production, prisons began to once again incorporate principles of reform—instead of punishing offenders retributively, rehabilitation was a primary goal. The prevailing sentiment regarding the efficacy of corrections, in terms of its corrective nature, was one of disappointment and disapproval. Neither policy makers, stakeholders, nor the general public had much faith in idea that offenders can leave prison and remain crime-free or be "improved." This report provided support for the continued probationary and paroling efforts of the criminal justice system.

Perhaps most condemning for the profession of law enforcement was the volume of the Wickersham Commission reports that discusses lawlessness in law enforcement, for example, corruption and misconduct. The *Report on Lawlessness in Law Enforcement* (volume 11) was the first investigation into the administration of justice and associated issues that was funded and disseminated publicly—specifically produced by and for a federal body. Misconduct and corruption in the police ranks were not new, nor were they something that was unknown to the public. However, the Commission was the first authority to report on these issues to a high level (President Hoover) and to a national audience. Furthermore, this volume was the first national-level study that examined the problem of police brutality, finding its widespread use. It would be another 30 years until another national level study reported on this issue.

The *Report on Lawlessness in Law Enforcement* explicitly detailed the use and abuse of police power, describing the behavior as being "a secret and illegal practice." Several behaviors and unlawful methods of police work were detailed in the report. These behaviors and methods include protracted questioning, physical and verbal threats, intimidation, brutality, illegal arrests and detention, and the restriction of access of an individual to his/her attorney. The Commission commonly referred to this lawless enforcement as the "third degree." These practices, in some instances, were quite severe. In order to obtain information about another individual or a crime officers would inflict—among other things—physical beatings with their hands or the use of objects. These practices were found to be directed at particular groups of people such as racial and ethnic minorities, the poor, activists, younger suspects or offenders, and members of specific political groups. Despite the ardent denial of these claims by police officials nationwide, including those of the 15 cities from which the data was gathered, the Commission held steadfast to its report. As a result, policy makers, stakeholders, and—perhaps most importantly—concerned and progressive police officials, took notice and made the issues presented a top priority in need of redress.

While these acts seem to be pervasive in metropolitan police departments across America, the task presented to the Wickersham Commission was not the broad investigation of the criminal justice system. Instead, the Commission was appointed for "A thorough inquiry into the problem of the enforcement of prohibition . . . together with the enforcement of other laws." The focus, then, was on the effects of alcohol prohibition and crime as mandated by the Eighteenth Amendment of the Constitution. The reports defined and detailed the issues surrounding the preceding influences of the amendment, crime, prohibition's influences on crime, and the administrative and logistical issues related to the effective implementation of the federal regulation.

The Commission outlined and discussed the corruption as it related to the prohibition of alcohol. Though it noted that such corruption was evident prior to Prohibition, the *Report on Lawlessness in Law Enforcement* indicated that across the country it had been revealed that numerous criminal prosecutions had taken place involving police and the prosecuting and administrative agencies involved in the regulation of alcohol production and distribution. In this volume, several contributions to the perceived failure of the National Prohibition Act were discussed in detail. These include the "emotionalism" that characterized the era in which the act was passed (during a *great war*), the underestimation of the logistical requirements needed for enforcement, the lack of experience of federal enforcement, the

Constitutional rights that may be abridged in the enforcement of the law, the political influence involved in the Act's legislation, constant changes in the statutes, the lack of administrative oversight, the lack of coordination of the several federal agencies involved in enforcement, and the lack of promotion of public observance of the Act.

As the first national study of the administration of justice, the 14 volumes of the Wickersham's Commission served as a foundation for future studies and as a basis for change—used, mostly, by civic activists, academics, and progressive law enforcement administrators. Despite its discussion on the effects on crime, specifically the relatively ineffectiveness of Prohibition and its stimulation of organized crime—as well as the correspondingly high national rates of homicide, some policy recommendations were disregarded or rebutted immediately thereafter. It would take quite some time before the reports would have any traction at the national level. For example, the next national-level study to investigate the problem was the U.S. Civil Rights Commission of 1961—some 30 years after the report was first published. Subsequent commissions continued to discuss the issue of police brutality through the early to mid-1960s. Moreover, the study was very influential in the genesis and implementation in 1965 of the President's Commission on Law Enforcement and Administration of Justice. The final report of this commission noted the impact of the Wickersham reports in systematically examining the issue of police brutality and related behavior—an issue that continues to be studied today.

Kaitlyn Clarke and Philip D. McCormack

See also: Corruption; J. Edgar Hoover (1895–1972), Director of the FBI; International Association of Chiefs of Police; Kerner Commission Report on Race Riots and Police Response; Knapp Commission; Uniform Crime Reports; Wiretapping

Further Reading

Eighteenth Amendment to the U.S. Constitution.
"National Commission on Law Observance and Enforcement." *Report on Criminal Statistic.* Washington, DC: Government Printing Office, 1931.
"National Commission on Law Observance and Enforcement." *Report on Enforcement of the Prohibition Laws of the United States.* Washington, DC: Government Printing Office, 1931.
"National Commission on Law Observance and Enforcement." *Report on Lawlessness in Law Enforcement.* Washington, DC: Government Printing Office, 1931.
"National Commission on Law Observance and Enforcement." *Report on Penal Institutions, Probation, and Parole.* Washington, DC: Government Printing Office, 1931.
Twenty-First Amendment to the Constitution.
"United States Commission on Civil Rights." *1961 United States Commission on Civil Rights Report.* Washington, DC: Government Printing Office, 1961.

BROWN V. MISSISSIPPI

Brown v. Mississippi was a critical U.S. Supreme Court decision regarding the admissibility of coerced confessions during a trial in a state court. At the time this case was decided, the section of the Fifth Amendment that prohibited a suspect from having to be a witness against oneself did not apply in state criminal trials. The prohibition applied only in the federal courts. This case involved three suspects being tortured by law enforcement into confessing to a murder. They were tried and convicted based on their confessions, and then they were sentenced to death. When the case was appealed to the U.S. Supreme Court, the convictions were reversed based on the Fourteenth Amendment's Due Process Clause. The clause applies to all states. Therefore, for the first time, the use of coerced confessions at state trials was determined to be unconstitutional, and it was no longer allowed to be used against a defendant at trial.

Brown v. Mississippi involved three Black defendants who had been convicted of murdering a White man. They were subsequently sentenced to death. The state used confessions by all three men as evidence that they killed this man. They all confessed to the crime only after they were brutally beaten by law enforcement involved in the investigation in order to get the defendants to confess. The defendants appealed their convictions to Mississippi's Supreme Court, but their appeal was denied. It was determined that their confessions were admissible at trial because the Mississippi state courts were able to determine their own procedural policies. However this decision was not unanimous and Judge Virgil Alexis Griffith (1874–1953) laid out the facts of the case in his dissenting opinion:

> The crime with which these defendants, all ignorant negroes, are charged, was discovered about 1 o'clock p.m. on Friday, March 30, 1934. On that night one Dial, a deputy sheriff, accompanied by others, came to the home of Ellington, one of the defendants, and requested him to accompany them to the house of the deceased, and there a number of white men were gathered, who began to accuse the defendant of the crime. Upon his denial they seized him, and with the participation of the deputy they hanged him by a rope to the limb of a tree, and, having let him down, they hung him again, and when he was let down the second time, and he still protested his innocence, he was tied to a tree and whipped, and, still declining to accede to the demands that he confess, he was finally released, and he returned with some difficulty to his home, suffering intense pain and agony. The record of the testimony shows that the signs of the rope on his neck were plainly visible during the so-called trial. A day or two thereafter the said deputy, accompanied by another, returned to the home of the said defendant and arrested him, and departed with the prisoner towards the jail in an adjoining county, but went by a route which led into the state of Alabama; and while on the way, in that state, the deputy stopped and again severely whipped the defendant, declaring that he would continue the whipping until he confessed, and the defendant then agreed to confess to such a statement as the deputy would dictate, and he did so, after which he was delivered to jail.
>
> The other two defendants, Ed Brown and Henry Shields, were also arrested and taken to the same jail. On Sunday night, April 1, 1934, the same deputy, accompanied by a number of white men, one of whom was also an officer, and by the jailer, came to the jail, and the two last named defendants were made to strip and they were laid over chairs and their backs were cut to pieces with a leather strap with buckles on it, and they were likewise made by the said deputy definitely to understand that the whipping would be continued unless and until they confessed, and not only confessed, but confessed in every matter of detail as demanded by those present; and in

this manner the defendants confessed the crime, and, as the whippings progressed and were repeated, they changed or adjusted their confession in all particulars of detail so as to conform to the demands of their torturers. When the confessions had been obtained in the exact form and contents as desired by the mob, they left with the parting admonition and warning that, if the defendants changed their story at any time in any respect from that last stated, the perpetrators of the outrage would administer the same or equally effective treatment.

Further details of the brutal treatment to which these helpless prisoners were subjected need not be pursued. It is sufficient to say that in pertinent respects the transcript reads more like pages torn from some medieval account than a record made within the confines of a modern civilization which aspires to an enlightened constitutional government.

At the trial all three defendants testified to the torture they received. The state's witnesses included a deputy and two other officers of the state who participated in the torture. When the deputy was asked about the whipping of one of the defendants he stated, "Not too much for a Negro; not as much as I would have done if it were left to me." The other two officers admitted that the defendants were tortured. The defendants' confessions were the only evidence presented by the state.

Compulsion to confess is the litmus test in determining whether a confession can be used at trial. The Fifth Amendment to the Constitution says, in part, that "no person . . . shall be compelled in any criminal case to be a witness against himself" (commonly known as the right against self-incrimination). However the amendment had applied only in federal courts, and states had not been required to adhere to the provisions of any of the Bill of Rights, including the Fifth Amendment. Thus, the state of Mississippi argued that a forced confession could, in fact, be used against a defendant. The U.S. Supreme Court needed to decide, in *Brown v. Mississippi*, if the Supreme Court of Mississippi had erred when it had determined these confessions could be used at a state criminal trial to convict the defendants.

The U.S. Supreme Court focused on due process, which means the rights of a defendant in a criminal trial are protected, and a just and fair trial will be held. A defendant is presumed innocent until proven guilty beyond a reasonable doubt, using only evidence that is obtained legally.

The U.S. Supreme Court first considered the power a state has to regulate its courts and in which ways it may regulate its courts. The state had argued that "exemption from compulsory self-incrimination in the courts of the States is not secured by any part of the Federal Constitution and the states were free to withdraw the privilege against self-incrimination and put the defendant on the stand as a state's witness." The court stated this argument was not applicable.

The court acknowledged the state could control court procedures, according to the state's policies, unless a line was crossed, obstructing some fundamental tradition of the people in Mississippi. The freedom of the state to establish its own policy is limited by the requirement of due process of law. Thus the court stated that a trial by ordeal is not constitutional. "The rack and torture chamber may not be substituted for the witness stand. . . . Nor may a State, through the actions of its officers, contrive a conviction through the pretense of a trial . . . and the trial equally is a mere pretense where the state authorities have contrived a conviction resting solely upon confessions obtained by violence . . ." The court rebuked the state of Mississippi and claimed "the due process clause requires 'that state action, whether through one agency or another, shall be consistent with the fundamental principles of liberty and justice which lie at the base of all our civil and political institutions' . . . it would be difficult to conceive of methods more revolting to the sense of justice than those taken to procure the confessions of these petitioners, and the use of the confessions thus obtained as the basis for conviction and sentence was a clear denial of due process."

The U.S. Supreme Court, in its decision that the Mississippi court had erred, quoted a prior decision in the case of *Fisher v. State*, 145 Miss.116 by the Supreme Court of Mississippi: "Coercing the supposed state's criminals into confessions and using such confessions so coerced from them against them in trials has been the curse of all countries. It was the chief inequity, the crowning infamy of the Star Chamber, and the Inquisition, and other similar institutions. The constitution recognized the evils that lay behind these practices and prohibited them in this country. . . . The duty of maintaining constitutional rights of a person on trial for his life rises above mere rules of procedure and wherever the court is clearly satisfied that such violations exist, it will refuse to sanction such violations and will apply the corrective." The U.S. Supreme Court reprimanded the Mississippi court because the Mississippi court had been well aware of the circumstances surrounding how the confessions were obtained, knew there was no other evidence against the defendants, and still allowed a conviction and sentence of death. Thus, the U.S. Supreme Court dissolved the sentences and convictions.

The Supreme Court's decision in *Brown v. Mississippi* was important because, for the first time in history, murder convictions of three "Negro" men accused of murdering a White man had been reversed. This had been based on the Fourteenth Amendment. The court had used the amendment to determine the confessions of the Black men had not been made freely and voluntarily. Instead, they had been coerced through physical violence. Therefore, the confessions could not be used as evidence in a state court criminal trial based on the concept that all persons are constitutionally guaranteed due process of law.

This case and many others that were decided subsequently were instrumental in the decision by the U.S. Supreme Court in the case of *Miranda v. Arizona*, 384 U.S. 436 (1966). The court in Miranda determined that to avoid the possibility of psychological compulsion during an in-custody interrogation, the defendant must be given the Miranda warning prior to interrogation so that the defendant understands the rights guaranteed by the U.S. Constitution.

Regarding compulsory self-incrimination, the case of *Brown v. Mississippi* was one of the most important U.S. Supreme Court decisions. The court determined that the brutal beatings of three suspects in order to get them to confess to a murder rendered the confessions inadmissible because they were not given freely and voluntarily. As a result, the Court prohibited the confessions to be used against the suspects because the beatings and brutality deprived the defendants of their constitutional rights to due process of law.

Cathie Perselay Seidman

See also: Crime Control versus Due Process; Fifth Amendment

Further Reading

Brown v. Mississippi, 297 U.S. 278. (1936).

Cloud, Morgan. "Torture and Truth," *Texas Law Review* 74 (1996): 1211.

Cortner, Richard C. *A "Scottsboro" Case in Mississippi: The Supreme Court and Brown v. Mississippi.* Jackson: University Press of Mississippi, 1986.

Kassin, Saul M., Steven A. Drizin, Thomas Grisso, Gisli H. Gudjonsson, Richard A. Leo, and Allison D. Redlich. "Police-Induced Confessions: Risk Factors and Recommendations." *Law and Human Behavior* 34, no. 1 (February 2010): 49–52.

Leo, Richard A., and George Conner Thomas. *Confessions of Guilt: From Torture to Miranda and Beyond.* New York: Oxford University Press, 2012.

Wallace, Paul S. "Repealing Miranda? Background of the Controversy over Pretrial Interrogation and Self Incrimination" in *Criminal Justice and Law Enforcement Issues* (75), Katherine A Neumann, editor. New York: Nova Science Publishers, 2002.

NATIONAL FIREARMS ACT

The 1920s and 1930s were decades rife with highly publicized violence that was sensationalized by the media and captured on film, celebrating the exploits of gangsters and criminals such as John Dillinger and Alphonse Gabriel "Al" Capone. The publicized nature of the criminal violence and the desire of law enforcement to quash the illegal activities that coincided with the violence during the Prohibition era led to the first federal mandate to regulate the manufacture and sale of firearms in the United States. The National Firearms Act of 1934 was the first legislation of its kind and has since affected the restrictions imposed upon and the process by which one procures certain types of firearms, most notably those of which were commonly used in the era of gangsters and criminal enterprises.

Following the Eighteenth Amendment of the U.S. Constitution, along with its corollary the Volstead Act, criminal enterprises quickly rose to power. These "gangs" and "mobs" effectively ruled the eras of the Great Depression and Prohibition by setting up illegal outfits that profited from the production and sale of alcohol, illegal gambling, and more violent crimes such as bank robbery. The Federal Bureau of Investigation (FBI) estimates that by the mid-1920s as many as 1,300 gangs operated in Chicago, Illinois, alone and that gang violence was largely responsible for an inordinate amount of violence—such as the more than 12,000 homicides taking place annually (a number that would not be seen again until the late 1960s).

The violence associated with the criminal enterprises of the 1920s and 1930s was not restricted to the large cities in which they occurred, such as Chicago. Accounts of criminal exploits such as those of Al Capone and Bonnie and Clyde were popularized and broadcast nationwide by various media outlets. Sensational journalism allowed these criminals and their alleged acts to become nationally recognized. Not only were newspapers circulating with increased popularity, but the newsreels of the 1930s were perhaps the most popular way of gathering news. Newsreels were shown before feature films in theaters across the United States and provided re-creations and dramatic depictions of stories of the time. As a result, the general public—not only law enforcement—was made keenly aware of the crime and violence that was occurring across the nation.

Further exacerbating the concern about the violence depicted in the media was the nature of the weaponry used. Gangsters and individual criminals used high-powered firearms such as the Thompson submachine gun, or the "Tommy Gun," and other similar automatic firearms. These weapons were far more powerful than the standard department-issued pistol supplied to law enforcement agents at the time, though some departments—specifically federal agencies—purchased these types of weapons in small quantities. Thus, law enforcement agencies at both the state and federal levels were at a significant disadvantage when responding to these criminals.

The laws at the time did not afford much protection for the country in terms of the distribution of the firearms, particularly the automatic weapons often used by criminals. There was very little, if any, record keeping and few restrictions were in place to limit the ability of gangsters and mobsters from getting their hands on these types of firearms for illegal use. After years of increasing violence, media portrayals, and resultant fear on behalf of the American public, Congress worked toward drafting legislation that would place restrictions on certain firearms and lay the foundation for future gun control initiatives. The first piece of legislation enacted was the National Firearms Act of 1934.

The act regulated firearms indirectly, insofar as it did not address the manufacture of higher-powered weapons such as the Tommy Gun. Rather, the act provided means by which the U.S. government could tax and impose restrictions on the sale and transfer of particular firearms and machine guns. In drafting this piece of legislation, Congress specified the particular types of firearms that it wanted to address: shotguns, rifles (less than 18 inches in length, such as those whose barrels are "sawed off"), and "machine guns"—which was meant to encompass any weapon that could shoot automatically or semi-automatically.

In specifying these particular types of firearms in the act, Congress was responding directly to law enforcement—and the public—and the collective desire for a legislative response to the increasing violence in American society. The way in which the legislation enacted restrictions on these weapons was indirect. It has been argued that due to the likely backlash and opposition that would result if Congress chose to address manufacturing, the members of the House and Senate opted to enact an administrative law as to not potentially infringe upon—or have the appearance of infringing upon—the Second Amendment right to bear arms. In the act, there is no mention of the elimination or reduction in the manufacturing of shotguns, rifles, or "machine guns." Instead, it focuses on the *individuals* involved in the manufacture and distribution of these weapons. Distribution refers to a variety of functions such as dealing (selling)—including wholesalers and pawnbrokers—importers, transporters, and those who dispose of these types of firearms.

The act was the first to implement a federal tax on firearm manufacturers and distributors. Going into effect almost immediately following its enactment, the act provides several conditions and stipulations by which importers, manufacturers, and dealers in firearms must abide. First, these individuals (and companies/groups) must register with the Internal Revenue Service (IRS) within the district(s) in which they are located and conduct business. Following this registration, the individuals and companies/groups are subject to a mandatory tax, based on two conditions: (1) whether the registered party is an importer or manufacturer, pawnbroker, or dealer other than a pawnbroker, and (2) the proportion of the fiscal year those engaging in business are registered. In essence, the tax is based on the type of business one is involved in and it is pro-rated based on the proportion of the year the business has been registered with the IRS. The act specifically outlines that the failure to register with the IRS when required to do so, as well as the failure to pay the corresponding federal tax, and continuance of the manufacture and distribution of firearms is considered unlawful and the individual will be subject to criminal penalty.

Not only was this law impactful in the sense that it required all of those in the firearms business to register with the IRS and pay taxes, but the registration requirements were quite substantial and the taxes required, at least for that era, were quite high. According to the Bureau of Labor Statistics, the rate at which each individual firearm was to be taxed ($200) would have the same buying power today as approximately $3,500. This tax is nearly as much as the cost of the weapon itself if purchased directly from the manufacturer in 1934. The registration requirements set forth in 1934 have had a lasting effect in the American firearm marketplace: several of the conditions of registration proscribed in the National Firearms Act of 1934 are still in effect today, at least in principal. For example, in order for the transfer of a firearm from one individual to another be considered a legal transaction, it must be accompanied with a written order and application from the transferor, for example, the dealer, manufacturer, or seller, and it must be approved by the appropriate authority (in 1934, the authority was the commissioner of the IRS). In addition to this application, the documentation of the applicants' fingerprints and photograph was mandated. As a result, the initial documentation and collection of personal identification information as related to the manufacture, sale, and transfer of firearms initiated with the act in 1934.

At the time, there was also very little, if any, oversight in the registration and monitoring of the manufacture and distribution of individual firearms. As a result, the act also included a provision that mandated the recording of the "manufacturer's number or other mark" that identifies each individual firearm. This is the first instance of a Congressional mandate that requires the identification and recording of individual firearms for the purpose of monitoring legislative compliance. Not only must the number or mark be recorded and included in the written orders and applications submitted when transferring a firearm, but these orders and applications must also be approved and returned to the applicants by the appropriate authority (in 1934—the Commissioner of the IRS). Subsequent provisions—related to registration—include the submission of the applicant's name and address. Not only can individuals be linked to specific firearms, but the location of these individuals (and, ultimately, the firearms) can be linked to specific locations.

In addition to the mandate that the manufacturer and importer provide a number or identification mark, the National Firearms Act explicitly states that this number or mark cannot be tampered with. Specifically, it is unlawful for anyone to "obliterate, remove, change, or alter" the identification. It is also deemed unlawful for individuals to possess firearms that have had identification number(s) and mark(s) tampered with. The issues of unlawful possession extend beyond that of firearms with tampered identifying numbers and marks. The act also states that the importation or transfer of firearms into the United States or its territories is unlawful, if not compliant with the act's conditions, as well as the possession of firearms that have come into the United States because of unlawful importation via purchase, sale, concealment, or any other form of receipt. Furthermore, the mere possession is sufficient evidence to authorize the conviction of the individual(s) involved, and the burden of proof, then, to prove innocence rests on the defendant(s). These provisions also apply to interstate commerce and distribution, where a firearm is shipped, carried, or delivered across state or territorial lines within the United States.

The penalties associated with violation of the act or failed compliance of any of its sections or provisions therein are fines of up to $2,000 and/or imprisonment up to five years. For context, according to the Bureau of Labor Statistics, a fine of $2,000 in 1934 has the same buying power in the early 2000s as approximately $35,000. Much like the taxes, the penalties imposed were not minor. The only individuals or groups that are exempt from the National Firearms Act are those that conduct business in the transfer of firearms to the federal government, any individual state, U.S. territory, or the District of Columbia. Therefore, the act is specifically directed at private citizens and organizations in terms of its regulation. Governments groups and organizations, such as law enforcement departments and federal agencies, are not subject to the same taxes, registration requirements, and penalties for failing to comply with the act.

During an area of increasing violence, public fear, and a marked disadvantage between law enforcement and criminals, Congress passed the first act addressing high-powered weapons such as short-barreled rifles, shotguns, and "machine guns." Although the National Firearms Act of 1934 did not directly affect the manufacturing of these types of firearms, it significantly affected the distribution and documentation of these firearms insofar as mandating the serialized identification of each individual weapon, the application (and subsequent approval) to transfer these weapons, and the regulation of transfer via the imposition of taxes. Since the act was passed, additional limitations on the distribution of specific weapons have been imposed at the federal level, and additional taxes have been required. Not only was this act the first of its kind, but it also set a standard that is followed today: Congressional mandates regulate private manufacture and distribution of firearms while exempting law enforcement departments and federal agencies from their conditions.

Kaitlyn Clarke and Philip D. McCormack

See also: Gangsters of the 1900s; Teddy Roosevelt's Fight against Police Corruption; Wickersham Report on Soaring Crime during Prohibition

Further Reading

"Brady Handgun Violence Prevention Act." Bureau of Alcohol, Tobacco, Firearms, and Explosives. https://www.atf.gov/rules-and-regulations/brady-law.

"Gun Control Act of 1968." Bureau of Alcohol, Tobacco, Firearms, and Explosives. https://www.atf.gov/rules-and-regulations/gun-control-act.

"H. R. 1025: Brady Handgun Violence Prevention Act." Congress.gov. https://www.congress.gov/bill/103rd-congress/house-bill/1025.

"History of Gun-Control Legislation." *Washington Post*, December 22, 2012. https://www.washingtonpost.com/national/history-of-gun-control-legislation/2012/12/22/80c8d624-4ad3-11e2-9a42-d1ce6d0ed278_story.html.

"Key Congressional Acts Related to Firearms." Law Center to Prevent Gun Violence, May 21, 2012. http://smartgunlaws.org/key-federal-acts-regulating-guns.

"National Firearms Act." Bureau of Alcohol, Tobacco, Firearms, and Explosives. https://www.atf.gov/rules-and-regulations/national-firearms-act.

Zimring, Franklin E. "Firearms and Federal Law: The Gun Control Act of 1968." *Journal of Legal Studies* 4 (133). http://scholarship.law.berkeley.edu/cgi/viewcontent.cgi?article=2114&context=facpubs.

POLICE MISCONDUCT DURING THE L.A. ZOOT SUIT RIOTS

The notorious Los Angeles "Zoot Suit Riots" of June 1943 involved violent clashes between Mexican American youth and predominantly White servicemen. The riots were further complicated by the actions of officers in the Los Angeles Police Department (LAPD). The events marked a high point of long-standing tensions in the city and festering hostilities forged by racism, classism, and cross-cultural and intergenerational misunderstandings, as well as political and economic strain and resentment. The riots lasted roughly a week, and although they resulted in no fatalities, there were numerous injuries and hundreds of arrests (mostly of Mexican American youth). The most controversial element of the riots was the formal response of the LAPD and military police that were deployed to assist them. Historical sociologists and criminologists have described them as heavy-handed perhaps as an effort to demonstrate the increased emphasis on professionalism within the agency (after years of corruption) as well as a mirror of anti-Mexican sentiments within the Anglo community.

Mexican Americans in Los Angeles

Like many major municipalities within the United States, Los Angeles was heavily segregated by race and ethnicity during the 20th century—in terms of both residency patterns as well as employment opportunities. There had been a strong Mexican cultural presence for centuries, and it remained after the United States acquired the territory, which eventually became the state of California at the end of the Mexican-American War in 1848 (with Mexican citizens who resided in the new United States territories being offered American citizenship). After the war, Mexican Americans and Mexican immigrants were economically disadvantaged and had few options available to them other than low-status and poorly paid jobs. The Great Depression brought an explosion of anti-immigrant sentiments and prejudices, culminating in federal and state-based legislation that discouraged employers from hiring immigrants. The immigrant community was subjected to mass deportations during the notorious "Mexican Repatriation" between 1929 and 1936; these efforts primarily targeted Mexican immigrants, but many Mexican American citizens were forcibly removed, as well. In the face of these hardships and humiliations, an emerging Mexican American youth culture began to assert itself. These youth (often referred to as *pachucos*) proudly and unapologetically affirmed their unique identity: not fully Mexican and somewhat alienated from those cultural roots, but simultaneously marginalized as Americans. The *pachucos* also expressed a defiant attitude toward authority figures.

Male and female members of this subculture became identified by their chosen attire—the zoot suit (or in the cases of *pachucas*, a modified version thereof)—although technically, not all self-identified *pachucos* wore zoot suits and not all

Mexican Americans lined up outside a Los Angeles jail en route to court after the Zoot Suit Riots, June 9, 1943. The cause of these racial attacks was based on conflict between American servicemen who were stationed in Southern California and Mexican American youth. (Library of Congress)

who favored zoot suits considered themselves *pachucos*. The zoot suit was not invented by the *pachuco* subculture, and in fact had enjoyed some measure of popularity among other ethnic groups, but it quickly became associated as an identifying symbol of rebellious Mexican American youth. This flamboyant and distinctive way of dress was characterized by oversized, padded-shouldered coats paired with baggy high-waisted tapered trousers, often accessorized by porkpie or fedora hats, long decorative chains, and slicked-back hairstyles. *Pachucos* spoke in a unique slang known as *Caló*, the use of which solidified their unique identity and their alienation from, and resistance to assimilating into, the majority Anglo culture.

Many Los Angelenos—and Anglo residents in particular—took a dim view of the *pachuco* subculture. Such attitudes were encouraged not only by the LAPD, which publicly blamed *pachucos* for rising rates of juvenile delinquency (although this was a trend that was not unique to Los Angeles), but also local news media. Tabloid publications as well as more respected venues such as the *Los Angeles Times* frequently published pieces that disproportionately focused on crime and delinquency perpetrated by zoot-suiters, specifically, and Mexican American youth in general. *Pachucos* were often portrayed as a unified gang that was heavily involved in violence and deviant behavior, and posed a genuine threat to law-abiding citizens. Although there were certainly self-identified *pachucos* who engaged in crime and delinquency, such activities in no way represented the majority. However, the characterization of "zoot-suiters" as dangerous gangsters and hoodlums took root.

LAPD

As with many other large police departments in the United States, the LAPD had been troubled since its inception. These troubles included poor management and oversight of patrol officers; weak or nonexistent hiring, training, and promotion criteria; and, eventually, serious allegations of corruption, graft, and political patronage (with the department essentially serving the interests of powerful local politicians and other elected officials—and in the case of the LAPD, also doing favors for prominent "legitimate" businessmen as well as organized crime figures such as bootleggers and racketeers).

The 1920s and 1930s marked the beginning of the nationwide professionalism movement within law enforcement that stressed many new things. These consisted of the establishment of standards for quality policing, the elimination of political influence and preferential treatment of those in positions of economic or political power, the strengthening community trust by demonstrating fair and equal treatment regardless of social status, and an emphasis on the goal of crime control. However, the LAPD had become notorious not only for the atmosphere of corruption that seemed to be deeply entrenched, but also for the utter powerlessness of its often-changing leadership to reform the agency. The department experienced unusually frequent turnover in its top administrative positions, as well as among its rank-and-file officers (somewhat reflecting the political turmoil within the offices of the mayor and the Los Angeles City Council).

The department engaged in activities that were somewhat unusual among its peer agencies, including cracking down on labor unions (at the behest of local business leaders) and other indications of politically "subversive" activities. Meanwhile, the department successfully implemented some standard elements of the police professionalism movement. In particular, it eagerly adopted new technologies and state-of-the-art investigative tools as they became available. These included the collection and utilization of crime statistics, the implementation of a complex dragnet system for apprehending offenders, and the adoption of one of the nation's most advanced radio communications and remote dispatch systems.

The department, therefore, possessed some tangible accoutrements of police professionalism, but had not managed to assume or apply many of the fundamental philosophies of the movement. By the late 1930s, some reform-minded administrators had attempted a dramatic restructuring of the department in a targeted effort to improve the agency's effectiveness and reputation, but the agency remained mired in challenges. Among its issues was evidence that it had not fully embraced the tenets of the police professionalism model that advocated for equal treatment across racial, ethnic, and socioeconomic lines, with allegations that the department continued to target minority groups (including Mexican immigrants and Mexican Americans) with undue and disproportionate scrutiny.

Repercussions of U.S. Involvement in World War II

The entry of the United States into World War II was followed by an immediate need to fill jobs previously held by men who had been enlisted or drafted into military service. To address these shortages, which greatly affected the agricultural and unskilled labor sectors, the United States and the Mexican government entered into an agreement that allowed for entry (on a temporary basis) of Mexican laborers. The U.S. government justified this action because of economic necessity, but it was not universally popular among the White populace and likely fostered resentment in communities that were already experiencing dramatic upheaval due to the war. Meanwhile, the LAPD was weathering numerous challenges of wartime. When its ranks were significantly diminished by drafts and enlistments, the agency was forced to compromise standards in training in order to quickly prepare new recruits. Los Angeles was considered potentially vulnerable to an attack, so in addition to focusing on routine crime-fighting and order maintenance, its officers were expected to be vigilant against signs of enemy invasion.

Meanwhile, nationwide austerity measures were implemented in order to preserve available materials that might be needed by American troops, and to support the war effort. Among these initiatives were regulations issued by the War Production Board, the federal agency responsible for rationing. In 1942, that agency limited the availability of wool and other fabrics, which affected the manufacturing of zoot suits. These directives did nothing to curb consumer appetite for zoot suits, particularly given the anti-authoritarian, defiant attitudes that defined the *pachuco* subculture, and bootleg tailors were willing to meet the demand. Mexican

American youth who donned zoot suits, then, were viewed with resentment and hostility by the dominant Anglo culture. The Anglos, who already believed the Mexican Americans were thuggish gangsters, now interpreted their actions as blatantly flouting cultural conventions, as well as purposely undermining the war effort. Because of their attempts to assert their cultural identity, zoot-suiters were regarded as unpatriotic, disloyal, and essentially un-American.

Sleepy Lagoon Murder Trial

Given the depth of anti-Mexican prejudice among the Anglo community and the history of local elected officials and law enforcement in perpetuating or even encouraging prejudice, the outrage surrounding the infamous "Sleepy Lagoon" murder in August 1942 was not unsurprising. The incident involved the killing of Jose Diaz, a Mexican immigrant who was found gravely injured after attending a party near a reservoir at the outskirts of Los Angeles. He later succumbed to his injuries. Although the exact cause of death was never conclusively determined, he had been discovered unconscious in the aftermath of a violent confrontation at the party between rival groups of zoot-suiters.

In response to this confrontation, the LAPD rounded up 600 Mexican American young men and women for interrogation, eventually charging a number of them with a variety of serious offenses (most of which were unrelated to Diaz's death). Ultimately, 17 young zoot-suiters (identified as members of the "38th Street Gang") were indicted and put on trial for murder. The defendants were all tried together in a bizarre proceeding in which they were denied access to their attorneys. Prosecutors presented "expert witnesses" who expressed blatant anti-Mexican sentiments, emphasizing the threat of the *pachuco* and zoot-suiter subculture specifically, and Mexican culture generally. Twelve of the defendants were convicted for either first- or second-degree murder; the remainder were convicted of related offenses. Although these convictions were ultimately overturned on procedural grounds, the trial atmosphere and surrounding events exemplified the power of prevailing anti-Mexican sentiments and the extent to which those in positions of authority exploited them.

Zoot Suit Riots and Aftermath

It was within this environment that long-simmering tensions between Mexican Americans and the dominant Anglo community finally exploded. In the summer of 1943, Los Angeles was a popular destination for (primarily White) military personnel on leave. Many of these personnel harbored hostilities that were stoked by not only anti-Mexican prejudice, but also resentment over the sight of flamboyantly dressed zoot-suiters who were openly defying the collective efforts of wartime rationing. Indeed, the presence of zoot-suited *pachucos* might have been interpreted as a personal affront, particularly among individuals under the influence of alcohol and in a raucous state of mind. A number of reported altercations occurred between servicemen and zoot-suiters during this period, but the most dramatic of these took place on the evening of June 3, 1943, when a group of sailors claimed that they had been brutally attacked by Mexican Americans in zoot suits. They reported the assault to the LAPD, but also sought retaliation on their own.

This set in motion an extraordinary series of events. Thousands of revenge-minded White servicemen and civilians, as well as off-duty LAPD officers who dubbed themselves the "Vengeance Squad" sought out, pursued, and physically attacked not only zoot-suiters (some as young as 12 years old) but also racial or ethnic minorities they happened to come across who weren't wearing zoot suits at all. The following evening, the attacks continued, with a mob of sailors initially focusing their attention on zoot-suiters. Once those targets were exhausted, the sailors moved on to terrorize Mexican American neighborhoods.

These events continued over the course of the next several days. The LAPD did little to intervene, reluctant to take formal action against servicemen and, perhaps, viewing the men's actions as justified. When officers did respond, it was primarily to arrest hundreds of Mexican Americans. Local news media seemed to encourage the servicemen's actions, depicting them as bravely protecting the city from dangerous elements. Military commanders were aware of these events, but initially did very little to control the actions of the men under their watch. The situation continued to escalate, with the original mob of sailors eventually joined by soldiers, Marines, and other sailors who traveled from more distant military bases to take part.

Approximately five days after the initial altercation that set the riots into motion, military officials finally took decisive action. Los Angeles was deemed off-limits to all military personnel and military police were instructed to take into custody any servicemen who violated standards of conduct. The violence eventually dissipated. The most significant official governmental response in the immediate aftermath of the riots was the decision of the Los Angeles City Council to pass a resolution that banned zoot suits. Later in the year, the governor of California (and future Supreme Court Justice) Earl Warren commissioned a citizens' investigatory committee to examine the circumstances that contributed to the Zoot Suit Riots; its report primarily blamed racism as well as an ineffectual response by the LAPD. The Los Angeles mayor's office, however, rejected these findings. Ultimately, despite criticisms of their performance, there were no significant repercussions for the LAPD or its leadership.

Miriam D. Sealock

See also: Deadly Force; Police Accountability; Police Brutality; Police Ethics; Racial Profiling

Further Reading

Escobar, Edward J. *Race, Police, and the Making of a Political Identity: Mexican-Americans and the Los Angeles Police Department, 1900–1945.* Berkeley: University of California Press, 1999.

"History of the LAPD." Los Angeles Police Department Web Site. http://www.lapdonline.org
    /history_of_the_lapd.

Mazon, Mauricio. *The Zoot Suit Riots: The Psychology of Symbolic Annihilation*. Austin: Uni-
    versity of Texas Press, 1988.

Moore, Joan W. *Homeboys: Gangs, Drugs, and Prisons in the Barrio of Los Angeles*. Philadel-
    phia: Temple University Press, 1978.

Pagan, Eduardo O. *Murder at the Sleepy Lagoon: Zoot Suits, Race, and Riot in Wartime L.A.*
    Chapel Hill: University of North Carolina Press, 2003.

Shelden, Randall G., Sharon K. Tracy, and William B. Brown. *Youth Gangs in American Soci-
    ety*. Boston, MA: Cengage Learning, 2012.

Starr, Kevin. *Embattled Dreams: California in War and Peace, 1940–1950*. New York: Oxford
    University Press, 2002.

Vigil, James D. *Barrio Gangs*. Austin: University of Texas Press, 1988.

UNIFORM CRIME REPORTS

Crime is a fundamental concept in justice administration—mostly notably in law enforcement. When looking to create, modify, or eliminate policies, programs, and training, law enforcement officials use crime and crime data to assist in making data-driven decisions and suggestions on best practices. These practices, in turn, guide both the development and oversight of functions that help the police to be more proactive and the judicial and corrections systems to be more efficient and effective.

Common misconceptions about crime and the law enforcement response to crime is due, in part, to the public's heavy reliance on the news and social media. The types of crimes illustrated in the news often indicate inverse relationships between actual crime and what is presented by the media. Murder, for example, is statistically the least likely to occur, but it is the crime most often presented in the news. "If it bleeds, it leads" has been the war cry of the news media for decades; however, this coverage serves to skew the statistical picture of what really goes on around the country.

Another misconception about crime and criminality comes from the public's fascination with popular TV crime dramas such as *CSI* (Crime Scene Investigation) or *NCIS* (Naval Criminal Investigative Services). In providing a statistical overview of crime in America and, further, special categories of crimes of interest, these numbers, unlike TV drama, represent real people, victims, and suspects, as well as the real loss and pain attributed directly to crime.

Official statistics and *victimization* statistics are the primary sources of data used to understand both the crime picture and to drive social policy decisions in the United States. Crime data are collected for purposes of monitoring, agency accountability, and research, and crimes known to the police have been the most significant and widely used measure. The most well-known and cited source is the Uniform Crime Reporting (UCR) published by the Federal Bureau of Investigation (FBI). The UCR is an annual report called *Crime in the United States* that lists major crimes in America. These statistics are compiled from reports by victims "to" the police.

The UCR was created in 1929 by the International Association of Chiefs of Police (IACP) and, through Congressional authority, the FBI has been collecting and reporting crime statistics known to law enforcement since 1930. In its first year of operation, the FBI reported crimes from 400 cities in 43 states (Schmalleger 2015). Today, nearly 16,000 law enforcement agencies voluntarily submit information about crimes reported to them to the FBI's Criminal Justice Information Services (CJIS) division.

To have uniformity in the UCR's reporting (as its title suggests), the FBI created standardized definitions of criminal acts. The goal of the original UCR was to provide a comparative study over time of crime and crime rates through what is known as the Crime Index. It amassed reports covering seven major offenses (murder, aggravated assault, rape, motor vehicle theft, robbery, larceny-theft, and burglary). More detailed information about homicides (the killing of a human by another human) was added to the UCR in 1961, and in 1979 an eighth offense was added: arson. In the early 2000s, the FBI developed an incident-based reporting system (National Incident-Based Reporting System, or NIBRS) that was gradually being adopted across the nation.

As a statistical advancement since 1930, the UCR has assisted researchers, police administrators, and other public policy officials to identify shifts in crime and crime rates over time. The first shift was a reduction in crime after young males (statistically the most crime-prone) entered the military service in large numbers during World War II. A second shift was a dramatic increase of crime following the postwar "baby boom" generation entering their teenage years (also considered prime crime years) during the 1960s. Yet another shift occurred in the 1980s with the increase of drug-related violent crimes—peaking in 1991—followed by a general decline in most categories of crime during the 1990s. A new shift noted by researchers of the Police Executive Research Forum (PERF) indicated a contemporary trend of high crime rates in larger cities across the United States in the early 2000s.

The Crime Index was once a comprehensive measure of the UCR that looked closely at the violent and property crimes categories. It was intended to be a tool to compare crime rates state-to-state and year-to-year (number of crimes per unit of population). It was discontinued in 2004 due to weighting of the larceny-theft category, which created less of a lens on changes in rates for more violent crimes.

The UCR, in 2016, evolved to divide offenses into two groups. As noted previously, police agencies submit information on known, reported crimes, including those solved by arrest as well as demographic variables such as race, age, and gender of persons arrested. Part I crimes are more serious than Part II offenses. With Part II, agencies report data related to incidences in which a person is arrested and charged with a crime. This is set apart from Part I crimes due to differences in how crimes are defined differently from state to state. Part II crimes are also called social order or "victimless" crimes.

There are eight Part I offenses:

Murder: Defined as "the unlawful killing of a human being" (UCR 2016). There are different degrees of murder—including first and second—and there are also different degrees of manslaughter—manslaughter and involuntary manslaughter. Statistically, murder is the smallest category of Part I offenses, but the most solved. Murder is most likely to occur in warmer months, committed with a large percentage of guns, mostly by people the deceased knew.

Forcible Rape: Defined as "unlawful sexual intercourse achieved through force and without consent (UCR 2016). Rape can apply to a variety of sexual attacks by different genders. Statistically, there is no age barrier to this crime and is the least reported of all offenses. Criminologists believe that more rapes occur than what is reported due to embarrassment, fear, and poor handling by the justice system.

Robbery: Defined as "the unlawful taking or attempted taking of property that is in the immediate possession of another by force or violence and/or by putting the victim in fear" (UCR 2016). Statistically, robbery is an urban offense in which those arrested are usually male and members of minority groups. Individual citizens living in urban areas are typical targets of robbers where guns are presented but discharged very rarely.

Aggravated Assault: Defined as "an unlawful attack by one person upon another" (UCR 2016). In some states, aggravated assault is the attempt to inflict serious injury or great bodily harm on another person; in other states, the actual completion of the crime is called aggravated *battery* and not assault. Modern usage groups them together and the clearance rates (crimes solved by the police) are typically high.

Burglary: Defined as "the unlawful entry of a structure to commit a felony or a theft" (UCR 2016). Burglary is a property crime with very high annual losses (by dollar amount) and very low clearance rates.

Larceny-Theft: Defined as "the unlawful taking or attempted taking, carrying, leading, or riding away of property, from the possession or constructive possession of another" (UCR 2016). It is the most common of the eight Part I offenses, but reported little due to smaller dollar value amounts. Theft of motor vehicle parts is reported the most.

Motor Vehicle Theft: Defined as "the theft or attempted theft of a motor vehicle" (UCR 2016). It is further defined as a "self-propelled road vehicle that runs on a land surface and not on rails." Because insurance companies require that thefts be reported, it has a higher reporting rate.

Arson: Defined as "any willful or malicious burning or attempt to burn, with or without intent to defraud, a dwelling house, public building, motor vehicle or aircraft, or personal property of another" (UCR 2016). The burning of structures, not vehicles, is the most reported category of arson.

Part II offenses include crimes indicated in the following table:

Table 1   Part I and Part II Offenses (UCR 2016)

Part I	Part II
Murder	Forgery
Forcible Rape	Fraud
Robbery	Embezzlement

(continued)

Table 1   Part I and Part II Offenses (UCR 2016) (*continued*)

Part I	Part II
Aggravated Assault	Stolen Property
Burglary	Vandalism
Larceny-Theft	Weapons Violations
Motor Vehicle Theft	Prostitution
Arson	Gambling
	Driving Under The Influence
	Drug Abuse
	Sex Offenses (not forcible rape)
	Offenses Against Family & Children
	Liquor Laws
	Drunkenness
	Disorderly Conduct
	Curfew/Loitering
	Runaways

While the UCR provides a general understanding of the crime problem, any statistical reporting structure will have assumptions and limitations that make the actual numbers vary in accuracy and, ultimately, their purported "truth." For instance, the FBI compiles its UCR figures from data submitted by city and county law enforcement agencies. As a result, the FBI must rely on the willingness of local and state agencies to submit reports (and to submit them accurately).

In measuring quality, there are several reasons that the FBI's reports are flawed. Because they reflect crimes reported to the police, they do not account for crimes that go unreported. For example, a drug dealer is unlikely to file a report that he or she was assaulted and had a drug supply stolen that could translate into theft, robbery, or aggravated assault. Likewise, a prostitute is unlikely to file a report of rape for fear of being hurt or losing "business." Even a victim of theft may not file a report because the amount on the deductible on the insurance may exceed the amount of the loss.

Generally, many citizens do not report crimes due to involving the actual police. Social status, embarrassment, fear of retaliation, or the belief that law enforcement cannot (or will not) do anything about it are reasons often cited for not reporting crime.

As neither an exclusive nor exhaustive measure, the *quality* of data that is submitted can be questionable as well. Clerical errors, data processing errors, and even politics can play a part in how crimes are reported and sent up the hierarchy. Consider the practice that if multiple crimes are reported in one incident, only the most serious offense is counted in the UCR.

All of these factors are reasons that reduce the accuracy of data produced by the UCR. It has then become common for the news media to either report inclines or declines in the overall crime rate in the United States based off of *official* statistics. Changes or rates of other crimes, then, depend on the news or social media outlet.

The analysis of crime data can yield distinct patterns of crime and victimization rates and the demographics of both crime victims and criminals. It becomes easily detectable, then, to view changes in frequency, scope, and types of crimes in specific geographic regions as well as changes in specific demographics of groups of people in criminality. The UCR provides a unique measure of crime developed for specific policy, training, and research purposes. Whether law enforcement agencies conduct crime analysis with their own in-house records or use national data produced by the UCR, there exist many different measures of crime with each having its own strength and weakness. Although statistics are necessary and important, it is critical to temper face value of such information with its assumptions, limitations, and illustration of how crime affects people (in terms of a person's ability to physically, emotionally, or psychologically recover). Most important, perhaps, is the big picture of how effective the criminal justice system was able to respond to take care of personal needs as well as promote both safety and best practices for law enforcement agencies across the United States.

Brian Kinnaird

See also: Crime Control versus Due Process; Crime Prevention Techniques; International Association of Chiefs of Police; Police Ethics

Further Reading

Blueprints for Violence Prevention, http://www.ncjrs.gov/html/ojjdp/jjbul2001_7_3/contents.html.
Bureau of Justice Statistics, https://www.bjs.gov.
Bureau of Justice Assistance, https://www.bja.gov.
Crime and Victims Statistics, http://www.ojp.usdoj.gov/bjs.
FBI Hate Crime Statistics, http://www.fbi.gov/ucr/.
Police Executive Research Forum, http://www.policeforum.org.
Schmalleger, Frank. *Criminology Today: An Integrative Introduction*, 7th ed. New York: Pearson, 2015.
Schmalleger, Frank. *Criminal Justice Today: An Introductory Text for the 21st Century*, 14th ed. New York: Pearson, 2013.
Sourcebook of Criminal Justice Statistics, http://www.albany.edu/sourcebook.
UCR/NIBRS, fbi.gov/ucr-program-data.
Uniform Crime Reporting Statistics, https://ucrdatatool.gov.
Uniform Crime Reporting (UCR), https://ucr.fbi.gov/.
Violence Policy Center, http://www.vpc.org.

WIRETAPPING

Over the years, many techniques have been implemented to learn about criminal behavior in order for law enforcement to intervene before a crime has occurred. The government has attempted to accomplish this goal while balancing it with the protection of due process rights. Such techniques include the use of wiretapping and eavesdropping devices. Wiretapping involves any interception of a telephone transmission, including the recording of conversations that are monitored unofficially or officially. It can be accomplished by taping a third-party conversation without any of the parties involved in the conversation knowing, or it can actually be recorded by one of the parties. Eavesdropping can occur when one overhears, records, amplifies, or transmits any part of a private conversation of others (without the consent of at least one person involved in the conversation). Electronic eavesdropping involves the use of electronically transmitted devices to monitor these conversations.

History

Telephone communication began in 1876 and, after the invention of the telephone recorder in the 1890s, telephone wiretapping was developed. Until the late 20th century, a phone "tap" was a very simple process, where a few wires were attached to a speaker. Early 20th-century law enforcement used it extensively, especially during World War I. After the war, state laws limited the power of local police to continue to eavesdrop. However, this practice remained particularly common during Prohibition (when the police knew that bootleggers communicated via the telephone). The federal government had to control its use and abuse. Hence, in 1924, U.S. Attorney General Harry M. Daugherty (1860–1941), with the support of the public, banned wiretaps.

Bruce Sewell, Apple's general counsel, Susan Landau, professor, Worcester Polytechnic Institute, and Cyrus Vance Jr., district attorney, New York County, are sworn in during a House Judiciary Committee Hearing on Apple's denial of the FBI's request to provide a way to hack into one of the San Bernardino terrorists' phones, Washington, D.C., 2016. (Samuel Corum/Anadolu Agency/Getty Images)

Yet, law enforcement still violated the law, and the public was concerned. The Federal Bureau of Investigation (FBI) published a 1928 manual stating that wiretapping was improper and unethical, but they continued to do it. By 1934, the Communications Act made it a federal crime to tap telephones. Yet, it still persisted with the wiretapping of suspected criminals, suspected communists, union leaders, religious groups, and civil rights activists.

In the 1950s, local police departments actually expanded wiretapping (now including public phone booths). One investigation after another found Fourth Amendment violations, but it remained legal to intercept email messages through phone lines until 1986 (when the Electronic Communications Privacy Act was passed). The U.S. Supreme Court ruled in 1967 that a warrant was required to wiretap, and in 1968, a law was passed to require warrants for those investigations. In 1978 the Foreign Intelligence Surveillance Act led to the creation of a secret federal court authorized to issue wiretap warrants in national security cases. In 1995, the first court-ordered Internet wiretap took place in the United States. It was performed by a Naval Criminal Investigative Service special agent. His name was Peter Garza, and he was investigating Julio Ardita.

In 1994, the Digital Telephony Act assisted with facilitating wiretaps by requiring all fiber-optic–based switches to be equipped on phones. The American Civil Liberties Union (ACLU) and the public were not supportive of this ruling because it included voice communication in digital format, and texts and data transferred between computers, including work email. Each administration that followed increased the use of federal wiretaps (Reagan, Bush, and Clinton). Presidents Bush and Obama gave the National Security Agency (NSA) significant surveillance authority, and after the USA FREEDOM Act was instituted, authorities were allowed to obtain calling records directly from the phone company. This act was implemented in the case of the San Bernardino shooting offenders (Syed Farook and Tashfeen Malik) in 2015.

Legality

Federal law enforcement officials can tap telephone lines only if probable cause exists to show that there was unlawful activity. Then they need to obtain a court order, which is limited to surveillance of communications related to the unlawful activity, for 30 days on average. There are restrictions on tape-recording conversations, especially by non-law enforcement officials. Federal law does allow recording of phone calls (and other electronic communications) if there is consent from at least one party. Some states require all parties to consent.

However, these laws do not apply to law enforcement investigations, emergencies, or unlawful behavior. Court orders are needed for some of the devices necessary to wiretap. When conducted by nongovernment employees (unofficially), it may not be illegal. For example, the telephone company can also listen to your conversations if it needs to monitor the quality of service or if it needs to protect against service theft or harassment. It can also use it to inspect the telephone system. The telephone company can use these devices without a court order in the name of protection (against fraudulent use of the telephone, harassment protection for customers, and theft of telephone services). Further, employers can record their employees' phone conversations.

When the U.S. Supreme Court banned the warrantless use of GPS tracking devices, law enforcement changed tactics, using cell phone tracking programs without a warrant. As can be seen from each of these examples, even though there are laws banning wiretapping, there are many ways around those laws.

How It Is Accomplished

Early on, wiretaps between a switchboard and the subscriber were made by connecting extra wires. Today, much more sophisticated techniques are being used, including radio scanners and pen registers (the device can record the phone number being dialed out). Even baby monitors can be used to record conversations. Monitoring phone conversations can be accomplished on a recording device or via recording software. It can also be recorded manually or automatically, and can be done in an undercover fashion (covertly), or out in the open (overtly). In order to "tap" a line, the phone jack connects to a wall socket connected to an adaptive socket. Then the audio plug connects to a computer or tape recorder.

Prevalence

In 1999, electronic surveillance for criminal and national security was up, and the primary targets were mobile devices. By 2004, electronic surveillance had reached an all-time high. State and federal courts all logged more than 1,700 wire, oral, and electronic communication and no applications for wiretapping were denied. The vast majority of wiretaps are issued in narcotics arrests, and surveillance requests are rarely denied. Most common (94 percent of the time), is the use of wire surveillance via telephone (land line, cell, cordless, or mobile), and 89 percent of wiretaps take place in six states (New York, New Jersey, California, Nevada, Florida, and Colorado). The number of state and federal state wiretaps is up 17 percent from 2014 to 2015, and more than 4,000 were conducted in 2015.

Problems

Not only is it clear that wiretapping is being conducted more prevalently, but it is also clear that its use needs to be monitored. There are indications that initial applications for wiretaps have been too broad, and there has not always been full disclosure. In fact, the Administrative Office of the Courts issued a Wiretap Report in 2013 detailing the use of surveillance by law enforcement. The report explained the use of wiretapping and provided information on the use of technology and encryptions. One complaint has been the perceived lack of transparency in email interceptions, phone recording collecting, and data management. In addition, phone companies have sued the FBI over wiretapping laws. Regulations have shifted from the FBI to the telephone companies directly, including the cost of paying for phone equipment upgrades in order to wiretap. Google, for example, intercepts and collects private wireless data, and they were fined for obstructing investigations and potentially violating the Wiretap Act via their use of their Street View feature.

Technological Improvements

As technology improves, signals can be located farther away. Even satellites can be used to receive transmissions. The signal can be recorded at the site of the tap or via phone wires and even transmitted via radio. Newer concerns have been raised about law enforcement's access to communication as it becomes possible to get greater resolution for phone locations when Wi-Fi information from a number of cells surrounding a location are combined for better precision. When Internet wiretapping occurs, users can encode (or hide) any file in another. This technique, called steganography, was used by Osama bin Laden when he communicated with his terrorist cells. There are programs online that make this easy to accomplish, such as TextHide. This is just one example that demonstrates a need to regulate use in order to protect privacy and constitutional rights.

Today

Today, there are more than 1 billion landlines and 6 billion cell phones, making wiretapping a concern. Within hours of the USA PATRIOT Act being signed into law, the Department of Justice obtained a new surveillance process. It has vastly expanded government investigative authority, especially with Internet access, under the Anti-Terrorism Bill.

Wiretapping has become a hot-button issue after September 11, 2001, but even before then, the government had the ability to "track" or use surveillance techniques and measures to detect crime. In the 30 years prior to 9/11, the concept of government wiretaps had a 70- to 80-percent disapproval rating; after 9/11, that disapproval rating dropped to 44 percent, with crime control superseding due process and civil liberties.

Rules have eased for police to access phone records, and the Federal Communications Commission (FCC) has approved FBI location tracking requests. It is clear that judicial supervision is necessary to determine that recordings are relevant, and there has to be a balance between due process rights of individuals and the interests of society and the government in protecting victims and preventing crime. In addition, we need to determine whether or not NSA surveillance is a necessary and effective tool.

Gina Robertiello

See also: ACLU; Crime Prevention Techniques; Fourth Amendment; Understanding Probable Cause

Further Reading

Miller, Joshua Rhett. "Cell Phone Tracking Can Locate Terrorists—But Only Where It's Legal." *Fox News*, March 18, 2009. http://www.foxnews.com/story/2009/03/18/cell-phone-tracking-can-locate-terrorists-but-only-where-it-legal.html.

Flaherty, Anne. "What the Government Pays to Snoop on You." *USA Today*, July 10, 2013. http://www.usatoday.com/story/money/business/2013/07/10/what-government-pays-to-snoop-on-you/2504819.

Messmer, Ellen. "Apple IOS Apps Subject to Man-in-the-Middle Attacks." *Network World*, October 29, 2013. http://www.networkworld.com/article/2171269/network-security/apple-ios-apps-subject-to-man-in-the-middle-attacks.html.

Part 3: Law Enforcement in an Era of Political and Social Upheaval (1950–1975)

MIRANDA V. ARIZONA

Miranda v. Arizona is an important U.S. Supreme Court decision that set out "bright line" rules regarding when police may ask questions of persons suspected of crimes. Miranda is important, as it represents a clear effort by the federal judiciary to impose constitutional constraints on police power, and it is also a prime case study showing how legal protections for the accused can be resisted, reworked, and even subverted through the efforts of law enforcement officials, public outcry, and appointments to the bench.

Prior to the Miranda ruling, the primary test for determining whether a confession to a crime (or some other incriminating admission) was admissible in court was whether the statement was voluntary. Thus, a number of pre-Miranda cases established that physical force was an impermissible way to obtain a confession, as were some forms of deception and psychological coercion (such as threatening to take a suspect's spouse into custody). But these decisions left judges and police, as well as citizens accused of crimes, with considerable uncertainty about how voluntariness would be defined and determined in individual cases. *Miranda v. Arizona* represents a deliberate effort to replace this ambiguity with clear guidelines for police and judges.

In 1963, Ernesto Miranda, who was a laborer and a drifter, was arrested in Phoenix, Arizona. He was thought to have abducted and sexually assaulted a 17-year-old girl. Miranda was taken to the police station and questioned for two hours, after which he signed a statement indicating that he "voluntarily" confessed to the crimes of rape and kidnapping. His statement was presented as evidence at trial, and Miranda was sentenced to 20 to 30 years in prison for each count. Three years later, the Supreme Court reviewed Miranda's conviction, taking up the question of whether his constitutional rights had been violated by police, specifically his Fifth Amendment protection against self-incrimination.

In 1966, in *Miranda v. Arizona*, a narrowly divided Supreme Court maintained that when individuals are taken into custody, or deprived of their freedom in a "significant way," they must be made aware of certain rights before being questioned. In particular, the ruling explained that before police can interrogate persons accused of crimes, the supposed criminals need to be informed about four constitutional "procedural safeguards." These protections include (1) a right to remain silent; (2) anything a person says to police can be used against them in court; (3) the right

In the *Miranda v. Arizona* case (1966), Ernesto Miranda listens as the jury deliberates in Phoenix, Arizona. The Supreme Court made major revisions to the now familiar Miranda warnings this year, changing the ways that police, lawyers and criminal suspects interact amid what experts call an attempt to pull back some of the rights that Americans have become used to over the past few decades. (AP Photo)

to an attorney; and (4) the stipulation that if a person can't afford an attorney, the state will provide one for them, prior to any questioning. Most jurisdictions in the United States have added a fifth provision, indicating that the accused may end questioning at any time, but this is not formally required by the *Miranda* decision itself.

Miranda v. Arizona left intact the previous constitutional requirement that confessions must be voluntary, and it added the four new explicitly provided protections. Suspects can waive or relinquish these rights only through an intelligent (informed and knowing) and voluntary decision. Any statement a suspect makes to police without first hearing the so-called "Miranda warnings" must be excluded from trial, with only a few notable exceptions, such as the decision in some states to allow sentencing determinations to include non-Mirandized statements.

Miranda was remarkable, given both its timing (in the mid-1960s, crime rates were climbing and becoming an increasingly salient political issue) and its sweep. Few, if any, decisions of the Supreme Court have given such specific instructions to law enforcement officials about what they must say and do. While court decisions following *Miranda* have given some leeway in precisely how the warnings can be phrased, the decision mandates that suspects taken into custody must be clearly informed of their right to have counsel and their right to protection against self-incrimination.

Court decisions after *Miranda* clarified a number of aspects of the decision. At its heart, the case requires law enforcement authorities to announce the specified protections prior to "custodial interrogation." Custody includes arrest, but it is not limited to that. During a criminal investigation, and if a person is being restrained by law enforcement (physically or by circumstance), police must provide Miranda warnings before questioning. On the other hand, police do not need to "Mirandize" citizens when asking general questions at the scene of a crime (since police have not yet focused on a particular suspect), or during routine traffic stops and stop and frisk encounters (on the assumption that these are brief and not especially invasive deprivations of liberty). In other words, not all forms of police questioning count as interrogation under the *Miranda v. Arizona* framework.

In addition to these points, not every utterance automatically triggers the warnings. Thus, volunteered statements can be admitted into court without *Miranda*. This is true even when law enforcement has a role in facilitating incriminating admissions and confessions, so long as police do not create the "functional equivalent" of an interrogation. Thus, courts have sanctioned the practice of police arranging and recording a conversation between a suspect and his wife without first providing the Miranda protections. *Miranda's* rules concerning custodial interrogation by authorities generally permit private citizens to pose questions so long as these individuals are not working with and for police.

When the *Miranda* case was first handed down, police, prosecutors, and skeptical leaders predicted it would hamstring law enforcement and lead to fewer convictions. But while there is some scholarly evidence that the decision led to a measurable decrease in confession rates, other research suggests that over time police have learned to adapt to the new rules, with the result that few convictions are lost simply because of *Miranda's* requirements. Among other strategies deployed, law enforcement officials will sometimes delay charging or arresting a suspect with the hope that the person may say something incriminating during this pre-warning phase. So long as the investigating authorities can convince a judge that this questioning is generalized (and not yet focused on a particular person), the technique is usually upheld.

Moreover, police can sometimes convince suspects that their cooperation and confession will lead to better judicial outcomes, such as a reduced sentence, even though police have little direct influence over charging decisions and almost no impact on punishment. U.S. courts have also sanctioned various forms of pressure and deception as part of police efforts to convince suspected criminals to waive their Miranda protections and make incriminating statements. For example, authorities may inform a suspect that he or she has failed a lie detector test, that a witness has identified them, or that police have specific evidence linking a detainee to a crime—whether or not any of this information is true. In addition to these points, the confines of the interrogation room and the associated psychological and social stresses it produces are often beyond the reach of Miranda's protections. Thus, police may freely inform a person accused of a crime that his volunteered statements will speed up court proceedings and help him move on with his life. Taken together, these factors help explain why scholars estimate that more than three-quarters of criminal suspects waive their Miranda rights and talk with police.

In recent decades, the judiciary, led by the Supreme Court, has further limited the impact of *Miranda* by identifying other exceptions and boundaries to the decision. To begin with, in order to exercise *Miranda's* protections, suspects must clearly and affirmatively indicate their intent. Therefore, even if a court has appointed an attorney to represent a defendant, unless the accused requests a lawyer, police may seek a Miranda waiver when the attorney is not present. Similarly, an individual who wants to exercise his right to remain silent must do so explicitly; mere silence does not indicate that a person is exercising this Fifth Amendment protection.

Other Court decisions have allowed police to seek a Miranda waiver, even if it was initially refused, so long as they wait a sufficient period (at least 14 days). Further, in the 1984 decision of *New York v. Quarles*, the Supreme Court decided police can ask questions of suspects in custody without first providing Miranda warnings, if a specific "public safety" threat (such as an undiscovered handgun) is close at hand. This public safety exception to *Miranda* was invoked in 2013 when police questioned Dzhokhar Tsarnaev, one of the two men responsible for a bomb attack at the Boston Marathon that year.

Notwithstanding these limitations, courts have consistently upheld the core holding of *Miranda* and set aside some efforts by police to circumvent the decision. Thus, in *Missouri v. Seibert* (2004), the Court invalidated a "question-first," two-step method for getting around *Miranda*. Law enforcement personnel would question citizens and obtain their confessions without informing them of their constitutional rights, but would then ask the suspects to repeat their incriminating statements after receiving the Miranda warnings. The Court held that this practice violated *Miranda* and made its protections "ineffective."

Perhaps the most serious threat to *Miranda* emerged in 1999 when a federal appeals court ruled that a law passed by Congress effectively overturned the decision by permitting voluntary incriminating statements in federal court whether or not Miranda warnings were first provided. The law, originally passed in 1968 as a reaction to the *Miranda* decision, had been dormant, unenforced by the government until the 1990s. The Supreme Court reviewed and rejected the appeals court decision, finding the Miranda warnings were constitutional rules that could not be overturned by Congress. As the Court put it, "Miranda has become embedded in routine police practice to the point where the warnings have become part of our national culture."

The Court's judgment is consistent with the evolving views of the public. At the time *Miranda* was handed down, the decision was hardly popular. A poll found that 57 percent of Americans thought it was a wrong decision, and only 30 percent approved of it (Peabody 2016). But over time, the ruling became entrenched in the courts and law enforcement circles. The Miranda warnings became a recurring feature of news reporting and even popular television shows and movies. This familiarity seems to have leveraged widespread acceptance in public opinion. By 2000, a robust 94 percent of those polled expressed support for the proposition that when the police arrest someone they should "be required to inform that person of their constitutional rights."

The eventual judicial, popular, and police acceptance of the basic *Miranda v. Arizona* decision has not foreclosed controversy. Legal scholars, political pundits, and popular commentators continue to debate the effectiveness of the case in both ensuring the basic rights of criminal defendants and protecting the public. Civil libertarians point to police practices and case law that provide numerous opportunities for making the Miranda protections less than meets the eye, especially for the most vulnerable suspects such as the poor and uneducated. At the same time, proponents of crime control and law enforcement contend that the suspects most likely to invoke the warnings are the most hardened and dangerous, and, in any event, the Miranda warnings serve primarily to diminish individuals' responsibility for engaging in criminal acts.

Despite this ongoing political and legal controversy, *Miranda* remains influential. Indeed, the Miranda warnings represent one of the more successful criminal law exports of the United States. A number of other nations (including South Africa, Switzerland, and New Zealand) have adopted similar rules in their judicial systems. Moreover, more than 50 years after it was first handed down, *Miranda* has been broadly implemented. It is possibly the most recognized case in U.S. criminal law and a familiar referent in American judicial proceedings, media accounts, and even popular culture.

Bruce Peabody

See also: Constitutional Mandates; Fifth Amendment; "Law and Order" as a Popular Political Slogan; Police Authority to Detain

Further Reading

Baker, Liva. *Miranda: Crime, Law and Politics.* New York: Atheneum, 1984.

Cassell, Paul G. "Miranda's Social Costs: An Empirical Reassessment." *Northwestern University Law Review* 90 (1996): 387–499.

Davidson, Amy. "What Happened to the Miranda Warning in Boston?" *New Yorker*, April 21, 2013.

Hall, Matthew E. K. *The Nature of Supreme Court Power.* New York: Cambridge University Press, 2013.

Leo, Richard A., and George C. Thomas III. *Confessions of Guilt: From Torture to Miranda and Beyond.* New York: Oxford University Press, 2012.

Peabody, Bruce. "Fifty Years Later, the Miranda Decision Hasn't Accomplished What the Supreme Court Intended." *Washington Post*, June 13, 2016. https://www.washingtonpost.com/news/monkey-cage/wp/2016/06/13/your-miranda-rights-are-50-years-old-today-heres-how-that-decision-has-aged.

MAPP V. OHIO

The 1961 *Mapp v. Ohio* decision reflected an era where the Supreme Court deliberately engineered uniformity in the application of individual constitutional rights and due process under the law. The court's decision extended the Fourth Amendment prohibition on "unreasonable search and seizure" used in federal court to all state courts (Wohl 2011, 1). After 55 years, the controversy over what happened, how, and why the Supreme Court ruled in favor of Mapp, and ultimately the consequence of the decision on police behavior and the public's response continues today. The debate is classic, reflecting those adherents in favor of the Crime Control Model of criminal justice wanting the decision overturned and those in favor of the Due Process Model arguing for its continued retention. While the debate about the effectiveness of the amendment's "exclusionary rule" continues, the Supreme Court's decision forever changed police procedure in the U.S. criminal justice system.

According to the Supreme Court's syllabus ("Mapp v. Ohio" 1961), the basic facts of the *Mapp v. Ohio* case are as follows:

On May 23, 1957, in Cleveland, Ohio, a 32-year-old African American single mother named Miss Dollree Mapp (1923–2014) was on the second floor of her two-family home with her daughter, when she heard the police knock on her door. Three officers from the Cleveland Police Department's Bureau of Special Investigations requested access to her home based on the suspicion that a suspect in a recent bombing incident had sought refuge there. In addition, there was suspicion of illegal gambling paraphernalia being at the residence. During the early 1960s, tensions were high between the African American community and the police in Cleveland, Ohio (Landmark Cases 2015). Miss Mapp, having already hired a

lawyer for a separate civil issue, told the police that she would need to talk to her lawyer before giving them access to her house. The police officers waited for Miss Mapp to speak with her attorney. The lawyer told her to ask the police if they had acquired a search warrant to search her house. (A search warrant is a written document signed by a judge or magistrate based on probable cause, authorizing police to search a particular location for a specific person or object [Neubauer and Fradella 2013, 289].) Miss Mapp then asked the police if they had a search warrant, and their response was that they did not. She then denied them entry into her house. The police informed their headquarters and established surveillance of the property.

Mapp v. Ohio (1961) was a landmark case involving Fourth Amendment rights. The U.S. Supreme Court determined that evidence obtained in violation of the Fourth Amendment is considered an illegal search and seizure. (AP Photo)

After three hours, four additional police officers arrived at her house and also attempted to gain access. Reportedly, shortly thereafter, a police lieutenant telephoned Miss Mapp and told her she needed to allow the police to search her home. In response, Miss Mapp called her attorney who told her that he would come over to her residence.

Almost simultaneous with the arrival of her lawyer, the police forcibly entered her property. At the time, Miss Mapp was standing on the staircase between the first and second floors. Meanwhile, the police outside were preventing her lawyer from entering the house, and her lawyer told the police that they were breaking the law. When Miss Mapp insisted on seeing a search warrant, one of the officers held up a piece of paper. Miss Mapp grabbed the paper and stuffed it into her blouse. After a short scuffle, the police forcibly recovered the paper and handcuffed a visibly upset Miss Mapp. She was escorted upstairs to her bedroom and told to sit on down on her bed.

The police began to search her bedroom and the other rooms on the second floor, including her daughter's bedroom, for evidence. Nothing of consequence was located in the upstairs search. They then continued the search in the basement, where the police located an old trunk. Inside this trunk, they found books and pictures that they claimed were obscene and violated Ohio state law. The police seized the material and arrested Miss Mapp, per a revised code in Ohio, for possessing obscene materials (Ohio Anti-obscenity Statute 1958). The code stated, "No person shall knowingly have in his possession or under his control an obscene, lewd or lascivious book, magazine, pamphlet, paper, writing, advertisement, circular, print, picture, photograph, or pictures and stories of immoral deeds, lust or crime." But Mapp was arrested, despite her efforts to convince the police the books and photos belonged to a former tenant.

During the trial, Miss Mapp entered the plea of "not guilty." Her lawyer, A. L. Kearns (1937–2005), argued that the evidence—the books and pictures—was not admissible because they were illegally acquired based on the lack of a search warrant. His argument was in line with *Weeks v. United States* (1914), which argued evidence seized illegally was not admissible in federal court. This was called an "exclusionary rule." Unfortunately for Miss Mapp, in 1949 the Supreme Court found in *Wolf v. Colorado* "that the states need not observe the federal rule, which excludes from criminal prosecution evidence obtained by illegal search" (Desky 1950, 498). At the time, adoption of the rule was voluntary at the state level, and only about 50 percent of the states had done so. On September 4, 1958, the Ohio Court of Common Pleas acquitted Miss Mapp of the gambling paraphernalia charge but found her guilty of violating the obscenity law and sentenced her to seven years in prison. The conviction was upheld by the intermediate court of appeals. Two years later, on March 23, 1960, the Ohio State Supreme Court reviewed the appeal and narrowly upheld the lower court's decision. Four of the seven judges on the Ohio Supreme Court voted in favor of overturning the decision of the lower court of appeals, citing the obscenity law on which Miss Mapp was convicted was unconstitutional. However, the Ohio state constitution mandated if more than one judge rules in favor of the constitutional question, then the lower court ruling is affirmed.

Based on this constitutional question, Mapp's lawyer appealed her conviction to the U.S. Supreme Court. Almost one year to the day, on March 29, 1961, the case went before the court.

A. L. Kearns argued the case for the appellant, Miss Mapp. Gertrude Bauer Mahon (1904–1979) argued for the appellee, the State of Ohio, and Bernard A. Berkman presented the case for the American Civil Liberties Union (ACLU), urging the court to support a reversal of the Ohio Supreme Court decision. The Supreme Court chief justice at the time was Earl Warren (1891–1974) (*Mapp v. Ohio* 1961, 1). The case for Kearns and Berkman primarily centered on the First and Fourteenth Amendments: that the Ohio State obscenity law was far too broad and therefore infringed on Miss Mapp's constitutional First Amendment rights of freedom of speech.

Shortly after the judicial conference, after hearing the oral arguments, justices Tom C. Clark (1899–1977), Black, and Brennan, reportedly had a conversation in an elevator about the merits of the case. During this conversation, they entertained using the Mapp case as the vehicle to overturn *Wolf v. Colorado,* thereby making the exclusionary rule applicable to all states. Upon gaining the support of both Warren and Douglas, the three had the majority to do so. On June 19, 1961, in a 5–3 vote, the U.S. Supreme Court voted to overturn the conviction. Justice Stewart did not vote; rather, he wrote a memo stating he agreed in part with Justice Harlan's dissent while at the same time thought the ruling of the lower court should be overturned.

Justice Harlan wrote the dissenting opinion. At issue was the decision of the court to use the Fourth Amendment as the foundation of their decision, even though it was not the central argument posed by Kearns or Berkman. Since the decision, there has been almost nonstop controversy as to the true intent behind the decision. The Fourth Amendment states:

> The right of the people to be secure in their persons, houses, papers, and effects, against unreasonable searches and seizures, shall not be violated, and no warrants shall issue, but upon probable cause, supported by oath or affirmation, and particularly describing the place to be searched, and the persons or things to be seized. (National Archives)

Some would argue that the foundation of the exclusionary rule is the uniform application of constitutional rights. For others, it is about curtailing police abuse of power. Regardless of its interpretation, the law has been under constant scrutiny with several cases serving to dismantle some of its foundation. In *Nix v. Williams* (1984), the Supreme Court determined evidence obtained by illegal means may be admissible if it is established that the evidence would have been discovered inevitably without the unlawful methods being used. Again, in *United States v. Leon* (1984), the court maintained the exclusionary rule should not be applied when evidence obtained is based on a search warrant issued by a neutral magistrate, which is later found to be invalid (*Mapp v. Ohio* 1961). In *Murray v. Carter*, the Supreme Court determined evidence obtained by violating the Fourth Amendment might be admissible in court, but only if that evidence came from an independent source (not related to the violation).

Then, in 2009, the court found in *Herring v. United States* an exception to the exclusionary rule, allowing illegally obtained evidence into court only if mistakes from the police lead to evidence as a result of good faith—as opposed to a total disregard of constitutional requirements (*Herring v. United States* 2009). The Fourth Amendment continues to adapt to both the social and technological changes in our society. In 2014, in *Riley v. California*, the Supreme Court determined that police cannot seek out digital information on a cell phone that was seized from someone who has been arrested, either without their consent or without a warrant (Robinson 2014, 438).

The impact of these decisions on police procedure has only made law enforcement more deliberate and sophisticated in their approach. Establishing probable cause and the application of search warrants have made current law enforcement officers more professional. The ongoing concern is the uniform application of the Fourth Amendment on the ever-changing digital and virtual environment. With cell phones protected by the exclusionary rule, the next challenge will be the digital cloud, a repository of unimaginable amounts of (personal) data, which is not currently under the protection of the Fourth Amendment. Law enforcement and criminal procedure continues to seek the balance between rule of law, security, and civil liberties.

The exclusionary rule's impact on crime also remains questionable with some touting no dramatic impact and others citing a definitive rise in crime but with a correlated reduction in wrongful convictions. As long as there are adherents to both the Due Process and Crime Control models of criminal justice, the Fourth Amendment's exclusionary rule will always be debated.

Frank Hall

See also: Crime Prevention Techniques; Fourth Amendment; *Mapp v. Ohio*

Further Reading

Desky, Robert M. *Wolf v. Colorado and Unreasonable Search and Seizure in California*, 38 Cal. L. Rev. 498. August 1950. http://scholarship.law.berkeley.edu/cgi/viewcontent.cgi ?article=3474&context=californialawreview.

Herring v. United States 555 U.S. 135 (2009).

Landmark Cases. C-SPAN National Constitution Center. Performed by Carolyn Long, Renee Hutchins, with host Susan Swain. Washington, DC: C-SPAN, National Constitution Center, Educational Discussion—Book Review, Nov 30, 2015.

Long, Carolyn. *Mapp v. Ohio: Guarding Against Unreasonable Searches and Seizures.* Lawrence: University Press of Kansas, 2006.

Mapp v. Ohio. 367 U.S. 643 (1961) http://images.ulib.csuohio.edu/cdm/compoundobject /collection/law/id/2920/rec/8.

Neubauer, David W., and Henry F. Fradella. *America's Courts and Criminal Justice System*, 11th ed. Belmont, CA: Wadsworth. 2013.

Ohio Anti-obscenity Statute. Ohio revised code: 2905.34–.35 (Supp. 1958). http://images
    .ulib.csuohio.edu/cdm/ref/collection/law/id/2627.
Robinson, David J. "The U.S. Supreme Court Says 'No' to Cell-Phone Searches Incident to
    Arrest." *Illinois Bar Journal,* Illinois State Bar Association 102, no. 9 (September 2014):
    438. https://www.isba.org/ibj/2014/09/ussupremecourtsays'no'cell-phonesea.
"Supreme Court Landmark Case *Mapp v. Ohio.*" C-SPAN, November 30, 2015. http://www
    .c-span.org/video/?327718-1/supreme-court-landmark-case-mapp-v-ohio.
Wohl, Alexander. "Mapp v. Ohio Turns 50." *Slate.com.* June 7, 2011. http://www.slate.com
    /articles/news_and_politics/jurisprudence/2011/06/mapp_v_ohio_turns_50.html.

TERRY V. OHIO

Terry v. Ohio is the Supreme Court case that says police may conduct brief investigational stops when they have adequate belief that someone may be planning or has
recently been engaged in criminal activity. Furthermore, when there is adequate belief
the suspect might be armed, a concern for officer and public safety allows a police
officer to pat down the suspect, but only in a limited way, to search for potential weapons. Together, these are known as a "stop and frisk," and the Court's approval of this
procedure has proved to be both a very effective and, at times, controversial investigative power for law enforcement.

This case began on October 31, 1963, when John Terry and his friend Richard
Chilton were observed by Police Detective Martin McFadden in downtown Cleveland, Ohio. The two African American gentlemen were at a street corner and caught
the eye of Detective McFadden, who observed them for around 10 minutes as
the men took turns walking down the block, stopping in front of a nearby store to
peer in through its front window, and then walking back. At one point, the two
men were approached by a Caucasian man named Carl Katz, who briefly conferred
with them before heading down the street. Chilton and Terry followed, before all
three men stopped to talk together once more. At this point, Detective McFadden,
who had patrolled the area for 30 years searching for pickpockets and shoplifters,
felt that the men might be planning an armed robbery, and he decided to intervene.

Detective McFadden approached the three men and told them to stop, keeping
their hands out of their pockets. After asking the men to identify themselves, he
turned Terry around and patted him down, at which point he felt a pistol in the
left breast pocket of Terry's overcoat. McFadden then ordered all three men into a
local store, where he patted down the other two men while the owner of the store
called for a police wagon. In that search, Detective McFadden found a .38 revolver
on Chilton, but Katz did not have any weapons. Katz was later released, but Chilton
and Terry were charged with carrying concealed weapons.

At the trial, the defendants challenged Detective McFadden's search, arguing that it
was not based on probable cause—the standard the law required to justify an arrest.
In order to have probable cause, Detective McFadden would have needed enough
evidence to support a reasonable belief that Terry and Chilton were either about
to commit, or were committing, a crime. Although the two men were behaving

suspiciously, probable cause was completely lacking. Since *Mapp v. Ohio* (1961), the normal court response to an illegal search would be to refuse to hear evidence related to the handguns found on the two men, essentially guaranteeing that charges would be dropped; however, the trial and appeals courts refused to consider the search illegal because they felt Detective McFadden's actions were reasonable, and both men were convicted.

On appeal to the Supreme Court, Chief Justice Earl Warren (1891–1974) represented an 8–1 majority that upheld Terry's conviction. The Court announced a new rule in criminal procedure, which said that the Fourth Amendment was not violated by brief investigatory stops that were based on reasonable suspicion that "crime was afoot," that is, that a crime had just occurred, was taking place, or was about to be committed. Furthermore, a police officer was permitted to do a basic pat down of a suspect, searching for weapons, but only if there was a plausible suspicion that the person might be armed. In this case, the Court believed that Detective McFadden's actions were very reasonable, and they found that the stop and the search that he conducted were legal. Similar stops made in the future based on this ruling would come to be known as "Terry stops" or sometimes as a "stop and frisk."

There are two important elements to a valid Terry stop: first, that the officer has reasonable suspicion that crime is afoot and, second, that the officer has reasonable suspicion that the suspect might be armed. To understand the rule this case laid out, it is important to recognize that these two questions are separate inquiries.

An important aspect of the Court's holding was announcing the "reasonable suspicion" standard, which is met by a lower level of certainty than what is required for probable cause (the standard required for most arrests and searches). Reasonable suspicion is more than just a gut feeling, and it is sometimes called a "reasonable *articulable* suspicion." This means that an officer must be able to describe the factors that created their suspicion, and the court will judge whether these factors, taken as a whole, meet the required standard. This is called the "totality of circumstances" test. Factors that are commonly listed in this analysis include the extent of the officer's experience, special training received, and features of the neighborhood or suspect's behavior that made the officer suspicious. The test is very fact-specific and can be quite flexible, which has at times drawn criticism of the rule.

As mentioned before, a Terry *frisk* is not an automatic part of a Terry *stop*, although the justification for a frisk is not frequently a primary reason to challenge a stop, as courts tend to be deferential to police on this factor. Furthermore, because officers need only a reasonable suspicion that a person might be armed, this suspicion does not necessarily need to be tied to the suspected criminal behavior that justified the stop. Odd shapes in a person's pockets or waistband, even how a person walks, have all been taken as justification for a Terry frisk.

The more commonly challenged aspect of a Terry frisk is the scope of the search conducted. The case itself involved a quick pat down similar to what you might encounter going through airport security, and the Supreme Court has been careful to limit the search to something like that. However, if, during a frisk, an officer feels either something they know to be a weapon or, if they're unsure an object might be a weapon, the officer is permitted to pull the object out for closer inspection without violating the Fourth Amendment. This means that, if an officer is unsure what an object is, but it does not feel like a weapon, such as a baggie with some pills in it, the officer is not permitted to pull that baggie from a suspect's pocket without either first obtaining the suspect's consent or securing a warrant. However, if an officer was unsure about a different object, say a glasses case, which could be a case concealing a weapon, the officer would be justified in removing the object for further inspection.

It might be somewhat surprising that the same Chief Justice that pushed for criminal justice reform and due process in the *Miranda v. Arizona* and *Mapp v. Ohio* decisions would hand down this pro-police decision, but the rule announced in *Terry* has been well-regarded in the years since. There have, however, been questions about the facts of *Terry* itself, as some commentators point out that Detective McFadden had little to no experience with armed robbery and may have singled out the men because of their race. However, Richard Chilton died in a shoot-out over a botched drug store robbery in 1967, so McFadden's intuition may have seemed retroactively well-founded by the time of the Court's ruling in 1968 (Katz 2005). Police actions relying on *Terry* have been mixed as well, with many officers' lives saved and criminals apprehended balanced against instances of abuse and police overreach, such as the controversial use of stop-and-frisk actions in New York City, which led to a 2013 civil rights lawsuit (Gay 2014).

Donald Roth

See also: Fleeing Felon Legislation; Fourth Amendment; Police Authority to Detain; Racial Profiling; Understanding Probable Cause

Further Reading

Gay, Mara. "Federal Court Greenlights New York Stop-and-Frisk Overhaul." *Wall Street Journal*, October 31, 2014. http://www.wsj.com/articles/federal-court-greenlights-new -york-stop-and-frisk-overhaul-1414783716.

Katz, Lewis R. "Terry v. Ohio at 35: A Revisionist View." *Mississippi Law Journal* 74, no. 2 (2004): 423–500. http://www.olemiss.edu/depts/ncjrl/pdf/katzmslj04.pdf.

Stop & Frisk: Terry v. Ohio. *Flex Your Rights*. https://www.flexyourrights.org/terry_v_ohio.

Terry v. Ohio. 392 U.S. 1 (1968). https://www.law.cornell.edu/supremecourt/text/392 /1#writing-USSC_CR_0392_0001_ZO.

KERNER COMMISSION REPORT ON RACE RIOTS AND POLICE RESPONSE

The 1960s was a decade rife with civil unrest, one that epitomized the concept of *social revolution*. Several movements developed and gained traction this time, focusing on issues that affected individuals across the United States. The decade saw a rise in counterculture, in which various groups refused to align themselves with the status quo and, alternatively, chose to make change in society. These groups and movements sought (and subsequently saw) change in women's rights, environmentalism, constitutional rights, the treatment of marginalized groups such as the disabled and the lesbian, gay, bisexual, and transgender (LGBT) community, and civil rights as it related to the marginalization of racial groups—specifically African Americans.

A byproduct of the marginalization of racial groups was increased racial tension, as well as disorder, across the United States. The areas of the most severe unrest and disorder were metropolitan areas, particularly those in which there was racial segregation, economic plight, and the combination thereof. In the 1960s, these cities included Newark and New Brunswick, New Jersey, and Detroit, Michigan. These cities experienced increasingly high levels of racial tension, which ultimately led to protests, demonstrations, and—in some instances—riots. In response to these incidents, in 1967, President Lyndon B. Johnson established the National Advisory Commission on Civil Disorders (NACCD), which was also known was the Kerner Commission.

The 11-member panel was referred to as the Kerner Commission due to the leadership by its chair, Illinois governor Otto Kerner. He had an illustrious career in public service, leading up to his selection as chairman of the committee. Academically, he was Ivy-league educated (at Brown University) and had studied at Northwestern University School of Law. Kerner was also a decorated veteran, having enlisted in the National Guard and serving in in the Field Artillery branch of the U.S. Army toward the end of World War II. Kerner reached the rank of general and retired with multiple medals and commendations for service. During this time, he also served as a U.S. district attorney and, subsequently, a Cook County (Illinois) judge. Following these positions, he served two terms of office as governor of Illinois (1960–1968). In 1967, President Lyndon B. Johnson commissioned several national advisory panels that investigated the relationships between social conditions and crime. Kerner was considered the most appropriate person to lead the NACCD and to study the patterns and causes of, and responses to, racial disorders in the United States.

The commission was directed to answer three questions related to the summer of 1967 that saw racial disorders, such as protests and riots, across the United States: (1) What happened? (2) Why did it happen? and (3) What can be done to prevent it from happening again? The commission was focused on describing the events that transpired, providing an explanation of the root cause(s), and providing policy recommendations for the prevention of future disorders. To answer these questions, the commission gathered information in several ways. First, members of the commission visited the places in question (Newark, New Brunswick, and Detroit) to have a first-hand view and experience of the conditions of the respective city. Second, members of the commission began a dialogue with members of the community who witnessed the disorders. Finally, the commission sought out leading experts across the country with practical and academic experience to provide insight and counsel to the commission's endeavor.

In the response to the first question, the commission discussed the specific cases of Newark and New Brunswick, New Jersey, and Detroit, Michigan—though disorders permeated the American landscape during the same time. From July 12th to the

17th, residents in Newark reacted to a purported case of police brutality that involved the arrest of an African American taxi driver. Protesters initiated the several-day event by protesting the arrest, only to be dispersed by the Newark police. Later in the evening, more protesters created havoc in the city's business district by setting fires—then rioters and looters joined the fight. The mayor had to call for support from the National Guard and state troopers. At the end of the nearly week-long incident, 26 people were dead, more than 1,000 were injured, and more than $10 million in property damage had been incurred.

In Detroit, Michigan, a similar set of circumstances resulted in a similar series of incidents. After a police raid of an unlicensed club, several onlookers and witnesses to the raid (which resulted in the arrest of more than 80 African Americans in attendance) surrounded the police as they loaded the arrestees into transport vehicles. After a rumor circulated through the crowd of brutality during one of the arrests, a glass bottle was thrown at police. The riot had begun. More bottles were thrown, at both officers' and patrol cars, and within an hour thousands of people filled the area. Fires were set, firefighters and police officers were attacked, and looting began. From July 23 to 27, more than 7,000 people were arrested. Forty-three individuals were killed and more than 1,000 injured. More than 1,700 stores were looted, 1,400 buildings burned, and more than $50 million in property damage had been incurred.

The preceding events were quite similar to those in New Brunswick, New Jersey. However, the outcome was far from similar to the riots seen in Newark and Detroit. In fact, no riot transpired in New Brunswick in the summer of 1967. On July 17th and 18th, hundreds of young African Americans vandalized and looted several businesses in the downtown district of the city. However, this activity never reached the level of rioting—almost all of the criminal activity was focused on the damage of property, not physical violence. On the second day, a crowd of nearly 200 African Americans walked to the police station and demanded to speak with the mayor about racial discrimination and the instances of police misconduct that had been mishandled (or not handled at all). The crowd also demanded that everyone who had been arrested on the first night of protests be released from jail—and they demanded proof. Despite the reassurance by the mayor that all those arrested had indeed been released, the crowd would not disperse without objective proof. The mayor, then, allowed representatives from the crowd to inspect the city jail—providing evidence that, indeed, they were empty. The crowd dispersed and widespread violence had been averted.

Although the commission focused on just three major metropolitan disorders—two of which resulted in riots—the entire nation experienced events like these. In the first nine months of 1967 leading up to the panel commission, 164 disorders were reported. The commission noted that the protesters and rioters were not "counter-culture" in the sense that they disagreed with American society; they, instead, sought their place in it—one with equal treatment and equal opportunity.

Not all cities experienced the same social conditions, nor were all minority groups in those cities disadvantaged to the same extent. However, the commission found several themes consistent across cities involved in disorders in 1967. These "grievances" were classified into three levels by their "relative intensity." The primary grievance, at the top of the list in the first level of intensity, was police practices. Similarly, the eighth (of twelve) grievance listed—in the third level of intensity—was that of discriminatory administration of justice. The commission noted that the principal official response to the disorders had not been the redress of the underlying conditions for the violence but the training and equipping of police with more sophisticated weapons. In fact, the police were described as becoming a symbol of "White power, White racism, and White repression" for members of the African American community. Further exacerbating these feelings was the widespread belief that police engaged regularly in brutality and a "double standard" of justice—based on the color of one's skin.

The commission committed an entire chapter of the executive report to the discussion of police. Chapter 11, *Police and the Community*, provided several recommendations for municipal governments and police agencies. The intent of these recommendations was to improve city, police, and community relations, which, in turn, would decrease the potential for future disorder. The commission suggested the following: the review of police operations in the "ghetto" to eliminate misconduct; additional police protection be afforded in poorer areas; the establishment of effective mechanisms for grievances against police; the adoption of policy guidelines for situations of high tension; the development of community support for law enforcement through programs; recruitment of African Americans into law enforcement, as well as the promotion of those already employed; and the establishment of a junior officer program to provide services specifically in "ghetto" neighborhoods. In addition to the suggestions provided in this chapter of the executive report, the commission also suggested specific training and improvement of procedures as it related to the police response to incidents that could lead to disorders, as well as the implementation of emergency plans in which all facets of the criminal justice system would work collaboratively.

Based on the events that preceded the riots in Newark and Detroit, the protests in New Brunswick, and the more than 160 additional disorders across the nation, the Kerner Commission identified the primary issues associated with racial tension in America and the violent uprisings that had occurred in the summer of 1967. The Commission's report was the culmination of years, if not decades, of failed public policy meant to address the continued racial tension and disadvantage observed in urban areas across the United States. At the heart of this racial tension was the unjust and unequal treatment of African Americans by police and others in position to administer justice. Police, particularly those in metropolitan areas, were operating using a "double standard," one unfairly based on an individual's race. Law enforcement not only treated African Americans differently than Whites, but the locations in which African Americans were more likely to live were patrolled less, experienced longer delays after calls for service, and experienced a general apathy on the part of officers following a police response. The *Report of the National Advisory Commission on Civil Disorders* was instrumental in broadcasting the conditions that the poor, specifically the poor African American, community faced, and the poor relationship it shared with public agencies such as the police.

Kaitlyn Clarke and Philip D. McCormack

See also: Knapp Commission; Wickersham Report on Soaring Crime during Prohibition

Further Reading

Knopf, Terry Ann. *Rumors, Race, and Riots*, 2nd ed. New Brunswick, NJ: Transaction Publishers, 2009.

National Commission on Law Observance and Enforcement. *Report on the Enforcement of the Prohibition Laws of the United States* (Volumes 1–14). Washington, DC: U.S. Government Printing Office, 1931.

Rasmussen, Chris. "A Web of Tension: A 1967 Protests in New Brunswick, New Jersey." *Journal of Urban History* 40, no. 1 (2014): 137–157.

U.S. Riot Commission. *Report of the National Advisory Commission on Civil Disorders*. Washington, DC: U.S. Government Printing Office, 1968.

U.S. Commission on Civil Rights. *1961 United States Commission on Civil Rights Report*. Washington, DC: U.S. Government Printing Office, 1961.

CHICAGO POLICE DURING THE 1968 DEMOCRATIC NATIONAL CONVENTION

The 1968 Democratic National Convention became a flashpoint symbolizing tensions between the youthful anti-war counterculture and the political and cultural status quo. The event was punctuated by tension, chaos, and dramatic police response. The convention took place in Chicago, Illinois, from August 26th to the 29th, 1968, with the purpose of solidifying the party's official platform and formally choosing the Democratic Party's presidential candidate for the national elections in November. The convention itself was a culmination of a difficult, tumultuous period for the Democratic Party (with embattled incumbent president Lyndon Johnson choosing not to seek reelection) and the nation as a whole, reaching a peak with the assassinations of Senator Robert F. Kennedy (who was running for president) and civil rights leader Martin Luther King, Jr. It was a chaotic year defined by civil unrest, clashes between law enforcement and the public, and urban riots, which were often precipitated by police-citizen confrontations gone awry.

Meanwhile, police departments across America were experiencing the repercussions of the movement toward police professionalism, which had begun decades earlier and had influenced local law enforcement strategies and practices in the years since. A cornerstone of this movement was a belief that familiarity with members of the community was not in the best interest of high-quality policing and that maintaining a "professional distance" from the public should be of paramount importance in order to avoid interactions that could result in favoritism or greater vulnerability to corruption. This approach was aided by technological innovations such as improved field communications and availability of patrol vehicles, which allowed officers to emphasize reactive crime-fighting by more efficiently responding to calls for service or disturbances in the field while avoiding any unnecessary interactions with the public. The goal was to essentially isolate police from the community in an effort to protect officers from temptations that might compromise them and their crime-fighting mission. The danger of this approach, however, was that in many municipalities, police became so detached from the communities they were tasked to serve that they were increasingly viewed as untrustworthy outsiders who were ignorant of the unique needs and concerns of residents.

The repercussions of this approach reached a tipping point in the mid-to-late 1960s, when civil rights and anti-war demonstrations challenged the reserves and standard protocols and practices of urban law enforcement agencies nationwide. Compounding the complexity of these interactions was a dramatic cultural divide. Patrol and administrative police department personnel remained primarily White and rooted in working-class communities, and their experiences and perspectives clashed dramatically with both Black Americans participating in civil rights demonstrations and anti-war activists who were often young, college-educated, and drawn from middle-class or upper-class backgrounds. Activists distrusted the police and were contemptuous of the governmental power and authority they represented. In turn, law enforcement was wary of the demonstrators' and activists' motives and deeply concerned about the potential of social movement leaders to employ anti-police rhetoric to incite and encourage violent resistance among their followers. The counterculture surrounding the anti-war movement represented an affront to the "traditional"

Police rout a big throng of hippies and yippies as they try to clear Grant Park during the Democratic National Convention in Chicago on August 28, 1968. Witnesses reported the Chicago Police force was unnecessarily aggressive and numerous innocent protestors were injured. (AP Photo)

values and mores of the political establishment, as well as those serving in law enforcement. Police had difficulty distinguishing among relatively benign "flower children" and more blatantly rabblerousing political agitators.

Within this greater context, Chicago political leaders and police prepared themselves for the upcoming Democratic convention. The rioting that had followed Martin Luther King, Jr.'s assassination the previous spring was still very fresh in residents' minds. Mayor Richard J. Daley had openly criticized the Chicago Police Department's handling of the situation. He accused the agency's leadership of exacerbating problems with an overly cautious approach and stated that officers should have been instructed to kill arsonists or maim or cripple looters. The Democratic National Convention already promised to be a contentious affair, with no definitive consensus at the outset regarding its nominee. The party was fractured along ideological lines, particularly in regard to its position on continued involvement in the Vietnam War. Among the remaining candidates, the two front-runners were viewed as philosophical opposites on the subject of the war. Senator Eugene McCarthy was an opponent of the war and an advocate of incorporating a "peace plank" into the party's official platform. Vice President Hubert Humphrey represented the party's orthodoxy and was strongly associated with outgoing President Lyndon Johnson's policies of continued involvement in Vietnam.

Chicago city administrators and law enforcement personnel were aware of the plans to disrupt the convention with rallies, marches, and other events, most notably by such groups as the Youth International Party (known popularly as the "Yippies"), the National Mobilization Committee to End the War in Vietnam (MOBE), and the Students for a Democratic Society (SDS). The Yippies, led by Jerry Rubin and Abbie Hoffman, thrived on media attention and engaged in outrageous stunts and street theater intended to raise their public profile. They announced a youth-oriented "Festival of Life" to be held in Lincoln Park, which would coincide with the week of the convention and was expected to draw thousands of individuals sympathetic to the anti-war movement.

Mayor Daley—a Democrat who was highly active and influential in national party politics and had a vested interest in a Democratic presidential victory in November—did not want these activities to interfere with the convention, and wanted order to be maintained in the city as much as possible. There had been incidents of violence at the recent National Republican Convention in Miami, and he was resolute that there not be similar disruptions under his watch. In his welcoming address opening the convention, he assured attendees by pledging, "as long as I am Mayor of this city, there will be law and order in Chicago." Meanwhile, protest groups began to converge on the city in the week prior to the start of the convention and made plans to gather at locales around the city including Grant Park, Lincoln Park, Soldier Field, and the Chicago Colosseum, as well as in the vicinity around the convention site at the International Amphitheatre.

Expecting the worst, Daley ordered that permits for marches and gatherings be restricted and that police strictly enforce an 11:00 p.m. curfew. The city was on a state of high alert, anticipating a deluge of protestors who might be unwilling to obey the restrictions that were being put into place. Mayor Daley made clear that violence and disorder among protestors would not be tolerated and troublemakers should expect a quick and dramatic response, as befitting any other significant threat to the community's wellbeing. Alarming rumors quickly spread about anarchic plans by radical groups for violence and, most notoriously, to poison the city's water supply with LSD. The 12,000-member Chicago Police Department was fully engaged, effectively doubling the amount of officers typically deployed in the field and placing them on 12-hour shifts.

The police were assisted, at the city's request, by close to 6,000 Illinois National Guardsmen with thousands more at the ready if needed. They were also assisted by hundreds of representatives from federal law enforcement agencies, including the Secret Service and the Federal Bureau of Investigation (FBI), and more than 6,000 U.S. Army troops who were stationed in the suburbs of the city out of concern that mayhem might spread beyond city limits. There were patrols in streets, public parks, and highways, with helicopters monitoring the events by air. Law enforcement officers were prepared to freely utilize batons, mace, and tear gas in order to maintain order, disperse crowds, or gain compliance from individual protestors, while National Guardsmen were outfitted with grenade launchers and machine guns to have at the ready in the event of a riot. Meanwhile, Mayor Daley also restricted media access to the convention by limiting press passes issued to journalists wishing to enter the convention floor.

A few days before the official start of the convention, the Festival of Life began, and crowds converged in Lincoln Park. There was discord between police and festivalgoers almost immediately, and when officers cleared the park in accordance with the evening curfew and attendees (as well as journalists who were present to cover the event) poured into the street, police kept order via physical force and the aggressive use of their batons. In the days that followed, tensions continued to escalate. By the opening day of the convention, law enforcement focused in earnest on stringent crowd control at the marches and demonstrations taking place around the city, employing batons and tear gas against individuals both antagonistic and non-compliant as well as the seemingly law-abiding. Meanwhile, the atmosphere was not appreciably more civil within the convention itself. Some speakers were openly and controversially criticizing the actions of Chicago police officers, and convention-floor disagreements were deteriorating into fistfights.

Skirmishes between police and the public increased in frequency and intensity as the week continued, culminating with particularly violent and chaotic encounters during the final two days of the convention. Most notorious of these was the "Battle of Michigan Avenue" of August 28th. Thousands of protestors had attempted to march toward the convention site, but were blocked by Chicago police and National Guard soldiers. Police were under orders to clear the streets, which they attempted to do by using their batons and mace against protestors as well as bystanders. Some resisted police or fought back, and the encounter escalated into a full-scale riot that was recorded by news media and broadcast to a nationwide viewing public.

All told, there were hundreds of arrests made during the week of the convention. There were no recorded fatalities as a result of violence between protestors and police, but there were a multitude of reported injured officers, demonstrators, journalists, and others. The precise number of individuals injured was difficult to determine, and varied depending on the source. Most of the injuries that were sustained, however, were relatively minor in nature and did not require hospitalization.

Meanwhile, the hostilities that emerged during the convention did nothing to heal the serious pre-existing rifts within the Democratic Party. The anti-war movement's favored candidate, Senator McCarthy, failed to earn his party's nomination, and the candidate more clearly identified with the status quo establishment, Vice President Humphrey, became the formal nominee. The fractured party was perhaps too damaged to effectively unite behind its candidate, and Humphrey was defeated in the general election by Republican candidate Richard Nixon.

The Aftermath

Due to the vivid media coverage of the clashes between police and demonstrators, anti-war activists were convinced that there would be a groundswell of public support for their cause. Whether broad sentiments were dramatically affected, however, is debatable. More certain is the fact that there were relatively few formal repercussions (in terms of internal departmental disciplinary action or criminal investigations and charges) for officers who clashed with demonstrators and other members of the public. The Justice Department and Attorney General Ramsey Clark were initially more interested in pursuing charges against police than against protestors, but 1969 ushered in the start of President Nixon's term and the appointment of Attorney General John Mitchell, and in March 1969, federal prosecutors announced criminal charges against police officers as well as protestors. Eight officers of the Chicago Police Department were indicted by a grand jury; seven of those officers were charged with assaulting demonstrators and the eighth with perjury.

Ultimately, charges against one officer were dismissed, and the seven remaining officers were all acquitted at trial. Mayor Daley had urged federal prosecutors to pursue criminal action against protestors, and at the same time as the announcement of the indictments of the eight officers, the grand jury handed down indictments against a group of high-profile individuals who had influential leadership roles within various activist organizations that attempted to disrupt the convention. These defendants, known as the "Chicago Eight" (including, among others, high-profile Yippies Rubin and Hoffman), were charged with conspiracy and intent to start a riot while crossing state lines, among other offenses. The trial proceedings devolved into a bizarre and acrimonious media circus that resulted in the defendants and one defense attorney being held in contempt of court. The outcome of the trial proceedings was a mixed bag, with acquittals for all defendants on the conspiracy charges and convictions (eventually overturned on appeal) for five of the defendants on the incitement to riot charges.

Findings of the *Walker Report*

In the aftermath of the convention, the National Commission on the Causes and Prevention of Violence (originally created by President Johnson after the assassinations of Kennedy and King) appointed Chicago-area attorney (and future governor of Illinois) Daniel Walker to lead the Chicago Study Team task force. This initiated an investigation of the conflicts between police and protestors. The final report, released in December 1968, involved an examination of statements from thousands of eyewitnesses as well as a review of extensive film and photographic footage of the events.

The report's conclusions were highly critical of law enforcement's response to the demonstrators, controversially characterizing their actions as tantamount to a "police riot." The report acknowledged the challenging circumstances confronting police officers, describing them as "the targets of mounting provocation by both word and act" during the course of the week. It concluded that the tactics utilized by police to quash the disturbances were unnecessarily harsh and heavy-handed. It also condemned the police for engaging in "unrestrained and indiscriminate" violence against not only protestors who provoked them, but also "peaceful demonstrators, onlookers, and large numbers of residents who were simply passing through, or who happened to live in, the areas where confrontations were occurring" and that journalists were "singled out for assault." The report characterized the actions of the Chicago Police Department's officers on the scene as criminal and critiqued the department in its decision to not discipline the officers as well as state and federal prosecutors' failure to successfully pursue criminal charges against the officers involved. The report also blamed Chicago's leadership for fostering a mindset among police that "violence against demonstrators, as against rioters, would be condoned by city officials."

These conclusions, however, contrasted dramatically with public sentiment among Chicagoans, as well as the general American public. According to separate nationwide surveys conducted by the Gallup organization, *The New York Times*, and the University of Michigan in the months following the convention, the majority of respondents supported the law enforcement response and the notion that police were simply doing their jobs. Respondents expressed the belief that appropriate levels of force were used given the difficult circumstances (an opinion perhaps bolstered by the fact that, ultimately, there were no deaths attributed to police actions during the week of the convention). Although journalists and cultural observers wrote pieces in the aftermath of the convention that were highly critical of the actions of police, many within the general public were sympathetic to law enforcement, and attitudes toward the anti-war movement and prominent activists within it perhaps suffered a more immediate dramatic negative impact.

Miriam D. Sealock

See also: Police Accountability; Police Brutality; Police Ethics; Police Mistreatment in Cases of Civil Disobedience; "Thin Blue Line": Police as a Guard against Anarchy

Further Reading

Farber, David. R. *Chicago '68*. Chicago, IL: University of Chicago Press, 1994.
Kusch, Frank. *Battleground Chicago: The Police and the 1968 Democratic National Convention*. Chicago, IL: University of Chicago Press, 2004.

Schultz, John. *No One Was Killed: The Democratic National Convention, August 1968.* Chicago, IL: University of Chicago Press, 2009.

Walker, Daniel. *Rights in Conflict: The Violent Confrontation of Demonstrators and Police in the Parks and Streets of Chicago during the Week of the Democratic National Convention of 1968.* New York: E. P. Dutton, 1968.

Walker, Samuel. *A Critical History of Police Reform.* Lexington, MA: Lexington Books, 1977.

Walker, Samuel. *The New World of Police Accountability.* Thousand Oaks, CA: Sage Publications, 2005.

INCREASE IN VIOLENT CRIME RATE AND RISK TO LAW ENFORCEMENT

The committing of a violent crime is a complex phenomenon, as is understanding why people commit them in the first place. Utilizing both victim surveys and official police data can be useful in painting the most realistic picture. To explain violent crime and the risks involved, it's necessary to first state what violent crime is.

Various acts are considered violent crimes, but they generally fall within one of four categories. Murder, or homicide, is the killing of another human being with conditions and consequences specifically covered under the law. Violent crime may also consist of rape and sexual assaults—sexual interactions that are forced upon the victim. A third type of violent crime is aggravated assault, in which one person attacks another person, with or without a weapon, and seriously injures the victim. Robbery is the forceful taking of someone's property against his or her will.

Degrees of Violent Crimes

The law defines different degrees of culpability in relation to violent crime. Willful killing is the most serious, but one can commit a violent crime via gross negligence (defined as negligent manslaughter). And while robbery involves the taking of something of value from another, it can include the threat or use of force. Also, the definition of rape has expanded to include a more broad definition, including more forms of sexual assault. Aggravated and simple assaults involve bodily harm, and the degree of harm—and the aggravating and mitigating circumstances surrounding the encounter—determines how the crime is defined. Therefore, while it may appear that crime rates in general are increasing, more and various acts and definitions of crime have expanded the overall definition of the crime. The rate of violent crime has actually gone down over the last 20 years.

Reducing Violence

According to most research, the increase or reduction in violent crime rates cannot be attributed to one single factor. Rather, there are several factors, depending on the nature of the crime. Neighborhood conditions, genetics, socialization within an area, and the law enforcement tactics that are used all contribute to the rate of violent crime in any particular area. Due to these varieties of factors, there is no singular way to decrease violent crime, but there are many things that can be used to decrease violent crime. Some options are difficult to implement due to financial, political, and moral restrictions. Multiple strategies must be implemented in order to address the variety of sources that contribute to violent crime rates.

Community Policing

Community policing is an innovative policing technique that is used to increase voluntary compliance and improve relationships between the public and the police. Community policing techniques include community meetings, door-to-door contacts, or "storefronts." Storefronts are police kiosks set up in neighborhoods to make it more convenient for citizens to report crime or other behavior in a quick and easy way. The assumption behind this technique is that increasing the quality and quantity of citizen-police interaction will reduce crime. This will not only make the community safer for residents, but it will also make the community safer for police to patrol.

Community policing also offers a promising remedy for problematic police/minority relations. However, the wide appeal of community policing across America has not totally solved strained police/minority relations in disadvantaged neighborhoods.

These areas remain dangerous for both residents and the police, and violent crimes are more problematic there than in middle-class neighborhoods and continue to plague law enforcement officers and residents.

Many cities have failed to implement community policing strategies due to criticism of the effort or political reasons. In order to enhance police legitimacy, produce effective results, and improve safety, community policing programs should be carefully planned and implemented.

Neighborhood Watch Program

Another effort to increase citizen involvement and improve social control is to implement neighborhood watch programs. These bring a stronger sense of community into an area and can improve pride and perceptions in one's neighborhood, leading to more respect for others. This effort can assist with decreasing the violent crime rates. However, since many people may not know their neighbors, there may be less allegiance to one's surroundings. Theoretically, if more individuals are given the responsibility of promoting the safety of those around them, they will also be more inclined to respect and support the area and the community members. Then, as these individuals play more important roles in their "neighborhood watch," they will have a higher stake in the overall safety of their neighborhood and will want to help prevent crime. This, in turn, can help decrease crime. Neighborhood watch programs can strengthen the community's communication with local law enforcement. However, most individuals do not know the police officers in the area, and as a result, they might have little trust in the police. Unfortunately, some lack of concern for one's neighbors can lead to disrespect for one's surroundings, and controversy between the public and the police may accentuate the problems.

Community-based programs and neighborhood watches have two main goals: to help keep kids off the streets and to keep families safe. Many of these programs attempt to decrease gang violence and understand the reasons for the gang members' involvement in crime in the first place. With community help from parents and teachers, organizational workers can talk to gang members in person in order to try to guide them in a different direction. However, some research has shown that neighborhood watch doesn't work and that the sending of information from police to citizens doesn't reduce violence.

The most promising conclusion is that the public's trust in the police is important. Citizens' trust in the police affects public support and cooperation, which are significant elements in reducing crime. A lack of trust in the police has led to an increase in certain violent crimes. One important way people determine whether the actions of police are fair involves perception of fairness during decision-making processes. This depends on several criteria including dignity and courtesy, but these are vague terms.

Some police tactics could be successful in reducing crime. If those tactics generate distrust between the police and the public, however, will those tactics still be considered effective? Research indicates if citizens feel that police are not concerned about their well-being and are not honest, citizens will be more likely to break the law. This lack of respect and trust may lead the police to change their tactics.

Problem-Oriented Policing

The Violent Crime Task Force is perceived as a successful group that has been able to target violent crime in a unique way. In order to solve challenging violent crime cases, the task force utilizes mapping software, cell phone records, and data-mining techniques in its investigations. As technology improves, police lack some of the advantages they once had, and criminals can sometimes be one step ahead of them.

Raising visibility of the police can give potential offenders a reason to stay away from a specific area because their risks of being caught may be substantially increased. Furthermore, raising the visibility of police may result in less disorder. When there is less disorder, people may feel that an area is safe and well taken care of, and as a result, they may look for a less-monitored place to commit crime.

Crime mapping—a way of monitoring crime patterns in a particular area—becomes extremely useful for the police so that they can see where they should be patrolling more frequently, and what time violent crimes are most likely to occur, so they can make themselves more visible to deter crimes from happening.

While some policing strategies continue to reduce violent crime, there may still be a serious threat to the security and safety of residents and law enforcement. Evidence suggests violent crime is most common in low-income, minority neighborhoods, and residents who live in these areas are the most resentful toward the police. This creates tension, so offering individuals low-cost community-based activities might reduce violent crime. Policy interventions to reduce violent crime rates are the most successful when everyone from the community as well as the government contributes to a coordinated effort.

Some research revealed that California reported a 10-percent increase in violent crimes from 2014 to 2015, although in 2015 overall crime in the 30 largest cities remained roughly the same as in 2014. Projections are for an overall annual decrease of 5.5 percent. Murder rates in these 30 cities are about the same as they were in 2012. These cities are the ones experiencing higher projected violent crime. In fact, Baltimore and Washington, D.C., account for almost half of the nation's increase in murders.

Violent crime, overall, is actually down, even though the public does not believe it is. The rates of some violent crimes are increasing, though, such as crimes against the homeless. And violent crime is on the rise in Washington, D.C., Baltimore, Detroit, and Chicago. Thus, the focus on decreasing violent crime should focus on these major cities and the community members who live and work in these neighborhoods. That, in turn, will help improve the safety of the officers who work in these neighborhoods.

Emirhan Darcan and Gina Robertiello

See also: Community Policing Today; Control Theory; Corruption; Crime Prevention Techniques; Impact of the War on Drugs; Police Ethics; PTSD and Family Issues among Officers; Uniform Crime Reports; Wilson and Kelling's Broken Windows Theory; Zero Tolerance Policy

Further Reading

Bachman, R., and L. E. Saltzman. *Violence against Women*, Vol. 81. Washington, DC: US Department of Justice, Office of Justice Programs, Bureau of Justice Statistics, 1994.

Davey, M., and M. Smith. "Murder Rates Rising Sharply in Many U.S. Cities." *The New York Times*, August 31, 2015. http://www.nytimes.com/2015/09/01/us/murder-rates-rising-sharply-in-many-us-cities.html?_r=0.

Farrington, D. P., D. L. MacKenzie, L. W. Sherman, and B. C. Welsh, eds. *Evidence-Based Crime Prevention*. New York: Routledge, 2003.

Felson, M. "The Topography of Crime." *Crime Prevention & Community Safety* 4, no. 1 (2002): 47–51.

Lopez, German. "The Murder Rate Went Up in 2015: It's Still Half of What It Was 25 Years Ago" *Vox*, September 16, 2015. http://www.vox.com/identities/2016/9/26/13055102/murder-rate-2015-ferguson-effect.

Lum, C., M. M. Haberfeld, G. Fachner, G., and C. Lieberman. "Police Activities to Counter Terrorism: What We Know and What We Need to Know." *To Protect and to Serve*, 101–141. New York: Springer, 2009.

Sherman, L. W., J. W. Shaw, and D. P. Rogan. "The Kansas City Gun Experiment." *Population* 4 (1995): 8–142.

Sunshine, J., and T. R. Tyler. "The Role of Procedural Justice and Legitimacy in Shaping Public Support for Policing." *Law & Society Review* 37, no. 3 (2003): 513–548.

Uniform Crime Reports. Federal Bureau of Investigation. https://www2.fbi.gov/ucr/ucr.htm.

Welsh, B. C., and D. P. Farrington. "Public Area CCTV and Crime Prevention: An Updated Systematic Review and MetaAnalysis." *Justice Quarterly* 26, no. 4 (2009): 716–745.

Wimmer, A. "Using Technology to Help Solve Crimes." *FBI Law Enforcement Bulletin* 77, no. 12 (2008): 7–10.

CONTROL THEORY

The control theory is one of the oldest and most popular criminology theories that seeks to provide tangible explanations, mostly from a conservative perspective, as to why people engage in criminal and deviant behaviors. Control theory operates on the assumption that all human beings are by nature capable of committing crimes. Therefore, all human beings possess the desire to commit crime if it serves their selfish interests. Underpinning this thinking is an Enlightenment idea proposed by Thomas Hobbes about the true nature of human beings. Hobbes was an English social philosopher who wrote during the 17th century. The crux of his argument is that human beings are selfish by nature, and without some external constraints the strong among us are likely to trample upon the rights of the weak in society. Therefore, there is a need for an overarching authority in society to regulate the behaviors of people for maintaining law and order.

The state, as an institution through the social control, assumed the role of law and order maintenance in society. The state derives its mandate from the people to exercise this authority. The state, however, must be accountable to the people and perform its social control functions, reflecting the will and interest of the people. A problem arises, however, when the state, through the police department, exercises its social control functions that the community or a section of the community find to be high-handed, abusive, and oppressive, thereby raising questions about the legitimacy the state, in general, and of the police, in particular.

One major proponent of the control theory was French sociologist Emile Durkheim, who observed that all societies are capable of generating deviants, and that there is no society, including convents, that can achieve full conformity among its citizens. He argues that crime is a normal phenomenon, as it is obtainable in all societies, and that people can simultaneously participate in both conventional and unconventional behaviors. Deviance, according to Durkheim, is functional in society, as it facilitates the definition of moral boundaries and the maintenance of social order. Society's negative response to deviant behaviors further reinforces the moral boundaries and reassures law-abiding citizens of their shared indignation against criminal acts. However, he argued that uncontrolled deviant behaviors can lead to a state of anomie and the breakdown of law and order in society.

The newer control theories emerged in the 1950s in response to the prevailing criminological theories that explained criminal and deviant behavior as deriving from structural conditions. Other theories also explained criminal behavior as emanating from interactional patterns or learned from one's close associates. Some theories argued that people who engaged in criminal behavior had ready-made rationalizations for their behaviors. Even though the control theories also seek an understanding of the aspirational motivations of deviants, the theories start from the premise that it is conformity rather than deviance that should be the primary focus of criminological inquiry. It is fair to argue that control theories locate the problem of criminal behavior primarily on the individual, against the socio-economic conditions of society. Control theories further argue that we would all engage in criminal behavior if we lacked both internal and external controls. Travis Hirschi's social bond theory, Gresham Sykes and David Matza's neutralization theory, Michael Gottfredson and Hirschi's self-control theory, and Walter Reckless's containment theory are some of the criminological theories within this paradigm.

Hirschi's (1969) social control theory identified the components of the value systems that bind youth to the society's moral order, including attachment, involvement, commitment, and belief. Attachment is considered the most important part of this bonding and describes the effects the youth's positive ties with parents, friends, schools, and religious groups may have on his or her behavior. It is believed that the stronger the attachment the individual has with others, the less likely he or she is to deviate from the social norms, as deviation from the norms of society are likely to weaken their standing in the community and could chip away the love and relationships he or she has from others. Commitment refers to the investment an individual makes in conventional pursuits such as education and career. The understanding is that people would not want to engage in behaviors that would cost them the benefits they stand to gain from their investments in education and career. Involvement describes the efforts an individual invests in conventional activities such as education, sports, and career—such that they would not have any time left to spare to engage in deviant activities. Belief refers to the extent to which we share in the values and norms of our society. Simply put, if people believe in the justness and purpose of a particular law or norm, they are more likely to obey it, thereby conforming to societal standards.

Reckless, in 1967, introduced another theory of social control called the containment theory. There are two components of the containment theory—*internal and external* containments. Through this theory, Reckless sought to explain why people seek conformity instead of deviance, despite the pressures and opportunities to do so. He attributed this resistance to deviant acts to other factors, such as good family upbringing. The values and identity acquired through family life are further reinforced and rewarded by other institutions, such as schools and religion. The inner containment aspect of the thesis was emphasized by Reckless as the more instrumental in regulating behavior, which includes goal orientation, self-concept, frustration tolerance, and norm retention. People with a good self-concept of themselves as being law-abiding and obedient, according to this perspective, tend to have stronger insulation against involvement in deviant acts. Having an orientation toward legitimate goals and aspirations that are realistic helps steer an individual toward conforming behavior instead of deviant acts that might undercut the expected gains of the individual's investment of time and efforts. And people with high tolerance for frustration and with a strong commitment to societal values and norms are more likely to be law abiding.

Sykes and Matza argued, in their neutralization theory, that offenders do subscribe to societal norms and values but choose to deviate from these norms by adopting the techniques of neutralization to overcome their guilt and responsibility feelings. One example of the techniques of neutralization, according to the theory, is denial of responsibility where offenders justify their deviant actions on the grounds of poverty or lack of resources. In other words, they did not choose to steal, for example, but resorted to stealing to avert starvation. Offenders also deny injury to their victims by claiming that their actions do not have untoward effect on their victims. For example, they justify stealing from a departmental store on the grounds that their loss would have little or no impact on their finances and that also corporations' losses are either written off in taxes or they get compensation from their insurers. The third technique of neutralization according to this perspective is of offenders denying a victim by suggesting that the victim of their assault, for example, deserved it by being drunk in a public place. Offenders also justify their criminal acts by, instead of taking responsibility or feeling any guilt for their harmful acts, blaming others who are inclined to pass negative judgment on their action by condemning the condemners. Through this line of argument, offenders criticize law enforcement agents or other members of the society who have issues with their deviant acts by asserting that law enforcement agents and other members of the society are corrupt or fail to live above board and are only hypocrites for condemning them for their deviant acts. Some offenders also seek defense or justifications of their deviant acts by appealing to higher loyalties. They can lay claim to the fact that their acts were carried out to protect their family or gang members who were in danger of some kind of harm if they did not take the action they took, including committing murder.

Gottfredson and Hirschi's general theory of crime, in 1990, was the latest social control theory that sought to explain deviant behavior. The thrust of the general theory of crime's argument is that individuals who lack self-control and are unable to consider the consequences of their actions, especially long term, are more likely to engage in deviant behavior. They are also likely to be impulsive, risk-seeking, self-centered, and temperamental—behaviors that offer immediate gratification and quick thrills. And they are therefore more likely to engage in illicit sex and drug use. They are often unable to defer gratification. They are also likely to lack diligence and tenacity, which is required to succeed in legitimate career pursuits. Since crime is a risky and thrilling activity, people with low self-control find it alluring and rewarding. Low self-control is a result of early childhood socialization. The theory argues that inadequate child-rearing practices, such as by those raised by parents who fail to monitor their children's behavior, are not capable of recognizing inappropriate behavior, and inconsistently punish aberrant behavior of their children, are likely to have low self-control. Therefore, low self-control is not an inherited trait but an acquired characteristic. The general theory of crime seeks to account for all types of criminal behavior, including white collar and blue collar criminal types.

In 1995, Charles R. Tittle introduced the latest control theory, called control-balance theory. This theory was originally intended as an integrative theory, but it is often also classified under the control theory. The thrust of the control-balance theory's argument is that, both too little and/or too much control can precipitate deviant behavior. This is because, as humans seek to control other humans, they are in the process of being controlled by others as well, which negates the human desire for autonomy. Furthermore, the amount of control people are able to exercise is related to the type and amount of crime they can commit. According to the theory, the relationship between control and balance correlates with conformity, whereas the control and imbalance is associated with deviance. Therefore, the amount of control people are able to exercise determines their level of conformity or deviance. For deviance to occur, however, depends on other factors, including the predisposition of the individual to deviance, situational factors, the opportunity for deviance response, the lack of constraints, and the individual's ability to translate desire for criminal acts into action. To illustrate, the theory identified six major forms of deviance. The following types of deviance are likely to occur when there is little or no control for the following:

- Predation—theft, homicide, sexual harassment, rape, and fraud
- Defiance—political protests and vandalism
- Submission—allowing oneself to be abused, and passive obedience

The following deviance types occur when people have power and control in abundance to exercise:

- Exploitation—profiteering, corporate price-fixing, or endangering workers
- Plunder—organizations pursuing their own interests without regard to others
- Decadence—irrational pleasure or debauchery (Newburn 2013, 245)

These control theories are the conservative criminologists' response to the labeling and conflict theories that were prevalent in the 1960s. The theories locate the problem of crime in the individual, peer groups, and family structures. Unlike other criminological theories that start their inquiry on what makes people commit crime, control theories instead seek an explanation to conformity, claiming that people are naturally self-centered and driven to selfish pursuits, regardless of what other people desire. Control theories therefore seek to understand the factors that prevent people from engaging in criminal or delinquent behavior. Socialization patterns and social bonds of society, according to this perspective, are important, as unsocialized and unrestrained people and those without strong bonds to society are likely to operate without consideration to society's rules and norms and the feeling of others. Another important tenet of social control theories is that people with little power as well as those with a lot of power are those more likely to deviate from the norms of society. People with little or no power often have weak ties to society and also do not have much to lose. People with economic and political power are able to circumvent the system to serve their parochial interests.

O. Oko Elechi, Sherill Morris-Francis, and Rochelle McGee-Cobbs

See also: Corruption; Fleeing Felon Legislation; Increase in Violent Crime Rate and Risk to Law Enforcement; Police Authority to Detain

Further Reading
Durkheim, Emile. *The Rules of the Sociological Method.* Translated by Sarah A. Solovay and John H. Mueller. New York: Free Press, 1895, reprinted 1965.

Hirschi, T. *Causes of Delinquency.* Berkeley: University of California Press, 1969.

Hirschi, T., and M. Gottfredson. "Age and the Explanation of Crime." *American Journal of Sociology*, 89 (1983): 522–584.

Sykes, G. M., and D. Matza. "Techniques of Neutralization: A Theory of Delinquency." *American Sociological Review*, 22 (1957): 664–670.

Tittle, C. *Control Balance: Toward a General Theory of Deviance*. Boulder, CO: Westview Press, 1995.

KNAPP COMMISSION

The decade of the 1960s ushered in an era of social revolution, one that involved heightened awareness of social issues at the time: civil rights, women's rights, and the mistreatment of individuals at the hands of civic authorities. During this time, the American population was experiencing a shift of demographics, one propelled by the "baby boom" generation. The voice of the counterculture was that of the youth—the group that chose to "fight back" instead of taking the path of passive resistance. Many efforts and movements were fueled by the angst and actions of young Americans. However, baby boomers were not the only ones intent on "fighting back" and addressing wrongdoing of civic leaders. Individuals within the corruption systems, themselves, were working to bring transparency and legitimacy to their respective organizations. One such case involved Officer Frank Serpico and the corruption he found within the New York Police Department.

Despite several commissions, most of which were the result of presidential appointment, the issues found and reported were rarely addressed. Both the McCone Commission of 1965 and the Kerner Commission of 1967 produced voluminous reports that discussed the deleterious effects of the racial segregation and mistreatment—specifically at the hands of the police. Not only was police misconduct in the form of brutality a regular phenomenon across the country, but so, too, was corruption—at both the individual and organizational level. Officer Frank Serpico witnessed this first-hand.

Serpico was a New York City police officer from 1959 until 1971. Throughout his time in the department, Serpico witnessed countless instances of corruption and bribery by fellow officers. The extent of the corruption was not limited to his partner or his superiors. It would soon be discovered that the corruption was pervasive across all five boroughs of New York City. Having been transferred to different precincts several times throughout his time with the department, Serpico would continually encounter the same illegal behaviors committed by his fellow officers. Multiple attempts to call attention to this problem, as well as his refusal to partake in the illegal activity, resulted in the distrust and even disdain of his fellow officers. This ultimately led to the refusal of officers to provide "back-up" to him after he was shot during a drug raid. The shot was nearly fatal, instead having lasting physical effects, including the loss of hearing in one ear. Serpico was lucky to live, only being saved as the result of a bystander finding him and calling for help—not as a result of help from his fellow officers. This culminating event prompted official investigation. In 1970, the mayor of New York City commissioned an independent, five-member panel called the Commission to Investigate Alleged Police Corruption—or the Knapp Commission.

The panel was known as the Knapp Commission because Whitman Knapp was its chair. He was chosen to head the panel as a result of his extensive legal experience, particularly that which related to the investigation of corruption. Upon graduation from Yale and then Harvard Law School, Knapp began to practice law, and he became an assistant district attorney in New York City. He was hired by, and worked under the leadership of, District Attorney Thomas Dewey—whose reputation for investigating corruption and organized crime was already established. Knapp later became counsel to Dewey when he became New York's governor. Years later, Knapp would obtain the relevant experience as counsel for the Waterfront Commission of New York Harbor. This commission was charged with investigation instances of corruption in the port district of New York, ensuring compliance with criminal and civil codes.

Following Serpico's near death, along with a series of local media reports detailing the illegal activities of its police force, the New York City Police Department was finally examined. These reports were not recent phenomena by any means. As the panel's official title suggests, the commission was directed to investigate possible instances of police corruption. This *alleged* police corruption was investigated for nearly two years, from April 1970 when the panel was commissioned to December 1972 when the final report was issued.

The Knapp Commission discovered numerous incidents of corruption within the ranks of the New York City Police Department. Its report outlined the corrupt practices that were widely practiced and deeply rooted in the department's operation—practices that have been in place for quite some time. In fact, the first recorded complaints about the department were filed in the first year of its existence: 1845. The panel discovered that police officers across the city, regardless of rank or precinct, were collecting bribes. These officers were collecting money for "protection." And this protection ensured that the individuals supplying the bribes to the officers could continue their other illegal activities, such as drug distribution, prostitution, or illegal gambling. Officers taking bribes would ensure that these criminals would not be investigated or arrested.

The commission's findings were reinforced by the testimony of Frank Serpico and his supervisor, Sergeant David Durk. Durk was a police detective who, along with Serpico, provided first-hand accounts of the widespread corruption in the New York City Police Department. The testimony provided by Durk and Serpico were just part of the dozens of others seen in public hearings beginning in late 1971. Witnesses, corrupt officers, and even the criminals providing the bribes testified before the panel. Particularly concerning was the (lack of) enforcement of narcotics laws. The preceding decade saw New York City experience a substantial influx of heroin. By the time of the Knapp Commission, lax enforcement of all drug offenses was an issue that even upper-level administrators in the department acknowledged. Some of these issues consisted of the following: confiscating and keeping money and drugs after an arrest or raid, selling drugs to informants in exchange for information or goods, transferred drugs to informants for distribution (e.g., sale), planting drugs on an individual in order to have an arresting offense, accepting money or drugs for information, and involvement in heroin transactions. One such practice was called "padding," in which an officer might add narcotics from his person to an offender's in order to increase the violation to felony status. Not only could this benefit the officer if he chose to make an arrest, but it could be used as further leverage in continuing his corrupt behavior.

The Knapp Commission found that the most common form of corruption, however, was relatively minor. Most of the peripheral offenses involved in the bribery of police officers were vice-related: prostitution, gambling, and low-level drug crimes. The commission described these types of corrupt police officers as "grass eaters," a term referring to those who engage in minor levels of illicit behavior—committed by police when under pressure from fellow officers. These officers would willingly accept bribes, free meals, or other gratuities, but they would not actively pursue such payments. Alternatively, police officers who were engaging in more severe forms of illicit behavior were called "meat eaters." This term refers to those who engage in major levels of illicit behavior—actively and aggressively seeking out situations that could financially benefit them or those in which they would receive something based on their position of authority.

The commission issued a preliminary report in August of 1972, and its final executive report—all 264 pages of it—in December of that same year. Perhaps unsurprisingly, the commission found numerous instances of corruption that was endemic to the New York City Police Department. The issues discovered through investigating and relayed through testimony found corruption to be a systematic problem in the department was not confined to one individual or group. As a result, the commission put forth several recommendations, some general and some specific. First, the commission suggested the individual officers, alone, should not be held responsible for illicit behavior. Instead, supervisors within the department must also be held accountable and subject to disciplinary measures similar to their corrupt subordinates. Second, the department's commanders should periodically review conditions that could promote corruption and report to the department's administration. The additional formal review of corruption should also be undertaken by a special prosecutor outside of New York City to eliminate possible partiality. Related, the commission suggested that the Internal Affairs Bureau reorganize and set up offices in every precinct, as well as take advantage of the use of the department's network of undercover informants. Finally, in order to change police culture and behavior, the commission suggested that the department change the methods by which it recruits, screens, and selects individuals for hiring, as well as address the professional culture of the department.

The Knapp Commission and any subsequent punishment was focused on lower-level police officers in the department. The commission was unable to obtain any "hard evidence" against anyone in the department that was above the rank of lieutenant. Furthermore, the commission noted that it did not have the resources to investigate officials outside of the agency—such as those in related municipal departments—that may have been participating in the same illicit behaviors.

The Knapp Commission dedicated nearly two years of resources to the investigation of police corruption within the ranks of the New York City Police Department.

The discoveries were influential in the widespread dissemination of Serpico's testimony, along with altering public sentiment toward the authority of the police and influencing changes, albeit ineffective, in the agency. Despite changes in the department's structure and operations, relatively little changed after the commission's report. Only 20 years later, another commission was formed to investigate similar improprieties on behalf of the New York City Police Department. Despite these multiple commissions, investigations, and structural changes, there continues to be problems with graft within the ranks of the police department. The Knapp Commission, though essential in bringing many of these issues to the forefront of the public eye, was largely unsuccessful in having lasting effects.

Kaitlyn Clarke and Philip D. McCormack

See also: Corruption; Frank Serpico (1936–); Kerner Commission Report on Race Riots and Police Response; Wickersham Report on Soaring Crime during Prohibition

Further Reading

Armstrong, Michael F. *They Wished They Were Honest: The Knapp Commission and New York City Police Corruption.* New York: Columbia University Press, 2012.

Braziller, George. *The Knapp Commission Report on Police Corruption.* New York: George Braziller, 1972.

Chin, Gabriel J. *New York City Police Corruption Investigation Commissions.* New York: William S. Hein & Co, 1997.

Maas, Peter. *Serpico: The Classic Story of the Cop Who Couldn't Be Bought.* New York: William Morrow Paperbacks, 2005.

Walker, Samuel E., and Carol A. Archbold. *The New World of Police Accountability*, 2nd ed. Thousand Oaks, CA: Sage, 2013.

FRANK SERPICO (1936–)

Francesco Vincent (Frank) Serpico began his career as a probationary officer with the New York Police Department (NYPD) in 1959. As with many police departments, for several months, he went through an obligatory training period under the supervision of a more seasoned police officer. On-the-job training is crucial because this is where the unofficial rules of the department and streets are learned. He subsequently passed his probationary period and became a full-time patrolman in March 1960. However, within a few years, he observed a pattern and practice of police officers committing crimes. His journey in reporting the internal corruption caused him to be retaliated against, and it almost cost him his life. Historically, he later became the first NYPD police officer to testify before an investigatory commission. This courageous act opened the doors for subsequent investigations of widespread corruption within the NYPD and afforded future police officers a blueprint to becoming a whistleblower.

Serpico was born in Brooklyn, New York, in 1936 to Italian immigrant parents from Naples, Italy. As a young boy, Serpico shined shoes in his father's shoe-repair shop. His father, Vincenzo, was a World War I prisoner of war (POW) who had aspirations of becoming a *carabineer* (Italian national military police) but chose to be a craftsman instead. However, his uncle was a carabineer, and Serpico observed the respect his uncle received and was impressed. Nevertheless, Serpico wasn't naïve to just how bad some police officers were capable of being. He reported that when he was a young boy, he observed a police officer physically beat an elderly Black woman while she lay on a parkway bench. Yet he was also influenced, early on, by some good police officers that he had encountered and knew that was what he wanted to be when he grew up.

In 1953, at the age of 18, Serpico enlisted in the U.S. Army and served two years in Korea. Once he returned, he went to college and studied law enforcement, while at the same time trying to offset the cost of tuition by working as a part-time private investigator and youth counselor. After four years, he graduated from John Jay College.

The early 1960s and 1970s witnessed the struggle of racial riots in several inner cities in the United States. Law enforcement played a crucial role in how the minority community was treated. Many Americans resented the police because of the systemic abuse of power, sometimes without the officers being punished. The NYPD would be no stranger to the controversies.

Serpico's first assignment was in the 81st precinct, which covers Bedford-Stuyvesant, an Italian community that changed, in the late 1960s, to a densely populated African American community. From all accounts, he was a good officer and made a lot of arrests. He was eventually transferred to the Bureau of Criminal

Frank Serpico with Ramsey Clark before Knapp Commission hearing, 1971. Serpico is a retired New York cop who blew the whistle on police corruption. He was portrayed by Al Pacino in a movie about his life in 1973. (Jim Garrett/NY Daily News via Getty Images)

Identification to assist with fingerprint classification. He remained in this bureau for approximately two years before moving on and becoming a plain-clothed undercover officer.

At the time, he lived in Greenwich Village, which was known for its very free-spirited residents. He grew a beard and wore casual clothes. Although a loner, he made friends with other students at John Jay College and was affectionately given the nickname "Paco."

Working in plains clothes afforded Serpico an opportunity to freelance and take advantage of his changing appearance. He blended into the city's environment due to his ability to speak different languages as well as some of the disguises he wore while undercover. For example, Serpico sometime dressed as a butcher, a rabbi, a sheik, and a vagrant.

His primary assignment had been to arrest drug dealers, prostitutes, and those involved in illegal gambling. He traveled back and forth between Brooklyn and the Bronx, working in some very dangerous communities. Unfortunately, it was while working in this assignment that he observed his fellow officers accept bribes, steal drug money, fail to log evidence, and let criminals go. Serpico was approached on numerous occasions by his fellow officers and requested to take payoffs, which he repeatedly refused. For his reluctance, he was shunned, physically assaulted, and received numerous death threats by officers who didn't trust him.

No longer able to stand by and watch the ongoing corruption, he reported his concerns to his supervisors. They assured him that his allegations would be investigated. However, they ignored him, and nothing was done to correct the problems.

Nonetheless, starting in 1967, Serpico made his concerns official and reached out to high-ranking NYPD officers and influential politicians. He violated a cardinal sin of law enforcement and disregarded the "Blue Wall of Silence" that is meant to protect police officers from external forces. His coming out made him an official whistleblower, an individual who reports on a particular person or organization engaged in illegal activity. He wasn't looked upon as a savior of the department. Many of his corrupt colleagues portrayed him as a traitor and a snitch. His commanding officers attacked his character, and deemed him a malcontent and a weirdo. Again, they failed to investigate any of his allegations.

Serpico's solo attempt at exposing internal corruption was ineffective until he teamed up with an NYPD detective, David Durk, who imagined, like most police officers, that he'd be able to make a difference.

Durk, a graduate of Amherst College who studied law at Columbia University, joined the NYPD in 1963. During this timeframe, educated police officers were a rarity. Over the years, after making numerous arrests of muggers and pickpockets, Durk was promoted to detective in the Chief of Detective's office.

Durk and Serpico initially met in 1966 while attending a class for incoming plain-clothes officers. They were polar opposites. Serpico was laid back and resembled a hippie; Durk was clean cut, donned conservative suits, resided on the Upper West Side, and had prominent friends in politics and the news media. But just like

Serpico, Durk had witnessed superiors taking payoffs from gamblers and drug dealers, and officers providing protection for merchants and mobsters. Yet, what disturbed him most was that in as much as the corruption was known among even the "good" officers, the pervasive Blue Wall of Silence was destroying morale. Durk, too, refused to take money and was threatened with physical harm.

They complained to the district attorney's office, which was an agency outside the purview of the NYPD. Their idealism of any meaningful resolution was short-lived, as the investigation went nowhere.

In 1970, after several frustrating years of fighting the internal bureaucracy, their concerns were published in a *New York Times* front-page article. Based on a six-month inquiry, reporter David Burnham revealed that millions of dollars had been paid yearly to NYPD officers. As a result of the embarrassing and damaging column, Mayor John V. Lindsay was pressured to impanel a special commission to investigate the allegations of widespread corruption by police officers, detectives, and supervisors within the NYPD.

Mayor Lindsay appointed a Wall Street attorney, Whitman Knapp, a Harvard law graduate, to chair a five-member commission (named the Knapp Commission), to conduct an extensive investigation into the NYPD. Cyrus Vance, Arnold Bauman, Franklin Thomas, and Joseph Montserrat were the other members assigned to the bipartisan and racially diverse commission, which was formed in April 1970. The investigation started in June 1971 and public hearings began a few months later.

While the investigation was ongoing, Serpico continued working in his undercover capacity with some of the detectives that had previously accused him of being a snitch.

On February 3, 1971, Serpico and other detectives were conducting surveillance of alleged drug dealing at 778 Driggs Avenue, an apartment building in South Williamsburg, Brooklyn, in what was supposed to be a routine heroin "buy and bust" detail. After confirming that an initial drug transaction had taken place and the necessary password to gain the confidence of the dealer had been secured, Serpico took on the role of a potential drug buyer and approached the drug dealer's apartment door.

With backup nearby, Serpico knocked on the door, and while speaking in Spanish blurted out the password and requested to purchase some drugs. As the door opened, Serpico attempted to forcibly gain entry but was thwarted, as the perpetrator immediately pinned him between the door and doorframe. Serpico called out for help from the back-up detectives, but no one responded. Within moments and at close range, he was shot in the face but was able to shoot the perpetrator in the hand. He would lie on the floor bleeding profusely until an elderly tenant of the building called 911.

Serpico was subsequently transported to Greenpoint Hospital by a police squad car. However, the officers had no idea that it was Serpico they had been transporting due to his undercover identity and bloodied appearance. While hospitalized, Mayor Lindsay and police commissioner Patrick Murphy visited him, but members of NYPD harassed him afterward by checking up on him on an hourly basis. According to

Serpico, not one of the approximately 39,000 NYPD officers volunteered to donate blood. Ironically, the detectives who were supposed to back up Serpico were later awarded medals for saving his life.

Serpico would eventually recover from the shooting, but he was left permanently deaf in his left ear and has bullet fragments lodged in his head just beneath his brain. He claimed that there was never a serious investigation into the circumstances surrounding how he was shot.

In the latter part of 1971, Serpico, Durk, and other frustrated police officers testified before the commission. They reported what they had observed over the course of their respective careers regarding internal corruption. They revealed the names of the police officers who they observed taking bribes and committing other crimes. In his testimony, Serpico said that police corruption couldn't exist without it being tolerated at the highest level.

The aftermath of the commission's final report, which was concluded by a 30-person staff, established that a pattern of corruption existed throughout the five boroughs within New York City. It faulted the Lindsay administration and (then) police commissioner Howard R. Leary for repeatedly failing to hold the NYPD responsible for its internal problems, despite overwhelming evidence of widespread corruption. The most alarming crime that they found was police officers had collected "protection money" and were on the "pad," which meant they accepted bribes and allowed illegal activities to continue without any police intervention. It also cited the inadequacies of the NYPD Internal Affairs unit, which consistently failed to probe allegations of corruption and administer punishment to those found guilty of departmental charges. While there were several indictments, there were only a few subsequent convictions.

Ultimately, one of the commission's leading recommendations was to appoint a permanent special prosecutor from outside of New York City to investigate police corruption. It also recommended that the NYPD Internal Affairs Division be reorganized and hold high-ranking police officials responsible for corrupt officers under their respective command.

In May 1972, Serpico received NYPD's highest honor, the Medal of Honor, but without an official ceremony. He equated it to being handed a pack of cigarettes. One month later, he officially retired. Afterward, he traveled to Europe to recuperate. After his return, author Peter Maas wrote a biography about Serpico, which sold more than 3 million copies. The book ultimately became the screenplay for the 1973 movie, *Serpico*.

Serpico returned to the United States in 1980 and has since resided in Columbia County in upstate New York. He has lectured at police academies where he shares his experiences with police officers who may be struggling with comparable issues. Today, he speaks out against police brutality and continues to be a staunch advocate for whistleblowers or "lamplighters," as he affectionately refers to them, who are being retaliated against.

Brian L. Royster

See also: Corruption; Kerner Commission Report on Race Riots and Police Response; Knapp Commission; William Bratton (1947–), Police Commissioner; Wilson and Kelling's Broken Windows Theory

Further Reading

Armstrong, M. F. *They Wished They Were Honest: The Knapp Commission and the New York City Police Corruption.* New York: Columbia University Press, 2012.
Knapp, W. *Report of the Commission to investigate alleged police corruption.* New York: George Braziller, 1972.
Maas, P. *Serpico.* New York: Viking Press, 1973.

SUMMERDALE SCANDAL

The Summerdale scandal was a ring of burglary, theft, and police corruption in Chicago, Illinois, in 1958 and 1959, during which eight city police officers ("The Summerdale Eight") joined forces with convicted criminal Richard Morrison to burglarize and steal merchandise from retail establishments in the Summerdale district of Chicago's North Side. According to Morrison's confessions, he and the Summerdale Eight were responsible for more than 150 burglaries in the district, stealing property and cash in excess of $100,000 (Thomas 1960). The crime ring ended on July 30, 1959, when Morrison was arrested and subsequently offered to reveal information about his partnership with Chicago police in exchange for leniency.

In 1958, at the age of 22, Chicago native Richard Morrison was a highly skilled and accomplished burglar. Since he had committed his first theft at the age of 15, he'd had eight years of experience and had developed sophisticated burglary tactics. He crafted ladders out of rope so he could gain access to premises through skylights and ventilation systems (Lindberg 2002). By posing as a customer shopping for commercial vaults and safes, he had schooled himself in the art of safe-breaking ("Master Thief Tells his Tale" 1959), and with the help of willing salespeople, familiarized himself with the location of the tumblers, the thickness of the steel, and the vulnerabilities of strong boxes (Lindberg 1991). He carried armor-piercing bullets that could blow the locks off even the strongest of safes (Lindberg 1991). Morrison had also established himself as an escape artist and wore a handcuff key around his neck—taped to the back of a St. Christopher medal. However, for all of his stealth and skill, Morrison was not fully immune from detection by law enforcement and had already been arrested, convicted, and served time for possession of burglary tools, burglary, and prowling in Chicago, California, and Las Vegas.

After completing his sentence in Las Vegas, Morrison returned home to Chicago in 1957. Arrested for petit larceny shortly thereafter, he served a few months in the Bridewell—Chicago's house of corrections. Once released, Morrison took a job delivering pizza and by his own accounts was attempting to maintain a law-abiding lifestyle (Thomis 1960). However, Morrison's reputation among Chicago police was still that of a burglar and thief, and police did not hesitate to issue parking tickets to his car, as well as to the other vehicles double-parked outside of Wesley's Pizzeria.

In an attempt to minimize the number of parking tickets issued outside of the restaurant, the owner of Wesley's began to offer free meals to certain Chicago police officers, and soon Richard Morrison was delivering complimentary food and pizza to the officers at Summerdale's 40th District.

The free-pizza arrangement between Wesley's and the Summerdale police created a familiarity that provided both the environment and the opportunities for illicit propositions. In June 1958, during a chance encounter, Officer Frank Faraci asked Morrison to "Cut us guys in on some of your jobs. . . . After all, we like nice things too" (Lindberg 1991). Morrison initially declined the offer of a joint venture in crime with the police, but after repeatedly being asked by Faraci and others to steal a set of golf clubs for Officer Allan Brinn, Morrison relented. On the evening of July 31, 1958, with the rationale that he would be stealing for a cop, Morrison set out in search of a set of golf clubs. Estimating that "about twenty percent of the new cars had golf clubs in them" (Thomis 1960), he had no luck in Summerdale. Consequently, he traveled into the neighboring district of Evanston, where he spotted a set of clubs inside of a parked car. However, Morrison's plan backfired; he had stumbled into a sting operation by Evanston police and was being observed while attempting to commit the theft. Although he initially escaped, he was arrested the following day and charged with auto looting (Thomis 1960).

Morrison needed money to pay for his defense in the Evanston case, so in mid-September 1958, he agreed to form an alliance with officers Frank Faraci and Alex Karras. Morrison said, "I figured I might as well go in with the Summerdale cops since I was in trouble again anyway" (Thomis 1960). "I told them I would give them one day a week for opening up any store in the 40th [Summerdale] district they wanted . . . they could have anything in the store, but I wanted the cash to pay for my lawyers" (Thomis 1960).

Each evening, Morrison met Summerdale police officers in a restaurant or saloon, and they planned the night's burglaries. Officers would case stores and submit wish lists to Morrison, who would break in, steal the desired items for the officers, and take cash for himself (Benzkofer 2013). In the beginning, police acted as lookouts while Morrison broke in and looted retail establishments, providing necessary interference if security guards or other police officers became suspicious or aware of Morrison's presence. As time passed, the officers became more active in the burglaries, entering premises themselves and taking and hauling away merchandise in their squad cars. Sometimes, Morrison would wait outside in a squad car while officers committed burglaries. The corrupt cops even offered Morrison a police uniform to wear during the heists to help him avoid detection, but he refused because it would be "too much trouble changing back and forth" (*Chicago Tribune*, June 23, 1960). The targeted businesses were numerous and diverse, and the spoils included furniture, meat, auto parts, hunting and boating equipment, and electronics. Burglaries in the area were so frequent that they came to be expected, and business owners had trouble getting insurance for items that were on the shelves (Lindberg 1991).

During his partnership with the Summerdale Eight, Morrison was arrested multiple times, but he was usually able to pay officers to "fix" the cases, so the charges would be dismissed. However, on July 30, 1959, Morrison was arrested and held in custody on charges that withstood Cook County corruption. When it was clear that the charges against him would be retained, Morrison realized that he would have to negotiate for leniency. In November of 1959, Morrison gave a 77-page statement to state attorneys, detailing his partnership with the Summerdale police and confessing to "150 or more" burglaries in the Summerdale area (Thomis 1960). For this, the Chicago press bestowed upon him the title of "Babbling Burglar."

Based on Morrison's information, the homes of the eight police officers were searched on January 14, 1960, and six truckloads of stolen merchandise, including sporting goods, furniture, electronics, and hunting equipment were recovered from seven of the homes (Farrar 1965). All eight officers were arrested and charged with conspiracy to commit burglary, burglary, and receiving stolen property. Patrick Groark, Jr., Frank Faraci, Sol Karras, Alex Karras, Peter Beeftink, Allen Brinn, Henry Mulea, and Alan Clements were all found guilty at trial. Faraci, the Karras brothers, and Clements were sentenced for one to five years and released on parole after 21 months. Brinn was sentenced for one to three years and released on parole after one year. Groark was sentenced to and served six months, and Beeftink and Mulea were each fined $500 ("Free 4 Summerdale Cops" 1967).

However, participants in the Summerdale scandal were not limited to the "Summerdale Eight." There were a number of other officers who were purportedly involved in some of the burglaries but never charged. Additionally, five officers were arrested and charged with extortion or conspiracy in connection with the scandal. George Raymond, Robert Ambrose, and Jackson Whelan were charged with accepting a $3,500 payoff from Morrison to suppress evidence in a burglary case against him. John Peterson, known as "the fixer" at the Summerdale station, and his partner, Glenn Cherry, were also arrested and charged (Thomis 1960).

The burglary charges against Morrison were dropped in exchange for his cooperation and testimony against the 13 officers. After the trial of the Summerdale Eight, he relocated to Florida, where he made the headlines as both a burglar and a robbery victim.

The Summerdale scandal sparked major reforms in the Chicago Police Department. Immediately following the sudden retirement of police commissioner Tim O'Connor in January 1960, Chicago Mayor Richard Daley assembled a panel to select a replacement who would bring integrity and professionalism to the profoundly dishonored department. Chairing the panel was Orlando W. Wilson, the former chief of police from Wichita, Kansas, and dean of the School of Criminology and professor of police administration at the University of California, Berkeley. At the conclusion of the search, Professor Wilson, who had studied under August Vollmer, the founder of the professional policing reform movement, was appointed superintendent of police in Chicago. During his seven-year tenure, Wilson reorganized the department, created an Internal Investigations Division (IID) to "police the police," implemented promotional exams, and brought 20th-century technology to the department (Lindberg 2002). Wilson, who is regarded as one of the most influential police leaders in history, retired in 1967.

Ironically, the wholly self-serving acts of Richard Morrison and the Summerdale Eight caused a reform that brought a multitude of positive changes within the Chicago Police Department, benefitting the residents of the nation's second most populous city, and serving as an example to police administrators everywhere.

Kari Larsen

See also: Corruption; Police Ethics; Teddy Roosevelt's Fight against Police Corruption

Further Reading

Benzkofer, Stephan. "A Police Scandal Breaks." *Chicago Tribune*, July 7, 2013.

Farrar, Fred. "Summerdale Scandal Draws to Close." *Chicago Tribune*, October 31, 1965.

"Free 4 Summerdale Cops." *Chicago Tribune.* September 19, 1967.

Lindberg, Richard C. *To Serve and Collect: Chicago Politics and Police Corruption from the Lager Beer Riot to the Summerdale Scandal.* New York: Praeger, 1991.

Lindberg, Richard C. "The Babbling Burglar and the Summerdale Scandal: The Lessons of Police Malfeasance." 2002. http://richardlindberg.net/articles/summerdale.html.

"Master Thief Tells his Tale—Hours of It!" *Chicago Tribune*, August 1, 1959.

Thomis, Wayne. "Cops Turn Burglars! City Horrified." *Chicago Tribune,* February 23, 1960.

Weidrich, Robert. "Morrison Blames 8 Cops for His Crimes." *Chicago Tribune*, June 30, 1961.

CHURCH COMMITTEE INVESTIGATION OF FBI SURVEILLANCE

The Cold War era (1947–1991) was a time marked by heightened paranoia, secrecy, and tension in foreign affairs, fueling of proxy-wars, the specter of communism, suspicion of secret agents infiltrating our society, and the threat of nuclear annihilation. In sum, U.S. politicians feared that our society and way of life would be the victim of an existential threat if certain steps were not taken to enhance national security. As a result of the escalating tensions and nuclear proliferation between the United States and the Soviet Union, the American government and its politicians took a *laissez-faire* (leave it alone) approach to domestic and foreign intelligence and law-enforcement activities conducted by the National Security Agency (NSA), the Federal Bureau of Investigation (FBI), and the Central Intelligence Agency (CIA).

Although the work of the intelligence community during the Cold War was of paramount importance in preventing and disrupting threats to our national security and economic interests, the lack of transparency and accountability of the intelligence community led to numerous, widely publicized instances of corruption, abuse of power, and extra-judicial (not legally authorized) and unsanctioned criminal activity among members of the political and intelligence communities. In essence, some of the work being conducted by our very own intelligence agencies was considered to be contrary to our national and democratic values, unlawful, and may very well have undermined our efforts to protect national security, which continues to be the main mission of U.S. intelligence agencies. Without transparency and

Senator Frank Church chaired the committee officially known as the United States Select Committee to Study Governmental Operations with Respect to Intelligence Activities. The committee was known informally as the "Church Committee" and was considered the first to police U.S. intelligence. (Photo-Quest/Getty Images)

accountability, U.S. intelligence assets were used to further the political ambitions of individual leaders, persecute political opposition, suppress civil liberties and minority communities, and essentially caused more harm than good by negatively effecting the public's perceptions of legitimacy and integrity regarding the authority of government.

In light of intelligence failures in the early 2000s, many U.S. Congressional and Senate committee investigations have been conducted to examine events and policies orchestrated by the intelligence community. These investigations include "blowback" from funding and arming the Mujahedeen in Afghanistan against the Soviet Union in the 1980s, the Iran-Contra affair in 1985, the 9/11 terrorist attacks in 2001, fabrication of a "smoking-gun" leading to the invasion of Iraq in 2003, the torture allegations pinned to the Enhanced Interrogation Program of enemy combatants from the War on Terror, Operation Fast and Furious between 2006 and 2011, and allegations of domestic spying and warrantless wiretapping—revealed in 2013 by Edward Snowden. The formal precedent and paradigm for investigating the intelligence community dates back to the Church Committee. Therefore, it is important to take a step back and historically observe how the American government and its citizens have previously responded to intelligence failures that threatened to undermine the democratic ideals, constitutional rights, foundations of justice, and public safety within the United States.

"Dark Figure of Justice" and Investigating Intelligence and Law-Enforcement Agencies

In the fields of criminology and sociology, researchers often refer to the "dark figure of crime" when describing the amount of unreported or unrecorded crime and victimization occurring in society among citizens. Various methodological and statistical techniques have been developed to estimate the dark figure of crime, using the official crime reports of law enforcement and comparing their numbers with self-report and survey data from research studies.

However, similar research or statistical methods are difficult to employ when studying the unlawful policies, unethical practices, and criminal activities being conducted within the justice system by law enforcement and intelligence agencies because of the official embargo on information, data, and documentation. Due to security classifications and clearance restrictions, it is not possible to enter a government bureau, request documents or information, and walk out with a load of information. Although security restrictions are an undeniable necessity for facilitating investigations, protecting identities, and protecting ongoing operations, they present a dilemma for members of the government and the greater public on holding accountability and maintaining ethical oversight when transparency is limited or completely restricted. In effect, allowing intelligence agencies too much discretion in their use of secrecy may provide a cover for corruption, as well as cover-ups within agencies.

Freedom of Information Act (FOIA) requests have been used successfully for yielding documents and data on unethical or unlawful behavior, but oftentimes the information is heavily redacted, and the names of individuals listed in the documents are censored and removed, particularly in regard to information managed by our intelligence community. Therefore, I have coined the term "dark figure of justice" to highlight many of the redacted, covered-up, unknowable, unrecorded, or undocumented activities that may qualify as unethical or criminal activities, which cannot be measured due to the configuration and compartmentalization of information being withheld by the justice system, the intelligence community, and politicians. These institutions often believe that they are protecting the public by keeping information secret. However, as history has repeatedly demonstrated, overwhelming secrecy in intelligence and law-enforcement operations, combined with minimal transparency and limited oversight, can lead to disastrous consequences for civil and human rights and can compromise public safety and national security.

A few of the primary methods for shedding light on the "dark figure of justice" are the use of testimony from whistle-blowers, external watchdog groups, and internal investigations conducted within agencies or by the larger government to facilitate transparency and accountability. Results and findings from investigations are then shared with the public through public hearings, publication of investigation results, news reports and documentaries, and academic research. If the investigations are successful, they can lead to a change in laws, accountability, prosecution of unlawful behavior, demotion or resignation of public officials, and transformation of public policy.

The formation of the Church Committee in 1975 is a prime example of the government reining itself in by bringing accountability and transparency to the intelligence community, which previously lacked such standards. The government wanted to publically address accusations of its tax-payer-funded intelligence agencies having gone "rogue." An accumulation of accusations and evidence indicating widespread illegal and unconstitutional activities, conducted under the premise of national security by the intelligence community, would be closely investigated by the Church Committee.

Investigation of the Intelligence Community

In 1975, Senator Frank Church (D-Idaho), chaired the 14-member bipartisan committee officially known as the United States Select Committee to Study Governmental Operations with Respect to Intelligence Activities. The committee was known informally as the Church Committee and was considered the first to comprehensively examine U.S. intelligence. It is a predecessor to what is officially known as the U.S. Senate Select Committee on Intelligence. The primary task of the Church Committee was to investigate alleged illegal and unconstitutional activities occurring within the U.S. intelligence community by the CIA, NSA, and FBI. After requesting information and documents from the heads of various intelligence agencies, countless fact-finding investigations, collecting testimony at open hearings, and deliberating on recommendations for improving the ethical and judicial oversight of the intelligence community, the committee published 14 exhaustive investigational reports. These were made available to the public, and the committee listed 96 recommendations in its final report.

The formation of the Church Committee was the indirect result of years of mounting evidence and public outcry that the intelligence community was engaging in activities that were not only illegal and unconstitutional, but also threatened to undermine the foundations of U.S. democracy and the sovereignty of other nations. In a 2014 video interview with the Brennan Center for Justice, the chief counsel to the Church Committee in 1975 and 1976, Frederick A. O. Schwarz, stated:

> How was it that the investigation happened when it did for the first time in 1975–1976? I think the events of Watergate, and the furor about the Vietnam War, and the leaks, such as the Pentagon Papers, had led to a pent-up interest in what the secret government had been doing, so instead of "don't ask, don't tell," it was "please let us know." (Brennan Center for Justice 2014)

Schwarz proceeded to discuss how the resignation of former president Richard Nixon over the Watergate scandal in 1974, combined with the death of the former director of the FBI in 1972, J. Edgar Hoover, created an environment with fewer obstacles to pursuing the truth and minimized fears of political reprisal for interrogating and investigating the intelligence community.

The activities of particular interest to the Church Committee included allegations of executive branch support of extra-judicial intelligence activity, assassination attempts of leaders of foreign governments, supporting unsanctioned coups d'état of foreign governments, harassment and intimidation of civil rights leaders, warrantless investigations, domestic spying on political opposition and activists, secret mind- and behavioral-control experiments on humans using psychoactive drugs and psychological manipulation, and the intelligence community secretly working with political leaders to further individual political ambitions or cover-ups.

It is often difficult to distinguish between the activities of foreign and domestic intelligence agencies within the U.S. government, particularly in the 21st century, due to the "war on terror," where transnational terrorist organizations act as non-state actors who operate without observing borders and target innocent civilians. As a result, intelligence agencies have had to adapt to these contemporary threats by engaging in joint task forces, intelligence sharing, and utilizing the NSA's drag-net of database information to identify red flags. With the line between domestic and foreign intelligence agencies being blurred, Frederick A. O. Schwarz reminds us by stating the following:

> I concluded that our FBI investigation was even more important than our CIA investi-gation and NSA investigation, because to really simplify it, what the FBI was doing threatened democracy in America and what the CIA was doing . . . injured our repu-tation in the world. Between the two you have to worry more about Democracy being undermined. (Brennan Center for Justice 2014)

Investigation of the FBI

The creation of the FBI in 1908 by Attorney General Charles Bonaparte, along with the executive support of President Theodore Roosevelt, was a landmark decision in the history of the intelligence community. This was because of its controversial role as a law-enforcement and intelligence agency managed at the federal level with interstate jurisdiction. It was also the investigative appendage to the U.S. Department of Justice. The FBI intended to serve as a politically disinterested law-enforcement body to investigate and prosecute state- and local-level corruption.

However, the Church Committee investigations revealed that, during the tenure of director J. Edgar Hoover in the 1960s, the FBI had become involved in the inves-tigation of civil rights activist and anti-war movements across the country. By the time the Church Committee started its investigation, the FBI's covert operations against political dissident groups was already considered by many academics, jour-nalists, and the general public as a move to shape political discourse and suppress political opposition through fear, intimidation, and disenfranchisement through the creation of blacklists, criminal records, and the incarceration of persistently out-spoken activists. Better known as the Counter Intelligence Program (COINTEL-PRO), it was arguably the most controversial element of the FBI's investigative projects during the 1960s. This was due to its highly politically influential nature and its use of covert and illegal projects to conduct surveillance of individuals or groups deemed subversive, infiltration of groups using undercover agents, discrediting of individuals and groups through propaganda campaigns and character assassination, and disrupting political activity among domestic civil rights and anti-war organ-izations. In sum, the FBI sought to control the national narrative by using aggressive, controversial, and unethical and unlawful policing and intelligence techniques.

The controversy of COINTELPRO is highlighted by the FBI's complete disregard for First Amendment rights by deterring freedom of speech. They did this through explicitly fueling fears among activists of being prosecuted or investigated for engag-ing in discourse that ran contrary to the government's agenda. This was achieved through implicitly sending a message to the masses that there is an "agent behind every mailbox" (Swire 2003). It was achieved by targeting "speakers, teachers, writers, and publications themselves" (Swire 2003)," which had the desired effect of generating paranoia and suspicion among political activists who feared being interviewed, surveilled, or detained for their ideological leanings and political associations. Of particular interest to the FBI were civil rights groups and activist leaders, such as the Black Panthers and Martin Luther King, Jr. The Church Committee reported, "No holds were barred. . . . The program to destroy Dr. King as the leader of the civil rights movement included efforts to discredit him with executive branch officials, Congressional leaders . . . and the press" (Swire 2003). The FBI sought to portray Dr. King as a public enemy, which ironically undermined their own legitimacy as a law-enforcement agency and ultimately led to them and other local law-enforcement agencies becoming alienated and distrusted by the larger African American community, as they were perceived by many in the minority community as a menacing and Orwellian presence (Tyler 2005).

The Church Committee's investigation and final report of domestic spying and covert operations revealed the FBI headquarters held more than 500,000 files on domestic intelligence, excluding the files held by FBI field offices scattered throughout the country. In 1972 the FBI opened 65,000 domestic intelligence files. Even within the files there are more individuals and organizations listed and named than the total number of files that exist, indicating widespread surveillance and violation of constitutional protections. Between 1940 and 1966, in eight U.S. cities, more than 130,000 first-class letters were secretly opened and copied by the FBI. In the event of a "national emergency," the FBI kept a list of 26,000 individuals that should be detained (Swire 2003). The descriptive statistics on the extent of the FBI's domestic surveillance and intelligence gathering capacity are a window into the wide-spread abuses to civil rights occurring within the larger intelligence community during that era.

Ultimately the most startling revelation presented by the Church Committee was the belief by executive branch officials and members of the intelligence community that "Crimes on behalf of 'national security' had been moral and necessary" (Bernstein 1976). Testimony contained within the Committee's final report reveals that agent William C. Sullivan, who led the FBI's Intelligence Division for 10 years and was integral in the campaign to discredit Martin Luther King, Jr., stated:

> Never once did I hear anybody, including myself, raise the question: 'Is this course of action which we have agreed upon lawful, is it legal, is it ethical or moral?' We never gave any thought to this line of reasoning, because we were just naturally pragmatic. The one thing we were concerned about, will this course of action work, will it get us what we want, will we reach the objective we desire to reach. (Swire 2003; Medsger 2014)

When used appropriately, proper safeguards, checks and balances, and the vetting of data and information collected by the intelligence community can provide the President, political representatives, law enforcement, and military decision makers with important information and intelligence about possible threats to national security, foreign interests, and economic interests (Swire 2003). Significantly unethical behavior was occurring rampantly throughout the government, but fundamentally the distortion of data and intelligence being presented to the president by the intelligence community, by exaggerating the threat of communist infiltration in the civil rights and anti–Vietnam War movements, not only undermined democracy and the U.S. Constitution, but may have also displaced valuable intelligence resources away from emerging or unforeseen threats.

The abuses perpetrated by the intelligence community were the byproduct of an overwhelming fear by politicians and scholars that the masses were not capable of protecting the public good; that only faith in elite executives would allow the United States to remain strong and vigilant against all threats foreign and domestic. Bernstein (1976) states that the popular sentiment among the politically and intellectually elite, which called for "an activist Executive defining the national interest, subduing or avoiding the passions of the electorate and the legalism-moralism of earlier policy, and overriding the localism and parochialism of Congress."

Bernstein (1976) discusses how the dominant ideology among the politically elite and intelligentsia had a pronounced belief that "the people were usually wrong and the experts were usually right." Bernstein (1976) states that the political commentator Walter Lippmann declared, "The unhappy truth is that the prevailing public opinion has been destructively wrong at the critical junctures." These beliefs and sentiments that were held among the politically elite ultimately set the foundations for a jingoistic monopoly of the intelligence community that facilitated and protected unquestioning and blind obedience to authority, covert actions against political opposition, acted as an appendage for supporting the political ambitions of political executives, and led to the widespread disregard of constitutional rights guaranteed to both individual citizens and political groups. The actions of the intelligence community were not simply the result of agencies going rogue, but they were the direct result of the vast socio-political distances being held between the executives who oversaw the national security and interests of the United States and their lack of faith and distrust in the capacity of the public for expressing political opinions on matters of national interest that ran contrary to the political agenda presented by the executives. In essence, discourse and debate on governmental operations and national interests were not only discouraged by the political elite, but were outright prohibited.

Legal and Policy Outcomes

By many measures, the Church Committee was successful at raising critical questions and documenting the constitutionality and extent of the intelligence community's domestic and foreign spying and covert operations using information gathered directly from files and testimony collected from the agency leadership, intelligence employees, and victims. Previously considered "untouchable," it was the first time the executive branch of the government was forced to acknowledge and willingly admit that numerous presidential administrations failed to provide procedural safeguards for protecting civil liberties as a direct result of systematic failures in self-policing plaguing the bureaucratic management of the intelligence community. However, the Church Committee's greatest success and legacy is that it set a precedent and laid forth the foundations for having a permanent intelligence investigative committee installed within the U.S. Senate with the primary purpose of maintaining transparency and accountability, and preventing excesses and abuses of civil rights occurring in the name of national security.

Sriram Chintakrindi

See also: J. Edgar Hoover (1895–1972), Director of the FBI; Police Accountability; Wickersham Report on Soaring Crime during Prohibition

Further Reading

Bedan, Matt. "Echelon's Effect: The Obsolescence of the US Foreign Intelligence Legal Regime." *Federal Communications Law Journal* 59 (2006): 425.

Bernstein, Barton J. "The Road to Watergate and Beyond: The Growth and Abuse of Executive Authority since 1940." *Law and Contemporary Problems* 40 (1976): 58–86.

Best, Jr, Richard A. "Proposals for Intelligence Reorganization, 1949–2004." Library of Congress, Washington, DC: Congressional Research Service, 2004.

Brennan Center for Justice. "Frederick A. O. Schwarz Part 1: Formation of the Church Committee." YouTube, December 2014. https://www.youtube.com/watch?v=TNV37Jg3Lsk.

Church Committee. "Intelligence Activities and the Rights of Americans: 1976 US Senate Report on Illegal Wiretaps and Domestic Spying by the FBI, CIA and NSA." St. Petersburg, FL: Red and Black Publishers, 2008.

Dycus, Stephen. "The Role of Military Intelligence in Homeland Security." *La. Law Review* 64 (2003): 779.

Elijah, J. Soffiyah. "Reality of Political Prisoners in the United States: What September 11 Taught Us about Defending Them." *Harvard Black Letter Law Journal* 18 (2002): 129.

Greene, Dorian D. "Ethical Dilemmas Confronting Intelligence Agency Counsel." *Tulsa Journal of Comparative International Law* 2 (1994): 91.

Haines, Gerald K. "Looking for a Rogue Elephant: The Pike Committee Investigations and the CIA." *Inside CIA: Lessons in Intelligence.* APH Publishing: New Delhi, 2004.

Jeffreys-Jones, Rhodri. *The FBI: A History.* New Haven, CT: Yale University Press, 2007.

Lobel, Jules. "The War on Terrorism and Civil Liberties." *University of Pittsburgh Law Review* 63 (2001): 767.

Martin, Kate. "Domestic Intelligence and Civil Liberties." *SAIS Review of International Affairs* 24, no. 1 (2004): 7–21.

Medsger, Betty. *The Burglary: The Discovery of J. Edgar Hoover's Secret FBI.* New York: Vintage, 2014.

Ott, Marvin C. "Partisanship and the Decline of Intelligence Oversight." *International Journal of Intelligence and Counterintelligence* 16, no. 1 (2003): 69–94.

Pickard, Daniel B. "Legalizing Assassination: Terrorism, the Central Intelligence Agency, and International Law." *Georgia Journal of International and Comparative Law* 30 (2001): 1.

Schwartz, David A. "Woodward, Bernstein Revisit Watergate." February 20, 2014. *Sun Sentinel.* http://articles.sun-sentinel.com/2014-02-20/florida-jewish-journal/fl-jjps-woodstein-0226-20140220_1_bob-woodward-nixon-presidential-library-museum-watergate.

Smith, W. Thomas. *Encyclopedia of the Central Intelligence Agency*. New York: Infobase Publishing, 2003.

Snider, L. Britt. *Recollections from the Church Committee's Investigation of NSA*. Central Intelligence Agency, Washington, DC: Center for the Study of Intelligence, 2000.

Swire, Peter P. "The System of Foreign Intelligence Surveillance Law." *George Washington Law Review* 72 (2003): 1306.

Tyler, Tom R. "Policing in Black and White: Ethnic Group Differences in Trust and Confidence in the Police." *Police Quarterly* 8, no. 3 (2005): 322–342.

Varghese, George P. "A Sense of Purpose: The Role of Law Enforcement in Foreign Intelligence Surveillance." *University of Pennsylvania Law Review* 152, no. 1 (2003): 385–430.

Warner, Michael, and J. Kenneth McDonald. *US Intelligence Community Reform Studies Since 1947*. Central Intelligence Agency, Washington, DC: Center for the Study of Intelligence, 2005.

Wiebe, Matthew C. "Assassination in Domestic and International Law: The Central Intelligence Agency, State-Sponsored Terrorism, and the Right of Self-Defense." *Tulsa Journal of Comparative and International Law* 11 (2003): 363.

POLICE AUTHORITY TO DETAIN

The police have the authority to temporarily detain an individual for investigative purposes. This limited seizure is known as an investigative detention. A brief detention of this nature must be based upon an officer's reasonable suspicion of the individual. Generally, reasonable suspicion refers to an officer's ability to believe criminal activity may be afoot and that the subject may potentially be involved. Although reasonable suspicion does not have the same level of importance as probable cause (the standard required for a custodial arrest), it is more than a mere hunch. During a detention, an officer is permitted to ask questions that are geared toward the particular criminal investigation. There is not a predetermined minimum or maximum length of time associated with such a detention. An acceptable duration of such an encounter may be any length of time considered objectively reasonable for an officer to determine the purpose of the stop.

Reasonableness, according to each particular situation, is evaluated by considering all the surrounding circumstances. Hence, the entire encounter shall be guided by the facts surrounding that situation, including the reason for the initial stop and the circumstances that may or may not evolve therefrom. Should probable cause against the individual develop as a result of the detention, the officer may lawfully arrest the subject based upon that probable cause. However, should the original reasonable suspicion of the officer cease or be otherwise diminished, the investigative detention must be terminated. Subsequently, any continued communication between the officer and the individual would be at the sole and voluntary discretion of that individual, as the officer would no longer have any legal authority to detain.

In a free society, people have the right to live and associate without unreasonable police interference. Consistent with that philosophy, the Fourth Amendment to the U.S. Constitution sets forth ". . . the right of the people to be secure in their persons, houses, papers, and effects, against unreasonable searches and seizures." Its objective is to protect individuals from unreasonable government intrusion. As police act as agents of the government, their conduct is subject to this constitutional scrutiny.

A search and seizure, in this context, constitutes a governmental intrusion. While the Fourth Amendment does not protect people from all searches and seizures by government, it does safeguard against those that are considered unreasonable. For example, such an intrusion would be unreasonable if it limited the liberty of the individual without any legal justification. Thus, a nonconsensual detention is tantamount to a depravation of liberty as the person is being held, even briefly, against his own will. However, the restriction of liberty, or "seizure" (under the Fourth Amendment), would be considered unreasonable if it were unsupported by the law.

In this context, a seizure takes place when, by virtue of police authority, a person is of the reasonable belief she is not free to leave. To avoid the potential deficits associated with subjectivity, the objective standard is applied to the analysis. Specifically, the reasonable belief of the individual is not measured by her perception of the situation but rather the legally constructed perception of an average person in the same situation. This construct attempts to place the circumstances within a more generalized meaning rather than within the potentially influenced or otherwise possibly flawed perceptions of the subject.

An individual is not considered under a seizure (according to constitutional standards) by any and every communication with law enforcement. There is an incalculable number of interactions between members of the public and the police. In fact, such informal dealings are even encouraged as an integral part of many community policing initiatives. As such, a friendly, social conversation or a casual question does not constitute a seizure. Should that not be the case, not only would it be rather unrealistic, but every communication between the police and the public would be deemed investigatory in nature and be required to meet constitutional standards.

An arrest, as noted above, is the highest level of seizure, as a person is forcibly taken into custody by police. Therefore, a custodial arrest requires the police to have a substantial basis or justification for such a high level of governmental intrusion and deprivation of liberty. The substantial justification is known as probable cause. Simply stated, probable cause is the reasonable belief that a crime has been committed and the individual being arrested committed it. Conversely, a hunch is merely intuitive in nature and does not justify a seizure or intrusion of any kind. It is not based on facts or other such objective information but rather only the subjective beliefs of the officer. In between the extremes of probable cause and a hunch lies what is known as reasonable suspicion. Reasonable suspicion is more than a hunch but less than probable cause. Essentially, it is the justification for briefly holding, or detaining, a person because of a criminal investigation based upon the reasonable belief that a crime may be taking place or has already occurred. This type of a stop or temporary investigative detention is based upon the holding in the landmark case of *Terry v. Ohio* (1968). Accordingly, this type of seizure is also commonly known as a "Terry stop."

In *Terry v. Ohio* (1968), the U.S. Supreme Court maintained that police may lawfully detain an individual for investigatory purposes if they have reasonable and particularized belief of criminal activity. The Court believed the limited and temporary intrusion of a person's liberty was justified in order to prevent suspected criminal activity. The intrusion may include questioning and other nonintrusive investigatory methods such as the use of narcotic-sniffing dogs. Pursuant to a separate and distinct legal justification, detaining officers may also pat down a person's outer clothing when searching for weapons. The officers may conduct this frisk, or "Terry frisk," only if they reasonably fear for their safety or the safety of others. Such fear will provide the officers with the reasonable suspicion necessary to justify the additional intrusion of liberty. It must be noted that this pat-down is not for evidentiary purposes but rather for safety purposes only. However, should non-weapon evidence be discovered in the routine course of a lawful safety frisk, it may be used in court.

Reasonableness associated with police detentions of an individual is also based upon the objective standard. Similarly, unlike the subjective standard that examines the actual belief of the particular officer involved, the objective standard considers a fictitious collective belief of the "average" officer with similar training and experience in the same or similar situation. As with the reasonable belief of the person subjected to the seizure, this legal fiction is also constructed and adopted in order to avoid the potential pitfalls (unreasonableness) that may inherently be associated with the individual subjectivity of the particular officer. In effect, the reasonableness of the seizure will be assessed by an analysis of the privacy rights of the person being detained and balanced against the governmental interest of the police to protect society from alleged criminality. The U.S. Supreme Court has determined the analysis shall consider the "totality of the circumstances" involved. Therefore, all facts and circumstances surrounding the event must be taken into consideration for the legal determination to be made.

The justification for the police's authority to seize a person is reflected on a very broad spectrum. In a custodial arrest, an officer uses his or her authoritative position to take the subject into custody. While the denial of freedom may emanate from a physical or verbal assertion, the results are the same. In a stop or temporary detention, the police have the authority to briefly detain the subject for investigatory purposes. Although this action does constitute a seizure, it is not considered as restrictive regarding liberty and therefore may be conducted on a less stringent legal basis. Nonetheless, in order to be lawful, the extent of the seizure must correspond to the basis for the intrusion. In other words, a higher level of seizure requires a higher level of justification for that seizure.

Investigatory detentions may take place in various situations, most notably stops on the street and stops in a motor vehicle (traffic stops). The required reasonable suspicion may be based upon a variety of factors, including the observation of the officer, an informant's tip, or information obtained from a police radio dispatch. Should the basis be from a known informant, the officer may reliably act upon the information provided. However, should the informant be anonymous or unknown to the officer, the information must be successfully corroborated before it may meet the legal standard. Perhaps more common is information received via police radio dispatch. In a representative scenario, the dispatcher transmits information based upon a reasonable belief that a crime may be taking place or it has already occurred. The information contained in the transmission enables the officer to make a lawful related stop.

However, what is specifically legally required to conduct a stop is much less conclusive. Perhaps among the most notable of subsequent criticisms of the holding in *Terry* was the lack of specificity regarding what specifically constitutes reasonable or "articulable" suspicion. In general terms, the legal guideline offered by the court to determine reasonableness was merely a balance of the societal need for the intrusion against the personal right to liberty. As a result, the decades that followed this landmark decision have been active with legal challenges and subsequent rulings that address the functional meaning of reasonable suspicion.

What the courts consider reasonable is subject to interpretation and modification. Over the years, courts have interpreted the factors associated with the reasonableness of a stop to include a consideration of the particular officer's training and experience, presence in a high crime area, association with people known by police to be criminals, and even "innocent" behavior. Critics suggest that such perceived expansions of legal doctrine provide law enforcement with very broad discretion from which to interpret the attending circumstances of the stop. Another such example is "flight" or running away from officers. Although, by legal interpretation, a person is not seized if he is free to walk away, running away or flight from a scene may be considered a factor from which to determine reasonable suspicion.

In the end, challenges to the police authority to detain are likely to continue based upon evolving interpretations of existing law and the degree to which society determines to maintain the delicate balance between public safety and personal privacy.

Thomas Lateano

See also: Community Policing Today; Fourth Amendment; Police Ethics; *Terry v. Ohio*

Further Reading

Hodges, Scott C. "Twenty-Hour Detention Based on Reasonable Suspicion Is Not a Minimal Intrusion: A Case for Amending Arizona's SB 1070." *Arizona Summit Law Review* 7 (2013): 411.

Levchak, Philip J. "Do Precinct Characteristics Influence Stop-and-Frisk in New York City? A Multi-Level Analysis of Post-Stop Outcomes." *Justice Quarterly* (2016), 1–30, doi:10 .1080/07418825.2016.1162320.

Meares, Tracey L. "Programming Errors: Understanding the Constitutionality of Stop-and-Frisk as a Program, Not an Incident." *University of Chicago Law Review* 82 (2015): 159–179.

Tyler, Tom R., Jeffrey Fagan, and Amanda Geller. "Street Stops and Police Legitimacy: Teachable Moments in Young Urban Men's Legal Socialization." *Journal of Empirical Legal Studies* 11, no. 4 (2014): 751–785.

Weisburd, David, Alese Wooditch, Sarit Weisburd, and Sue-Ming Yang. "Do Stop, Question, and Frisk Practices Deter Crime?" *Criminology & Public Policy* 15 (2015): 31–56.

Wooditch, Alese, and David Weisburd. "Using Space–Time Analysis to Evaluate Criminal Justice Programs: An Application to Stop-Question-Frisk Practices." *Journal of Quantitative Criminology* 32L (2015), 1–23.
Woods, Jordan Blair. "Decriminalization, Police Authority, and Routine Traffic Stops." *UCLA Law Review* 62 (2015): 672.

CORRUPTION

Police corruption has been a major problem in American policing for a long time. It began in the earliest days of colonization, when policing was characterized by a variety of law enforcement roles that had been practiced in Britain. Then corruption continued through the time of the colonial sheriffs and watchmen. When professionalism entered American policing in the 19th and earlier part of 20th centuries, policing in America was plagued by poor performance and corruption. The range of corrupt activities included soliciting for bribes, extortion of money from drug dealers, theft of drugs, planting of evidence, beating of arrestees, bank robbery, false imprisonment, and fabrication and planting of evidence (Rennison and Dodge 2016; Newburn 1999).

Corruption and misconduct have undermined the development of police institutions around the world (Bayley and Perito 2011; Rotimi, 2001). According to Transparency International, the police are the fourth most corrupt public institution in 86 countries after political parties, public officials, and parliaments and legislature (2010). Other countries, such as India, ranked the police highest among the nine public services on its corruption index (Bayley and Perito 2011). In the United States, police corruption is harshly regressive in that the very poor and racially marginalized members of the society often report police abuse and paying bribes to the police under duress (Bayley and Perito 2011; Smith 2007). The history of American policing has continued to depict corruption as one of the major problems that "washes resources, undermines security, makes a mockery of justice, slows economic development, and alienates populations from their governments" (Bayley and Perito 2011, 2). From 1950 to the early 2000s, police corruption has continued to destabilize the rule of law, equal access to justice, fair elections, fair trials, cultural expressions, social and economic opportunities, and access to the necessities of life (ICHRPTI 2009). To tackle this institutional problem, government set up various commissions to investigate the numerous allegations of police corruption and make suggestions for reforms.

In the early 20th century, the Prohibition Act under President Woodrow Wilson's administration contributed to the hike in police corruption, as a lot of money was being made by bootleggers. They would, in turn, pay police officers to allow their illegal activities to continue (U.S. National Archives 2008). The Wickersham Commission in 1929 found Prohibition unenforceable due to its associated social and political problems and the potential for police corruption. Additionally, the civil rights movements of the 1960s and 1970s were laden with numerous incidents of police brutality and corruption. Many White police officers were grossly involved in racial injustices and violations of the constitutional rights of individuals. Notably, during the Birmingham Campaign of 1963–1964 and the Selma-to-Montgomery marches of 1965, the police were involved in several acts of brutality and misconduct. Similarly, the Kerner Commission investigated the numerous acts of police misconduct and corruption and suggested many reforms in 1965, focusing on eradicating racial discrimination and inequality.

Particularly, around the 1970s, the Knapp Commission discovered many in the New York Police Department were involved in payoffs from brothels, narcotics, gambling, and bribery. The commission recommended prosecution for this police corruption, but it was not very effective, as misconduct and corruption continued to be widespread. According to the Mollen Commission, the New York Police Department's corruption took a more serious turn in the 1990s when a group of officers were not only involved in extortion, but they were also involved in trafficking illicit drugs, conducting illegal searches and seizures, and falsifying records (Mollen Commission 1994). The commission recommended the police department hire an external oversight committee; however, corruption continued to thrive. Similarly, from 2000 to 2002, and then in 2011, officers of the Baltimore and Los Angeles police departments were found to be involved in receiving kickbacks, drug dealings, perjury, tampering with confessional evidence, false imprisonment, and other acts of corruption (Walker and Katz 2013). Still, corruption continued.

Researchers agree that police corruption is difficult to define (Roebuck and Barker 1974; Sayed and Bruce 1998; Porter and Warrender 2009). Roebuck and Barker loosely defined it as behavior by a police officer that is dishonest, deviant, unethical, or improper (1974). Goldstein's definition involved two key elements, namely personal gain and misuse of authority (1975). By his definition, police corruption refers to "acts involving the misuse of authority by a police officer in a manner designed to produce personal gain for himself or for others" (3). This definition recognizes that the specific purpose of corruption may be for the benefit of a wider group. Apart from personal gains, corruption may also involve "organizational gain," which may penetrate the higher levels of a police department. Klockars refers to this as the "dirty means" to achieve a "legitimate end" (1985). Hence, from a broader perspective, McMullan (1961) aptly included activities that qualify an act as corrupt by stating that "a public official is corrupt if he accepts money or money's worth for doing something he is under a duty to do anyway, that he is under a duty not to do or to exercise a legitimate discretion for improper reasons" (183–184).

From a narrower perspective, Wilson (1968) distinguished police corruption in terms of corrupt behavior, such as acceptance of bribes as well as criminal but not corrupt behavior—committing acts of burglary while on duty. Wilson's distinction of bribery entails the exploitation of authority, whereas burglary does not necessarily involve exploitation of authority but a criminal behavior in the line of duty.

Roebuck and Barker, and Punch, identified nine types of police corruption, including corruption of authority, kickbacks, opportunistic theft, shakedowns, protection of illegal activity, the fix, direct criminal activities, internal payoffs, and flaking or padding (1974; 1985).

Table 1   The Nine Types of Police Corruption

Types	Characteristics
Corruption of authority	When officers receive gratuities by virtue of their position as police officers (free meals, free dry cleaning, discounts on purchases, etc.); the Knapp Commission in the 1970s distinguished between grass eaters (who passively accept what is offered to them) and meat eaters (who aggressively demand favors) (Walker and Katz, 2013).
Kickbacks	When an officer receives money, goods, or services in return for providing help in a secret and dishonest business deal
Opportunistic theft	When officers take advantage of opportunities by stealing from traffic accident victims, arrestees, dead bodies, or citizen's properties
Shakedowns	Also referred to as bribes; accepting bribes not to enforce the law, for example, taking money instead of writing a traffic ticket or not making an arrest in lieu of money
Protection of illegal activity	Officers involved in protecting citizens engaged in illegal activities (illegal drug dealing, prostitution, and gambling)
"The fix"	When officers intentionally destabilize criminal investigations because of ulterior motives
Direct criminal activities	Officers involved in criminal activities against citizens for personal gains (theft, burglary, or sexual misconduct)
Internal payoffs	Referred to as internal corruption where promotions, holidays, or favored assignments must be sold or purchased with bribes
Flaking or padding	Falsifying or planting of evidence, especially on drug-related investigations

Sources: Roebuck and Barker (1974); Punch (1985); Newburn (1999)

The typical forms of police corruption according to Walker and Katz (2013) are gratuities, bribes, internal corruption, theft and burglary, and corruption and brutality. Prenzler and Ransley (2002) also categorized police corruption and misconduct into classic corruption, process corruption, brutality, and miscellaneous conduct. Classic corruption represents bribery or graft, which involves a police officer receiving personal gain for not doing his or her duty, for example, accepting money for waiving a speeding ticket. Process corruption involves the fabrication of evidence in order to distort the course of justice. This could be in the form of falsifying evidence. Brutality, a newer form of corruption, is composed of violent threats and assaults that eventually lead to personal benefits such as when officers brutally beat drug dealers, steal their drugs and money, and sell the drugs to make gain. The last clas-sifications of police corruption, according to Prenzler and Ransley (2002), are miscellaneous conducts such as harassment, drug abuse, racial slurs, maltreatment of detainees, use of abusive language, and drunk driving while on duty.

Theories of Police Corruption

Police corruption is not peculiar only to the American criminal justice system. Australia and the United Kingdom have also encountered the problems of police corruption (Newburn 1999; Orole, Gadar, and Hunter 2015). Literature reviewed indicates elements of criminological theories that explain police corruption in general (Orole, Gadar, and Hunter 2015; Walker and Katz 2013; Akers 2000). Various theories have been influential in understanding the proliferation of police corruption: social learn-ing theory, organizational/occupational culture theory, and individual bad apple theory.

Social Learning Theory

The basic principles of the theory toward social behavior are founded on four variables: differential association, definitions, reinforcement, and modeling. Differ-ential association plays an important role in social learning. According to Akers, an individual's ability to develop either favorable or unfavorable definitions to devi-ance depends on interactions with their peers (2000). Akers's argument on social learning is buttressed more when a learning process is followed by positive or neg-ative reinforcement through rewards or punishments.

Social learning theory maintains that officers develop and model peer groups within the department. These peer groups have the tendency to form a subculture if their learning processes support nonconventional deviance behavior. Therefore, when new officers learn definitions unfavorable to positive police culture such as acceptance of bribes, it increases their chances of appreciating standards and norms favorable to police subculture or criminal behavior (Bernard, Snipes, and Gerould 2010). Obviously, the nature of police work exposes police officers, and co-workers to learn, accept, and internalize the definitions shared by other officers in a police occupational setting.

Organizational/Occupational Culture Theory

According to Orole, Gadar, and Hunter (2015), organizational culture is one of the underlying factors contributing to police corruption. The attributes of police culture that define the department might include similar values, customs, practices, and tra-ditions among officers. The quality of leadership, management, and supervision deter-mines the values and the practices in a department. Hence, police corruption tends to thrive in departments that tolerate violations of rules. For example officers are more likely to derogate or give in to corruption if they believe that the punishment for deviating from the norms will not be harsh. Culture can play an important role in reducing opportunities for corruption. Klockars, Ivkovich, Harver, and Haberfeld

(2000) examined the impact of organizational culture and degree of police intolerance for corrupt behavior in various police departments across the country. The result indicates that more officers in departments that are serious about organizational integrity tend to expect severe punishment if caught committing any act of corruption than officers in departments that care less about violation of organizational integrity. This suggests that police officers in departments that hardly tolerate corruption are more likely to conform to organizational values, norms, and practices, thereby avoiding opportunities for corrupt activities than officers in organizations with loose integrity.

Individual Bad Apple Theory

The bad apple theory is a traditional occupational explanation of police corruption where officers of the police organization believe that police corruption is the product of one or more individuals and not the entire organization per se. The bad apple theory allows police agencies to blame a small number of corrupt officers in the department without having to investigate larger problems in the department. This leaves the impression that the corrupt few do not represent the standard exhibited by the department.

Experts criticized the bad apple theory for failure to explain most police corruption adequately. The Knapp Commission, specifically, condemned the organizational idea that police corruption resulted from activities of a few bad apples in the department. The commission rejected the doctrine by stating:

> According to this theory, which bordered on official Department doctrine, any policeman found to be corrupt must promptly be denounced as a rotten apple in an otherwise clean barrel. It must never be admitted that his individual corruption may be symptomatic of underlying disease. . . . A high command unwilling to acknowledge that the problem of corruption is extensive cannot very well argue that drastic changes are necessary to deal with the problem. . . . The rotten apple doctrine has in many ways been an obstacle to meaningful reform . . . (and) the commission examined and rejected the premises upon which the rotten apple doctrine rested. (Knapp 1972, 6–8)

Obviously, the Knapp Commission discovered systematic corruption within the New York Police Department. However, a more recent inquiry into police corruption by the Mollen Commission in the 1990s found traditional forms of organized corruption and other devious forms of criminal activity (Newburn 1999). Therefore, for effective reform strategies, explanations of police corruption must be based on the examination of the whole police system and not just the few cases that come to the public's attention through the reporting by citizens who are victims of police corruption.

Ifeoma E. Okoye, O. Oko Elechi, and Dorothy Aerga

See also: Kerner Commission Report on Race Riots and Police Response; Knapp Commission; Police Accountability; Police Ethics

Further Reading

Akers, R. L. *Criminological Theories: Introduction, Evaluation and Application.* Los Angeles: Roxbury, 2000.

Bayley, D., and R. Perito. "Police Corruption: What Past Scandals Teach About Current Challenges." *Special Report* (294). Washington, DC: United States Institute of Peace, 2011.

Bernard, T. J., J. B. Snipes, and A. L. Gerould. *Vold's Theoretical Criminology.* New York: Oxford University Press, 2010.

Goldstein, H. *Police Corruption: A Perspective on Its Nature and Control*, 47 (6). Washington, DC: The Police Foundation, 1975.

International Council on Human Rights Policy and Transparency International (ICHRPTI). *Corruption and Human Rights: Making the Connection.* Geneva Switzerland: ICHRP, 2009.

Klockars, C. B. *The Idea of Police.* Beverly Hills, CA: Sage, 1985.

Klockars, C. B., S. K. Ivkovich, W. E. Harver, and M. R. Haberfeld. *The Measurement of Police Integrity.* Washington, DC: National Institute of Justice, 2000.

Knapp, W. *Report of the Commission to Investigate Alleged Police Corruption.* New York: George Braziller, 1972.

McMullan, M. "A Theory of Corruption." *Sociological Review* 9 (1961): 181–201.

Mollen Commission. *Report of the Commission to Investigate Allegations of Police Corruption and the Anti-Corruption Procedures of the Police Department.* New York: Mollen Commission, 1994.

Newburn, T. "Understanding and Preventing Police Corruption: Lessons from the Literature." *Police Research Series, Paper 110*, 1999. Research Development Statistics.

Orole, F., K. Gadar, and M. Hunter. "Influencing Factors and Theoretical Perspective of Police Corruption in Nigeria." *International Journal of Social Science and Human Behavior Study* 2, no. 2 (2015): 197–202.

Porter, L. E., and C. Warrender. "A Multivariate Model of Police Deviance: Examining the Nature of Corruption, Crime and Misconduct." *Policing and Society: An International Journal of Research and Policy* 19 (2009): 79–99.

Prenzler, T., and J. Ransley. *Police Reform: Building Integrity.* Annandale, New South Wales: Hawkins Press, 2002.

Punch, M. *Conduct Unbecoming: The Social Construction of Police Deviance and Control.* London: Tavistock, 1985.

Rennison, C. M., and M. Dodge, *Introduction to Criminal Justice: Systems, Diversity, and Change.* Thousand Oaks, California: Sage Publications, Inc., 2016.

Roebuck, J. B., and T. Barker. "A Typology of Police Corruption." *Social Problems*, 21 (1974): 423–437.

Rotimi, G. *The Police in a Federal State: The Nigerian Experience.* Ibadan, Nigeria: College Press. 2001.

Sayed, T., and D. Bruce. "Police Corruption: Toward a Working Definition." *African Security Review* 7, no. 1 (1998): 3–14.

Smith, D. J. *A Culture of Corruption: Everyday Deception and Popular Discontent.* Princeton, NJ: Princeton University Press, 2007.

Transparency International. *Global Corruption Barometer.* Berlin, Germany, 2010.

U.S. National Archives. "Teaching with Documents: The Volstead Act and Related Prohibition Documents." 2008. http://www.archives.gov/education/lessons/volstead-act.

Walker, S. and Katz, C. *The Police in America: An Introduction.* Columbus, Ohio: McGraw Hill Education, 2013.

Wilson, J. Q. *Varieties of Police Behaviour.* Cambridge, MA: Harvard University Press, 1968.

RICO ACT

The Racketeer Influenced and Corrupt Organizations (RICO) Act is a provision of the Organized Crime Control Act (OCCA) of 1970, a law designed to enhance the U.S. government's effort to combat organized crime. The OCCA made significant reforms to the criminal justice system based on the recommendations of the 1967 President's Commission on Law Enforcement and Administration of Justice, including revamping the federal grand jury system, authorizing judges to grant immunity to obtain testimony over objections about self-incrimination, providing physical facilities to protect witnesses, and other provisions. However, it would take the U.S. federal government nearly 10 years to effectively use RICO to prosecute high-level organized crime figures. Yet despite the U.S. government's use of RICO to cripple organized crime, it remains a very controversial criminal statute, given its wide application and severe criminal penalties.

Organized crime in the United States gained significant public attention during the early 1950s following the Kefauver Committee's investigation into the mafia's involvement in interstate commerce and the discovery on November 14, 1957, of a meeting between high-ranking members of the American mafia from across the United States in Apalachin, New York. The discovery at Apalachin was believed to have provided evidence of a nationwide conspiracy and even forced Federal Bureau of Investigation (FBI) director J. Edgar Hoover to finally acknowledge the existence of the mafia. The discovery of the 1957 Apalachin meeting occurred when the U.S. Senate was investigating allegations of the American mafia's infiltration of the International Brotherhood of Teamsters, a powerful trade union. This investigation by the U.S. Select Committee on Improper Activities in Labor and Management, which was also known as the McClellan Committee after its chair, U.S. Senator John L. McClellan, was initiated on January 30, 1957.

These highly publicized events and subsequent Senate hearings held by Senator McClellan in the early 1960s, which included testimony from mobster Joseph Valachi regarding the existence of a national mafia commission in 1963, led to the creation of the President's Task Force on Organized Crime in 1967. The task force was created in 1965 as part of President Lyndon B. Johnson's Commission on Law Enforcement and Administration of Justice. The recommendations made in 1967 by President Johnson's commission would lead to two significant pieces of legislation: the Safe Streets Act and the Omnibus Crime Control Act, which authorized wiretapping of suspected criminal offenders under Title III of the Act, and the Organized Crime Control Act of 1970, which included RICO.

The OCCA consists of 12 titles, each designed to enhance the federal government's capabilities in its efforts to combat organized crime in the United States. Title I of the OCCA establishes special grand juries to hear government witnesses and other evidence against alleged organized crime figures in closed sessions and return indictments against the accused. Title II authorizes "use immunity," which protects a witness from prosecution directly or indirectly using the witness's testimony or anything directly derived from it against the witness. Title III codified civil contempt procedures by authorizing the detention without bail of witnesses, who refused to comply with court orders, for up to 18 months. Title IV authorized a conviction for perjury. Title V authorized the attorney general to protect federal and state witnesses and their families. Title VI authorized the use of depositions in criminal cases. Title VII limited to five years the circumstances within which evidence could be challenged as inadmissible and required court review of the disclosure of government records in connection with such a challenge. Title XIII declared it a federal crime to plot to obstruct state law through corruption of officials. Title IX declared it a crime to use income from organized crime to acquire or establish a business engaged in interstate commerce. Title X provided for increased sentences for dangerous adult special offenders. This generally extended sentences for organized crime members who committed a felony. Title XI established more federal controls over interstate and foreign commerce in explosives through licensing and permits. Title XII established the National Commission on Individual Rights to review federal laws and practices.

While many of the provisions of the OCCA provided the U.S. government with enhanced tools to combat organized crime, Title IX, which is referred to as RICO, expanded traditional conspiracy laws in the United States by making it illegal to be in, or part of, an enterprise that is engaged in a pattern of racketeering activities. Racketeering activities include 32 predicated offenses enumerated in RICO. These criminal offenses include murder, extortion, drug trafficking, gambling, money laundering and related offenses; obstruction of justice; acts of terrorism; human smuggling; and other offenses often associated with organized crime. A pattern of racketeering occurs when there are two or more of the enumerated offenses within a 10-year timeframe. However, the most recent offense for prosecution must have been committed within the previous five years. In addition, each of the offenses must be demonstrated to have been committed as part of an ongoing criminal enterprise. The term "enterprise" is defined as any legal or illegal ongoing business or group that is used to facilitate criminal activity.

RICO's strength is in providing federal law enforcement officials a tool to subject leaders of criminal organizations to prosecution for the criminal activity of their associates. Prior to RICO's passage, it was difficult for U.S. attorneys to secure a criminal conviction for high-ranking members of a criminal organization. Under RICO, it is possible to hold the leaders of a criminal organization responsible for the actions of their associates even if they are not directly involved in the criminal act. In addition, RICO provides for enhanced criminal penalties for committing the predicate offenses as part of an ongoing criminal enterprise. Penalties include up to 20 years in prison and/or a fine of up to $20,000 for each criminal violation. Many of these same criminal violations would result in a lower sentence if convicted under traditional penal codes.

RICO also provides for criminal asset forfeiture. Provisions of RICO state that an offender forfeits all interests in an enterprise when convicted for racketeering. This provision has been interpreted to mean that the U.S. government can seize the assets of an organized crime figure if the assets are derived from the profits made from a criminal enterprise. The provisions for asset forfeiture do provide federal law enforcement with powerful tools to combat organized crime because organized crime groups primarily seek to survive by making money. Likewise, criminals join criminal organizations in part to enhance their opportunities to increase their personal wealth and status. Therefore, the asset forfeiture provisions are designed to give federal law enforcement officials the ability to deprive criminals of their illicitly derived money and material goods, such as expensive homes, yachts, and sports cars.

Yet, despite Congress's efforts to provide federal law enforcement with the tools to combat organized crime, RICO was underutilized by the federal government for nearly a decade. It was underutilized because of the reluctance of U.S. attorneys to use the law because of concerns about its constitutionality. The FBI, under J. Edgar Hoover, remained distant from mob contacts, as did a number of U.S. attorneys general under U.S. presidents Richard Nixon, Gerald Ford, and Jimmy Carter. During these presidencies, eight U.S. attorneys general led the Department of Justice. By 1979, only 200 RICO cases had been tried, and not one of them was against an organized crime figure. In response to this situation, the former chief counsel of the Subcommittee on Criminal Laws and Procedures of the Senate Judiciary Committee, G. Robert Blakey, would subsequently publish a law journal article in 1980 advocating its use and hosting numerous seminars for FBI agents and U.S. prosecutors at Cornell University Law School (where Blakey was a law professor). Blakely was the primary author of the RICO legislation in consultation with Senator McClellan, who had led the Subcommittee on Criminal Law and Procedures,

It was at one of G. Robert Blakey's RICO seminars that then U.S. attorney Rudolph Giuliani was introduced to its concepts and application. In 1985, Giuliani would use RICO to pursue the most ambitious prosecution of the American mafia in U.S. history. Giuliani sought to prosecute the heads of New York's Gambino, Bonanno, Lucchese, Genovese, and Colombo crime families in what was dubbed the "Mafia Commission" trial. Giuliani would indict 11 members of the 5 New York crime families, including Anthony Salerno, the boss of the Genovese crime family; Paul Castellano, the boss of the Gambino crime family; Carmine Persico, the boss of the Colombo crime family; Anthony Corallo, the boss of the Lucchese crime family; and Phillip Rastelli, the boss of the Bonanno crime family. However, Castellano would be murdered while out on bail, Rastelli would be tried in a separate RICO trial with his underboss Joseph Massino, and Aniello Dellacroce, the underboss of the Gambino crime family, would die of natural causes. Despite these setbacks, the remaining eight defendants would be convicted and receive lengthy prison sentences, ensuring the defendants, given their ages, would die in prison. The mafia bosses, in particular, all received 100 year prison terms.

The "Mafia Commission" trial would mark the first successful large-scale RICO case against the American mafia. With its success, the U.S. federal government—armed with RICO—continued its efforts to cripple the American mafia. The prospects of lengthy prison terms under RICO, coupled with offers for personal security under the U.S. Marshal's Witness Protection Program (Title V of the OCCA), caused more mafia members and associates to cooperate with federal agents, breaking the mafia's *omerta,* or code of silence. One of the most notorious mafia turncoats was Sammy "the Bull" Gravano. Gravano, who was the underboss of the Gambino crime family and the government's highest ranking mafia turncoat, would be a key government witness against Gambino crime boss John Gotti, dubbed the "Teflon Don" by the media because previous criminal charges did not stick. However, Gravano's testimony at Gotti's 1992 trial would secure Gotti's conviction and life sentence.

Despite the many successes attributed to RICO against organized crime, a number of concerns have been raised about the legislation, raising concerns about its potential misuse and abuse. These concerns include the sweeping application of the law beyond the mafia, the severity of the penalties, and the potential for double jeopardy and other constitutional violations. In fact, the first 200 RICO cases brought to trial did not involve the mafia, and many cases since the U.S. government's efforts to attack the mafia have invoked RICO. This can be attributed, in part, to the fact that the OCCA did not define the term "organized crime," but rather used vaguely defined terms of "enterprise" and "pattern of racketeering." As a result, RICO has been invoked in a number of investigations involving public corruption, computer theft rings, street gangs, terrorists, and others.

In addition, appeals have been made to the courts about the severity of the penalties associated with RICO, suggesting the penalties may violate the Eighth Amendment of the U.S. Constitution, which is the right against "cruel and unusual" punishment. These challenges are rooted in the fact that the criminal acts defined as racketeering activities under RICO are carrying a 20-year prison sentence, yet many of these violations, if charged outside of RICO, would not carry a 20-year prison term. Therefore, it is argued that the sentences are disproportionate. This, coupled with the fact that most individuals charged under RICO must by definition have two or more criminal violations to establish a pattern of racketeering, has led to prison terms amounting to life in prison.

Another concern about the penalties is related to the provisions on asset forfeiture. Assets seized by the federal government are often sold at auctions with the profits from the sale being used to supplement the law enforcement agency's budget. In addition, seized property has been maintained and used by the federal government for undercover operations. It is less suspicious if an undercover agent appears to own an expensive home, sports cars, and so forth when developing his or her bona fides with a drug trafficker or others. Nonetheless, this has raised the concern by some that the government may use RICO in order to generate a profit or some other benefit, amounting to what critics suggest are profit-driven incentives on what cases to investigate and prosecute.

Other claims of constitutional rights violations stemming from RICO have included violations of the First Amendment's right to assembly and the Fifth Amendment's right not to be tried twice for the same offense (i.e., the double jeopardy clause). For instance, an element of RICO that must be proved by the U.S. government is that the defendant was associated "in fact" with the criminal enterprise. This element has been criticized as a violation of the First Amendment right to assembly because the law in essence makes it a crime to be a member or associate of a criminal enterprise. RICO has been challenged on the notion that it violates the Fifth Amendment's right against double jeopardy, as well, because the government must prove that the defendant committed two or more criminal offenses over a 10-year period. This has raised the prospects that previous criminal offenses, which the defendant has already been punished for, may be used in a new trial to demonstrate that the offender has been engaged in a pattern of racketeering. Despite the numerous challenges brought against RICO, the U.S. Supreme Court has continuously upheld the provisions of RICO, at times suggesting it was up to Congress, not the courts, to restrict or correct any problems with the legislation.

RICO is a powerful legislative tool for federal law enforcement in its efforts to combat organized crime. It has been successfully used to cripple the American mafia in the United States and has been used to bring terrorists from the Black Liberation Party, gang members from Mara Salvatrucha (MS13), and others to justice. However, the law is not without controversy. A number of constitutional concerns have been raised since the law was first enacted in 1970. Since its inception, many have called for legislative reform, and others have called for it to be abolished or its use restricted.

David A. Marvelli

See also: Fifth Amendment; J. Edgar Hoover (1895–1972), Director of the FBI; Wiretapping

Further Reading

Blakey, G. R., and B. Gettings. "Racketeer Influenced and Corrupt Organizations (RICO): Basic Concepts—Criminal and Civil Remedies." *Temple Law Quarterly* 53 (1980): 1009–1043.

Marion, N. E. *Government versus Organized Crime.* Upper Saddle River, NJ: Pearson, 2008.

Raab, S. *Five Families: The Rise, Decline, and Resurgence of America's Most Powerful Mafia Empires.* New York: Thomas Dunne Books, 2006.

U.S. Department of Justice. *Criminal RICO: 18 U.S.C. §§ 1961–1968: A Manual for Federal Prosecutors.* Washington, DC: U.S. Government Press, 2009.

Part 4: A New Mandate for Exercising Police Power (1975–2000)

WILSON AND KELLING'S BROKEN WINDOWS THEORY

"Broken windows" is a criminological theory by George Kelling and James Q. Wilson. It describes a socio-psychological process by which perceptions of social and physical disorder lead to more serious levels of crime. It states that the reduction of petty offenses and disorderly conduct such as vandalism, littering, and public drinking will reduce and prevent more significant crimes. Police have used the theory to justify a variety of interventions—from zealous stop-question-frisk practices, to 3-1-1 call centers to report disorderly conditions, and police-led neighborhood beautification projects. As an influential idea in urban policing, the broken windows theory is not without controversy.

Kelling and Wilson (1982) use the metaphor of a building with a broken window to describe how, if a window is broken or damaged and then left unrepaired, additional windows will soon be broken. Some areas are frequented by determined window-breakers. Other areas are populated by window-lovers. The unrepaired broken window signals that no one cares about the area. Breaking more windows costs nothing. Broken windows signify to the public that negligence is acceptable on that property and that they are free to do as they please. The same applies to the link in communities between disorderliness and more serious crime.

The broken windows theory suggests public forms of physical and social disorder (i.e., graffiti, litter, aggressive panhandling, and solicitous prostitutes) increase fear and crime, both directly and indirectly. Neighborhoods and their appearances are significant to those who live and socialize within the borders of the community. A community's appearance has long been thought to directly influence an individual's perception and actions. For example, if a neighborhood appears to be shabby and run down, people in the community may act negatively. This usually instills fear in residents. However, the fear of crime is usually more rampant than the actual likelihood of it. Due to the fear, though, a psychological distress affects people in these communities and invites would-be criminals.

Due to such a great fear of crime, personal activities within the neighborhoods become restricted, dissatisfaction lingers through the neighborhood, and the overall quality of life diminishes. Kelling and Wilson stated that residents living in deprived areas become less attached to their neighborhoods, thus creating a cycle of fear and withdrawal from the community. A broken window represents uncontrolled, deviant behaviors that can attract offenders. It also suggests to the non–criminally inclined that they should stay away.

Intellectual Roots of Broken Windows

The broken windows theory derives from Kelling's experience with two seminal police experiments—the Newark Foot Patrol Experiment and the Kansas City Preventative Patrol Experiment. The preventative patrol experiment was conducted in 1972, and it concluded that this ubiquitous patrol tactic—police patrol in automobiles—had no effect on crime or citizen satisfaction. This groundbreaking study encouraged other forward-thinking police chiefs to consider other ways of policing their communities and opened the door to further research on police efficacy.

In 1981, Kelling and his colleagues published their findings of a similar study—this time of foot patrols in Newark. By varying the amount of foot patrols in each beat, Kelling found no effect on crime. They did find, however, that police foot patrols increased citizen satisfaction and reduced their fear—both worthwhile outcomes for the police profession as it moved toward a stronger community orientation. Kelling's observations of foot patrol officers negotiating with citizens the rules of the

Detroit police chief Ralph Godbee and author George Kelling are interviewed in Detroit. Kelling, a senior fellow from the New York–based Manhattan Institute for Policy Research, visits Detroit twice each month and consults with Godbee on the benefits of putting more officers on foot patrol and focusing on issues that might appear insignificant in a city with one of the highest crime rates in the nation. (AP Photo/Carlos Osorio)

streets inspired the broken windows metaphor that he and Wilson wrote about in 1982.

Kelling and Wilson were not, however, the first to posit a link between fear, crime, and disorder. Famous Stanford Prison experimenter Philip Zimbardo, for example, conducted an experiment in 1969, which demonstrated the broken windows process in action. In it, Zimbardo explained the relationship between different neighborhood environments and crime. He began by stripping two cars of their license plates, opening their hoods, breaking a single window in each, and leaving them in two different environments—one defined by anonymity (the Bronx), the other more representative of a conscientious community (Palo Alto). In the Bronx community, in which anonymity was more prevalent, people stripped and vandalized the car within minutes. No further damage was done to the car parked in Palo Alto over the five-day experiment. This experiment laid the groundwork for the broken window theory's explanation of the relationship between lower levels of disorder, more serious disorder, and the processes people follow in helping to maintain order or in contributing to disorder.

Kelling also attributes his ideas about the theory to the work of urbanologist Jane Jacobs, whose influential book *The Death and Life of Great American Cities* about the relationship between city environments and human behavior. In her book, Jacobs describes how the layout of city streets and sidewalks affect the flow of personal interactions that can produce pro-social or deviant activities. In 1979, sociologist Nathan Glazer wrote about the interplay among subway car graffiti, perceptions of uncontrolled environments, and the sense of danger they produce.

Though Kelling and Wilson's 1982 article was not the first to discuss such relationships, their broken window metaphor went hand-in-hand with the increasingly popular community policing movement to make change more palpable to police departments looking to improve their service to the community. Their metaphor aided police administrators in understanding the relationship between fear, crime, and disorder. It also suggested to line-officer supervisors tangible tactics they could employ in carrying out the theory.

Skogan (1992) later expanded upon the process of neighborhood disorder, its detrimental effects, fear, and crime and described nontraditional ways for police to deal with community concerns over what are sometimes referred to as quality-of-life offenses. More recently, Wagers, Sousa, and Kelling (2008) assessed the main ideas of broken windows and offered greater insight into the theory's implications for crime, policing, and neighborhood order.

Practical Applications of Broken Windows

The theory itself echoes many of the bedrock principles and practices established by the founder of modern policing, Sir Robert Peel, whose police sought to prevent crime and disorder through non-forceful community engagement. In the modern United States, police departments' applications of the broken windows theory have taken various forms. They are all generally motivated by the goals of reducing crime and fear and enhancing the quality of life for residents. One of the most enthusiastic and well-known champions of broken windows policing is William Bratton, who has served as commissioner or chief of police departments in Boston (1993–1994), New York City (1994–1996; 2014–current), and Los Angeles (2002–2009). He also served as chief of police for city transit police in Boston and New York. From 1983 to 1986 Bratton was the Massachusetts Bay Transportation Authority chief of police, and from 1990 to 1992, he served as chief of the New York City Transit Police.

In each of these posts, Bratton heralded the core notion of the broken windows theory—signs of social and physical disorder lead to heightened fear and more serious criminal activity. Each of Bratton's tenures is defined by his encouraging the police department to engage the community, and to pay attention to petty crimes such as vandalism, graffiti, and public drunkenness. This resulted in reduced levels of crime and fear. Many of Bratton's subordinates have carried on his broken windows police tactics in their own tenures as leaders in police departments in Philadelphia, Miami, Newark, and Chicago.

One of the pejorative names applied to broken windows policing is zero-tolerance policing. As the name suggests, this policing tactic takes away the ability of the patrol officer to use his or her judgment when responding to a lower-level offense, which is often a highly discretionary police activity. Under a zero-tolerance approach, police officers can sometimes be seen as using their power aggressively, brutally, and relentlessly. Oftentimes, the zero-tolerance approach forces police to make arrests or write citations for lower-level offenses, instead of using alternative methods of responding to and preventing such illegal behavior.

There are times, however, when such an implementation of the broken windows theory may be appropriate. The New York City Transit Authority's zero tolerance for subway car graffiti in the late 1980s is a good example of how zero tolerance for such disorderly acts can prevent disorder from spiraling out of control. A few years later, in conjunction with a zero tolerance approach to subway car graffiti, police famously used multiple tactics to respond to the lower-level offense of fare-beating and, in turn, helped to usher in a precipitous decline in the numbers of serious crimes such as aggravated assaults, robberies, and homicide. The key to determining which application of broken windows policing is most appropriate depends upon police having productive relationships with their communities.

An important constitutional, but increasingly controversial, method of responding to quality-of-life offenses is commonly referred to as "stop and frisk," but a more accurate name for the tactic is "stop, question, and frisk." It is sometimes known as a Terry stop, from the 1968 Supreme Court case *Terry v. Ohio*, which ruled police can stop a person if there is reasonable suspicion that the person is involved in criminal activity. If the officer determines through a person's actions and answers to the officer's questions that he or she may be carrying a weapon, then the officer has the right to frisk the subject for said weapon for safety reasons.

In practice, and as supported by the broken windows theory, the Terry stop is used to prevent more serious crimes (especially urban gun violence) in three ways. By engaging citizens whom police have reasonable suspicion to believe are involved in an offense sets the tone that someone cares about an area and that further offending will not be tolerated. To relate it to the broken window metaphor, someone is fixing the broken window because they care about maintaining an orderly area. Secondly, when stopping citizens for a lower-level offense, police may find probable cause of even more serious wrongdoing, such as an illegally held firearm or a person with an arrest warrant. Finally, Terry stops also have a deterrent effect. When people know that police will take such behavior seriously, there is less chance people will engage in criminal behavior such as illegally carrying a firearm.

Jenkins and DeCarlo (2015) demonstrate how police departments have used the broken windows theory in communities to drastically reduce serious crime in Boston, Los Angeles, Milwaukee, and Newark. In Milwaukee, for example, police increased the number of pedestrian and motor vehicle stops, while at the same time reducing street robberies, motor vehicle offenses, *and* citizen complaints against the police. Kelling and Coles (1996) present multiple, successful, community-based approaches for preventing crime and enhancing the quality of life in cities by attending to physical and social disorder.

Terry stops (and broken windows policing, by proxy) came under fire in 2013 when a federal court ruled in *Floyd v. City of New York* that the practice as enacted by the New York Police Department (NYPD) was racially biased and, therefore, unconstitutional. Subsequent events in Ferguson, Missouri, Staten Island, New York, and North Charleston, South Carolina, where Black men died as a result of police stopping them on probable cause that they committed minor offenses, have led some to conclude that broken windows policing leads to police abuse of power. Indeed, much of the current debate about police power revolves around the extent to which police target individuals based on extra-legal, non-behavioral factors or whether police operate in areas of crime and disorder hotspots that also happen to have higher concentrations of socio-economically disadvantaged and non-White residents.

One way to ensure that police respond in the appropriate ways and to the right types of problems is the technological and administrative innovation of Computer Statistics (CompStat). Created by the NYPD in the 1990s, CompStat is a computerized system of tracking, mapping, and analyzing commonalities among crimes. The information is then used to inform administrative and strategic goals related to the allocation of resources and tactics based on where crime concentrates. This practice developed contemporaneously to the height of broken windows policing in New York City and helped police see for the first time how crime and disorder clustered in certain areas and at specific times. A similar and new program, called RespectStat, allows police to better understand the affect their practices have on community perceptions of the police. The CompStat and RespectStat programs can be used together to define the quantity and clustering of crime, while also ensuring that police and the community have common definitions of what constitutes a problem and a worthwhile intervention.

To this day, Kelling and Wilson's broken windows theory is regarded as one of the most important theories to be applied to policing. Its underlying idea—take care of little things and the big things follow—makes intuitive sense to many. For that reason, it has influenced other parts of everyday life. From keeping a clean workspace, to improving one's health, or fighting piracy, the broken windows metaphor has been cited as useful in explaining how attention to minor acts results in payoffs in other, more substantial areas. Although various applications of the broken windows theory to policing will remain topics of debate, there is little doubt that police will continue to do precisely as the theory suggests—pay attention to community concerns regarding signs of physical and social disorder, the so-called minor offenses that deteriorate the fabric of neighborhood life.

John Sember and Michael J. Jenkins

See also: Community Policing Today; Eric Garner Case in New York City and Subsequent Tensions; Sir Robert Peel and Principles of Modern Policing; *Terry v. Ohio*; William Bratton (1947–), Police Commissioner; Zero Tolerance Policy

Further Reading

Glazer, Nathan. "On Subway Graffiti in New York." *National Affairs* 54 (1979). http://www
.nationalaffairs.com/doclib/20080528_197905401onsubwaygraffitiinnewyorknathan
glazer.pdf.

Jacobs, Jane. *The Death and Life of Great American Cities.* New York: Vintage, 1992.

Jenkins, Michael J., and John DeCarlo. *Police Leaders in the New Community Problem-Solving Era.* Durham, NC: Carolina Academic Press, 2015.

Kelling, G. L., and C. M. Coles. *Fixing Broken Windows: Restoring Order and Reducing Crime in our Communities.* New York: Martin Kessler Books, 1996.

Kelling, G. L., and J. Wilson. "Broken Windows: The Police and Neighborhood Safety." *Atlantic Monthly* (March 1982): 29–38.

Skogan, W. *Disorder and Decline: Crime and the Spiral of Decay in American Cities.* Los Angeles: University of California, 1992.

Wagers, M., W. Sousa, and G. Kelling. "Broken Windows." In *Environmental Criminology and Crime Analysis*, edited by R. Wortley and L. Mazerolle, 247–261. London: Willan Publishing, 2008.

FLEEING FELON LEGISLATION

The phrase "fleeing felon legislation" describes laws that reflect the appropriate behavior of police officers, including the amount of discretion they possess, while in pursuit of individuals who are believed to have committed felony offenses. These laws often focus on the amount of force that law-enforcement representatives may use under specific circumstances. In many situations, officers may utilize deadly force during their pursuits of people who are thought to have engaged in felonious or serious criminal behavior. This does not apply, however, to individuals who are accused of misdemeanors, infractions, violations, or other less serious offenses. Policies about how police are supposed to behave during encounters with suspects who are running away from them are commonly outlined by law enforcement agencies and tend to be more restrictive than statutes or written laws passed by a legislative body. Some states have enacted laws that enhance criminal penalties for suspects who evade or flee police. When challenging fleeing felon legislation, critics often assert that law enforcement's use of force was unwarranted and cite violations of the Fourth and Fourteenth amendments. Several U.S. Supreme Court cases have helped define how police are supposed to act when dealing with suspects who are running away or escaping. What is considered "reasonable" force is often the issue at hand.

The use of deadly force by police may be defined as the action taken to shoot and kill suspects who are threats to the safety of victims, officers, or the public. Before the mid-1980s, there were four established deadly force rules that law enforcement agencies recognized in the pursuit of fleeing suspects, including the Any Felony Rule, Defense of Life Rule, Forcible Felony Rule, and Model Penal Code. The Any Felony Rule allowed officers to use any means necessary to prevent felony suspects from escaping arrest. It was the most commonly followed rule across jurisdictions the United States, although most law enforcement agencies had stricter internal guidelines that superseded it. The Defense of Life Rule allowed officers to use deadly force, but only when it was justifiable to save human lives. The Forcible Felony Rule allowed officers to use deadly force, but only in circumstances in which suspects had committed forcible felonies or serious offenses where violence or physical force against others was used. Examples included murder, rape, arson, kidnapping, and armed robbery. The Model Penal Code allowed officers to use deadly force, but only when deadly force was used or threatened by suspects while engaging in crime and if substantial risk of death or serious bodily harm existed from failing to immediately apprehend suspects. Many observers believed that the Forcible Felony Rule and Model Penal Code together served as a balance to an extreme found in the Any Felony Rule and Defense of Life Rule.

The use of deadly force was considered a legitimate police response to suspected felony offenses until it was addressed by the U.S. Supreme Court in *Tennessee v. Garner* (1985). On the evening of October 3, 1974, Memphis police officers Leslie Wright and Elton Hymon responded to a call from a woman who claimed that her neighbor's house had been burglarized. At the scene, Hymon came across a young man who was believed to be around the age of 17 and about 5'6" in the backyard. Hymon called out to the teen and ordered him to stop, but the young man ran toward the fence surrounding the backyard and attempted to jump it. In response, Hymon shot at the young man, hitting him in the back of the head. The young man, Edward Garner, subsequently died. Garner was 15 years old, 5 feet 2 inches tall, and weighed 110 pounds. He had stolen $10 and a purse. At the time, Hymon's decision to fire his weapon was authorized under Tennessee law, as well as the Memphis Police Department's policy guidelines. Nonetheless, Garner's father filed a lawsuit against the city of Memphis and Hymon for Fourth Amendment violations, arguing that Garner's death did not afford him due process. The District Court found that Hymon was acting in good faith, and the Tennessee statute, which permitted officers to use all necessary means to apprehend fleeing suspects, was constitutional. The Court of Appeals for the Sixth Circuit subsequently reversed this decision. In a 6–3 decision, the Supreme Court affirmed the Sixth Circuit, finding the Tennessee statute unconstitutional because it allowed police to use deadly force against unarmed, fleeing felons. The Supreme Court decided the Fourth Amendment declared deadly force illegal unless it was necessary to stop the escape of fleeing felons and unless officers have probable cause to think suspects present threats of violence. With this decision, the Court essentially abolished the common law rule for deadly force and supported the Model Penal Code with respect to apprehending fleeing suspects. The Supreme Court also established a "reasonableness requirement" in this case, which called for a balance between the intrusion of suspects' rights and government's law enforcement interests. In other words, the Supreme Court pointed to a need to establish when it is worth violating a person's constitutional rights for the safety of police and the public.

Following *Tennessee v. Garner*, many cases defined the reasonableness requirement. However, the Supreme Court used the reasonableness test in *Graham v. Connor* (1989), when Dethorne Graham sued police officers after sustaining injuries during his arrest. Graham was experiencing a diabetic reaction and stopped at a small store to buy some juice. When he realized the line was too long, he left suddenly, which caused officers at the store to become suspicious and decide to conduct an investigative stop of Graham. During the stop, Graham allegedly began to act belligerently and was handcuffed by officers before fainting. He awoke to find cuts on his wrist, a broken foot, and a bruised forehead. In ruling on the case, the Supreme Court determined that careful attention must be paid to each individual case. Details, such as the severity of the suspected criminal behavior, threats posed to officers and the public by suspects, and whether or not individuals are truly resisting or attempting to evade arrest, were said to be relevant. The Supreme Court also found that "objective reasonableness" should be considered. That is, in judging whether use of force was appropriate in a given situation, the viewpoint of an objective officer on the scene must be used, rather than an understanding of a situation after it has happened. In this way, this federal paradigm to judge the acceptability of police use of force acknowledges that police often need to make quick decisions in situations that escalate rapidly. Due to the recent high-profile cases of Eric Garner and Freddie Gray, who died during separate encounters with law enforcement, public attention to the reasonableness requirement, objective reasonableness, and police behavior toward suspects has increased.

More recently, in *City of Jackson v. Brister* (2003), the Mississippi Supreme Court found police officers liable for disregarding public safety when they engaged in a traffic pursuit of an individual suspected of forgery that ended in the death of a young woman. The Court ruled that the reasonableness requirement had not been met, as the fleeing individual was a nonviolent suspect and not an immediate threat to officers or the public. Another important case relevant to police behavior and fleeing persons was *Scott v. Harris* (2007). In March 2001, 19-year-old Victor Harris was recorded by police as driving at an excessive speed down a Georgia road. Although an officer attempted a traffic stop, Harris sped up and attempted to evade. Multiple officers were called into the subsequent pursuit, including Timothy Scott who became the driver of the lead pursuit vehicle. Following a mid-chase incident in which Harris collided with one of the patrol vehicles in a parking lot, Scott called for permission to ram the suspect's vehicle from behind with his car in an attempt to cause Harris to lose control. Scott's supervisor approved the request, and Scott attempted the maneuver, causing the car that Harris was driving to run off the road, overturn, and crash. Harris survived the crash, but he was left paralyzed from the neck down. He sued Scott for violation of his Fourth Amendment rights, stating that Scott had used excessive force.

Some commentators pointed out that speeding did not normally defend the use of deadly force, and some observers felt that Harris did not need to be seized at the time of the chase. And yet, others contended that Harris was a threat to the officers and to safety of public because he could have harmed other motorists or pedestrians. So, do law enforcement officers who stop a high-speed chase by ramming a fleeing suspect's vehicle violate the Fourth Amendment's protection against unreasonable seizure? Apparently, they do not. Using the reasonableness requirement, as well as objective reasonableness, the Supreme Court ruled in favor of Scott. The 8-1 decision stated that Scott's decision to end the pursuit by ramming the suspect's car stopped potential harm to other officers and citizens and a split-second decision was appropriate and necessary. In its ruling, the Supreme Court considered the need to prevent the potential harm that Harris posed alongside the high likelihood that he would be harmed by Scott's use of force. Thus, the Supreme Court held that police officers who utilized deadly force to prevent harm to innocent people were acting in a reasonable manner, even if that meant exposing a fleeing suspect to a serious risk of harm.

David Patrick Connor and Emily M. Malterud

See also: Deadly Force; Eric Garner Case in New York City and Subsequent Tensions; Fourth Amendment; Freddie Gray Case; Police Brutality

Further Reading

City of Jackson v. Brister, 838 So. 2d 274 (Miss 2003).
Graham v. Connor, 490 U.S. 386 (1989).
Scott v. Harris, 550 U.S. 372 (2007).
Tennessee v. Garner, 471 U.S. 1 (1985).
Tucker, Eric. "When Can Police Use Lethal Force against a Fleeing Suspect?" *PBS Newshour*, April 8, 2015. http://www.pbs.org/newshour/rundown/can-police-use-lethal-force -fleeing-suspect.
Walker, Jeffery T., and Craig Hemmens. *Legal Guide for Police: Constitutional Issues*. New York: Routledge, 2015.

RODNEY KING BEATING AND RIOTS

Rodney King (1965–2012) became famous in 1991 after receiving a brutal beating by Los Angeles police. A bystander videotaped the beating from his apartment window. This incident sparked much chaos and controversy at the time, and it is still discussed today, especially in light of more recent incidents in which White police

Brutally beaten by four White Los Angeles police officers after being pulled over while driving, African American Rodney King became a symbol of police brutality and racial prejudice. Angered by the acquittal of the officers, Los Angeles erupted into riots that lasted four days and left 54 people dead. Here, King meets with the press on April 29, 1992, in the midst of the riots, with a plea to the city: "Can't we all get along?" (AP Photo/Brennan Linsley)

officers have been accused of using excessive or deadly force on African Americans. Because Rodney King's beating was captured on video, it also marked one of the first times that the public was able to witness and weigh in on such behavior, becoming the impetus for rioting at the time and racial tensions that still persist today.

On March 3, 1991, Rodney King, who was on parole for robbing a convenience store, was speeding and driving erratically. The California Highway Patrol attempted to pull King over. However, instead of stopping, King led the troopers on a 110-mile chase. Eventually King exited the highway and drove into a Los Angeles neighborhood, at which point more police officers joined the pursuit. Four of the police who responded (officers Powell, Wind, Briseno, and Koon) did not realize they were being video-recorded, as they eventually dragged King from his vehicle and kicked and beat him until he was unconscious. George Holliday, an uninvolved citizen, recorded the incident from his nearby apartment window. Such video recording and "citizen journalism" (Maurantonio 2014, 741) was virtually unheard of in 1991, and this amateur-made video immediately became the focal point of a national conversation, a conversation that continues 25 years later. The video has been referred to as "one of the most watched pieces of amateur video in history" (Coffin 2012; as cited in Maurantonio 2014, 740).

The primary problem with the video is that it did not begin at the beginning of King's interaction with police. According to police reports, after police were able to stop King from driving, they ordered him to step out of his vehicle and lie down on his stomach on the ground. King allegedly refused to obey this order, at which point the officers attempted to physically force King to lie down. King, who was alleged to have been on several drugs, including PCP (commonly known as angel dust), which police would later report gave him "superhuman strength" (Vogelman 1993, 571), resisted police and became combative. At that point, Officer Koon drew his Taser and shot King with 50,000-volt Taser darts.

The point at which Officer Koon shot King with the Taser is the point at which the video begins. King then gets up and charges Officer Powell. The next several minutes of video show the officers swinging metal batons at King's face, knocking him to the ground, kicking him, and stepping on his back. Reports state that officers struck King a total of 56 times until he finally put his hands behind his back to be handcuffed. The beating left King with a shattered eye socket and cheekbone, multiple skull fractures, a concussion, broken teeth, injuries to both knees, kidney injuries, facial nerve damage that left his face partially paralyzed, permanent brain damage, and a broken leg. And after the incident, King had a permanent limp.

Eleven days later the four officers involved in the beating were indicted for assault. The defense argued for a change of venue for their trial and was successful in having it moved from Los Angeles County to Ventura County, which has a higher proportion of Caucasian residents, as compared with residents of color, and is more affluent. In April 1992, a jury that included no African Americans acquitted three of the four officers. The jury was not able to reach a verdict regarding Officer Powell, and a retrial ended in a hung jury. Ironically, the video that appeared to contain the most damning evidence possible against the police officers was primarily responsible for their acquittals. The video was dissected frame by frame during the trial, enabling the defense to make the case that King continued to be a threat to officers throughout their interaction, and justifying the officers' use of force.

The acquittals incited riots by angry African Americans in Los Angeles—riots that included looting stores and burning buildings. King was televised three days into the riots, asking perhaps one of the most famous questions in recent history in an attempt to end the violence: "People, I just want to say, you know, can we all get along?" The case raised questions of morality, of whether King was a victim or a hero, and of procedural justice. The change of venue and the acquittals of the officers had many in society questioning not only the fairness of police, but also that of the criminal justice system with regard to the outcomes and treatment of African Americans. The officers involved were eventually indicted for violating King's constitutional rights. Officers Wind and Briseno were acquitted, and officers Koon and Powell were convicted. The latter two were sentenced to two and a half years in prison.

Rodney King became an extremely well-known anti-hero following the incident. He won $3.8 million after suing the city of Los Angeles, as the city employed the officers involved. He had further run-ins with the law for crimes, including hit-and-run driving, driving under the influence, domestic assault, and the use of PCP. The world watched as King struggled with drug and alcohol abuse, appearing on television shows such as *Celebrity Rehab* in 2008 and *Sober House* in 2009. Ultimately, many were saddened to hear that, on June 17, 2012, King drowned at the bottom of his swimming pool at the age of 47. His drowning ended a life characterized by struggle—a life most would know nothing about if it were not for that amateur video captured by George Holliday in 1991. Long before society became accustomed to immediate access of information, the public had access to information that allowed them to judge the facts of the King incident for themselves, as the video was played and replayed.

The case was a fascinating harbinger of events to come; no one in 1991 could have anticipated that in another 25 years, video-recorded incidents between police and citizens would become so commonplace that police departments across the United States would be deciding whether they need to equip their officers with body cameras at all times. Anyone who remembers the Rodney King beating likely saw the video on news channels hundreds of times. Professors in social science classes in the 1990s played for their students VHS recordings of the incident, taped from their own televisions, to use as conversation starters about race relations and police brutality, conversations that are all too familiar to students in 2016. Now, video-recordings of African Americans killed by law enforcement are often immediately available via social media to anyone with a smart-phone or a computer, providing information and insight that increase the quantity and intensity of these conversations, regardless of the outcomes of the cases.

The Rodney King video sparked discussions of morality, of whether King was a victim, a hero, or a dangerous criminal whose "victimhood" was a myth created by the media. The subsequent trial, from its change of venue to its acquittal of the officers, led most Americans to question the validity of the court process and raised issues of procedural justice. But perhaps most importantly, it was the precursor to many years of discussions about the right for the public to view firsthand how police interact with civilians through the lens of race relations.

Deborah A. Eckberg

See also: Police Brutality; Racial Profiling; Use of Tasers

Further Reading

Balko, Radley. "As Ferguson Waits, Some Lessons from the Rodney King Riots." The Watch (opinion), *The Washington Post*, posted on November 18, 2014. https://www.washington post.com/news/the-watch/wp/2014/11/18/as-ferguson-waits-some-lessons-from-the -rodney-king-riots.

Maurantonio, Nicole. "Remembering Rodney King: Myth, Racial Reconciliation, and Civil Rights History." *Journalism and Mass Communication Quarterly* 91, no. 4 (2014): 740–755. doi:10.1177/1077699014550094.

Mullen, Elizabeth, and Linda J. Skitka. "When Outcomes Prompt Criticisms of Procedures: An Analysis of the Rodney King Case." *Analyses of Social Issues and Public Policy* 6, no. 1 (2006): 1–14.

Rabinowitz, Paula. "Street/Crime: From Rodney King's Beating to Michael Brown's Shooting." *Cultural Critique* 90 (2015): 143–147.

Vogelman, Lawrence. "The Big Black Man Syndrome: The Rodney King Trial and the Use of Racial Stereotypes in the Courtroom." *Fordham Urban Law Journal* 20, no. 3 (1993): 571–578.

"LAW AND ORDER" AS A POPULAR POLITICAL SLOGAN

Since its inception, the slogan "law and order" has influenced criminal justice legislation, policy and practices. Politicians rely on the slogan and other phrases related to it to demonstrate that they assume a tough stance on crime and through their influence will provide, through legislation, safety for their constituents. The theme of law and order is now more than 50 years old and has failed to achieve its stated objectives. Supporters have relied upon false or incorrect premises, which compound the confusion to general beliefs about crime, criminals, and justice. The law-and-order agenda has contributed to greater failure in the criminal justice system.

In his 1964 presidential campaign, Barry Goldwater introduced the idea of "law and order." Upon becoming the Republican candidate, he warned Americans that there was a "growing menace to personal safety, to life, to limb, and to property" and that there would be "rioting in the streets." The law and order campaign slogan would be, from that time forward, a repetitive election campaign theme for conservative Republicans and Democrats. Some notable candidates and future presidents, through their emphasis on the "law and order" message in their administrations, would ensure its political permanence. They included presidents Richard Nixon, Gerald Ford, Ronald Regan, George H. W. Bush, and Bill Clinton. The popularity of the slogan was not lost on other non-political figures. In 1989, Donald Trump bought full-page ads in four New York City newspapers with the headline "Bring Back the Death Penalty! Bring Back our Police!" This followed the Central Park Jogger case (1989), which resulted in the wrongful conviction of five young Black and Hispanic males. The influence of the law-and-order theme after more than 50 years has lost little of its clout.

Politicians have stood behind the "law and order" slogan, assuming a posture that they would not be soft on crime, that citizens were incapable of defending themselves, and that all crime should be dealt with swiftly and with certainty by law enforcement, corrections, and the courts. The rhetoric would lead to a shift in law-enforcement approaches from the Due Process Model to the Crime Control Model. The shift is notable in legislation and changes in policy and operations that would affect all aspects of criminal justice.

The late 1960s and 1970s saw the intersection of crime, riots, and racial activism as contributing factors to threats of safety. Crime was interpreted as pathological for Black males, who were presented as criminals, even if Whites committed the crime. With that interpretation, it appeared clear that law and order was needed to restore stability in the United States.

Rhetoric, followed by legislation and policy changes, became the tools of key decision makers in the state and federal legislatures and in the executive branch of government. New legislation would replace, augment, and create fundamental laws to ensure a more conservative Crime Control Model. The legislation provided enhancements for law enforcement, statutes that redefined crime, mandated harsher sentences, limited judicial discretion, eliminated or curtailed the use of parole, and restricted or eliminated correctional programming. Some examples of the legislation included the 1973 New York Rockefeller Drug Laws; the legalization of the death penalty; Clinton's Violent Crime Control and Law Enforcement Act of 1994; the 1994 Federal Death Penalty Act, which increased the number of offenses that would be death-penalty eligible to 60; and the Comprehensive Crime Control Act of 1984, which eliminated federal parole.

Of course, what was enacted as practice was mirrored in the news and popularized in the media, sensationalized by talk shows, and reinforced for the public in television and movies with little regard for content accuracy or for correct interpretation by the public. The media would headline scandal and crime that was the more astonishing, extraordinary, or exceptional. The appearance was that such crime was the norm and plagued us, and there was nowhere safe. Television shows and movies about crime and fighting crime not only became more graphic but also came to dominate the viewing screen. They gave the appearance that law enforcement was fighting an uphill battle to protect society from within and without. An early example would be *Miami Vice*. In time more crime-fighting dramas such as NCIS would become prominent as long-running series that would spin off other series with locations from coast to coast across the United States.

The theme of law and order progressively preyed on the basest fears of Americans. It emphasized that the crime rate (which fundamentally remained unchanged) confirmed that we were constantly threatened by a lawless society, that current criminal justice practices were a failure, and that a more conservative and punitive legal/correctional solution versus a social solution were required to combat crime. Resources were progressively directed to fighting crime while social services were cut or their funding reduced, including provisions for primary and secondary education.

The fear of crime gained greater force with the publicized and politicized events that blended truth and misconception. There is perhaps no greater example than the infamous declaration by Dr. Robert Martinson that "Nothing works." The phrase "Nothing works" attributed to an unknown academic, writing in a new academic journal (a source that normally has minimal popular readership) seemed to capture everyone's attention (the media, politicians, prosecutors, penologists, judges, and academics). The irony was that Martinson's comments would be taken out of context and misquoted and even published in college criminal justice textbooks. He never said, "Nothing works."

Penologists joined the discussion and decried the accusations that their work did no good. *Corrections Today*—the magazine of the American Correctional Association—published its longest article after interviewing every commissioner and secretary of corrections in the nation. The correctional administrators all argued that they did good work, but there was little of substance to support their contentions, or say just what their good work really accomplished, especially when reported recidivism rates ranged from about 40 percent to more than 60 percent. The quote continues to be used, although there has been greater clarification about its meaning. Nevertheless, it is "Nothing works" that keeps coming to the forefront in political circles, that is, it supports the claim that we are soft on crime, that crime is winning, that we need law and order.

A few years after Martinson, in 1986, what would be taken as personified proof that nothing works, a convict by the name of Willie Horton who was serving time for murder would not return from weekend prison furlough. In 1987 he would commit a brutal rape and pistol whipping of a couple.

The George H. W. Bush presidential campaign would capitalize on this event as perhaps no other in history, utilizing what have become known as the Bush/Dukakis attack ads. Michael Dukakis would be portrayed as a weak, ineffective governor who let a dangerous murderer out of prison to prey on society. Horton had the misfortune to have a countenance that could be identified as the face of crime—a face to fear. Race had already been implicated as a cause of rising crime, and now there was a Black man's face, a mug shot that would appear regularly on television, on the front page of newspapers and in textbooks. The Bush campaign went so far as to emphasize that his name was Willie and not William. Willie sounded more criminal than William, and Willie would not be forgotten. The name would repeatedly resurface and be associated with other scandals, as the example of what happens when we are not tough on crime. There have been several incidents in New Jersey where this has been the case. Either Governor Chris Christie has associated it with another politician (Senator Bonnie Watson Coleman), or it has been hurled back at him from spectators.

One of the other sensationalized crimes that would seemingly gain permanent traction nationally and internationally was the tragic case of Megan Kanka. To great fanfare, in 1994, then–New Jersey governor Christine Todd Whitman signed Megan's Law, which was the model for a national version and a law that other states would replicate. In 2016, New Jersey Congressman Chris Smith would see his bill for an international version of Megan's Law, which required the reporting of sex offenders (who might travel abroad) to other countries, go to President Barack Obama's desk for a signature. As a 2016 presidential candidate, Donald Trump would return to the law-and-order stage by proclaiming the need for it following a disturbance in Baltimore.

The consequences of politicizing law and order could not have been foreseen, nor could anyone have anticipated the enormous implications, including the establishment of a vast prison industrial complex. The new legislation never anticipated that it would be counterproductive, create homelessness, or be a burden on social services. The consequences of the law and order movement have affected the convicted, the accused, and society. The solutions to the threat of crime and criminals would be proposed by legislators and signed into law, even though it often would be oppositional to research. Policy would be written and made operational. The new solutions had every appearance of being pragmatic in their design and implementation. They included more effective police powers, better equipped police, and larger police forces, as well as criminal legislation that specifically defined more severe penalties and civil legislation that provided social consequences. What began with the drug laws to penalize drug offenders extended to education with the elimination of PELL grants to convicts and concomitantly reducing or eliminating education in prison. In addition, drug and other offenders would be additionally disenfranchised and could now be denied public housing, and all offenders would have to check the box that they had been charged with, arrested, or convicted of crime.

The fight for law and order through crime control that enhanced criminal and civil collateral consequences dominated the previous five decades while ignoring the underlying and systemic causes of crime as well as the evidence-based practices for prevention and reform.

The development of crime policy based on law and order has neither reduced crime nor contributed to public safety. The ideology scapegoated the lower class—specifically poor people of color—furthering racial and financial divisions. Once the sole province of conservative Republicans, the political agenda of law and order came to be adopted by Democratic politicians as well. The argument was no longer whether there should be a Crime Control Model or whether citizens should be accorded due process. The argument was how, to whom, and what measures the tools of the Crime Control Model could be applied. Some of the tools developed in order to achieve the goal of law and order include: increased elimination or curtailment of parole, increased use of the death penalty, mandatory sentencing, as well as the vilification of drugs (and those who use them). Another tool includes the creation of civil collateral consequences (which run into the hundreds for state and federal governments). This tool ensures that those who run afoul of the law could be disenfranchised and may not be forgiven, redeemed, or restored.

The politics of law and order have been remarkably successful for five decades, pushing to the side all challenges to the law-and-order agenda, even when empirical data demonstrated the falsehoods of the agenda and the failure that it created. Seemingly, the juggernaut of law and order would and has proceeded unabated. However, politicians and government officials did not anticipate the problem of how to shoulder the cost of that agenda.

The victories of law and order have come with a cost that was perhaps unforeseen in the beginning. Politicians and government officials alike would resort to tactics such as off-balance-sheet financing to hide the fiscal cost from voters. An example is to place the cost of vehicles in the treasury budget and not in correctional budget. The disenfranchisement of American citizens would be another matter as the ranks of the homeless in all major cities would grow, family members would become alienated from one another, and crime would continue unabated.

Since the recent election of Donald Trump, the call for law and order will probably gain prominence and remain a political platform staple.

Matthew J. Sheridan

See also: Chicago Police during the 1968 Democratic National Convention; Crime Control versus Due Process; Impact of the War on Drugs; Kerner Commission

Report on Race Riots and Police Response; Perceptions of Police Today; Police Misconduct during the L.A. Zoot Suit Riots; Racial Profiling; Rodney King Beating and Riots

Further Reading

Flamm, Michael W. *Law and Order: Street Crime, Civil Unrest, and the Crisis of Liberalism in the 1960s.* New York: Columbia University Press, 2005.

Hoffman, Peter B. "History of the Federal Parole System." U.S. Department of Justice, United States Parole Commission. May 2003 http://www.justice.gov/sites/default/files/uspc/legacy/2009/10/07/history.pdf.

Martinson, R. "What Works? Questions and Answers about Prison Reform." *The Public Interest* (Spring 1974): 22–54.

National Advisory Commission on Civil Disorders. *Report on Civil Disorders (The Kerner Report).* New York: Bantam Books, 1968.

Omnibus Crime Control and Safe Streets Act of 1968. Public Law 90–351.82 stat 197. (1968).

Platt, Anthony M. "Crime Rave." *Monthly Review: An Independent Socialist Magazine* 47, no. 2 (1995): 35–46.

Uniform Crime Reports. FBI. https://www.fbi.gov/about-us/cjis/ucr/ucr.

WILLIAM BRATTON (1947–), POLICE COMMISSIONER

William Bratton, former commissioner of the New York Police Department (NYPD), was born on October 6, 1947. At a young age, Bratton had a keen interest in law enforcement and management. He is known as an innovative leader who surrounds himself with the most competent talent available. Bratton has a reputation for transforming the culture and structure of his agencies, while simultaneously preventing and reducing crime. Bratton has served in numerous roles as a police officer and continues to be an influential force in American policing.

Career in Policing

Bratton has had a lengthy career in policing. His first law enforcement job was with the military during the Vietnam War. After graduating from Boston Technical High School in 1965, Bratton entered the U.S. Army where he served as a military police soldier for nearly five years. Although he was afforded the opportunity to participate in Officers' Training School, Bratton stayed true to his desire to become a police officer and turned down the offer.

In 1970, Bratton returned home from military service and was sworn in as a police officer with the Boston Police Department (BPD). He was promoted to the top of the BPD, becoming sergeant in 1975 and lieutenant in 1978. By 1980, Bratton became the youngest executive superintendent in the history of the BPD at the age of 32. Bratton has claimed that his time as second-in-command at the BPD allowed him to appreciate the role of data collection and analysis in assessing strategies to address crime. While the BPD was restructuring itself, Bratton was removed as executive

Police commissioner William Bratton speaks at a news conference May 9, 1994, in New York. Bratton was the former commissioner of the New York City Police (2014–2016), as well as Boston (1993–1994). He was Chief of the Los Angeles Police Department from 2002 to 2009. (AP Photo/Luc Novovitch)

superintendent and was subsequently assigned to a community liaison position. Some observers believe the reassignment of Bratton to a lower position on the BPD hierarchy was the result of him informing the media of his goal to ultimately become police commissioner. Bratton was later responsible for issues surrounding labor relations and 9-1-1 calls in a new liaison role.

Despite his misfortunes toward the end of his tenure at the BPD, Bratton persevered and became the chief of police for the Massachusetts Bay Transportation Authority (MBTA) in 1983. Bratton has described his time at the MBTA as a rewarding experience that allowed him to implement change and become an innovative leader. By 1986, however, he was ready for a new challenge and moved on to the Metropolitan District Commission Police (MDCP). Governor Michael Dukakis appointed Bratton as superintendent of the MDCP and asked him to focus on improving organizational integrity. Prior to Bratton's leadership, the MDCP had suffered from allegations of cheating by officers on promotion exams.

After restoring the positive reputation of the MDCP, in 1990, Bratton became the head of the New York City Transit Police (NYCTP). He was hired by the NYCTP to help establish effective crime control strategies on the subway system. In recent years, the subway system had experienced a significant increase in criminal and nuisance activities that made many community members feel uncomfortable and unsafe.

As a result, the number of people who utilized the subway system to travel had decreased. Crime rates drastically declined on the New York subway system only a few months into Bratton's reign.

In the early 1990s, Bratton returned to the BPD. He served as Superintendent in Chief of the BPD from 1992 until 1993, and he subsequently served as the Commissioner of the BPD for the last six months of 1993. Bratton brought Jack Maple, a former NYCTP lieutenant, with him to the BPD. Maple had created innovative crime-reduction strategies on the New York subway system under Bratton's supervision.

In 1994, Mayor Rudolph Giuliani appointed Bratton as the NYPD commissioner. Maple moved from the BPD to the NYPD with Bratton to serve as deputy commissioner. With the permission of Giuliani, Bratton adopted a broken windows approach to crime reduction. In other words, Bratton and his officers focused on the reduction and prevention of nuisance activities, as such efforts allegedly helped to create order and increase lawfulness, which was believed to stop more serious criminal behavior from taking place. Based on the ideas of James Wilson and George Kelling, the broken windows theory emphasizes the importance of focusing police efforts on smaller, petty offenses, such as aggressive panhandling, public intoxication, theft, vandalism, and possession of small amounts of illicit drugs, to deter lawbreakers from committing more serious crimes. The idea is that a focus on less serious offenses will lead communities to feel more secure, and potential perpetrators would become deterred as police presence increases. What is more, law-abiding citizens will begin to take pride in their communities and work with police to maintain law and order. At its core, broken windows theory seeks to empower community members to take back their neighborhoods from social disorganization and increase quality of life for citizens.

Maple also helped Bratton transform the NYPD through use of a new management system known as Computer Statistics (CompStat), which asserted that the use of timely and accurate data was important to the reduction and prevention of crime. CompStat utilized electronic crime mapping and analysis of detailed and up-to-date crime data to identify problem areas of the city. It required precinct commanders to oversee and be responsible for the crime rates in their districts. CompStat meetings were generally run by Maple and upper-level NYPD representatives, required precinct commanders to report on their districts' crime as well as what they were doing to address the problems, and provided a forum for data examination and alternative solutions. Many commentators have noted the intense questioning and interrogation that precinct commanders have endured during CompStat meetings.

In 1996, Bratton resigned from the NYPD. Some observers believe that his resignation came as the result of personal conflicts with Giuliani. It has been pointed out that Giuliani did not always support all of the reforms that were instituted by Bratton. However, others note that Giuliani did not appreciate that Bratton was getting most of the credit for New York City's decrease in crime. Before his departure from the NYPD, Bratton was under investigation for accepting several unauthorized trips from various businesses and individuals, and he was also under scrutiny for signing a book deal while serving as commissioner.

In 2002, Mayor James Hahn appointed Bratton as chief of the Los Angeles Police Department (LAPD). The overall crime rate in Los Angeles dropped for six consecutive years under Bratton's leadership. Despite his success in Los Angeles, Bratton has been criticized for absence on the job. According to some critics, Bratton was out of town for more than four months of the 2005 calendar year. Nonetheless, in 2007, he was reappointed by the Los Angeles Police Commission to an additional five-year term. However, after seven years at the LAPD, Bratton resigned from his position.

Bratton returned as the NYPD commissioner in 2013, and he stepped down on August 2, 2016. He was appointed by Mayor Bill de Blasio who ran on a promise of reforming stop-and-frisk practices and improving relations between minority communities and the NYPD. This appointment was surprising to some observers, as Bratton brought aggressive stop-and-frisk strategies to the NYPD during his previous reign. However, as evidence surfaced showing that the NYPD was stopping many law-abiding citizens each year (most of whom were Black and Latino), Bratton subsequently reversed his position on stop and frisk and contended that the approach was misused in New York City between 2002 and 2013 under Commissioner Ray Kelly. Many commentators have pointed out that the NYPD's stop-and-frisk practices raise serious concerns about legality, privacy, and racial profiling.

In March 2016, Bratton responded to Republican presidential candidate Ted Cruz who asserted that police should patrol and secure Muslim neighborhoods in order to prevent terrorist attacks. In his response, Bratton insinuated that Cruz was clueless with respect to effective policing strategies. Bratton also noted that providing police surveillance at each location where people congregate in a large jurisdiction like New York City would be impossible.

Reform Strategies

Throughout his career in policing, Bratton implemented unique reform strategies that frequently led to desired change. In the late 1970s, for instance, Bratton managed a BPD community policing program in the Fenway Park district. Although it was unusual at the time, Bratton held community meetings where residents could voice their concerns to his officers about problems in the neighborhood. Bratton quickly realized that what his officers saw as problems in the neighborhood were not always what local residents saw as problems. By gauging the perceptions of community members, Bratton learned that concerns often revolved around nuisance activities rather than criminal behavior. Some believe this may have inspired Bratton to adopt his broken windows approach to policing.

However, it was not until Bratton was the head of the NYCTP in the 1990s that he explicitly used broken windows principles. For example, at the time, the subway system transported many people who had not paid the fare to ride. Bratton organized a sweep of the subway system to target these violators. Plainclothes officers provided surveillance, arrested numerous violators at one time, handcuffed the violators together in a line, and walked them outside to a nearby mobile processing center.

Bratton instructed his media relations officers to promote the "bust bus" and shame fare violators. As it turned out, many of the violators who were arrested for fare evasion had outstanding warrants or weapons. This led to a 22-percent reduction in felonies in the subway system over a two-year period (Bratton and Knobler 1998).

In a span of 27 months during Bratton's initial tenure as the NYPD commissioner, major crime in New York City dropped more than 30 percent. From 1990 to 1998, murder rates in the city decreased 72 percent, and violent offenses were reduced by more than 50 percent (Shelden 2004). This trend began in the subway system and subsequently made its way to the streets. The sharp decrease in criminal behavior was attributed to Bratton's broken windows approach

The adoption and use of CompStat represented another unique way that Bratton accomplished crime prevention and reduction. Commonly utilized today by various law enforcement agencies, CompStat allows police to collect and analyze crime data in their communities, as well as identify "hot spots," which are areas on a map that indicate high crime intensity. In this way, Bratton and the NYPD were the first to systematically focus on problem areas in neighborhoods by utilizing dynamic data management procedures. Because of CompStat, New York City was said to be the safest large city in the United States in the 1990s. Community members began to feel safer, while police were able to gather information to arrest large criminal organizations. Bratton also required many of his officers to walk their designated areas of the city and actively engage with citizens. This strategy gave the look and feel of safety and enabled police to develop a working relationship with community members who may have been unwilling to otherwise interact with them.

Beyond broken windows and CompStat, Bratton's commitment to reducing police corruption and improving standards may have contributed to his effectiveness. Bratton reduced corruption by unveiling it and openly discussing it with internal investigators. Prior to Bratton's leadership, many commentators believed that corruption in the NYPD was largely hidden from public view, rarely examined, or seldom pursed. At the same time, some felt that the NYPD would often ignore illegal activities, creating an atmosphere of lawlessness. Bratton addressed these concerns by providing enhanced training programs for new recruits as well as seasoned officers. Trainings provided officers with methods to help reduce public disorder and target overt criminal behavior. Rookie officers were subjected to a combination of extensive field and classroom activities to help prepare them for real-life scenarios. In addition, Bratton developed more stringent hiring standards, increasing the minimum age of NYPD officers from 20 to 22 and requiring applicants to possess a two-year college degree.

Although Bratton's approaches to crime control often have been described in a positive light, some observers have criticized his methods. Critics of Bratton's broken windows strategy have stressed that such an approach produces a zero tolerance police culture marked with stop-and-frisk procedures that unnecessarily increase stop rates and often target poor, homeless, and minority communities. A study of the LAPD conducted by Harvard University researchers over the course of eight years (starting in 2002 while Bratton was chief) indicated that pedestrian and motor-vehicle stops rose from 587,200 to over 875,000 (Stone, Foglesong, and Cole 2009). Of all citizens who were stopped by police, Blacks represented 22 percent in 2002 and 23 percent in 2008. Hispanics represented 43 percent in 2002 and 48 percent in 2008. Only 18 percent of Whites were stopped in 2002, and this decreased to 15 percent in 2008.

David Patrick Connor and Jabril A. Hassen

See also: Corruption; Crime Prevention Techniques; Racial Profiling; Wilson and Kelling's Broken Windows Theory; Zero Tolerance Policy

Further Reading

Bratton, William, and Peter Knobler. *Turnaround: How America's Top Cop Reserved the Crime Epidemic.* New York: Random House, 1998.

Domanick, Joe. *Blue: The LAPD and the Battle to Redeem American Policing.* New York: Simon & Schuster, 2015.

Harcourt, Bernard E., and Jens Ludwig. "Broken Windows: New Evidence from New York City and a Five-city Social Experiment." *University of Chicago Law Review* 73 (2006): 271–320.

Shelden, Randall G. "Assessing 'Broken Windows': A Brief Critique." Center on Juvenile and Criminal Justice, 2004. http://www.cjcj.org/uploads/cjcj/documents/broken.pdf.

Stone, Christopher, Todd Foglesong, and Christine M Cole. *Policing Los Angeles Under a Consent Decree: The Dynamics of Change at the LMPD.* Cambridge, MA: Harvard Kennedy School, 2009.

RUBY RIDGE AND THE WACO SIEGE

As recently as the June 2016 Orlando, Florida, massacre—with the April 1999 Columbine High School carnage as a point of reference—and going back at least several decades, police response to criminal incidents in the United States that have involved armed adversaries resulted in siege events, which ended in disastrous results. Episodes such as these were often subjected to extensive media attention as well as governmental post incident inquiries and reports.

The Ruby Ridge (Idaho) and Branch Davidian (Waco, Texas) incidents were primarily the responsibility of federal law enforcement agencies; the assistance and support of local law enforcement were well documented during each of them and is common during such incidents.

In August 1992 the U.S. Marshals Service, and then the Federal Bureau of Investigation (FBI), attempted to apprehend Randy Weaver at Ruby Ridge, in Idaho. Weaver was a self-proclaimed survivalist and white supremacist who was wanted on a federal warrant for failure to appear in court for a weapon-related violation originally filed by the Bureau of Alcohol, Tobacco, Firearms and Explosives (ATF). While the U.S. Marshals were conducting a surveillance operation near Weaver's home in order to take him into custody, a confrontation ensued, resulting in the shooting death of a deputy U.S. Marshal and Weaver's 14-year-old son, Sammy. During the subsequent siege, Randy Weaver and Kevin Harris—one of

With guns drawn, agents of the Bureau of Alcohol, Tobacco and Firearms and the Idaho State Patrol place the first of five neo-Nazis under arrest near Naples, Idaho, August 25, 1992. Numerous weapons were found in the group's car (back, center) near a police barricade three miles from the site of a four-day standoff with white supremacist, Randy Weaver. (AP Photo/ Mason Marsh)

his followers—were wounded, and his wife, Vicki, was killed by FBI sniper fire (Johnston, July 13, 1995).

A Lexis Counsel Connect Internet report, *The Shooting at Ruby Ridge* (1996), contains extensive excerpts from U.S. Congressional Hearings and trial transcripts about the incident, which had occurred between August 21 and 31, 1992. This online service for attorneys provided the following information: Soon after the U.S. Marshals Service contacted the FBI about the incident, a decision was made to deploy the FBI Hostage Rescue Team (HRT) to the scene. According to the FBI Web site, HRT was established in 1983 to be a national-level counterterrorism unit. The team offers a tactical option for extraordinary hostage crises and other law enforcement situations within the United States ("Hostage Rescue Team" 2013).

Initially, FBI headquarters rejected an operational plan for Ruby Ridge because it did not contain a negotiation component. Prior to the submission of the rejected plan, FBI and local police negotiators played no role in its development. In fact, the HRT leader was quoted as having said this "would be no long siege." This led the lead FBI negotiator at the scene to believe that a tactical solution would be sought without negotiations. The negotiator reported no interest in negotiation on the part of the HRT commander, and "available records reflect insufficient consideration of negotiations strategy as compared to tactical approaches." After 10 days, Randy

Weaver surrendered to authorities based on the intervention of a third-party, non-government negotiator. A report on the incident in *The New York Times* noted, "A 1994 Justice Department report on the incident which has never been made public . . . shows that the FBI fought to keep its files closed to outsiders, even Federal prosecutors" (Johnston July 19, 1995, 14). A major point of contention was the determination of the "rules of engagement": a directive that delineates the limitations and circumstances under which force may be used against an adversary (Free Dictionary). The terminology is usually found in the U.S. military and federal law enforcement. On the local and state side of the equation, one would most probably be dealing with issues related to justification for the purpose of self-defense.

The policy that was used in this case was a "shoot on site" one, which led to a jury acquittal in the criminal trial. Both Weaver and Harris were charged only with failure to appear, and were later awarded a wrongful death settlement in the amount of $3.1 million for the Weaver family. Errors were made in judgment and procedure, as well as in intelligence assessment, by all three law enforcement agencies involved (ATF, the FBI, and the U.S. Marshals Service). An FBI supervisor was convicted of obstruction of justice, and the FBI sniper was indicted, but the local prosecutor declined to bring the case to trial.

Approximately six months after the Ruby Ridge events, another siege ended badly. The Branch Davidian compound, at Mount Carmel, near Waco, Texas, was the scene of a 51-day siege in 1993. ATF agents were attempting to serve a search warrant and an arrest warrant based on a year-long investigation into federal firearms' violations. This began on February 28th of that year. During the initial encounter, 20 ATF agents were wounded and four were killed. An unknown number of suspects within the compound were killed, and others, including their leader, David Koresh, were wounded. Although negotiations were somewhat successful during the siege, the event ended in the death of more than 70 additional individuals inside the compound on April 19th (Dennis Jr. 1993).

During the standoff, 35 individuals were negotiated out, including 21 children. Two additional people—Koresh supporters who had breached the perimeters and entered the compound—subsequently exited safely. Numerous other Koresh sympathizers tried to join him but were repelled by the surrounding authorities. One of those who did not make it into the compound was Timothy McVeigh (McVeigh was later found guilty and executed for the detonation of a truck bomb outside the Oklahoma City Federal Building, which killed 168 people and injured more than 600, on April 19, 1995). In an internal memorandum dated March 22, 1973, the FBI negotiating team stated, "The long-term prospect for a peaceful resolution remains good." As it turned out, no Davidian members were negotiated out after March 23rd (Dennis Jr. 1993, 18 and 28).

Alan A. Stone, a Harvard professor of law and psychiatry, conducted a review of the incident for the federal government and noted, "During the first phase of the FBI's engagement at Waco, a period of days, the agents on the ground proceeded with a strategy of conciliatory negotiation, which had the approval and understanding of the entire chain of command" (1993, 8). However, Stone also reported that a little more than a month into the siege, the FBI first "took a more aggressive approach to negotiation" and later "gave up the process of negotiation" and "was concentrating on tactical pressure alone" (Stone 1993, 10). Stone subsequently concluded that "the FBI command failed to give adequate consideration to their own behavioral science and negotiation experts" (Stone 1993, 1).

Another government reviewer, Ariel Merari (1993) of the University of Tel Aviv, noted that FBI agents reported that political considerations and embarrassment did not influence their decisions to change tactics. Merari believed such factors were relevant and legitimate and that they should have been acknowledged and discussed (Merari 1993, 7). Finally, Nancy T. Ammerman (1993) of Princeton University observed that the advice of the FBI negotiators was not heeded, in part because "there was an understandable desire among many agents in Waco to make Koresh and the Davidians pay for the harm they had caused. Arguments for patience and unconventional tactics fell on deaf ears" (Ammerman 1993, 4).

Although not fully accepted within the law enforcement community, these and other incidents illustrate that many academics and law enforcement personnel started to believe that formal negotiation strategies can be useful in the goal of reducing violent outcomes. In the past, more traditional tactics were used. However, the SWAT team and incident commanders in the Ruby Ridge and Waco incidents actually used more force than negotiations, with success. This was not necessarily the norm, as other organizational configurations exist, including a direct reporting line from the head of hostage negotiation to the incident commander. Also, there have been siege events in which local police or federal agents have engaged in hostage/crisis negotiation and the outcome was the preservation of the lives of hostages, law enforcement personnel, and perpetrators.

Another point should be considered when reviewing law enforcement events such as Ruby Ridge and Waco. Individualized "radicalization" is regularly discussed in terms of motivation for this attack or that. Consider Timothy McVeigh, the primary perpetrator of the Oklahoma City bombing in 1995. He was a sympathizer of David Koresh and selected the second anniversary of the end of the Waco Siege to use a vehicle-borne, improvised explosive device to kill 168 individuals. Most were federal employees. It would appear that one contributing factor that encourages law enforcement to proceed in an attack is the justification that they are using violence appropriately, because the U.S. government, law enforcement, or military uses violence. And many individuals believe that a personal or institutional grudge is appropriate justification for retaliation and vengeance.

It should be noted that the media reporting and governmental review of Ruby Ridge and Waco generally conclude that had different tactics or emphasis been followed, more lives would have been saved. A differing point of view is that if the law-enforcement response is not swift and sure, more lives will be lost. This perspective is being discussed and investigated in connection with the massacre of 49 individuals at the 2016 Orlando, Florida, nightclub. Many are asking this: Why did it take approximately three hours for the police to make a tactical entry? Time will tell.

The discussion and review of the April 1999 Columbine High School attack, which resulted in the death of twelve students and one teacher, prompted a major shift in police siege tactics. Because of Columbine, many of the 17,000 local and state police agencies in the United States now follow an "active shooter" protocol. According to the U.S. Department of Homeland Security:

> An Active Shooter is an individual actively engaged in killing or attempting to kill people in a confined and populated area; in most cases, active shooters use firearms(s) and there is no pattern or method to their selection of victims. Active shooter situations are unpredictable and evolve quickly. Typically, the immediate deployment of law enforcement is required to stop the shooting and mitigate harm to victims.

So, which is the most appropriate operational response to a life-threatening, siege-type situation? Wait and see and potentially experience casualties? Or go in and get them and potentially experience casualties? This dilemma may be expressed as the choice between an "action imperative" or to engage in "dynamic inactivity." Both of these phrases are open to interpretation and are defined by the situation presented. The answer is not simple. What is required is an organizational response that encompasses adherence to professional selection and training, adequate resources, communication and intelligence, and knowledge and respect for the rule of law as envisioned by the framers of the U.S. Constitution.

Robert J. Louden

See also: Fourth Amendment

Further Reading

Ammerman, N. T. *Recommendations of Experts for Improvements in Federal Law Enforcement after Waco.* Report to the Justice and Treasury Departments. Washington, DC: U.S. Department of Justice, 1993.

Dennis, E. S. G., Jr. *Evaluation of the Handling of the Branch Davidian Stand-Off in Waco, Texas.* Washington, DC: U.S. Department of Justice, 1993.

The Free Dictionary. "Rules of Engagement." http://www.thefreedictionary.com /rules+of+engagement.

"Hostage Rescue Team: Part 1: 30 Years of Service to the Nation." FBI News. 2013. https:// www.fbi.gov/news/stories/the-hostage-rescue-team-30-years-of-service-2.

Johnston, D. "No. 2 Man at F.B.I. Ousted From Post." *The New York Times,* July 13, 1995.

Johnston, D. "Director of F.B.I. Demotes Deputy." *The New York Times,* July 15, 1995. http:// www.nytimes.com/1995/07/15/us/director-of-fbi-demotes-deputy.html.

Johnston, D. "Documents Were Destroyed as F.B.I. Resisted Siege Investigation, Report Says." *The New York Times,* July 15, 1995.

Louden, R. J. "How Much Is Enough? How Much Is Too Much?" *Recommendations of Experts for Improvements in Federal Law Enforcement After Waco.* Washington, DC: U.S. Department of Justice, 1993.

Louden, R. J. "The Structure and Procedures of Hostage: Crisis Negotiation Units in United States Police Organizations." Ph.D. diss., City University of New York, 1999.

Merari, A. "Report for the Departments of Justice and Treasury's Review Board of Barricade Events." *Recommendations of Experts for Improvements in Federal Law Enforcement After Waco.* Washington, DC: U.S. Department of Justice, 1993.

Pitcavage, Mark. "20 Years Later, Shadows of Ruby Ridge Standoff Still Linger." Anti-Defamation League. 2012. http://www.adl.org/press-center/c/20-years-later-shadows-of.html.

Stone, A. A. *Report and Recommendations Concerning the Handling of Incidents Such as the Branch Davidian Standoff in Waco Texas.* November 10, 1993. Cambridge, MA: Unpublished.

U.S. Department of Homeland Security. *Active Shooter Preparedness.* October 25, 2016. https://www.dhs.gov/active-shooter-preparedness.

ZERO TOLERANCE POLICY

Zero tolerance approach is a popular and well-known policy especially implemented in the 1980s and 1990s in the United States. This policy included problem-oriented, community-oriented, order maintenance, the broken windows theory, and quality-of-life policing approaches, and it aimed to increase the quality of life by using aggressive policing techniques.

Zero tolerance policy is explained in three different categories. Being tough on crime means, "All laws will be enforced, that offenders will be apprehended and will not get away with crime, and that if convicted, an offender will face a harsh penalty." Strict, non-discretionary law *enforcement* means, "An aggressive law enforcement approach to policing, where no exceptions are made for the type of offenses being committed or the circumstances in which they occur." And police action against minor offenses and disorder means, "Police will not ignore minor crime and disorder but will specifically pay attention to so-called quality of life offenses such as public drinking, public urinating, graffiti, vandalism, begging, and vagrancy" (Marshall 1999, 2).

Police efforts concentrate on street and disorder offenses, believing this will reduce serious criminality. When reducing disorder in the streets, their prior effort is devoted to the quality of life. Using risk assessment methods, police proactively intensify operations that are directed to people, places, and properties.

Zero tolerance policy is mostly associated with the broken windows theory (Wilson and Kelling 1982), which states that if one of the windows of a building is broken and not fixed soon, then other windows can be broken. In other words, if minor offenses such as vandalism, public drinking, littering, graffiti, and begging are not controlled and prevented, then the streets or neighborhoods will be open to more serious crimes. In such a place, since disorderly attitudes are not prevented, then others will most likely move into the site. Then, drug dealers and prostitutes could come to the place, serious crimes such as street robberies could increase, property values could decline, and respectable and law-abiding people could be replaced with less respectful people. Eventually, disorder could invade the neighborhood.

Historical Developments

When then President Richard Nixon announced the "war on crime," use of drugs among youths was a significant problem in the United States. Some interest groups such as National Federation of Parents for Drug-Free Youth (NFP) and Parents Resource Institute for Drug Education (PRIDE) started campaigns against drugs and pressured the federal government to get involved. In 1982, President Ronald Reagan continued the war on crime by beginning his presidency with the slogan of "War on Drugs." In the 1980s, the federal government increased its efforts on enforcement against drugs. And under the pressure of interest groups, national drug policy shifted to stricter law enforcement. The budget for drug enforcement was increased five times, whereas the budget allocated for drug treatment was decreased four times (Newburn and Jones 2001).

These anti-drug policies gained larger publicity when First Lady Nancy Reagan visited an elementary school where she watched an anti-drug film. After that she said, "Let's just say no to drugs." Later, her quote became a nationwide slogan, and she became associated with the "Just Say No" campaigns against drugs. In addition to Nancy Reagan's involvement, the president acted accordingly and launched an "outspoken intolerance" policy for drug use. He then started a bipartisan effort to pass legislation known as the Anti-Drug Abuse acts of 1986 and 1988. The notion of "zero tolerance" for illegal drugs became the slogan of the 1988 presidential campaign in which George H. W. Bush took over the duty.

Apart from anti-drug campaigns, "zero tolerance" was used in many anti-crime and order maintenance campaigns. Zero tolerance against domestic violence, zero tolerance for any disorder at schools, and zero tolerance to crimes are among them. However, throughout the zero tolerance history, it is New York City's zero tolerance policy against crime and criminals that has become the most well-known.

Zero Tolerance Policy in New York City

Until the mid-1900s, New York City was known as the crime capital because of the high rates of serious crimes such as robbery, homicide, organized crime, and aggravated assault. Crime problems reached an all-time high during the 1993 mayoral election campaign. Rudolph Giuliani, a former prosecutor, claimed that New York needed a new approach to crime-solving. During his campaign, Giuliani focused on tough crime policies and quality of life for the city's residents. "The squeegee men, the petty drug dealers, the graffiti scribblers, and the prostitutes who ruled the sidewalks in certain high crime neighborhoods all were targeted in candidate Giuliani's campaign promise to reclaim the streets of New York for law-abiding citizens" (Greene 1999, 172).

In 1993, Giuliani was elected mayor of New York City, and he was reelected in 1997. His success is definitely linked to his police commissioner, William Bratton, who was appointed in 1994. Bratton had achieved success in eliminating fare evaders and minor offenses from New York City's subways in his early career. In fact, fare evaders were a real problem for New Yorkers, and every day almost 200,000 of them were illegally using the subway system. Further, beggars and homeless persons had invaded underground platforms. Bratton summarized the situation as "Graffiti, burned-out cars, and trash seemed to be everywhere; it looked like something out of a futuristic movie. Then as you entered Manhattan, you met the unofficial greeter for the City of New York, the Squeegee pest. Welcome to New York City. This guy had a dirty rag or squeegee and would wash your window with some dirty liquid and demand money" (Bratton 1997, 33–34).

Under the pressure of various negative problems of the city, Bratton, as the new commissioner of the New York Police Department (NYPD), published two strategies for the fight against crime. His first strategy was "Reclaiming the Public Spaces of New York," which would deal with the low-level disorder. The second was "Getting Guns off the Streets of New York" that was planned to eliminate gun violence. Both strategies were also interrelated—if the department could eliminate the guns and disorder, quality of life would increase, and serious crimes would decline. A starting point for the zero tolerance policing was the implementation of "stop and frisk" in the precincts.

Bratton also started a managerial reform in the department and took over the responsibility of the commanders at the precinct level. Besides this reform, his policing strategy at the neighborhood level was grounded in "traditional law enforcement methods and relentless crackdown campaigns to arrest and jail low-level drug offenders and other petty criminals" (Greene 1999, 175). Whatever its name—either quality of life or order maintenance policing—it was hyper-aggressive policing, especially toward petty criminals and drug dealers because it swept them off the streets and put them in jail.

Bratton also wanted to strengthen the authority of the police by decreasing the intervention of legal restrictions. Basically, law enforcement officers were stopping and searching citizens who were drinking beer in public or urinating, then checking possible warrants for them, questioning them about criminal activities in their neighborhoods, and looking for illegal guns or drugs. Bratton claimed that law enforcement could prevent the crime before it happened. As a result, stop-and-frisk implementation along with aggressive policing caused citizen complaints and civil rights violations to increase significantly.

Comprehensive Computer Statistics (CompStat) has been a strategic tool used in implementing zero tolerance policy. CompStat strategy includes rapid response of resources, timely and accurate intelligence data, effective tactics, and relentless follow-up. It was the starting point of collecting timely crime records in a shared databank when police executives recognized this urgent need and persuaded police departments to share information. The data, including the time and location of the crime, and encountering activities of the police, were presented to the CompStat unit. After submitting the data, the unit entered the data into the city-wide database, and it could then be analyzed by computer. This became the "Weekly Crime Report" of the city. These reports have been prepared weekly, monthly, and yearly ever since, and commanders and top-level managers can follow the trends and emerging problems of the city in terms of crime.

The NYPD's zero tolerance policing policy was evaluated by Kelling and Sousa (2001). They claimed that police influenced crime levels in neighborhoods, and they maintained that policing strategies, including decentralized problem solving, have had a significant impact. They also gave credit to the economics, demographics, imprisonment rates, drug use patterns, and weapon availability on declining crime rates; however, their argument was that such variables had a minor effect, while police activities had a major effect.

Based on the Uniform Crime Report statistics, from 1993 to 1999, crime declined 50 percent in New York City. Specifically, murder (66 percent), motor vehicle theft (66 percent), burglary (59 percent), robbery (58 percent), larceny-theft (40 percent), grand larceny (37 percent), aggravated assault (36 percent), and forcible rape (40 percent) declined in the city (Smith and Bratton, 2001). The crime reductions in New York City were well above the nationwide crime rates. For example, between 1993 and 2001, the reduction rate of property crimes in New York City was 56 percent, while it was just 23 percent nationwide (Demir et al. 2011). A more recent report also claims that murder rates have seen an 85-percent reduction in the city of New York between 1990 and 2013 (Fischer, 2015). NYPD's zero tolerance policy has received national publicity and has been credited with impressive improvements in neighborhood quality of life and reductions in crime.

Critiques of Zero Tolerance Policy

Main critiques on zero tolerance policy focus on two aspects: first, its aggressive police tactics that cause violations of civil rights; second, it is not the police but other factors that can reduce crime rates.

The first major critique is, "It does not fix broken windows. Instead it attacks poor and minority citizens by violating their rights and interfering with community policing while obfuscating the need for social justice" (Fischer 2015, 1). Abner Louima, for example, a 30-year-old Haitian immigrant, was an important figure against the aggressive police tactics of NYPD in the mid-1990s. He was arrested after a dispute between police and club-goers. During the transportation to the police station, he claimed to be assaulted two times and, once he arrived at the station, he claimed racist abuse, saying one officer shoved a broom into his rectum. After the assaults, he was taken to a hospital without any report. Only three days later, his situation was recognized by police managers and the public, when his nurse reported the incident to the Internal Affairs Bureau.

Aggressive policing has also been associated with the racist behaviors or torture against minorities. The study by Gelman, Kiss, and Fagan (2004) on NYPD's stop-and-frisk practices examines 175,000 pedestrian stops by NYPD over a 15-month period. The results suggest that Hispanics and African Americans are stopped more often than Whites.

Another criticism on the zero tolerance policy has been that it is not the aggressive policing tactics, but other factors, that reduce the crime level. Proponents of this idea claim that crime rates declined not only in New York City, but also in the whole nation after the mid-1990s, and, therefore, there should be other explanations to that. One explanation was that the use of cheap and epidemic crack cocaine that claimed to make an impact on the commission of serious crime such as homicide in the beginning of 1990s disappeared in the end of the century, and as a result the crime rates reduced. Another explanation was that, nationwide, the economy grew

30 percent between 1991 and 2001. When budgets of local governments increase, the amount of money to spend for prison and policing also increase, which indirectly affects crime rates.

Oguzhan Omer Demir

See also: Community Policing Today; Crime Control versus Due Process; Frank Serpico (1936–); Impact of the War on Drugs; Police Accountability; William Bratton (1947–), Police Commissioner

Further Reading

Bowling, Benjamin. "The Rise and Fall of New York Murder: Zero Tolerance or Crack's Decline?" *British Journal of Criminology* 39, no. 4 (1999): 531–554.

Bratton, William. "Crime Is Down in New York City: Blame the Police." In *Policing: Key Readings*, edited by Tim Newburn. London: Willan, 2005.

Burke, Roger Hopkins. "The Socio-Political Context of Zero Tolerance Policing Strategies." *Policing: An International Journal of Police Strategies and Management* 21, no. 4 (1998): 666–682.

Casella, Ronnie. "Zero Tolerance Policy in Schools: Rationale, Consequences, and Alternatives." *The Teachers College Record* 105, no. 5 (2003): 872–892(21).

Cunneen, Chris. "Zero Tolerance Policing and the Experience of New York City." *Current Issues in Criminal Justice* 10, no. 3 (1991): 299–313.

Demir, Oguzhan, Celik Omer, Cetin Ahmet, Cem Hakan, and Murat Ozkan. "Why Crime Dropped During Giuliani's Term in New York: A Glance at Crime Prevention Policies." *International Journal of Human Sciences* 8, no. 2 (2011): 250–264.

Dixon, David, and Phillip Cuffin. "Zero Tolerance Policing of Illegal Drug Markets." *Drug and Alcohol Review* 18 (1999): 478–486.

Fischer, Michael. "Zero-Tolerance Policing." In *The Encyclopedia of Crime and Punishment.* Edited by Wesley G. Jennings. Boston: Wiley-Blackwell, 2015.

Gelman, Andrew, Alex Kiss, and Jeffry Fagan. *An Analysis of the NYPD's Stop-and-Frisk Policy in the Context of Claims of Racial Bias.* Unpublished research granted by National Science Foundation SES-9987748 and SES-0318115. March 23, 2004. http://www.stat.columbia.edu/~gelman/research/unpublished/frisk6.pdf.

Greene, Judith A. "Zero Tolerance: A Case Study of Police Policies and Practices in New York City." *Crime and Delinquency* 45, no. 2 (1999): 171–187.

Kelling, George L. and William H. Sousa. *Do Police Matter? An Analysis of the Impact of New York City's Police Reforms.* New York: Center for Civic Innovation at the Manhattan Institute, 2001.

Levitt, Steven D. "Understanding Why Crime Fell in the 1990s: For Factors that Explain the Decline and Six that Do Not." *Journal of Economic Perspective* 18, no. 1 (2004): 163–190.

Marshall, Jayne. *Zero Tolerance Policing.* South Australia Office of Crime Statistics and Research, Information Bulletins. March 1999. http://www.ocsar.sa.gov.au/docs/information_bulletins/IB9.pdf.

Moore, Mark H. "Sizing Up Compstat: An Important Administrative Innovation in Policing." *Criminology and Public Policy* 2, no. 3 (2003): 469–494.

Moore, M. H. "The Limits of Social Science in Guiding Policy." *Criminology and Public Policy* 2, no. 1 (2002): 33–42.

Newburn, Tim, and Trevor Jones. *Policy Transfer and Crime Control: Some Reflections on Zero Tolerance*. Paper presented at the annual meeting of the American Political Science Association, San Francisco, CA, 2001.

Smith Dennis C., and William Bratton. "Performance Management in New York City: COMPSTAT and the Revolution in Police Management." In *Quicker, Better, Cheaper? Managing Performance in American Government*, edited by D. Forsythe. Albany, NY: SUNY Press, 2001.

Spitzer, Elliot. "*The New York City Police Department's 'Stop & Frisk' Practices: A Report to the People of the State of New York from the Office of the Attorney General*." New York State Office of the Attorney General. 1999. http://www.oag.state.ny.us/sites/default/files/pdfs/bureaus/civil_rights/stp_frsk.pdf.

Wilson, James Q., and George Kelling. "Broken Windows." *Atlantic Monthly* 249, no. 3 (1982): 29–38.

Zero Tolerance: Policing a Free Society, edited by N. Dennis. The IEA Health and Welfare Unit, Choice in Welfare No. 35, 1997.

"THIN BLUE LINE": POLICE AS A GUARD AGAINST ANARCHY

A common belief is that society in a condition of anarchy—without law or authority—would be in complete chaos. Disorder would rule, the innocent would be unprotected from society's predators, the strongest and richest would have everything, the weak and poor would have nothing, and morality would disappear. Although this a cynical viewpoint, the implication is that if human beings were left to their own devices, they would be deprived of something and revert to some animal state where the only thing that mattered was their personal satisfaction. Likewise, under government authority, police provide the checks and balances through enforcement of laws, thus creating or *restoring* order. People are safe, the planes fly on time, and balance is restored. Personal gain and self-satisfaction through animal instincts are tempered by agents of justice who stand between law and lawlessness—a thread that holds a disorderly society together. It is commonly held, then, that without the police, anarchy would prevail, and a society would tear itself down with a new one rising from its ashes.

The social contract (or social contractarianism) founded by Enlightenment-era philosophers John Locke (1632–1704), Thomas Hobbes (1588–1679), and Jean-Jacques Rousseau (1712–1778) is perhaps the most influential catalyst for both creating and understanding what has become known as the "thin blue line" between the police and the public. Born out of moral and political philosophy, the social contract states that in exchange for safety and security, a society must relinquish some of its civil liberties. It provides legitimacy of the state to use its authority to "keep people in check."

The caveat to the social contract, in any sense, are two basic principles: (1) authority must be respected, and (2) rights must be respected. It is very difficult to have lawful and legitimate authority without consequences for not following the rules, such as obeying traffic signs or not driving while intoxicated. At the same time, it is difficult to follow rules and laws when an authority figure, such as a police officer, uses illegal methods to stop your vehicle, cite you, or arrest you. It is in this respect that the social contract has been largely criticized because the imposition of order (even where legitimate) actually creates disorder. Where the public knows the laws and rules, and understands that they have a right to ask questions and seek clarification when the police intervene in their lives, situations tend to escalate when the police do not explain or say they have to explain. There is no longer a common bond of respect that is largely grounded in lawful authority, acknowledgment by the public of their wrongdoing, and good communication about it.

For the police, there also exists what is known as a "public paradox." It essentially means the public wants and needs the police; however, their attitude might be "don't pull *me* over." A community very much appreciates the police solving a string of car burglaries in their neighborhood but does not like police presence when they have been called to that neighborhood for a barking dog complaint, noise complaint, or ticketing vehicles that are parked illegally. Unlike firefighters, who may similarly respond to a car accident, the firefighter doesn't issue a citation or draw blood for intoxicants. Additionally, the public paradox creates a perception of double standards in which the social elite (affluent and powerful) own the police and their responses—especially as it affects them. This further creates a social class system where the poor have no rights (or can't stand up for them), and the rich "buy" their rights and have their way. In the middle, then, are everyday crooks and criminals who find ways to circumvent the criminal justice system while the rich and poor are busy at war with each other, the police, and the government, attempting to render the authority system impotent. Classic literary works that illustrate such dystopian societies, such as *Lord of the Flies* (1954), *1984* (1949), *Animal Farm* (1945), and *Brave New World* (1932) serve as potent reflections on how, without order or with too much or illegitimate order, a society becomes reckless, disobedient, violent, and individualistic.

The "thin blue line" is a catchphrase that came into use after a 1988 documentary film by the same name about the murder of a Dallas police officer. Closing arguments from the prosecutor at the end of the film discussed the thin blue line as a police "line" that separates the public from anarchy. This metaphor of a line drawn in the sand comes from a more historical account of the Crimean War and the Battle of Balaklava in 1854. The term "thin red line" was coined due to color of the regiment's uniforms and their formation prior to a battle charge.

The use of the term "thin blue line" has varied throughout the years but essentially retains two general meanings. It has always been an implicit understanding among cops as a band of brothers and sisters who stand between law and lawlessness, order and chaos, and good and evil. They help to separate law-abiding citizens from criminals. They exist as a *thread* that holds society together—ultimately at the price of their lives—and a thread is thinner than string or rope.

Civilians, supporters, advocates, and police benevolent groups have taken that understanding and expression of duty and helped to translate a police officer's paradoxical circumstances. In a society that says, "We need law and order, just don't pull me over," the phrase is now a symbol that depicts a thin, horizontal blue line against a black background. The black color on top is the law-abiding public and the black color on the bottom represents the criminals. The blue line symbolizes the men and women in law enforcement, historically whose uniforms were traditionally blue, and it is thinner than the black color because there are fewer officers than there are members of society. (There are roughly 800,000 sworn law enforcement officers for 320 million people in the United States.) It's also thin because they are strong yet weary, confronted with intolerable conditions, exasperated and depressed by a society that sometimes appears to be moving away from what is right and wrong. They act in support of their oath of office and upholding the Constitution, but, more-over, for the love of their communities and for each other.

Another interpretation of the thin blue line is the police stance between tyranny and a free society. As mentioned with the social contract and public paradox, people are often confused regarding the reasons for the existence of the police. The police are actively characterized as protecting people to maintain safety and order in society. They protect life and property and are called upon to perform every conceivable kind of service. While the phrase "To Protect and Serve" is found on police vehicles, the police *are* the vehicles by which the limits and permissibility of social tolerance are tested. They face glaring challenges in a multicultural and free society where they limit individual freedom by applying coercive force to change behavior. If people know right from wrong, then they should be able to recognize another's by their own understanding and experience. If one tries to exert domination over another, then they have overstepped the truth and entered into a false relationship. The nature and existence of the police, then, appears un-American because the system of govern-ment that sends them to the front lines is supposed to value individual freedom. This clash of conflicting viewpoints places law enforcement in an uncomfortable middle, not only between law and lawlessness on the streets, but between law enforcement and administration.

The thin blue line as a band of warriors is forever needed. The police must fight civil disobedience, and violence typically occurs around the climax of disorder. It highlights vulnerabilities where problems are unraveling and gaps are neglected, instead of being handled immediately and efficiently. By using the words fascism, totalitarianism, and dictatorships, some view the government and its agents as using tactics of oppression to beat down the poor and weak—the only answer for which is lawlessness, which leads to crime and violence.

Anarchists reject rules and people who seek to enforce them, because rules restrict an individual's freedom. They must, then, also reject government and its laws and the police whose job is to enforce those laws. Regardless of how democratic, no govern-ment is acceptable. They believe in a perfectibility of mankind who, left to themselves, would act voluntarily, ethically, and in a socially beneficial way. A free, unhampered life for one who governs themselves cannot be restricted in any way by authority.

The *State* is the embodiment of government and law. Anarchism is also consid-ered *antistatism* and those who believe in those principles are convinced that the State must disappear in order for mankind to be truly free. If this is true, then there is a clear distinction between a *society*, where people voluntarily and freely create their world, and the *State*, which is artificially created as a structured community for oppression through authority that limits behavior in accordance with customs and laws.

The only way for a new society to flourish is to destroy the State through violence, or slowly through education. As the population of America continues to grow through natural citizenship, immigration, and life expectancy, there is a similar increase in local, state, and federal government. As a result, more police are created or, even more, the authority and scope of policing increases as a way to control antisocial behavior.

Anger at mistakes, neglect, and indifference grows social unrest and anarchy. From fiscal crises, racial tensions, terrorism, and political divisiveness, the media goes on to serve as mechanisms of manipulation and instruments to form public opinion. Because the police are the most visible agents of the government, they are being targeted by the public at a scope and level never seen before in the annals of police history. Death by gunfire as a result of coordinated efforts to "take out" the police is often part of weekly headlines (Grinberg 2016). When citizens are free to prey upon each other, the police become an easy target. This is similar to the business model of "removing the middle man." It's similar to a game without referees and officials or someone to stop the fight. Because of the social unrest, the government then hyper-militarizes police with body cameras, audio devices, vehicles, equipment, and military-grade weaponry, often confusing the once firmly established and agreed upon mission and role of the police as public servants.

Our police stand, not as oppressors, but as hope during the toughest of times. William Straus and Neil Howe (1997) discussed the cycles of social development and revolutions, which historically repeat themselves, but run parallel with the thin blue line. They exist as historical "turns" such as the Truman, Eisenhower, and Kennedy eras (1943–1963) where there was a new civic order with a weakening of individualism and a strengthening of social, political, and religious institutions. A second turn (1963–1983) was where a strong awakening occurred, the civic order is attacked, and there is a passionate upheaval historically seen through what was called the "turbulent 60s." During the Reagan, Bush, and Clinton eras (1983–2003), yet another turn occurred in which individualism was strengthened, a cultural war unraveled and existing institutions became weak, leading to new values from a decaying civic order. The fourth turn is an upheaval of the entire system, which creates a new civic order thus leading to another "first" turning.

The long withstanding customs and laws that govern police behavior is pitted against American freedoms. Because the American police officer represents a decentralized government, they are public servants who are often toted as armed, occupying forces. The public is concerned about illegal search and seizure, police brutality, corruption, police shootings, racism, and cover-ups. The anti-cop rhetoric that comes from a never-ending battle of a "war on cops, crime, drugs, and terror" promotes a shift toward soldier mentality and tactics. As a result, a thin blue line could feel contempt for the public they serve as well as the government that employs them and for which they depend on for better response tactics. Tactics have always been consistent with laws governing police conduct and work to remain within the boundaries of a democracy and not that of totalitarianism.

The thin blue line police response to criminality and anarchy is and always will be in its training. Finding adequate training and funding for training, however, is problematic. Being decentralized requires local cops to work within local budgets, state for state and so forth. Many cops must fund their own training beyond the initial police academy and so in-service and continuing education training may not be adequate to handle the threats they face. This further stretches an already thin line. While American courts, special interest and lobbyist groups, and various political factions of government fight over crime control versus due process and civil rights, there is a consistent pull on the number of police officers who are equipped to safely and tactically handle civil discourse. There are continued debates about the rights and responsibilities of law enforcement and what policies and procedures are considered *legal* and *justified*.

A vicious cycle is currently underway as the thin blue line police take on a nation that may destroy itself if it believes the cops are not in support of the public. The police must protect themselves and others yet are tethered to unwinnable strategies by their own government and administrations. Is it the police who agitate a distraught public? Or are the police merely puppets with strings being pulled from above? Some members of the public have attempted to coordinate hate and smear campaigns that go viral on social media outlets. Militant groups, social movements, and national tragedies (such as the Trayvon Martin case and events in Ferguson, Missouri, and Baltimore, Maryland) have called for federal intervention to soften the core of what *used* to be the police. Will it be better? Will it be worse? Powerful considerations must be undertaken with a new social contract and new civic order. Cops want to help, but they also want to go home. The consequences, through changes in policies and training are yet unknown, but it is certain that the thin blue line is stretched thin. How much thinner can it go?

Brian Kinnaird

See also: Community Policing Today; Control Theory; Crime Control versus Due Process; Crime Prevention Techniques; Michael Brown Shooting and the Aftermath in Ferguson

Further Reading

Das, D., and A. Verma. *Police Mission: Challenges and Responses*. Lanham, MD: Scarecrow Press, 2003.

Grinberg, E. "Police officer deaths from guns up 78% from July last year." CNN Web site. July 28, 2016. http://www.cnn.com/2016/07/17/us/police-shooting-deaths-july-2016/.

Grossman, D. *On Combat: The Psychology of Physiology of Deadly Conflict in War and Peace*. Mascoutah, IL: Warrior Science Publications, 2008.

Jacker, C. *The Black Flag of Anarchy*. New York: Charles Scribner's Sons, 1968.

Straus, W., and N. Howe. *The Fourth Turning: An American Prophecy*. New York: Broadway Books, 1997.

Von Hoffman, N. *Radical: A Portrait of Saul Alinsky*. New York: Nation Books, 2010.
Whitehead, J. *A Government of Wolves: The Emerging American Police State*. New York: Select-
    Books, 2013.

IMPACT OF THE WAR ON DRUGS

The phrase "war on drugs" is commonly used to describe American policy toward reducing the supply of and demand for illegal drugs. Since the 1970s, billions of dollars have been dedicated toward drug prohibition despite critiques that tactics are ineffective, unconstitutional, and biased against certain populations. The effects of the drug war are wide ranging, impacting individuals, communities, and criminal justice system resources. Recent federal- and state-level reforms have led some experts to argue that the war on drugs has concluded, while others disagree based on the significant resources still dedicated toward the enforcement of punitive drug policies.

Background

For much of the 20th century, federal laws such as the Harrison Narcotics Act of 1914 and the Marijuana Tax Act of 1937 seemed to be effective in maintaining low

A member of the Hells Angels Motorcycle Club, with arms behind his back, is arrested by FBI agents in lower Manhattan, May 2, 1985. Attorney General Edwin Meese III announced the arrests of more than 125 people from over 50 locations for violations of the Controlled Substance Act and the Racketeer Influenced and Corrupt Organizations Act. (AP Photo/ Nancy Kaye)

levels of recreational drug use in the United States. Following World War II, rates of drug use remained modest. Drug abuse was not considered a major societal problem compared to other political concerns. The decade of the 1960s featured recreational drug use as one of the most identifiable characteristics. Rates of use increased for marijuana as well as several other drugs. In response to the perception that drug use was an emerging international problem, the Single Convention on Narcotic Drugs of 1961 was ratified. This international agreement prompted many nations to develop comprehensive drug laws. In the United States, the Controlled Substances Act (CSA) was passed in 1970 to combine several drug laws into a single piece of comprehensive legislation. The CSA established a method for scheduling drugs, which would determine punishment levels and impact availability for medicinal purposes.

Shortly after the creation of the CSA, in a 1971 press conference, President Richard M. Nixon claimed that drug abuse was the country's number-one enemy. Two years later, in 1973, the Drug Enforcement Administration (DEA) was created as an instrument to enforce federal drug laws. Subsequent efforts by the federal government to rid the country of illegal drugs were paralleled by municipal and state agencies around the nation. Governmental spending on drug enforcement continued to increase, leading to more arrests, higher incarceration rates, and immense controversy.

Characteristics

The War on Drugs is a multifaceted response that involves international and domestic partnerships. It addresses problems of drug use, distribution, and cultivation. Several approaches focus on keeping drugs out of the country, including crop eradication and intense patrols in transit zones and along the nation's borders. Although eradication efforts do occur within the United States, several of the drugs most commonly used for recreational purposes in the United States, such as heroin and cocaine, are grown only in other countries.

Crop eradication usually involves the use of herbicides, which often requires international cooperation. Specifically, eradication has been a key component of Plan Colombia—an alliance between Colombia and the United States, with the goal of reducing supply and raising prices. Another layer of supply reduction occurs in transit zones, such as the Gulf of Mexico where the U.S. Coast Guard attempts to interdict shipments of drugs coming into the country. Additionally, considerable resources are placed at the nation's seaports, road crossings, and along other passable locations at the Mexican border. Border Protection and U.S. Customs agents perform critical roles at this stage.

Within the country, several other approaches gained support during the early years of the War on Drugs. In order to make progress during investigations into drug trafficking, law enforcement agencies operate undercover using sting operations, confidential informants, and wiretaps. These operations are vital to gain information on trafficking networks but controversial due to their intrusiveness. Another tool for law enforcement is civil asset forfeiture, which allows law enforcement to seize assets associated with drug activity. Forfeiture provisions generate significant financial revenue for agencies, which enables police to conduct future operations. Critics argue that forfeiture laws do not provide enough protections for innocent citizens.

Perhaps the most impactful components of the War on Drugs are the sentencing laws applied to a variety of drug-related offenses. Mandatory minimum sentences and habitual offender laws reduce judicial discretion to ensure that individuals who plead or are found guilty of drug crimes receive substantial prison sentences. Specifically, additional penalties are associated with arrests that occur within specified distances of locations where children are likely to congregate, such as schools and daycare centers. Many of these sentencing laws apply to individuals punished for possession and distribution. The ramifications of drug convictions are not limited to the criminal sentence. Legislation passed toward the end of the 20th century allows individuals with drug convictions to be partially or fully restricted from accessing forms of social assistance including welfare, student aid, public housing, and food stamps.

The War on Drugs has also featured components that aim to reduce demand for illegal substances through education and awareness. Central to this effort is the Drug Abuse Resistance Education (DARE), a program led by law enforcement with a zero-tolerance message. Launched in the early 1980s, the DARE program spread across the country despite research that consistently demonstrates that the program is not effective in reducing long-term drug use for its participants. The rise to prominence of the DARE program occurred simultaneously with awareness campaigns that encouraged American youth to "just say no" to illegal drugs. Together, educational programs in schools and awareness campaigns in the media are some of the most familiar aspects of the War on Drugs for many citizens.

Impact

There are many dimensions to consider in evaluating the impact of the War on Drugs. Drug prohibition efforts are assessed for their effect on specific measurable desired outcomes. The impact of the War on Drugs can also be evaluated by the amount of resources that are dedicated to the enforcement and execution of drug laws in the criminal justice system. And it is important to consider unintended consequences of the drug war on individuals and communities.

The measurement of success in the drug war is very complicated. Specific desirable outcomes associated with success include reduced self-reported drug use, fewer fatal overdoses, higher drug prices, and less purity. Some of these outcomes are easier to measure than others. Rates of drug use are generally calculated using self-report surveys, such as the National Survey of Drug Use and Health or Monitoring the Future. Overdose fatalities are calculated by utilizing emergency room data and coroner reports. Estimates of the price of drugs and purity levels rely on more complex methodologies. The assessment of the War on Drugs also depends upon when one believes the strategy commenced. The term "war" was used in the 1970s, but some people consider the 1980s to be a more accurate starting point because of the sharp increase in funding.

In the Monitoring the Future survey of eighth-, tenth-, and twelfth-grade students, rates of annual drug use have experienced peaks and valleys throughout the duration of the drug war. Rates of illicit drug use initially declined during the 1980s, increased through the 1990s to peaks later that decade, and declined moderately in the years that followed. Usage rates for certain specific drugs have declined steadily since the early 1990s including LSD and cocaine, whereas other drugs, such as marijuana, have not shown such decline (Johnston et al. 2016).

Another method for assessing the success of the drug war is to examine data on fatal overdoses. Using overdose fatalities as a measure, the War on Drugs has not had a sustainable effect. Data from the Centers for Disease Control and Prevention (CDC) indicates a yearly increase in the number drug overdoses since 2000 (CDC 2015). Recent increases have been primarily driven by a jump in overdose deaths related to opioid prescription pain medications and heroin.

While data on drug use and overdoses serves as a measure of demand, other measures focus on how policy influences the price and purity of drugs. Because illegal drugs are grown and sold in an underground market by definition, data gathered on purity and prices are estimated. Research on the effect of supply-side reduction measures is mixed; however, a recently published study using government surveillance system data found that inflation-adjusted prices for cocaine, heroin, and marijuana actually decreased between 1990 and 2007 while purity increased (Werb et al. 2013).

The connections between specific components of drug prohibition and changing rates of drug use are affected by many factors. There are many other social, psychological, and biological variables that can impact drug use patterns beyond enforcement strategies. Therefore, it is difficult to parse out the individual reasons why drug use increases in one decade and decreases in the next. Supporters of the drug war will point to the decrease of drug use in the 1980s and some recent declines to suggest that some tactics are working. Drug war detractors will argue that if the drug war was effective, the gains would be more consistent across time and drug type.

Another impact of drug prohibition is the effect on criminal justice system resources. Law enforcement agencies are greatly affected by the focus on drug law enforcement. The creation of specialized narcotics unit can mean the transfer of personnel from other duties toward drug-related responsibilities. Beyond resource allocation, many of the tactics utilized in proactively enforcing the drug war are inherently dangerous. Law enforcement agents have been killed while making drug-related stops of citizens or working undercover. The increased focus on drug crimes also affects other parts of the criminal justice system. Courts become more congested due to the influx of drug cases. In response, there may be more pressure to resolve cases quickly and rely on plea bargains. In the corrections system, the focus on drugs has led to increases in the U.S. probation and prison systems. According to the Bureau of Justice Statistics (BJS), in 2014, 25 percent of adult probationers committed a drug offense (Kaeble et al. 2015). Likewise, BJS reports that at the end of 2013, about 16 percent of all prisoners and 50 percent of federal prisoners committed a drug offense (Carson 2015). These statistics indicate that increased attention on drugs by law enforcement has resulted in larger correctional populations.

The War on Drugs also impacts individuals and communities through unintended consequences. These consequences include fractured relationships between communities and law enforcement, unequal outcomes across demographic populations, and areas with a disproportionate number of young adults incarcerated.

The nature of aggressive policing tactics could create rifts between communities and law enforcement, and some communities may already be skeptical of governmental intentions. When individuals are stopped on the street or raids are conducted in private homes, communities may view police as an occupying force enforcing laws that they do not fully support. Although some aggressive policing tactics are necessary to achieve the basic goals of drug prohibition, many of the tactics are seen as intrusive. Further, there are cases when a person is stopped on the street who has no affiliation with drugs or when the wrong house is raided.

The impact of the drug war has had disproportionate effects on minority and lower-class communities. There are different reasons for the disparities. In some instances, law enforcement focuses resources to reduce drug distribution in areas where there is more violence and calls for service. Other reasons include drug-free school zone laws that often encompass entire dense urban cities, leaving all persons arrested for drug offenses facing mandatory charges while offenders in suburban and rural areas are far less likely to be arrested in these enhanced penalty areas. Lower-class arrestees of the drug war may also face longer sentences for a variety of other reasons. Crack cocaine was associated with much longer sentences than powder cocaine for decades at a federal level. In other situations, arrested offenders might face challenges in courts while relying on court-appointed lawyers. Ultimately, accusations of bias in the drug war are supported by surveys that show that racial minorities are generally less likely to use drugs than Caucasians, yet the results of drug enforcement often fall on minority communities disproportionately.

Because of decades of punitive drug law enforcement and punishment, many communities experience shortages of young adults who should be legitimate economic providers for families. This phenomenon has affected not only males but also females who have experienced significant increases in incarceration rates. When substantial proportions of communities are incarcerated, more social aid is needed to support children and other non-providing family members. Such communities are harmed by drug abuse and distribution, but the same areas may also be harmed by the long-term implications of aggressive enforcement.

Recent Reforms

Since the turn of the century, there have been many changes in drug-related law enforcement tactics, correctional approaches, and state laws that suggest a movement away from the drug war philosophy. In 2000, the Civil Asset Forfeiture Reform Act was passed to address complaints about the use of forfeiture across the country. More recently, several states have modified their civil asset forfeiture provisions to provide more protections to citizens. One of the more well-known policing approaches, conducting "stop and frisk" searches, has been reduced in some cities based on court orders and departmental guideline changes. In New York City, a District Court judge ruled the city's program allowing these searches must be overhauled.

The rapid spread of drug treatment courts also indicates changing attitudes about drug addiction. There are about 3,000 drug courts operating across the country. These courts provide specialized personnel to address drug addiction in a community-based setting. Such opportunities present chances for drug addicts to receive treatment opposed to harsher punishments that were associated with the drug war ideology. Politicians across the political spectrum now speak openly about their desire to funnel persons addicted to drugs toward treatment.

Sentencing reforms have also occurred at both state and federal levels. Two well publicized examples of reform are revisions to New York's Rockefeller Drug Laws and federal changes in crack cocaine sentencing. The Rockefeller Drug Laws, enacted under New York governor Nelson Rockefeller in the 1970s, had mandated lengthy prison sentences for possessing even small amounts of drugs. Recent amendments to the laws have provided more judicial discretion and opportunities for treatment. The infamous disparity in sentencing between crack and powder cocaine was a commonly used example of institutional racism in the fight against drugs. The Fair Sentencing Act reduced the 100:1 weight ratio between crack and powder cocaine that had existed for decades to trigger federal criminal penalties.

Finally, the most extreme forms of drug policy liberalization are found in states like Alaska, California, Colorado, Oregon, and Washington. These states have legalized marijuana, while many other states have decriminalized its use by removing criminal penalties. Although the federal government still outlaws marijuana under federal law, the Drug Enforcement Administration has conducted few raids in states that have modified marijuana laws. The legalization of marijuana directly contrasts with prohibitionist attitudes of the War on Drugs era.

These reforms suggest that major changes are occurring in U.S. drug policy. However, America is still embedded in the most comprehensive fight against drug use and distribution of any country in the world. The Office of National Drug Control Policy's budget allocation for domestic law enforcement and interdiction remain extremely high. About $9.2 billion was requested for funding in 2015 for domestic law enforcement with about $4 billion requested for interdiction. Harm reduction measures, utilized in countries such as Canada, Switzerland, and the Netherlands are not discussed as serious policy options. Although many drug sentencing laws are being reformed, some states are creating new sentencing laws that allow drug dealers who have distributed drugs leading to fatal overdoses to be charged with murder.

These conflicting signals complicate analyses of current drug policy and predictions about its future. While some signs point to a transition away from the War on Drugs, other evidence speaks to the American commitment to drug prohibition. The only point of consensus that cannot be argued is that the effects of our drug policies, whether positive or negative, will impact our society for generations to come.

Steven Block

See also: Fourth Amendment; Police Authority to Detain; Racial Profiling; *Terry v. Ohio*; Zero Tolerance Policy

Further Reading

Carson E. Ann. *Prisoners in 2014.* Washington, DC: U.S. Department of Justice, Office of Justice Programs, Bureau of Justice Statistics, 2015.

Caulkins, Jonathan P., Peter Reuter, Martin Y. Iguchi, and James Chiesa. *How Goes the "War on Drugs": An Assessment of U.S. Drug Problems and Policy.* Santa Monica, CA: RAND, 2005.

Centers for Disease Control and Prevention (CDC). *Drug Overdose Deaths Hit Record Numbers in 2014.* 2015. http://www.cdc.gov/media/releases/2015/p1218-drug-overdose.html.

Jensen, Eric L., Jurg Gerber, and Clayton Mosher. "Social Consequences of the War on Drugs: The Legacy of Failed Policy." *Criminal Justice Policy Review* 15 (2004): 100–121.

Johnston, Lloyd D., Patrick M. O'Malley, Richard A. Miech, Jerald G. Bachman, and John E. Schulenberg. *Monitoring the Future National Survey Results on Drug Use, 1975–2015: Overview, key findings on adolescent drug use.* Ann Arbor, MI: Institute for Social Research, University of Michigan, 2016.

Kaeble, Danielle, Laura M. Maruschak, and Thomas P. Bonczar. *Probation and Parole in the United States, 2014.* Washington, DC: U.S. Department of Justice, Office of Justice Programs, Bureau of Justice Statistics, 2015.

MacCoun, Robert J., and Peter Reuter. *Drug War Heresies: Learning from Other Vices, Times, and Places.* New York: Cambridge University Press, 2001.

Petrocelli, Matthew, Trish Oberweis, Michael R. Smith, and Joseph Petrocelli. "Assessing Police Attitudes Toward Drugs and Drug Enforcement." *American Journal of Criminal Justice* 39 (2014): 22–40.

Radosh, Polly F. "War on Drugs: Gender and Race Inequities in Crime Control Strategies." *Criminal Justice Studies* 21 (2008): 167–178.

Werb, Dan, Thomas Kerr, Bohdan Nosyk, Steffanie Strathdee, Julio Montaner, and Evan Wood. "The Temporal Relationship Between Drug Supply Indicators: An Audit of International Government Surveillance Systems." *BMJ Open* 3 (2013): 1–8.

CHRISTOPHER COMMISSION

The Christopher Commission was formed in response to the 1991 beating of Rodney King by Los Angeles Police Department (LAPD) officers, which was caught on videotape. The work of the Commission was a starting point for a broader movement relating to policing reform and monitoring the quality of police-community relations. The Commission's work served as a model framework for hundreds of subsequent police department investigations and evaluations in the 20th and 21st centuries. As a result of such commissions, national efforts to address police-community relations and excessive use of force have been created.

Early in the morning of March 3, 1991, George Holliday captured video of LAPD officers Laurence Powell, Timothy Wind, and Theodore Briseno beating 25-year-old King after a high-speed car chase. After stopping the car, officers ordered King, who had been driving, along with Freddie Helms and Bryant Allen to get out of the vehicle. Allen and Helms complied with the police commands and exited the vehicle. However, King did not, and he was subsequently Tased. Officers then continually kicked King in the head and body and further clubbed him with 56 baton strokes. Following the beating, King was taken by ambulance to the Pacifica Hospital of the Valley where he received 20 stitches and was treated for a broken leg, broken right ankle, and a broken cheekbone. While the beating was taking place, Sergeant Stacey Koon was present, but he took no action to stop it.

On March 4, 1991, Holliday went to the LAPD, intending to offer the video footage of the beating to the police as evidence of the excessive use of force during the incident. Holliday reported that after informing the desk officer that he had witnessed a motorist being beaten by LAPD officers, there was a lack of concern or interest for what he had witnessed. Holliday then left the police department without informing them of the existence of the videotape and subsequently arranged with a television station, KTLA, to have the footage broadcast.

The video was televised on March 4, 1991. Immediately following this, there was an overwhelming reaction by the public, with telephone calls inundating the police department, the mayor's office, and the media. Many city leaders, including Police Chief Daryl Gates, expressed shock that such an event could take place in Los Angeles. Mayor Tom Bradley said he was "shocked and outraged" by the events, adding, "This is something that we cannot, and will not tolerate" (Independent Commission of the Los Angeles Police Department 1991, 13).

Government officials responded quickly to the video of the beating. By March 6, 1991, the Federal Bureau of Investigation (FBI), the Los Angeles district attorney's office, and the LAPD's Internal Affairs Division had begun investigations. Powell, Koon, Briseno, and Wind were indicted on state charges soon afterward.

Intense public fury was exhibited because of the footage's release. The police department was immediately under scrutiny for what many believed had been a longstanding police brutality issue. In response to the widespread outrage that seriously undermined public confidence in the LAPD, Mayor Tom Bradley announced a 10-point plan that included the creation of an independent commission, chaired by former Deputy Attorney General Warren Christopher. The purpose of what became known as the Christopher Commission was to conduct a "full and fair examination of the structure and operation of the Los Angeles Police Department" (Bradley 1991, 2).

Work of the Christopher Commission

Beginning on April 1, 1991, the members of the Christopher Commission, which consisted of more than 60 lawyers who were supported by three data analysis and accounting firms, began what the Commission referred to as "an unprecedented inquiry into the use of excessive force by a police department" (Independent Commission of the Los Angeles Police Department 1991, ii). This investigation included testimony from more than 50 expert witnesses in 26 executive sessions, hearing from more than 150 additional private citizens and representatives of community organizations at five public hearings and interviewing more than 500 current and former Los Angeles police officers. Along with these witnesses, additional extensive analysis from a variety of police reports, legal documents, and other records was conducted. Although the Christopher Commission discovered the LAPD was mostly well organized and without corruption, there were nevertheless several significant problems noted within the department.

The identified problems fell under eight categories: (1) the use of excessive force, (2) racism and bias, (3) community policing, (4) recruitment, (5) training, (6) promotion and training, (7) officer discipline and personnel complaints, and (8) structural issues regarding the chief of police and the police commission.

One of the main problems identified by the Commission was the officers' use and misuse of force. The Commission found that certain officers misused force on multiple occasions and further repeatedly disregarded written policies. Several current and former high-ranking police officials stated this was a problem well known to supervisors but that the department failed to address the misconduct of these problem officers. The Commission reported the misconduct was allowed to continue, in part, because supervisory staff was not held accountable for the incidents of excessive force.

Among the electronic data provided by the LAPD, the Commission found a group of problem police officers that had posed a much higher risk of using excessive force compared to other officers. Specifically, the Commission found there was a group of 44 police officers who had had eight or more excessive force or improper tactics allegations brought up between 1986 and 1990. Further, a group of 63 police officers had been identified as being involved in 20 or more use-of-force reports between January 1987 and March 1991. An especially troubling finding of the Commission was that the personnel files of the police officers with at least eight improper tactics or excessive force allegations were mostly quite positive. The evaluations had an emphasis placed on every positive comment and gave little to no mention of any of the allegations of excessive use of force. The Commission concluded these performance evaluations were often quite misleading and failed to accurately describe the officers' history of discipline.

To address the problem of excessive force in the LAPD, the Commission made several specific recommendations. First, the leadership within the department needed to make curbing excessive use of force a priority. Second, a system wherein command officers were held accountable for excessive force of officers under their command needed to be developed. Third, the lieutenants and sergeants working with officers needed to be charged with monitoring the use of force of the officers they supervised and provide counseling to those who have histories of using excessive or unnecessary use of force. This would address the problem and, additionally, take care of any necessary disciplining. Finally, in a futuristic note, the Commission proposed that video and audio recordings of contacts between the public and the police could potentially hold promise for cutting back on excessive force.

Bias and Racism

An area the Commission found that aggravated the problem of excessive force within the Los Angeles Police Department was racism and bias already existing within the department. In a survey completed by 650 officers from the LAPD, close to a quarter believed "racial bias (prejudice) on the part of officers toward minority citizens currently exists and contributes to a negative interaction between police and community" (Independent Commission of the Los Angeles Police Department 1991, xii). Additionally, slightly more than one-quarter agreed with the statement, "an officer's prejudice towards the suspect's race may lead to the use of excessive force" (Independent Commission of the Los Angeles Police Department 1991, xii).

Additional evidence of racial bias was found through the Commission's review of more than 100,000 pages of computer-generated Mobile Digital Terminal (MDT) transcripts, which are used in public transit vehicles to communicate with a central dispatch office, that covered the days between November 1, 1989, and March 4, 1991. From this review, the Commission found that there were a substantial number of repeated and troubling racial remarks made by police officers while they were on duty. These remarks were also concerning in that the supervisors of these officers had direct access to the MDT comments that were made. However, they often were negligent in either properly monitoring the messages or in disciplining the officers who made the inappropriate remarks.

Several witnesses provided further evidence that racial prejudice and intolerance also occurred in the field. Numerous witnesses testified that the behavior of LAPD officers included acts that verbally humiliated and harassed minority suspects and included the use of invasive and humiliating tactics within minority neighborhoods. There was additional evidence presented that incidents of bias were not solely confined to the public who the officers' served, but also included other officers who identified with ethnic or racial minority groups. In addition to the findings of racism, the Commission also found evidence of bias based on gender and sexual orientation.

The Commission asserted that without active leadership by those at the top, the problems of racism and bias within the police department could not be eradicated. To address the problem, the Commission recommended that the chief of police implement concrete methods of ensuring the problems of racism and bias would not be tolerated in the department.

Community Policing

The Commission found that the organizational structure of the LAPD emphasized crime control over crime prevention, which isolated the police from the communities they were supposed to be serving. While this aggressive approach of detecting and responding to crime did produce results as far as clearing crimes went, it did so at the risk of alienating police officers from communities. To help tackle this issue, the Commission recommended a transition to a community-policing model involving increased interaction between officers and citizens on the street.

Recruitment

The Commission's investigation also revealed problems with the department's recruiting practices. Psychological evaluations and background investigations of potential candidates were not sufficient to flag those who were at risk of misconduct. In addition, those tasked with completing background investigations of candidates were overworked and inadequately trained. The Commission also believed that it was not enough to improve the process by which candidates were screened to manage these issues, because some police officers were well suited psychologically when they began their jobs but would subsequently suffer from issues such as problems with alcohol, burnout, and disenchantment. In its recommendations, the Commission proposed that officers should be retested periodically to identify psychological concerns, which may arise. Further, the Commission recommended supervisors understand that part of their responsibilities involved providing training and counseling options to help their officers better cope with problems.

Training

While the Commission was generally impressed with the training provided at the police academy for new recruits, there were nevertheless areas of concern. One area of concern was that little time was spent on cultural awareness in the academy. Other areas identified by the Commission involved deficiencies in the Spanish language program and the field training provided for new officers after completion of academy. One finding that may have been a contributing factor to use of excessive force was that there was no screening for those serving as field training officers. Thus, some with attitudes conducive to misconduct and with misconduct histories sometimes provided training to new recruits, serving as poor role models in the process.

Promotions

The Commission found the several issues relating to promotion and assignments likely contributed to use of excessive force. It found an officer's history of unstained complaints made against said officer was not being used in the determination of promotion. The Commission identified patrol assignment as significant in helping reduce uses of excessive force if officers were placed on assignment strategically. The Commission suggested that officers with histories of excessive force complaints should be paired with officers who had excellent communication skills, as a way to lessen the probability that use of force would occur.

Personnel Complaints and Officer Discipline

The issue receiving the greatest amount of adverse comments during the Commission's hearings had to do with the difficulties the public encountered when trying to file complaints against LAPD officers, especially complaints related to the use of excessive force. The Commission found there were numerous obstacles that people who wished to file complaints against police officers faced. One obstacle was that the intake officers who were in charge of taking reports often discouraged complaints from being filed or required long waits to complete the necessary forms to file a complaint. A second obstacle faced in heavily Latino divisions was that no Spanish-speaking officers were available to assist with the complaint. The Commission also found flaws in the way the department investigated many of the complaints and in how cases were adjudicated. The biggest single barrier the Commission found that prevented the effective investigation of complaints had to do with the officers' seemingly unwritten code of silence about the misconduct witnessed by their peers.

To address the issues of personnel complaints and officer discipline, the Commission believed that there needed to be substantial changes to the police department's disciplinary system. The Commission made several recommendations on how this could be accomplished. First, an office of the inspector general needed to be created within the police commission to be given the responsibility of overseeing the police disciplinary process. Second, the police commission needed to be given the responsibility of overseeing the complaint process. Third, excessive force complaints needed to be investigated by the internal affairs division. Finally, although the Commission believed the chief of police remains responsible for imposing discipline, they also felt that guidelines needed to be set by the chief of police and the police commission needed to be held responsible for following such guidelines.

Structural Issues

The Commission noted concerns relating to the structural constraints that limited the power the police commission had over the chief of police and other high ranking members within the police department. The police commission was limited in many ways, specifically because it was not an independent commission, one without influence by others within the police department. To address this issue, the Christopher Commission made recommendations that there be an independent civilian chief of staff who was in charge of the police commission's staff and that additional steps be taken to insulate them from outside political influence.

Brian E. Oliver and Raj Sethuraju

See also: Police Accountability; Police Misconduct during the L.A. Zoot Suit Riots; Racial Profiling; Rodney King Beating and Riots

Further Reading
Bradley, Tom. Letter to the Special Independent Commission. April 1, 1991.
Independent Commission of the Los Angeles Police Department. *Report of the independent commission of the Los Angeles Police Department.* Los Angeles, 1991.

ABNER LOUIMA CASE
When considering many of the issues related to questionable law enforcement behavior, particularly as it may relate to reports of unnecessary and excessive violence

Abner Louima, a Haitian immigrant, was arrested in a Brooklyn nightclub in 1997, and then tortured in a New York City police station house bathroom. (AP Photo/Richard Drew)

by the police, the quote attributed to Juvenal—the Roman poet and satirist (55–127 CE)—often comes to mind: *quis custodiet apsos custodies*. Who will guard the guards themselves?

This almost 2,000-year-old statement is certainly appropriate in 2016, as it was in the summer of 1997 when Abner Louima was arrested and then brutally assaulted in the 70th New York Police Department (NYPD) precinct station house in Brooklyn. The encounter that led to the arrest was a street fight. Louima's subsequent victimization while in custody was outrageous; he was sodomized and seriously injured with a wooden (toilet) plunger.

Volumes of media accounts, print and electronic, and governmental agency reports have documented what happened that night in Brooklyn in August 1997. Criminal and civil investigations have been conducted. Police operations, tactics, and training have been reviewed and revised. In a 10-year retrospective, *The New York Times* reported that Louima, a Haitian immigrant, had received $8.7 million in settlements from New York City and the Patrolmen's Benevolent Association (PBA) and relocated out of the city. The money received was reported to be the largest police brutality pay-out in the city's history. Louima continues to be involved in speaking out against police-related violence and Haitian immigrant issues.

The incident stood out as a stark illustration of police-related violence nation-wide and was taken as a sign of an anything-goes approach to crime control. In

November 2000, the U.S. Commission on Civil Rights published *Revisiting Who Is Guarding the Guardians? A Report on Police Practices and Civil Rights in America* and noted that the assault and beating of Louima, while in custody in a New York City precinct, stunned the country.

Although the proverbial police "blue wall" seemed to stymie the investigation into the matter and a potential cover-up was assumed, a thorough investigation was conducted resulting in the arrest of Police Officer Justin Volpe. Volpe pled guilty at his 1999 trial, leading to a 30-year sentence in federal prison. Other officers who were implicated in the attack were investigated and subjected to various criminal and departmental charges.

A positive project that was developed because of the Louima assault and the death of Amadou Diallo almost two years later was called *Streetwise: Language, Culture, and Police Work in New York,* which was conceived, developed, and originally delivered by the New York State Regional Community Police Institute. Regional Community Policing Institutes (RCPI) was established by the Office of Community Oriented Policing Services, U.S. Department of Justice, in 1997. It was designed for delivery to street-level police personnel and their supervisors.

The *Streetwise* project provided participants with cultural knowledge about different groups of people. Participants learned basic linguistic skills about groups such as the Chinese, Hispanics, and Russians, and they learned about the different LGBT communities. The training was accomplished with media presentations, case studies, and role playing. In addition, there were problem-solving exercises. The testimony of mentor officers was used to demonstrate how language and culture influence police officers' daily interactions with the community.

A program such as *Streetwise* is an important aspect of agency response in rebuilding citizen expectations and confidence. But there is a greater, more holistic need. The community deserves to be able to be confident that a sustainable system is in place that will better ensure that illegal and unacceptable attacks, such as on Abner Louima, will not be tolerated.

The Bureau of Justice Statistics quadrennial "Census of State and Local Law Enforcement Agencies, 2008" shows that there were about 765,000 sworn personnel, defined as those with general arrest powers, employed by 17,985 state and local law enforcement agencies (Bureau of Justice Statistics 2008). Each state sets its own minimum standards for law enforcement employment and training. There are many differences across state lines and sometimes within a given state. Because of the nature of governance in the United States, we will never achieve, and should not pursue, a national policing force. What we should expect—demand—is reasonable, informed standards for selection and training. Each agency must have an appropriately transparent system of supervision, management, and leadership including a proper plan for discipline and rewards. Organizations such as the International Association of Chiefs of Police (IACP) and the National Sheriffs Association (NSA) are professionally engaged in advocating for such activity and as was pointed out 50 years ago by former NYPD officer turned social psychologist, Morton Bard, greater cooperation and collaboration between law enforcement agencies and the social and behavioral sciences is imperative.

In April 2015, Loretta Lynch was confirmed by the Senate to become the U.S. Attorney General. Of interest, in 1999 she was an assistant U.S. attorney in the Eastern District of New York (EDNY) and was part of the team that prosecuted Justin Volpe, and other officers for covering up the incident. Later she became the U.S. attorney for the EDNY and conducted a pattern or practice investigation concerning police violence and potential civil rights abuses. Lynch's elevation to the head of the U.S. Department of Justice (DOJ) positioned her to build on the experiences in the EDNY, as she oversees the review or investigation of the numerous incidents that have occurred over the past several years. She also has the ability to greatly influence police practices and training through numerous DOJ functions.

In these times of heightened concern about officer behavior in several law enforcement agencies, police response to inappropriate behavior may need to be revised. A true collaboration between the DOJ, the state attorneys general, the IACP and NSA, and competent social and behavioral academic scientists should review legal and administrative directives influencing police operations. Only then may we be able to accomplish the important steps to operate fairly. For example, being able to identify the nature and extent of the problem is important. To adjust to the changing times and this "new reality," it is necessary to identify which legislative bodies are responsible for addressing the issues and which parties are charged with problem resolution. Further, there must be a responsibility for suggested changes in policy, procedure, and practices for the new reality. Agency organizational change(s) may be appropriate accompanied by adequate funding.

Robert J. Louden

See also: Amadou Diallo Case; Police Accountability; Police Brutality; Police Misconduct during the L.A. Zoot Suit Riots; Racial Profiling; "Thin Blue Line": Police as a Guard against Anarchy

Further Reading

Bureau of Justice Statistics. "U.S. State and Local Law Enforcement Agencies Census 2008." *Alaska Justice Forum* 28, no. 2–3 (2011): 8–9. http://justice.uaa.alaska.edu/forum/28/2-3summerfall2011/f_lawenf_census.html.

Chan, Sewell. "The Abner Louima Case, 10 Years Later." City Room: Blogging from the Five Boroughs, posted on August 9, 2007. http://cityroom.blogs.nytimes.com/2007/08/09/the-abner-louima-case-10-years-laterk.

Childress, Sarah. "Policing the Police: As Attorney General, How Will Loretta Lynch Police the Police?" *Frontline*, April 23, 2015. http://www.pbs.org/wgbh/frontline/article/as-attorney-general-how-will-loretta-lynch-police-the-police.

Louden, R. J. "Policing Post-9/11." *Fordham Urban Law Journal* 32, no. 4 (2005): 757–765.

Louden, R. J. "Streetwise: Language, Culture, and Police Work in New York." *African Americans and Criminal Justice: An Encyclopedia*, edited by Delores D. Jones-Brown, Beverly D. Frazier, and Marvie Brooks. Santa Barbara, CA: Greenwood Publishing, 2014.

U.S. Commission on Civil Rights. "*Revisiting 'Who Is Guarding the Guardians?' A Report on Police Practices and Civil Rights in America*." U.S. Commission on Civil Rights Web Site. November 2000. http://www.usccr.gov/pubs/guard/main.htm.

AMADOU DIALLO CASE

In 1999, Amadou Diallo, a 22-year-old African immigrant, was killed by four New York police officers: Sean Carroll, Edward McMellon, Kenneth Boss, and Richard Murphy. The officers were driving an unmarked car and wearing plain clothes at the time of the shooting. They fired 41 shots outside of Diallo's apartment in the Bronx. Although the officers were charged with second-degree murder, they were not found guilty. Outrage followed Diallo's shooting in New York City and throughout the nation, raising issues related to racial profiling and police brutality.

Amadou Diallo had immigrated to New York City in 1996. During his time in the United States, he worked as a sidewalk vendor. On February 4, 1999, Diallo was believed to have gotten something to eat after returning home from work. As he was standing near the front door of his apartment, the officers drove by in an unmarked police car. Diallo matched the description of a young, African American man wanted for rape, so the police stopped the car and approached Diallo.

The men declared they were the police and requested that he "show his hands." Diallo did not stop at their request, but rather ran up the stairs to his apartment. The light outside the apartment was not on, so when Diallo reached into his jacket and pulled out a dark object, the police mistook the object for a gun. This caused Officer Carroll to yell out "Gun!" to his fellow officers. At the same time, Officer McMellon fell down the steps, making it appear as though he had been shot. The officers then began shooting at Diallo. Together, they fired the 41 shots, and Diallo was hit by 19 of them. It was reported that officers Carroll and McMellon fired 16 shots each, Boss fired 5, and Murphy fired 4.

There were no weapons found on or near Diallo immediately after the shooting, suggesting that he had been reaching for his wallet, not a weapon. The autopsy determined that Diallo died of gunshot wounds to the torso. The coroner also reported that some shots had entered Diallo through the soles of his feet, indicating that he was already down when the officers were shooting.

After the Diallo shooting, an internal investigation found that the officers did what they should have done in this situation—they were found to have acted according to police protocol. However, as more facts unfolded, many members of the community became outraged. It was established that the four police officers had been recruited to work with the Street Crime Unit, an elite squad aimed at getting guns off the streets and fighting street crime in New York. Some people argued that it would be unlikely that the officers were out looking for a suspect from a crime that was reported to have happened more than a year prior to Diallo's shooting. Because Diallo was innocent and had no criminal record, many people also believed that this case exposed the New York Police Department's aggressive policing strategies in minority communities.

News of the shooting was followed by angry demonstrations and protests throughout New York City. There has historically been a large population of African Americans, Hispanics, and immigrants in the Bronx. Because of Diallo's shooting, many residents of the Bronx believed that they could just as easily have become the victim of a police shooting. Many people were concerned that the Street Crime Unit was involved in excessive use of "stop and frisk" and for overstepping individual civil liberties to meet arrest quotas. Many also felt that Diallo was not just the victim of these officers but of aggressive policing strategies that were the result of Mayor Rudolph Giuliani's administration. Additionally, some people believed that Mayor Giuliani's support of these officers created additional strife among minority communities, showing little concern for Diallo's life.

Following Diallo's death, the grand jury indicted the officers on charges of second-degree murder on March 25, 1999. However, the location of the actual trial was changed from New York City to the New York Court of Appeals in Albany, because of the negative publicity associated with this case.

Justice Joseph C. Teresi presided over the trial in Albany, and the jury panel consisted of four African American women, two Caucasian women, and six Caucasian men. Because there were no civilian witnesses at the scene of Diallo's shooting, the jury had to rely primarily on the officers' testimony. As expected, there were differing accounts of the events that happened on the morning of Diallo's death. The chief prosecutor, Eric Warner, stated that the officers did not call out any warning prior to shooting Diallo. He also stated that the officers continued to fire after Diallo was already on the ground. Defense attorneys, on the other hand, stated that although Diallo's death was a tragedy, it was not a crime. They mentioned that Diallo was acting suspiciously when he did not stop at the officers' commands, and Diallo had pointed an object at them. Although the object turned out to be a wallet, at the time the officers believed it was a gun, which was when they began shooting in self-defense, as they were in fear for their own lives.

They were charged with two counts of second-degree murder. One stated they intentionally caused Diallo's death, while the other stated that they killed him through actions that demonstrated a depraved indifference to human life. Based on New York law, someone can use deadly force if he or she *reasonably* believes deadly force is needed for self-defense. The defense referred to the case of Bernhard Goetz, who shot and seriously wounded four young men riding the train in New York City in 1984. He was acquitted of the attempted murder charges, claiming that the shooting was in self-defense because he feared for his life, as he was being robbed. The jury found that there was a reasonable basis to believe deadly force was reasonable in this particular circumstance. Consequently, the question the Diallo jury had to contemplate was not whether the officers thought Diallo intended to use deadly force against them, but if the officers' belief was *reasonable*. That is, the testimony examined whether a reasonable person would have perceived Diallo to pose a lethal threat to the officers at the time of the incident.

After hearing all of the testimony, the jury delivered a verdict of "not guilty," and the officers were acquitted of the charges on February 25, 2000. The acquittal created public outrage, as many people criticized the verdict, and Diallo became a national example of racial profiling and aggressive policing techniques. There were protests and anti-police demonstrations in the streets of New York, following the acquittal of the four officers.

Diallo's death also brought to light questions regarding implicit bias and whether racial stereotypes can affect immediate decisions. It is impossible to know what

Diallo was thinking when he reached into his pocket instead of following instructions when the officers ordered him to raise his hands. It is likely that he misunderstood the order and intended to show the officers his identification. It was not until after the shooting that the officers realized Diallo was holding a wallet, not a weapon. However, the jury's verdict was that the officers acted *reasonably*, given the circumstances surrounding this case.

Francesca Spina

See also: Deadly Force; Eric Garner Case in New York City and Subsequent Tensions; Freddie Gray Case; Michael Brown Shooting and the Aftermath in Ferguson; Police Brutality; Racial Profiling

Further Reading

Fritsch, Jane. "The Diallo Verdict: The Overview; 4 Officers in Diallo Shooting are Acquitted of All Charges." *The New York Times*, February 26, 2000.

Gillers, Stephen. "Four Officers, One Likely Strategy." *The New York Times*, April 3, 1999.

Harring, Sydney. "The Diallo Verdict: Another 'Tragic Accident' in New York's War on Street Crime?" *Social Justice* 27, no. 1 (2000): 9–18.

Payne, B. Keith. "Weapon Bias: Split-Second Decisions and Unintended Stereotyping." *Current Directions in Psychological Science* 15, no. 6 (2006): 287–291.

Part 5: Intensive Debate about the "American Police State" (2000–Present)

DEADLY FORCE

The use of lethal or deadly force has been the defining feature of American policing throughout its history. The potential to inflict death is the core of police powers and one of the most contentious issues in modern policing. American police are different from law enforcement officers in other countries because of the weaponry used at all levels—from local police departments to state highway patrols to the Federal Bureau of Investigation (FBI). As a reflection of a strongly rooted gun culture, police are heavily armed and weaponized, which some people refer to as the "militarization of the police." U.S. law enforcement faces challenges in tempering the use of deadly force when a cycle of gun violence ensues (to deal with armed violent criminals produced by the wars waged against crimes, drugs, gangs, and terrorism most recently), avoiding an arms race that makes their jobs more difficult (access to guns is no barrier, as it makes any incident potentially deadly), and undermining efforts to increase trust and build better relations with communities (deadly force disproportionally used against particular segments of the U.S. population). Perceptions are more influential than reality in today's media-dominated society in which deadly force as a growing trend is accepted without any credible and strong evidence to supporting this assertion.

Using deadly force is seen as calibrated and necessary by law enforcement while viewed as disproportional and excessive by others (especially minority, poor communities, and populations). While deadly force is rarely used by the police, the visibility and attention given to any deadly force incidents magnify the use, causing citizens to perceive that deadly force is used more than it actually is. Law enforcement has become isolated from the public due to this issue, and this is likely to continue in the future. Evidence on the factors responsible for deadly force and its impact is inconclusive due to the absence of accurate data. Societal expectations of the police are greater and increasingly more critical in recent years. Citizens expect police to use force only when absolutely necessary and only as a last resort. Police view deadly force from the prism of officer safety and examine deadly force as reasonable when deadly threats to officers and citizens can be prevented. Deadly force is now a bigger political issue than ever before with proposed solutions complicated by extremist political debate.

Deadly force is referred to as the amount of force likely to cause serious bodily harm. Police officers may only use deadly force in specific circumstances. (Laryn Kragt Bakker/Dreamstime .com)

Deadly force and the potential to use it are considered vital to how police view their responsibilities. Police work on the frontlines, enforcing laws and protecting the innocent and vulnerable. They are the line between order and anarchy of predatory, violent criminals. Force and deadly force are options to be used; hesitations in deploying deadly force can be fatal. In justifying and legitimizing the use of force, police consider different types of force, the appropriate times for its application, and the quantity of force. Police are trained professionals and use deadly force as a last resort, only as necessary and appropriate to the specific incident. The level of force required varies by situation, circumstances, and specific persons involved, which seems to suggest achievement of a high degree of objectivity in police deadly force decision-making by proper training and policy. Quickly developing and potentially dangerous situations that require split-second decision-making make deadly force highly subjective. Training is difficult to simulate for many reasons. Replicating the stress, emotions, and physiological aspects of real-life incidents in artificial conditions is extremely difficult. Each decision is specific to the individual officer and his or perspective at the time.

Named as the split-second syndrome, which refers to the amount of time officers have to determine if deadly force is necessary, this subjectivity is unavoidable. The prospects of misunderstanding and misreading situations is possible even for highly trained officers. Until the landmark ruling of the dominant fleeing felon standard (in which police were justified in using deadly force to apprehend felons), the amount of autonomy given to the police in force decisions was substantial. The potential for abuse of these powers has emerged as a problem for police. Police brutality and use of force against ethnic minorities, particularly young African American males, were part of extensive criticism of the police from the 1960s until the landmark ruling from *Tennessee v. Garner* (1985).

Before 1986, the inclination to use more force than necessary has been seen as a major problem by citizens and due process proponents. After the ruling, there were more controls over the police. Police departments increasingly developed lethal force policies to avoid liability from failure to train or inadequate training of their officers. The success of these policies was widely acclaimed and preceded the Supreme Court's famous deadly force ruling. *Tennessee v. Garner* (1985) led to the development of the current standard of reasonable use in which deadly force is to be reserved for situations in which officers have probable cause of an unavoidable threat of death or serious injuries to officers and citizens. The ruling aimed to prevent deadly force to be used against fleeing, nonviolent, unarmed, felony suspects. Some argue that protection of life is at the core of the ruling and should be the main factor in determining use of deadly force. Officers' and citizens' loss of lives served as the dominant standard to judge the use of deadly force by police. Others argue that the new standard remains vague and unclear with considerable autonomy still given to the police. Officers could rationalize and justify decisions when they were given the benefit of doubt and in good faith. Not surprisingly, law enforcement felt little pressure to change their practices to avoid lethal force. Deadly force for self-defense remained part of the police officer's arsenal. New language about deadly force emerged from a subsequent case, *Graham v. Connor* (1989), including "objectively reasonable" (what is reasonable based on the facts and circumstances and not intent or motivation of officers) and "totality of circumstances" (the conditions known by an officer when making decisions about use of force).

The phrase "objectively reasonable" refers to information available at that time to the officer, and "totality of circumstances" present in the incident at that time. This standard for some is too subjective and gives significant latitude to the individual officer to use deadly force, providing little incentive for caution. From officers' perspectives, deadly force is warranted when officers do not have full information and have to respond quickly with the threat of being injured or killed. Legal standards are limited in their application during incidents and the courts have permitted officers to define what is reasonable from their perspective. Deference to law enforcement has also limited liability in criminal and civil cases. Shared values and reliance on the need to work together made the police and legal systems hesitant to directly challenge each other's professional expertise.

Despite all of the research explaining police use of deadly force, it is not conclusive, and definitive conclusions are limited because of the lack of systematic data. The race or ethnicity of suspects, physical resistance by suspects (surprisingly, verbal resistance and failure to comply with officer commands are factors as well), and whether or not suspects are armed (guns especially but even knives and other weapons) increase the likelihood of deadly force. Educated officers and effective supervision (more recently) have been identified as critical to minimizing deadly force, but the specific mechanisms and parameters to translate these into actual practice are exceedingly elusive. Requiring college education as a minimum requirement would decrease the number of recruits and limit policing as a career choice for some. Using the same logic, effective supervision would put supervisors in precarious positions of micro-managing, increase tensions between police officers and managers, and offer less appealing work conditions in the minds of street officers.

Earlier research indicated that suspect demeanor and lack of respect given to officers increased officer use of force. The escalation of force depended on citizen responses and interactions with law enforcement. Police, unlike citizens, were expected to rely on their training to use force judiciously and with sound judgement. As human beings, officers are impacted from lack of proper deference even in the face of citizen provocation and personalized. De-escalation as a preventative strategy for deadly force is not well documented, even though police try to avoid deadly force whenever possible to protect themselves and others.

There is a building consensus with some scholars and practitioners that excessive force is concentrated in a few problem officers; younger officers are prone to use force when unwarranted. No fool-proof methods to filter out problem officers are available. Police departments are more sensitive about excessive force in more recent decades and provision of citizen complaints and grievance mechanisms is more common. Holding police accountable is a growing priority in relation to excessive force. Non-lethal alternatives to deadly force, such as Tasers, are promoted as effective solutions but cannot prevent deadly force if dynamic and fast-evolving situations do not permit their use. Non-lethal alternatives offer little against weapons on the street and are not true alternatives to deadly force. Ideally, a use-of-force continuum would be considered; officers often need to make split-second decisions, so there is little time to "think" about how much force they are going to use.

Societal events and policy developments are responsible for making deadly force the most prominent issue in current policing. Deadly force is present in the intense coverage by the media and political attention given to gun control and lethal violence (mass shootings), stand-your-ground laws and specific cases (Trayvon Martin's shooting), the Black Lives Matter movement, the concentration of negative consequences of the punitive and get-tough-on-crime wars on crimes, drugs, gangs, and now terrorism. Advancements in social media, notably smartphones, single-handedly propelled deadly force into intense scrutiny. Some wondered about the extent to which police abused force of any kind, including deadly force powers, on a regular basis or followed the use-of-force continuum (this is a tool used for training police of how much and when to use force starting from no force to minimal to moderate to deadly force) in practice. Doubts have been raised on the secretive and subcultural nature of policing being responsible for police isolation and reluctance to discuss reforms to deadly force training, policy, and accountability.

Weapons training is still an important part of academy training for the police. The war-like mentality police learn in strict command-and-control settings reinforces the use of weapons and readiness to use deadly force for the battle on the streets. It is notoriously difficult to change police behavior via training when the command-and-control, para-military structure of policing academies and organizations emphasize controlling situations, obeying directives from upper management, and preparing to use deadly force to save lives as a necessity and requirement to join police ranks. As with many issues in policing, use-of-force training is dominated by legal concerns and requirements. Although legal checks on deadly force are essential (to ensure that lethal force is used only when absolutely necessary and appropriate), accountability on deadly force through legal means has supported the status quo of police expectations with holding themselves accountable (through their profession and departmental controls) and non-police parties expecting significant changes to reduce the levels of deadly force and their deadly consequences. Political solutions to the use of deadly force and its effects are largely symbolic and offer little in resolving this stand-off.

Sanjay Marwah

See also: Fleeing Felon Legislation; Michael Brown Shooting and the Aftermath in Ferguson; Militarization of Public and Campus Police Departments; Police Accountability; Trayvon Martin Shooting

Further Reading

Anderson, Jose Felipe. "From Fugitives to Ferguson: Repairing Historical and Structural Defects in Legally Sanctioned Use of Deadly Force." *Washington University Journal of Law and Policy* 69 (2015): 63–85.

Klinger, David. *Into the Kill Zone: A Cop's Eye View of Deadly Force.* San Francisco: Jossey-Bass, 2006.

Shjarback, John, and Michael White. "Departmental Professionalism and Its Impact on Indicators of Violence in Police-Citizen Encounters." *Police Quarterly* 19, no. 1 (2015): 32–62.

Terrill, William. "The Elusive Nature of Reasonableness." *Criminology & Public Policy* 8, no. 1 (2009): 163–172.

White, Michael. "Transactional Encounters, Crisis-Driven Reform, and the Potential for a National Police Deadly Force Database." *Criminology & Public Policy* 15, no. 1 (2015): 223–235.

POLICE ACCOUNTABILITY

Police accountability is about controlling police wrongdoing, whether the wrongdoing is a criminal violation or a violation of departmental rules, at the individual officer level, and ensuring that the police comply with rules and regulations and operate efficiently and effectively at the organizational level. Police wrongdoings involve corruption and misconduct. Corruption can be defined as offenses involving material and/or financial gains, while misconduct often does not involve such gains (Jiao 2010). Various control and oversight systems have been implemented to hold the police accountable, including internal policies and programs, managerial and supervisory schemes, police auditing, citizen review bodies, civil rights and civil liberties organizations, laws and regulations, courts, politicians, government officials, the news media, and the public (Jiao 2010). These methods, groups, and people often work together or complementarily to control, change, and reform the police.

Issues of police accountability arise due to inherent risk in officers' routine activities and underperformance at the organizational level. Police officers engage in high-risk situations and are susceptible to temptations, greed, danger, criminal behaviors, citizen injuries and deaths, civil rights violations, disciplinary actions, and system failures. These problems manifest themselves in the form of police corruption and misconduct and organizational inefficiencies. Corruption ranges from police taking bribes, overlooking illegal activities, drug-trafficking, to committing crimes directly in relationship to the drug trade (Jiao 2010). Misconduct ranges from sleeping on the job, disrespect for the dignity of individuals, unequal treatment of different groups, misuse and excessive use of force, to criminal homicide. Organizational issues stem from the inability of police agencies to deliver effectively the basic services such as crime control and order maintenance to their communities.

Critical ramifications exist due to poor police accountability, including loss of public trust, lack of cooperation and support in crime prevention and criminal investigation, and draining of financial and human resources. Police are often investigated for issues related to corruption, search and seizures, use of force, and probable cause. Whether a police organization and its programs are functioning economically, efficiently, and effectively is also a concern of police administrators, government officials, and the public. Police departments therefore not only need to define and enforce standards of conduct, but also gather accurate and objective financial and performance information to improve their operations and achieve effective management.

Various police accountability programs have been established to deal with police misbehaviors and underperformance. These measures can be broadly categorized into internal and external mechanisms. Internal measures involve police efforts, and external measures are created by institutions independent or semi-independent from the police (Jiao 2010). Police leadership's commitment to police policies is essential to their successful implementation. Internal policies and procedures may have an effect only when supported by a clear message from the leadership and management that they will be followed (Fridell 2015). The administrative commitment to police accountability comes in the form of various internal mechanisms, including rules and procedures, internal affairs investigation, use of force reporting, citizen complaints review procedures, an early intervention system, departmental rewards for desired behaviors, and special programs designed to improve efficiency and effectiveness. Police officers deserve effective policies, training, supervision, and a strong system of accountability.

External approaches include those provided by civilian and other governmental bodies outside the police, including citizen oversight systems, independent investigative programs, and monitoring agencies (Jiao 2010). Citizen oversight bodies include citizen complaint review systems and auditor models of citizen oversight. Investigative programs include government-appointed commissions and the U.S. Department of Justice pattern and practice suits. Monitoring agencies scrutinize activities of internal police investigations or an external oversight or investigative body.

The following is a list of some organizations and programs dedicated to strengthening police accountability: The New York City Civilian Complaint Review Board (NYCCCRB), New York City Commission to Combat Police Corruption (NYCCCPC), the National Association for the Advancement of the Colored People (NAACP), the American Civil Liberties Union (ACLU), Human Rights Watch, the United States Commission on Civil Rights, the U.S. Department of Justice, the Knapp Commission (1972), the Christopher Commission (1992), the Mollen Commission (1994), the Los Angeles County (California) Sheriff's Department's Office of Independent Review, Austin (Texas) Police Monitor, Nashville (Tennessee) Metropolitan Police Department's Office of Professional Accountability, Philadelphia Integrity and Accountability Office, and Computer Statistics (Compstat), which is an application developed by the New York Police Department (NYPD) to measure crime and police performance and improve accountability of police commanders.

A most prevalent police program dedicated to police accountability is the Internal Affairs Bureau (IAB). Internal Affairs officers consider the law, the labor contract, the police policy, and past practice in their investigations. The completed investigative report is usually submitted to the officers' supervisors and/or an internal review committee for review and recommendation. The chief or deputy chief of police reviews the report and recommendations and makes the final decision regarding disciplinary actions. In New York City, the IAB receives and investigates police corruption and is answerable only to the Chief. The IAB also engages in various proactive activities to prevent corruption such as analyzing complaint data to identify potentially corrupt units and carrying out secretive "integrity tests" to secure evidence against particular officers (Jiao 2010). The New York City Commission to Combat Police Corruption (NYCCCPC) was created through Executive Order to monitor anti-corruption activities. It performs audits and analyses of the NYPD's control systems and provides recommendations for improvement (Jiao 2010).

The New York City Civilian Complaint Review Board (NYCCCRB) handles allegations of police misconduct against NYPD officers. Its cases include use of force, abuse of authority, and discourteous use of language incidents. Its investigative staff, which is composed of civilian employees, conducts investigations of police misconduct. The CCRB's dispositions on complaints, including recommendations for disciplinary actions, are forwarded to the police commissioner (Jiao 2010).

Use-of-force reporting is another common practice for enforcing standards of conduct. This program requires that police officers fill out separate use-of-force reports for specific force types. Although agencies have different designations regarding reportable force, the International Association of Chiefs of Police (IACP 1999) model policy requires that physical force, chemical force, impact force, electronic equipment use, and firearm discharges be reported. "All use-of-force reports shall specify the actions of the suspect that necessitated the use of force, the reasons why the officer used force, as well as any suspect complaints of injury, medical treatment received, or refusal of medical treatment" (IACP 1999, IV.A.2). In conjunction with use-of-force reporting, police agencies have instituted open and accessible complaints process to receive, review, and investigate use-of-force complaints and provide for appropriate dispositions for sustained complaints (Walker 2005).

Early intervention systems are used primarily to identify potentially problematic officers. However, they do not focus on isolated or anecdotal incidents to determine whether an intervention is warranted. Rather, they involve collection and analysis of data for evaluation of officer performance and identification of problems. The early intervention systems databases usually utilize civilian complaints and the use-of-force reports to identify performance problems of individual officers. They serve as an important administrative tool for monitoring officer conduct and preventing more serious problems from happening.

Police auditing involves research and analysis by professionals with knowledge and expertise in policing and accounting. Police audits are done both internally by specialized police personnel and externally by independent auditors. Auditors measure compliance with departmental policies and procedures and the law, determine whether police are performing at an appropriate level, and recommend actions for improving management, organizational structure, and operating procedures. Because police auditing is used to not only examine financial and financial-related statements, but also evaluate police efficiency and effectiveness, a police audit is often referred to as a compliance audit or a performance audit. A variety of police audits exist ranging from a single focus on police purchasing to a comprehensive audit aimed at increasing police efficiency and effectiveness in an entire organization. Police auditing meets the need of the government, police, and public to know about the economy, efficiency, and effectiveness of police operations.

The Independent Police Auditor (IPA) is different from traditional audit functions performed by a city or state government auditor, an internal police auditor, or an independent external auditor. An IPA occupies a largely self-governing municipal office dedicated to auditing police investigations of citizen complaints. As an oversight body, it monitors police activities and determines if a police investigation is complete, thorough, and objective. It also serves as a resource for citizens of a city regarding police actions and standards. The office of the IPA is usually established through directives of a city council or mayor and reports directly to the city council or mayor. The creation and operations of the office is governed by a city charter section or ordinance. The IPA handles typically four types of cases: (1) use of unnecessary force or any force citizens believe to be wrong, including use of deadly force, shooting, and suspicious and wrongful deaths; (2) financial-related cases such as officer benefits, police staffing levels, off-the-book accounts, and impounds and property rooms; (3) misbehaviors such as discourteous treatment, verbal abuse, coercion, racial profiling, and sexual orientation bias; and (4) routine police operations such as call center operations, domestic violence response, and detective bureau reports.

The U.S. Department of Justice (DOJ) investigates police departments that demonstrate a practice or pattern of offenses that lead to civil rights violations. Such investigations often result in memoranda of agreement and consent decrees encompassing reform and improvement of police organization and operations. The legal authority of the DOJ to investigate police practices is based on federal statute 42 U.S.C. Sec. 14141, the Violent Crime Control Act passed by the Congress in 1994. The DOJ is authorized to initiate investigations focused on a pattern or practice that violates citizens' constitutional rights and other laws of the United States, collect statistics on police abuse, file civil litigation to address such illegal practices, and enter memoranda of agreement and consent decrees with local municipalities. Some state governments have a similar process in place to identify and reform police agencies to stop violations of state constitutional rights. The DOJ usually engages with an independent monitor to report progress or lack thereof to the district court to ensure the implementation of a consent decree. In many ways, implementing the consent decree is similar to the auditing process, which measures whether police activities such as arrests, search warrants, property/evidence rooms, confidential informants, use-of-force investigations, and complaint management systems are in compliance with policies, procedures, and laws.

Police litigation has been used to hold the police accountable through the use of Title 42 of the U.S. Code, Section 1983. This federal statute provides redress to individual citizens for deprivation of constitutional and federal statutory rights (Bickel 2001). The U.S. Supreme Court has passed rulings that allow financial liability lawsuits to municipalities based on the misconduct of police officers. Municipalities can be regarded as "persons" under Section 1983, giving rise to liability and a municipal government could be liable for actions of its officers providing that a plaintiff proves that a city policy or custom is the driving force behind a right violation perpetrated by an officer acting in the position of legal authority (Monell 1978). Private litigants are given a federal court remedy as a first resort rather than after state action (Monroe 1961). Section 1983 actions most commonly involve the Fourth and Fourteenth amendment issues such as use of force, search and seizure, and due process violations (Kean 1999).

These various internal mechanisms and external approaches established to ensure police accountability are not without concerns or controversies. A police organization must balance the need to curb norms that foster corruption and misconduct and the need to allow officers the flexibility to address the variety of situations they confront. The overuse of formal controls stifles individual initiatives and may cause some officers to evade accountability procedures. A significant issue for many police agencies is the hurdle of establishing performance measurements and collecting systematic data to assess their operations. The quasi-military organizational structure and strong occupational culture often make it difficult for them to engage in this process and create planned change. The auditor model of citizen oversight usually involves review of policies and procedures only without direct investigation of citizen complaints and thus suffers from a lack of credibility and public support. The independent auditor also faces challenges from various stakeholders and is often restricted by the authorities of the office. Most elected officials such as mayors and legislators do not understand the details of police administration, are subject to political pressures, and therefore are not able to provide proper guidance to police executives. Public demands for crime control often conflict with principles such as equal protection of the law and due process. Over the years, police accountability involves a constant tension between internal and external control and between police autonomy and external oversight.

Police accountability is about controlling police wrongdoing at both the individual and organizational level with various control and oversight mechanisms. Police officers may commit crime or violate departmental policies and police organizations may underperform or not be able to meet public demand for services and crime control. Police departments not only need to define and enforce standards of conduct, but also use financial and performance information to improve police management. Police accountability programs can be grouped broadly under internal and external measures, involving either the efforts of those established by independent or semi-independent institutions outside the police, or the efforts of the police themselves (Jiao 2010). The police administrative commitment to accountability comes in the form of internal mechanisms that convey to police officers that corruption and misconduct will not be tolerated. These internal means of promoting accountability include internal affairs investigation, use of force reporting, citizen complaints review procedures, an early intervention system, departmental rewards for desired behaviors, and special programs designed to improve police efficiency and effectiveness. External approaches include citizen complaint review systems, auditor models of citizen oversight, government-appointed commissions, the USDOJ pattern and practice investigations and consent decrees, monitoring agencies that scrutinize activities of an internal control program and an external oversight or investigative body, and police litigation using Title 42 of the U.S. Code, Section 1983. These various mechanisms and approaches often involve a complex and difficult process and a constant tension between police autonomy and external oversight but overall complement one another in achieving police accountability.

Allan Jiao

See also: ACLU; Christopher Commission; Corruption; Knapp Commission; Police Brutality; Racial Profiling

Further Reading

Bickel, William. "An Analysis of Section 1983 Litigation Dealing with Police Misconduct." In *Police Misconduct: A Reader for the 21st Century*, edited by Michael J. Palmiotto, 415–427. Upper Saddle River, NJ: Prentice Hall, 2001.

Dunham, Roger G., and Geoffrey P. Alpert, eds. *Critical Issues in Policing: Contemporary Readings*. Long Grove, IL: Waveland Press, 2015.

Fridell, Lorie A. "Use-of-Force Policy, Policy Enforcement, and Training." In *Critical Issues in Policing: Contemporary Readings*, edited by Roger G. Dunham and Geoffrey P. Alpert, 548–566. Long Grove, IL: Waveland Press, 2015.

International Association of Chiefs of Police (IACP). *Model Policy: Use of Force*. Arlington,
VA: IACP, 1999.

Jiao, Allan Y. "Controlling Police Corruption and Misconduct: A Comparative Examination
between Hong Kong and New York." *Asian Journal of Criminology* 5, no. 1 (2010): 27–44.

Jiao, Allan Y. *Police Auditing: Standards and Applications*. Springfield, IL: Charles C. Thomas,
2015.

Kean, Seth M. "Municipal Liability for Off-duty Police Misconduct under Section 1983: The
'Under Color of Law' Requirement." *Boston University Law Review* 79 (1999): 195–230.

Monell v. Department of Social Services, 436 U.S. 658, 663. 1978.

Monroe v. Pape, 365 U.S. 167. 1961.

Palmiotto, Michael J., ed. *Police Misconduct: A Reader for the 21st Century*. Upper Saddle River,
NJ: Prentice Hall, 2001.

Walker, Samuel. *The New World of Police Accountability*. Thousand Oaks, CA: Sage Publications, 2005.

POLICE BRUTALITY

Police brutality is a multifaceted term, the use of which signifies protest against conduct, policies, and practices that have resulted in individuals and groups feeling abused
or brutalized at the hands of police. Although their implications overlap somewhat
with phenomena of excessive force, officer misconduct, and system-wide racial disparities in criminal justice outcomes, charges of police brutality tend to transcend
procedural examinations of specific circumstances or individual incidents, drawing
attention instead to the overall climate of police-community relationships and high-
lighting the need for reform.

Police brutality occurs when officers willfully attack, beat, kill, or otherwise mistreat community members. Physical forms of excessive force represent the most
obvious basis of police brutality complaints. Officers have used batons, Tasers, pepper
spray, guns, and unsanctioned physical violence against community members for
what critics charge is the purpose of willful intimidation and intentional harm. A
closely related issue is the perceived lack of institutional intervention to rein in problem officers and effectively confront abusive behavior. Even police officers cite this
as a problem: two-thirds of police officers surveyed agreed that "an officer who reports
another officer's misconduct is likely to be given the cold shoulder by his or her
fellow officers" (Weisburd et al. 2000, 5).

While flagrant misconduct and high-profile fatalities drive news headlines, some
observers complain of a less visible but more pervasive system of brutality that tran-
scends individual incidents caused by "bad apple" officers. Brutality also presents
itself in less-obvious nonphysical forms, including psychological intimidation, verbal abuse, racial profiling, false arrests, political repression, and sexual abuse. Drawing attention to the ways that the overall enforcement apparatus compromises the
trust, security, and human dignity of marginalized (and non-marginalized) groups
and individuals, some observers note that brutality can even be found in the policies and statutes that drive enforcement work. Some of the specific enforcement
policies under attack in this context include lack of training in nonviolent solutions,

racially patterned police stops, aggressive stop-and-frisk policies, unequal (or nuisance) enforcement of low-level offences, assessment of fines that recipients are too poor to pay, and culturally homogenous priorities and staffing decisions made by police departments and city governments.

Reform-minded groups have also identified political and economic pressures that incentivize enforcement practices that deliver significant harm to already-disadvantaged groups and individuals. Some of the culprits include the now mostly discredited "War on Drugs" and "tough-on-crime" political platforms, once politically popular, both of have disproportionately impacted minority groups and individuals. Critics also point to conflicts of interest springing from public–private partnerships, government contracts, and political endorsements from police unions.

Beyond its reference to a specific set of behaviors and incidents, the term "police brutality" originates in citizen demands for corrective changes in the criminal justice system and beyond. This contrasts with discussions that focus on the related term "excessive force." Police leadership, prosecutors, and juries tend to focus on whether specific police policies or laws are broken in specific incidents; however, discussions of police brutality tend to take a more encompassing approach, drawing attention to policies, laws, professional practices, relevant institutional and political cultures, and accused "bad apple" officers. In contrast to related discussions about excessive force or officer misconduct, police brutality is often discussed as a systemic social problem manifesting in system-wide patterns of harm-doing and systemic accountability issues. Some advocates against police brutality call for criminal justice (and broader) reforms that would dismantle the broader set of circumstances that make brutality possible and relatively common.

Reform-minded citizen groups and the criminal justice system occupy vastly different paradigms of thought on the issue of police brutality, sharing little or no common ground for constructive discussion. Lack of common ground is especially apparent in the divergent responses to the topic of police use of deadly force against citizens. The Black Lives Matter (BLM) movement, for example, asserts that most police violence is unjustified and constitutes "deadly oppression" of African Americans, causing Blacks to be denied the justice and freedom that other groups enjoy. Whereas the Federal Bureau of Investigation (FBI) classifies the overwhelming majority of police shootings as "justifiable homicide," the BLM movement claims that "Black lives are systematically and intentionally targeted for demise," and that most police violence constitutes "deadly oppression," resulting in African Americans' being denied justice and freedom enjoyed by other groups (BLM 2016).

In contrast, criminal justice agencies have not tended to view police harm of civilians as a meaningful social problem. In fact, most state or local agencies do not widely collect or systematically analyze data about the most severe forms of police harm. Likewise, national criminal justice reporting systems do not endeavor to reliably track or analyze cases in which police activity caused serious harm or injury to civilians. The closest the federal government comes to such reporting is the FBI's report of justifiable homicide, which tracks only those cases in which a police officer killed a felon in the line of duty (FBI 2012). By many accounts, these reporting practices (or lack thereof) minimize and obscure most of the police-community incidents that result in serious harm to civilians. By their very design, official FBI reports leave out all cases in which fatalities or injuries may have been unjustified. Agencies are not required to submit data and do so only voluntarily. In fact, studies outside of law enforcement demonstrate that police are killing up to twice as many civilians as the FBI had reported. While, as of this writing, FBI leadership has indicated that reporting systems are a concern, a reliable reporting system is still lacking. Journalists and crowd-sourced datasets remain the best source of information on police shootings (Kindy, Fisher, Tate, and Jenkins 2015).

Data on less-than-lethal police misconduct is also sorely lacking. One of the most studied impediments to good data on brutality is the reluctance or inability of the justice system to hold misbehaving officers accountable, which keeps those cases out of the public eye and off the official records. Case information becomes public only in situations reaching the level of a public scandal, disciplinary action, or successful prosecution. The fact that scandal, discipline, and prosecution are rare in most cases of police brutality obscures the full picture of police brutality. In its study of 14 American cities, the organization Human Rights Watch (1998) noted a widespread failure of cities to adequately track and report serious police misconduct.

Some observers have called for policies that would prevent brutality by increasing accountability and providing better guidance to officers (and observers) regarding appropriate and inappropriate behavior, but such policies have not gained significant traction. Police agencies, police unions, prosecutors, oversight boards, courts, and federal and state statutes tend to grant broad license and discretion for officer use of force. By most accounts, internal and civilian oversight mechanisms are weak, and criminal courts tend to find police shootings permissible as long as the officer in question believed it necessary (Madar 2014).

While not especially proficient at monitoring or accountability measures, the federal government, especially the Department of Justice (DOJ), has carefully documented problems in specific law enforcement agencies after being called in after high-profile flare-ups. DOJ investigations have found evidence of police brutality (e.g., patterns of excessive force, discriminatory intent, clear racial disparities, and other means) in many major police departments, including New Orleans, Chicago, Los Angeles, Newark, Albuquerque, and Ferguson. Although the DOJ reports are often scathing, meaningful sanctions or the provision of resources to institute needed fixes are usually limited or nonexistent. For the most part, erring departments are provided with a set of recommendations and are entrusted to reform themselves (Berman and Lowery 2015; U.S. DOJ 2015; Rushkin 2014).

Because conceptions of police brutality hinge on interpretations of vague variables such as surrounding circumstances, officer mindset, and intent, understandings of what counts as "police brutality" are hotly contested and are shaped, at least in part, by demographics and collective histories, as well as by perceived group and professional interests. Surveys consistently show Blacks are less likely than Whites to trust local police and to treat both races equally. For example, 71 percent of Whites express confidence in equal treatment, whereas only 36 percent of Blacks do. Almost

60 percent of Blacks rated police performance as poor in terms of avoiding excessive force, compared with 23 percent of Whites. Of Blacks surveyed, 70 percent said police do a poor job of holding officers accountable for misconduct, compared with 27 percent of Whites (Drake 2015). Differing group conceptions of police brutality and surrounding issues make it beneficial to understand the unique histories of groups that have experienced intergenerational patterns of harm linked to criminal justice and law enforcement institutions.

Historically, individuals from marginalized communities have experienced police brutality most profoundly. By most accounts, harmful encounters with law enforcement continue to severely impact marginalized communities more than other groups. Over the course of U.S. history, disempowered groups and those protesting for or claiming civil or human rights violations have been disproportionately at risk for victimization.

Deeper understandings of police brutality require observers to keep in mind that throughout American history, activities that easily meet today's thresholds of police brutality—for example, enforcing slavery or racial segregation or suppressing peaceful civil rights and anti-war protesters—were once routine and mandatory aspects of police officers' jobs. Engaging in objectively brutal tasks constituted significant parts of the official mission of some police agencies, supported at taxpayers' expense.

Affected Groups

Whether dictated by law, policy, culture, or another social dynamic, a range of official law enforcement practices in the United States has caused patterned harm to specific communities—harm undoubtedly experienced as brutality by those subjected to it and by those who carefully consider the legacy of law enforcement's engagement with communities.

Although today's enforcement policies and policing practices are ostensibly blind to race and class, they continue to deliver disproportionate harm and negative impacts to marginalized communities. Because law enforcement serves as the overall justice system's main gatekeeper, those who experience hardship caused by imprisonment or having a criminal record experience it as police brutality. While police harm has victimized many Whites, the history of law enforcement shows a consistent presence of patterned force incidents concentrated in minority communities alongside the core activities of crime prevention and public safety. To the extent that data are available from the patchwork of surveys and oversight and complaint bodies, the same patterns are clear: minority males are disproportionately represented among those who complain about police brutality.

African Americans

Many observe that the challenging history of police-community interaction within the African American community has left a significant legacy of ill will and mistrust, one that transfers from one generation to the next. Although current tensions between the community and law enforcement are often construed as individual officer misconduct, some of the African American community's experience with brutality at the hands of law enforcement has been sanctioned or mandated by laws and official policies and delivered by officers who were dutifully performing their official functions.

In the Southern United States, for example, laws severely limiting the rights of African American slaves supported the institution of slavery. These laws were enforced by police forces known as slave patrols. To support the interests of plantation economies, police could—without permission—enter the residence of any person, Black or White, who was suspected of harboring escaped slaves in an effort to return individuals to bondage. The work of slave patrols was performed in compliance with the law but was undoubtedly experienced as police brutality. Dilemmas like these demonstrate the complicated relationship between law, policy, and the victims of police brutality.

Abolitionists and Suffragettes

Activists in the United States who worked to abolish slavery were targets of police violence because they spoke out in favor of emancipation. Similarly, some of the activists who advocated for women's voting rights in the early 20th century were victims of police violence during otherwise peaceful protests.

Native Americans

Though not well publicized, the rates of shootings of Native Americans by police are (for some age groups) consistently higher than those of shootings of Whites and other minority groups. Some observers note that this is one of various disproportionately negative impacts that the U.S. justice system has on Native American communities. In terms of probabilities, Native Americans are the racial group most likely to be killed by law enforcement. Native Americans make up only 0.8 percent of the population, but they account for almost 2 percent of all police killings. Both before and after receiving citizenship rights in 1924, Native Americans have experienced strained relationships with the justice system and law enforcement in general. For example, Native Americans are imprisoned at four to six times the rate of White Americans. Because law enforcement is the gateway to imprisonment, many see disproportionate imprisonment as a problem originating in discriminatory policing policies (Argost 2015).

Asian Americans

While police incidents in Asian American communities tend to be lower profile, some activists cite a need for greater awareness of police-community violence in Asian American communities. Bao Phi, who is a Minneapolis-based poet and activist, says, "[W]hile we do not experience racism in the exact same way as Blacks, Latinos, and Native Americans, I think we should look at cases of state-sanctioned violence and police brutality against Asian Americans . . ." (Wang 2014).

A recent example of fatal police contact with a member of the Asian American community is that of Fong Lee, whose death by police shooting prompted the trial of a Minneapolis police officer, who was acquitted. Minneapolis police leadership praised the exoneration, but some activists took another view, including community activist Tou Ger Xiong, who pointed out that the acquittal serves to condone police discrimination against people of color and implies impunity for unnecessary police violence. According to Xiong, the verdict "does nothing more than to reaffirm the fact that we should fear police and members of law enforcement. Because it is saying to us, 'Watch out, if a cop thinks you pose a threat, you will be killed, you will shot, you will be killed'" (Williams 2009).

Some observers note that within the Asian American community, as in other non-majority communities, challenges are linked to the justice system as a whole rather than the behavior or ethics of individual officers. The system, some say, encourages police misconduct by, among other things, failing to hold officers accountable. Speaking again of the Fong Lee case, Xiong lamented the fact that during the trial, the court did not admit convincing evidence of the involved officer's racial bias. Criticizing the overall process and calling the judge's rulings "prejudicial," Xiong said, "[T]oday's verdict was not only a slap in the face of the Lee family, but a disgrace to the community and the judicial process" (Williams 2009).

LGBT Communities

Perhaps the most well-known example of police brutality directed against the gay and lesbian community occurred during the Stonewall Riots of 1969. In the early hours of June 28th, police officers harassed a party of gay customers at the Stonewall Inn—which, at the time, was a popular gay bar in New York City—because of the customers' sexual orientation. The group tried to stand its ground, and a riot ensued. Soon, word spread throughout the city, which brought more members of the lesbian, gay, bisexual, and transgender (LGBT) community to the Stonewall. When they began to throw bottles and other objects at the police, extra officers arrived on the scene and began to beat the mob back. The next night, over 1,000 protestors returned. In the following days, more protests and riots spread throughout New York City. The Stonewall Riots of 1969 led to the creation of gay rights groups in many major cities in the United States.

Hispanics/Latino/as

Relationships between Latino communities and law enforcement are complex and in many cases difficult. A recent poll found that 68 percent of Latinos feared that law enforcement officials would use excessive force against them (Planas 2015). In New York City, Latinos have disproportionately been targets of impromptu street interrogations (NYCLU 2015).

Definitional and Measurement Issues

Measuring police brutality by looking only at successful prosecutions or disciplinary punishments of officers paints an overly rosy picture of police-community contact. Most allegations of police brutality are not successfully prosecuted or subject to agency discipline. Outcomes in civil proceedings paint a darker, though still murky picture of police wrongdoing. In many cases, civil payouts of thousands and even millions of dollars per case suggest that many unsuccessfully prosecuted cases of police harm are not entirely without merit. Again, the imprecision of the term "police brutality" and the lack of alignment with specific policies and practices make claims of brutality even more difficult to demonstrate than more specific forms of officer and departmental misconduct. One person's brutality can be another person's legitimate use of force.

Importantly, not all documented cases of excessive force or police misconduct constitute police brutality. Police work is dynamic, and its practitioners are subject to human error. The precise amount of force necessary to subdue a subject depends on a variety of factors, many of which are unknown to officers, including the subject's strength and vulnerabilities, as well as other aspects of a dynamic, unbounded, constantly evolving field setting. As in all professions, some decisions hold up better in hindsight than others. All practitioners make errors. Because law enforcement professionals are often required to act quickly, even when given imperfect information, evolving situations, stress, and strained community relationships, even the most effective recruiting, screening, training, oversight, and discipline will not ensure that all officers will always behave perfectly.

Anne Cross

See also: Perceptions of Police Today; Police Accountability; Police Mistreatment in Cases of Civil Disobedience; Racial Profiling; Use of Tasers

Further Reading

Argost, Matt. "Police Are Killing Native Americans at Higher Rate than Any Race, and Nobody Is Talking about It." The Free Thought Project. August 2, 2015. http://thefreethought project.com/police-killing-native-americans-higher-rate-race-talking.

Berman, Mark, and Wesley Lowery. "The 12 Key Highlights from the DOJ's Scathing Ferguson Report." *The Washington Post*, March 4, 2015. https://www.washingtonpost.com /news/post-nation/wp/2015/03/04/the-12-key-highlights-from-the-dojs-scathing -ferguson-report.

Black Lives Matter (BLM). "Guiding Principles." Black Lives Matter Web Site. 2016. http:// blacklivesmatter.com/guiding-principles.

Drake, Bruce. "Divide between Blacks and Whites on Police Runs Deep." Pew Research Center Fact Tank. April 28, 2015. http://www.pewresearch.org/fact-tank/2015/04/28/blacks -whites-police.

Federal Bureau of Investigation (FBI). "Crime in the United States 2012: Expanded Homicide Data." https://www.fbi.gov/about-us/cjis/ucr/crime-in-the-u.s/2012/crime-in-the -u.s.-2012/offenses-known-to-law-enforcement/expanded-homicide/expand homicidemain.

Hooper, Deona. "Ferguson Proves the United States Justice System Is Not Broken, but Working Perfectly as Designed." *Critical and Radical Social Work* 3, no. 1 (2015): 141–147.

Human Rights Watch. "Shielded from Justice: Police Brutality and Accountability in the United States." July 1, 1998. https://www.hrw.org/report/1998/07/01/shielded-justice /police-brutality-and-accountability-united-states.

Kane, Robert J., and Michael D. White. *Jammed Up: Bad Cops, Police Misconduct, and the New York City Police Department.* New York: New York University Press, 2013.

Kindy, Kimberly, Marc Fisher, Julie Tate, and Jennifer Jenkins. "A Year of Reckoning: Police Shoot Nearly 1000." *The Washington Post*, December 26, 2015. http://www.washing tonpost.com/sf/investigative/2015/12/26/a-year-of-reckoning-police-fatally-shoot -nearly-1000.

Madar, Chase. "Why It's Impossible to Indict a Cop: It's Not Just Ferguson—Here's How the System Protects Police." *The Nation*, November 25, 2014. http://www.theation.com /article/why-its-impossible-indict-cop.

New York Civil Liberties Union (NYCLU). "Stop-and-Frisk Data." Racial Justice. 2015. http:// www.nyclu.org/content/stop-and-frisk-data.

Planas, Roque. "Why the Media Pays Less Attention to Police Killings of Latinos." *Huffing-ton Post*, February 24, 2015. http://www.huffingtonpost.com/2015/02/24/police-killings -latinos_n_6739448.html.

Rushkin, Steven. "Federal Enforcement of Police Reform." *Fordham Law Review* 82, no. 6 (2014): 3189–3247. http://ir.lawnet.fordham.edu/flr/vol82/iss6/20.

Taylor, Clarence. "African Americans, Police Brutality, and the U.S. Criminal Justice System." *Journal of African American History* 98, no. 2 (2013): 200–204.

U.S. Department of Justice (DOJ). *Investigation of the Ferguson Police Department.* Civil Rights Division. 2015. https://www.justice.gov/sites/default/files/opa/press-releases/attach ments/2015/03/04/ferguson_police_department_report.pdf.

Wang, Frances Kai-Hwa. "Eric Garner Case Resonates among Asian Americans." *NBC News*, December 5, 2014. http://www.nbcnews.com/news/asian-america/eric-garner-case -resonates-among-asian-americans-n262406.

Weisburd, David, Rosann Greenspan, Edwin E. Hamilton, Hubert Williams, and Kellie A. Bryant. 2000. "Police Attitudes toward Abuse of Authority: Findings from a National Study." *National Institute of Justice: Research in Brief*, May 2000. https://www.ncjrs.gov /pdffiles1/nij/181312.pdf.

Williams, Brandt. "Fong Lee's Family Angered by Verdict." *Minnesota Public Radio*, May 28, 2009. http://www.mprnews.org/story/2009/05/28/fonglee_verdict.

POLICE MISTREATMENT IN CASES OF CIVIL DISOBEDIENCE

Under the U.S. Constitution, the right to assemble is a First Amendment promise. People are allowed to assemble in peaceful protest in order to address issues of neglect or abuse of civil rights by the government. Police officers are tasked with the duties to use their authority and power to protect citizens from criminals and other wrong-doers. Yet, in cases of civil disobedience, police officers often use their power to mistreat and abuse peaceful protesters. Police mistreatment is any abuse of police authority that is illegal and/or immoral. Although civil disobedience is a form of peaceful political protesting, government backlash has been known to be violent during certain eras of U.S. history (Earl 2011). Police mistreatment has involved harassment, illegal arrests, clubbing, fire hosing, tear gassing, pepper-spraying, using Tasers, executing chokeholds, and using police dogs, and even killing protesters.

Civil Disobedience in the 1960s and 1970s

In contemporary U.S. history, the Civil Rights Movement (1954–1968) often comes up when discussing police mistreatment in cases of civil disobedience. Though most forms of police mistreatment go unrecorded, during the Civil Rights Movement the media documented many forms of police abuse (History.com 2009). Some of the most infamous of these abuses involved police clubbing, fire hosing, tear gassing, and releasing police dogs to attack peaceful adult and child protesters during the 1963 March on Washington, the Freedom Summer of 1964, and the 1965 Selma to Montgomery March on the Pettus Bridge (Champion 2001; Marshall 2013).

The 1960s was a time of civil unrest within the United States. However, it was also a time of extreme conservatism. This clash of ideologies often resulted in social rejection of protesters. Aside from the Civil Rights Movement, the other most widely recognized social movements involving civil disobedience during this time was the anti-Vietnam War movement, which began as a middle-class college student movement in the mid-1960s and was initially led by the group Students for a Democratic Society. This was a time of anti-establishment, and protesters commonly represented the hippie and drug cultures so widely despised by most of society.

Most of the protesters were nonviolent. However, they did engage in never-before-used hostile tactics, such as name calling and profanity. Although only a small proportion of the protesters were violent, their violence worked to further taint the movement in the eyes of a conservative public that generally rejected the anti-Vietnam War movement. One common sentiment was that protesters deserved the violence they received from law enforcement and the National Guard (Gustainis and Hahn 1988). The anti-Vietnam War movement remained a nonviolent movement that involved teach-ins and sit-ins until 1967, when campus and local police stormed a student demonstration at the University of Wisconsin. During this demonstration, police with no riot training stormed the building and beat students with clubs. Law enforcement, which represented the working class, saw the middle-class protesters as traitors and did not hesitate to attack male and female students with clubs, beating them on the head, spine, and stomach. Some student protesters fought back. In the end, 47 students and 19 police officers were hospitalized.

The Cold War was at its height during the 1950s and 1960s, and U.S. citizens feared communism would destroy the American way of life. So fearful was the public that even the extreme police violence toward protesters during the 1968 Democratic National Convention in Chicago did not sway the public's rejection of protesters (Gustainis and Hahn 1988). During this protest, more than 27,000 Chicago police, and state and federal officers were unleashed, beating and gassing protesters and unlucky passers-by, placing hundreds in the hospital. So bad was the riot that the media identified it as a "police riot" (Lewis 2013). Still, national polls found that more than 80 percent of the public did not believe that the law enforcement used too much force. The Chicano Moratorium Movement, a sect of the anti–Vietnam War movement, experienced two protester deaths from Los Angeles police in 1970. Middle America did not support the Vietnam War protest until the death toll of American soldiers in Vietnam started to rise, Nixon implemented the draft in 1969, and the National Guard shot 13 students—four of whom died—at Kent State in 1970.

Civil Disobedience in the 1990s and 2000s

Civil disobedience continued as a form of protest throughout the years. However, the last three decades has seen an upsurge in civil disobedience. The November 29 through December 3, 1999, Seattle protest of the World Trade Organization (WTO) is perhaps the largest organized civil disobedience to occur in the last few decades. Part of the global-justice movement, labor activists, free trade activists, environmentalists, and human rights activists collaborated in a nonviolent demonstration of the Third Ministerial Conference of the WTO. It was estimated that by November 30th, referred to as N30, 40,000 protesters attended the Seattle protest (Murphy and Pfaff 2005). Though protesters were trained in and committed to nonviolent civil disobedience, police used tear gas against the crowds indiscriminately gassing protesters, shoppers, and WTO delegates alike. As police continued to assault the crowds with pepper and tear gas, the gas traveled into the homes of nearby residents and even affected police with ineffective equipment. As police attempted to push the crowd back, protesters locked arms and legs and covered their heads. Others put on goggles, vinegar soaked bandanas and even gas masks. Video footage shows police officers poking sitting protesters with batons, spraying people with pepper and tear gas, and even shooting smoke and concussion grenades and rubber bullets and bean bags into crowds of nonviolent protesters (Gillham and Marx 2000). By the second day of protests, the Mayor declared a state of emergency, brought in 200 National Guard soldiers, and 300 state police officers, implemented a curfew, and made it a felony for any non-law enforcement individual to be in possession of a gas mask. The violence lasted for three days and resulted in 500 arrests and $20 million in lost sales and property damage. In 2007, a federal jury determined that the city illegally arrested 200 protesters on December 1, 1999, violating their Fourth Amendment rights.

Following the WTO protests, the 2004 protest at the Republican National Convention was another large-scale, nonviolent protest met with police mistreatment. Protesters rallied against the selection of George W. Bush as the Republican candidate and the Iraq war. Jennifer Earl (2009) argues that when national leaders feel threatened, the result is political repression and violation of constitutional rights such as freedom of assembly and speech. She further points out that since the early 1970s, police have turned to the use of arrests instead of violence when "negotiation management" with protesters fails (Earl 2011). This can be seen in the case of the protests at the 2004 Republican National Convention in New York City.

Protest policing tactics at the convention entailed the use of metal barricades and batons to divide, subdue, and round up as many protesters as possible (Lovell 2009). They were then caught up in orange nets and incarcerated for an average of 24 hours in a temporary jail on New York City's lower Westside Pier 57. These police tactics swept up all people within reach, including protestors, passers-by, legal advocates, and journalists. The temporary jail came to be known as "Guantanamo on the Hudson" because the conditions of these detentions were deplorable and obvious civil rights violations. People were crowded in cells made of chain-linked fence surrounded by razor wire, 30 to 40 in a cell under extreme temperature conditions. The ground on which the detainees were held had oil and bus waste, which caused abrasions and lesions. As many as 1,800 people were arrested in the three-day event on charges such as disorderly conduct and resisting arrest. Eventually, 90 percent of the charges were dismissed or resulted in an acquittal. By 2014, the New York Police Department (NYPD) settled in an $18 million class-action lawsuit brought by 1,200 of the arrestees.

Civil Disobedience of the 2010s

The 2010s has witnessed an increased the criminalization of public demonstrations. Additionally, the upsurge of police brutality has once again become more prevalent within the decade. More importantly, due to the rise of social media activism, many of these accounts of police abuse have been documented and posted on social media outlets, online newspapers, blogs, and YouTube. The Occupy Wall Street and Black Lives Matter movements are undoubtedly two of the largest social movements of the 21st century. These political and social demonstrations propelled into national movements making news headlines across the world. To understand the dynamics of both movements, we must first juxtapose current tactics of police abuse and civil disobedience.

In 2011, the Occupy Wall Street movement became one of the largest social movements of the 21st century. Although it began in New York and is known as the Occupy Wall Street movement, it was a spinoff of the Global Justice movement and evolved into the global Occupy movement. We can see similarity between the current movement and the World Trade Organization protest. To date, Occupy demonstrations have occurred in more than 951 cities in 82 nations (Shrivastava and Ivanova 2015). Protesters are fighting against global economic inequality and oppression. Occupy Wall Street called into question the cultural-cognitive, normative, and regulatory legitimacy of capitalism, corporations, and governments that work to maintain power. Again, we find credence in Earl's (2009) earlier argument that when national leaders feel threatened, they will engage in political repression and violate constitutional rights such as freedom of assembly and speech.

Occupy Wall Street quickly became a social media sensation, broadcasting throughout the major American airwaves. Organizers used Facebook and created Web sites such as occupywallst.org and occupywallstreet.net, and Twitter hashtags such as #occupy and #ows, in order to quickly spread news of events. This practice worked to bypass the mainstream media, what Marxist cultural theorists call the ideological state apparatus used to reproduce the power elite (Shank 1999).

The Occupy movement became a voice for the economically marginalized and had a strong following by the middle class as well. In New York City's Zuccotti Park, hundreds of demonstrators shouted, "We are the 99 percent!" This chant became the theme of the movement. Occupy Wall Street demonstrators were eventually pushed out of Zuccotti Park by New York police, causing protesters to relocate to other parts of the city and disrupting the business of large corporations and banks. The majority of Occupy demonstrators were nonviolent activists who were protesting for social justice. Nevertheless, they were still met with high restraint and aggressive law enforcement that resulted in numerous accounts of escalated police use of force with batons and pepper spray.

One can review hours of video footage via YouTube of Occupy Wall Street demonstrators and police interactions. Footage provides evidence of peaceful, nonviolent protesters being assaulted, gassed and pepper-sprayed, and dragged by police officers (Occupy Wall Street 2011). One particular incident shows lines of kneeling, handcuffed demonstrators being repeatedly pepper-sprayed by an NYPD officer. This event shows that, even after being compliant and handcuffed, demonstrators still suffered repercussions. In another incident, a protester was put in a chokehold, slammed to the ground, and then dragged for shouting during a daytime demonstration. These and many more examples illustrate a significant degree of police brutality and mistreatment against nonviolent protesters who called into question the legitimacy of the government (Knuckey, Glenn, and MacLeon 2012).

Similar to the Occupy Wall Street movement, Black Lives Matter demonstrators dissented to the hegemonic pedagogies of the criminal justice system. However, the movement is reminiscent of the Civil Rights Movement of the 1950s and 1960s. It came about as a direct result of police use of excessive force against African American males, violating their civil rights. The civilian killing of 17-year-old Trayvon Martin triggered the movement via social media. This is when we first saw the Twitter hashtag #BlackLivesMatter. However, the 2014 police killings of unarmed Eric Garner and Michael Brown were precursors to taking this movement to the streets in national protesting.

Following the killing of Michael Brown on August 9, 2014, in Ferguson, Missouri, the community held a vigil but was interrupted by police with riot gear (Edwards 2016). Peaceful protesting by most protesters continued, but on the third day of protesting, police used tear gas to break up the crowd who did not disperse at nightfall. Similar to the events of the Republican National Convention, journalists were also caught in the crossfire. By August 18th, some protesters turned to violence and lootings, and police response was to bring out armed vehicles and tear gas, likening the event to a war zone. Following were countless events of police violence in which protesters in the Black Lives Matter movement were met with batons, pepper spray, and an ultra-militarized police force. Ferguson, demonstrators were met with an ultra-militarized police force fit to engage in "war" with the assembled proletariat. The Black Lives Matter demonstrations were a result of the lack of police accountability and the consequences of justifiable homicide or murders of Black bodies. Shehzad Nadeem (2015) points out that even though Black men are less than 7 percent of the U.S. population, they nevertheless made up 29 percent of police deaths in 2000. Nadeem points to this as evidence of institutional racism. The protesters demanded equality, better community relations, more training, and the recruitment and hiring of more people of color in law enforcement.

Dr. Jason Williams (2014) argues that the tumultuous relationship between African Americans and the police does not exist in a vacuum. Instead, the outcries of Blacks and the Black Lives Matter movement stem from the sociohistorical pathology of American policing and slave patrols. In addition, this condemnation and killing of Black bodies is reminiscent of the story line of *The Hunger Games* (Williams 2014). Ironically enough, the Black Lives Matter Movement does inherently resemble the same macabre background but with more realistic outcries of demonstrators and violent interactions with police authoritative power.

Nadeem (2015) describes police violence as a routine feature of American life that can be seen from city to city. However, when police protesting of the Black Lives Matter movement is compared to that of the 1999 World Trade Organization protest, the 2004 Republican National Convention protests, and the Occupy Wall Street movement, the concept of negotiated management discussed by Earl no longer applied. It would seem that when protesters are of a predominantly nonminority background and are calling into question the legitimacy of the government, the violations of their freedom of speech and assembly via arrests are much more likely to be the tactics used. On the other hand, when racial minorities call into question police legitimacy, these protests are more likely to be met with violence. Pressure was placed on the Cleveland and Ferguson police departments to revise their tactics after the killings of 12-year-old Tamir Rice and 18-year-old Michael Brown. Furthermore, the shooting of Akai Gurley and the chokehold death of Eric Garner and by New York City police officers have brought back the trauma of police killings of Amadou Diallo and Sean Bell. With constant media coverage of these murders, more and more activists are demanding a reorganization of policing.

In cases of civil disobedience, police response often results in continued conversation: civil disobedience results from a perceived violation of rights, and police mistreatment of protesters engaging in civil disobedience. Police actions tend to favor the more powerful segments of society and work to maintain the status quo (Gillham and Marx 2000). Witnessing repeat events of police mistreatment suggests that there needs to be reform in policing as well as reform in protest policing.

Venessa Garcia and Emmanuel Pierre-Louis

See also: Abner Louima Case; Amadou Diallo Case; Chicago Police during the 1968 Democratic National Convention; Deadly Force; Eric Garner Case in New York City and Subsequent Tensions; Freddie Gray Case; Michael Brown Shooting and the Aftermath in Ferguson; Militarization of Public and Campus Police Departments; Perceptions of Police Today; Police Accountability; Police Brutality; Racial Profiling; Rodney King Beating and Riots; Sean Bell Shooting; Southern Slave Patrols; Tamir Rice Shooting in Cleveland; Trayvon Martin Shooting; Walter Scott Shooting

Further Reading

Champion, Dean J. *Police Misconduct in America: A Reference Handbook*. Santa Barbara, CA: ABC-CLIO, 2001.

Earl, Jennifer. "Information Access and Protest Policing Post-9/11: Studying the Policing of the 2004 Republican National Convention." *American Behavioral Scientist* 53 (2009): 44–60.

Earl, Jennifer. "Protest Arrests and Future Protest Participation: The 2004 Republican National Convention Arrestees and the Effects of Repression." In *Studies in Law, Politics, and Society: Special Issue Social Movements/Legal Possibilities*, edited by Austin Sarat, 141–173. United Kingdom: Emerald Group Publishing, 2011.

Edwards, Sue Bradford. *Black Lives Matter*. Minneapolis: Abdo Publishing, 2016.

Foner, E., and J. A. Garraty. *The Reader's Companion to American History*. Boston, MA: Houghton Mifflin, 1991.

Gillham, Patrick F., and Gary T. Marx. "Complexity and Irony in Policing and Protesting: The World Trade Organization in Seattle." *Social Justice* 27 (2000): 212–236.

Gustainis, J. Justin, and Dan F. Hahn. "While the Whole World Watched: Rhetorical Failures of Anti-War Protest." *Communication Quarterly* 36 (1988): 203–216.

Knuckey, Sarah, Katherine Glenn, and Emi MacLeon. "Suppressing Protest: Human Rights Violations in the U.S. Response to Occupy Wall Street." New York: Protest and Assembly Rights Project, 2012.

Lewis, Penny. *Hardhats, Hippies, and Hawks: The Vietnam Antiwar Movement as Myth and Memory*. Ithaca, NY: Cornell University Press, 2013.

Lovell, Jarret S. *Crimes of Dissent: Civil Disobedience, Criminal Justice and the Politics of Conscience*. New York: NYU Press, 2009.

Marshall, James P. *Student Activism and Civil Rights in Mississippi: Protest Politics and Struggle for Racial Justice, 1960–1965*. Baton Rouge: Louisiana State University Press, 2013.

Murphy, Gillian H., and Steven Pfaff. "Thinking Locally, Acting Globally? What the Seattle WTO Protests Tell Us about the Global Justice Movement." In *Political Power and Social Theory*, edited by Diane E. Davis, 151–176. San Diego: Elsevier Inc., 2005.

Nadeem, Shehzad. "Black and Blue." *Context* 14 (2015): 12–14.

Occupy Wall Street. *Occupy Police Brutality Compilation*. YouTube.com, 4:40. November 22, 2011. https://www.youtube.com/watch?v=45VGFgiFu7Y&feature=youtube.

Shank, G. "Looking Back: Radical Criminology and Social Movement." *Social Justice* 26, no. 2 (1999): 114–134.

Shrivastava, Paul and Olga Ivanova. "Inequality, Corporate Legitimacy and the Occupy Wall Street Movement." *Human Relations* 68 (2015): 1209–1231.

Williams, Jason Michael. " 'The Hunger Games'-ification of US Police and the Community." Truthout.com. December 2014. www.truth-out.org/opinion/item/28151-the-hunger-game-ification-of-us-police-and-the-community.

TIMOTHY THOMAS'S DEATH

Timothy Thomas was 19 years old when he was shot and killed by a police officer in Cincinnati, Ohio. It was about 2 a.m. on April 7, 2001, in the "Over the Rhine" neighborhood. Thomas was apparently leaving the "Warehouse," a local nightclub, when the police identified him as an individual with outstanding citations. He was an African American and the father of an infant son. He was unarmed. Thomas had outstanding traffic warrants from 21 traffic violations. On that fateful night, Thomas took off running when he realized the police officer was coming after him. The officer in question, although off duty, called for back-up when he spotted Thomas. To evade police arrest, Thomas ran into a dark alley. According to the police report, an officer ran into the alley, and soon after a shot was heard. The officer's shot hit Thomas in the chest, and he was pronounced dead at about 3:02 a.m. The entire incident was

Angela Leisure, center, mother of Timothy Thomas, hugs sister-in-law Tanja Leisure, left, and husband Eric Leisure, right, after a Cincinnati police officer was acquitted of all charges in the shooting death of her son, September 26, 2001, in Cincinnati. (AP Photo/Al Behrman)

captured by the officer's car camera. Patrolman Stephen Roach, a 27-year-old Cincinnati White police officer, was the one who shot Thomas.

The killing of Thomas, who was an unarmed African American man, for unpaid traffic citations, ignited several days of street riots in Cincinnati. The riots lasted from April 9 to 13, 2001, and they were considered the largest urban riots in the United States since the Rodney King riots in Los Angeles, in 1992. For four nights, rioters were reported to have thrown objects at policemen. There was also extensive looting and vandalizing of businesses in and around the neighborhoods of downtown Cincinnati. The riots ended on April 13, 2001, after the city imposed a city-wide curfew. About eight hundred protesters were arrested. A few dozen people in the area also sustained injuries during the riots. The cost to the businesses in the area following the looting and vandalizing of their properties was estimated to be at $3.6 million. The city itself lost between $1.5 to $2 million in the course of the four nights of rioting. Downtown businesses were reported to have incurred an additional loss of about $10 million from the boycott of their businesses by shoppers in solidarity with African Americans who were perceived to be the victims of police brutality and racial profiling. Additionally, the rate of violent crime in the area increased for several years following the riots.

One question raised was this: Why would the death of an unarmed Black teenager, who had been trying to evade police arrest for traffic violations, elicit that kind of rampage response from mostly the Black community? To put it in proper context, it's necessary to examine Timothy Thomas's case, in particular, and the relationship between the police and the Black community. A brief overview of the socio-economic conditions of the African American community in the area will also help shed more light on both the remote and immediate causes of the riot. In about two months prior to his shooting death, Thomas was cited for 21 violations. According to the incident report, he was pulled over by the police 11 times. Six of the officers who pulled him over were White, whereas four of the officers who pulled him over were Black. The citations were for identical causes, namely, not wearing a seat belt and operating a motor vehicle without proof of auto insurance or a license. When the police accosted Thomas in the Over-the-Rhine neighborhood, the police sought to arrest him for the outstanding 14 nonviolent misdemeanor offenses, with 12 of them related to traffic citations according to the incident report. Thomas was chased by nine Cincinnati police officers for about 10 minutes before patrolman Stephen Roach joined the chase. Patrolman Roach caught up with Thomas in a dark alley and shot him in the chest at a close range. Patrolman Roach claimed that he shot at Thomas because he thought he was reaching for a gun in his waistband. It was later determined, however, through investigation, that Thomas must have been trying to pull up his sagging pants. Patrolman Roach also claimed that, at the time, he did not know that the charges against Thomas were for minor traffic offenses and, again, that Thomas had ignored his order to stop. Thomas later died at the hospital from the gunshot wound.

To appreciate why the African American community in the area may not have perceived the police killing of an unarmed teenager Thomas as an isolated incident, a brief review of police arrest records in the area is pertinent. According to the published report by *CityBeat*, a Cincinnati local newspaper, there is abundant evidence that suggests Black motorists are disproportionately targeted by the Cincinnati police. According to the newspaper's report, the Cincinnati police issued 141,000 traffic citations within a 22-month period. A review of the report, according to the newspaper, revealed that Black motorists were twice as likely to be cited for driving without a proper license and not wearing a seatbelt. The report points out that Black motorists are four times more likely to be cited for driving without proof of insurance. Other related statistics further underscore the Cincinnati African American community's misgivings and mistrust of the police. For example, since 1995, Thomas had been the 15th Black man shot and killed by the Cincinnati police. Four of the suspects killed by the police were only since November 2000. None of the suspects killed by the police during the period under review was White. Further exacerbating the problem was the fact that one of the victims of police summary execution, Roger Owensby, Jr., was alleged to have died of asphyxiation during a chokehold by a police officer on November 7, 2000. By the next day, another Black youth, Jeffrey Irons, died during a scuffle with the police. The perception of the African American community was that the officers responsible for the deaths of the two Black men were not fully held accountable. One of the officers charged for their murders was acquitted and the second officer's case failed as the trial was declared inconclusive. The officer was never brought back again for a trial; the first trial was proclaimed a mistrial. The police, in their own rebuttal, claimed that 10 of those men shot and killed by the police had pointed guns or fired at police officers.

A brief look at the social structure of the Over-the-Rhine neighborhood in 2000, the year preceding what is considered the worst racial riot in Cincinnati history in more than three decades, is instructive. The neighborhood's population was estimated at 7,368, of which 5,974 were of African American heritage. The city was in every respect decaying, with about 1,667 of the 3,594 housing units uninhabited. And 96 percent of the units that were occupied were by renters. The average annual income of the Over-the-Rhine residents was $8,600, compared to the $26,774 average income of the entire city. The neighborhood's high poverty and unemployment rates are often attributed to the collapse of manufacturing jobs, on which the city had depended for a long time. Many of the city residents who were unable to relocate to other parts of the city or country eked out a living through the underground economy of drug dealing and prostitution. This accounted for the high crime rate in the area.

Incidentally, about three weeks before the Cincinnati urban riot, a local group in collaboration with the American Civil Liberties Union (ACLU) filed a civil lawsuit against the city and the police department for the more than 30 years of racial profiling against the Black community. Additional lawsuits against the city and police department for discrimination and police brutality emerged. One notable example of the lawsuits filed against the city of Cincinnati was in 1999 by Bomani Tyehimba, an African American man. According to the lawsuit, the police had handcuffed and beaten him up during what was considered a routine traffic stop. He claimed that the police ordered him out of his car and threatened him with a gun pointed to his head.

As if to suggest that the April 2001 riots by some members of the Cincinnati community in reaction the death of an unarmed Black teenager being shot to death by police was justified, the judge in September 26, 2001, acquitted Patrolman Stephen Roach of the charges in the shooting to death of Thomas. Roach had been charged with negligent homicide and obstructing official business preferred against him. If convicted of both misdemeanor charges, Patrolman Roach would have served nine months in jail. The bench trial lasted seven days. Judge Ralph E. Winkler of Hamilton County Municipal Court justified his acquittal of Patrolman Roach, the White officer accused of shooting death of Thomas, argued that Patrolman Roach's action was reasonable. According to him, Patrolman Roach's shooting of Thomas was due to a quick reaction to what was otherwise a dangerous situation, which Thomas was responsible for creating. In addition, according to Judge Winkler, Patrolman Roach had an unblemished record as an officer. And in contrast, Thomas, according to him, was wanted on many violations. In addition, Thomas made the situation even more dangerous by refusing to stop when Patrolman Roach ordered him to stop, according to the judge. It is imperative to note that Patrolman Roach was the first officer from the Cincinnati police department to even stand trial for killing a suspect. The judge underscored this aberration by scolding the police department for charging Patrolman Roach for the killing of Thomas. Thomas's mother, Angela Leisure, walked out of the courtroom that day disappointed that justice had not been served by the judge's acquittal of Patrolman Roach in the killing of her son. She wondered what it would take for police officers to be held accountable for their actions in the same way other citizens were.

To appreciate why the police killing of Thomas seemed to be a breaking point for some members of the African American community in Cincinnati, a brief review of the factors that contributed to the distrust between the community and the police is necessary. First let us examine the particular case of Thomas's experience with the Cincinnati police. According to Thomas's mother, about two months prior to his death, Thomas had shared to his mother his encounter with the Cincinnati police officers. Thomas had complained to his mother that he received two tickets for supposedly the same traffic violations from one police officer. Later on that day, he received two more tickets from different police officers for the same traffic violations he received tickets for earlier all in their neighborhood. Many people in the community find these traffic violations tickets spurious and suspicious. For one thing, driving without a license and auto insurance are non-moving violations that can be detected only after one is pulled over by the police. Driving without a seat belt is also a secondary violation that the police can detect only when they look very closely at the motorist. This is unlike running a red light and driving over the posted speed limit, which the police can detect from a distance. The question then becomes was Thomas pulled over as other Black motorists are routinely pulled over because of who they are, rather than for their traffic infractions? These events are similar to the conviction of four police officers in New York for the torture of Abner Louima, a Haitian immigrant. There is also the case of the unarmed Amadou Diallo, an African immigrant shot dead by police with 41 bullets.

Also notable is the case of an unarmed African American motorist killed in Liberty City, Miami, which resulted in public protests. According to the police, the man, Arthur McDuffie, crashed his motorcycle and died during a police chase. However, the coroner claimed otherwise, as it appeared McDuffie had been beaten with flashlights. Police involved in the beating of Rodney King were acquitted. King was an unarmed African American motorist in Los Angeles. Other events include the investigation of 70 officers of the Los Angeles special anti-gang unit for drug dealing, witness intimidation, and other unwholesome corrupt practices. Not long after, there was the case of the Philadelphia police that burned down a housing block where five children and six adults perished.

Some studies reveal Hispanic and African American motorists are routinely singled out for stops and searches with or without traffic infractions. African Americans driving in supposedly White neighborhoods are likely to be stopped and searched more often than White motorists.

The police shooting of Timothy Thomas and the subsequent riots in Cincinnati reflect the mutual distrust between the African American community and the police and reinforces the perception, especially in the African American community, that Black minorities are more likely to be stopped and searched.

O. Oko Elechi, Dorothy Aerga, and Ifeoma E. Okoye

See also: Abner Louima Case; Amadou Diallo Case; Corruption; Police Accountability; Police Brutality; Police Ethics; Racial Profiling; Rodney King Beating and Riots

Further Reading

Bayley, D., and R. Perito. *Police Corruption: What Past Scandals Teach about Current Challenges* (Special Report No. 294). Washington, DC: United States Institute of Peace, 2011.

"Corruption and Human Rights: Making the Connection." International Council on Human Rights Policy and Transparency International. Geneva, Switzerland: ICHRP, 2009.

Goldstein, H. *Police Corruption: A Perspective on Its Nature and Control.* Washington, DC: The Police Foundation, 1975.

Jones, J. R., and D. P. Carlson. *Reputable Conduct: Ethical Issues in Policing and Corrections* (2nd Edition). Upper Saddle River, NJ: Prentice Hall-Pearson, 2004.

Milovanovic, D., and K. K. Russell. *Petit Apartheid in the U.S. Criminal Justice System: The Dark Figure of Racism.* Durham, NC: Carolina Academic Press, 2001.

Newburn, T. "Understanding and Preventing Police Corruption: Lessons from the Literature." *Police Research Series, Paper 110.* Research Development Statistics, *Journal of Research and Policy* 19 (1999): 79–99.

Withrow, B. L. *The Racial Profiling Controversy: What Every Police Leader Should Know.* Flushing, NY: Looseleaf, 2011.

MILITARIZATION OF PUBLIC AND CAMPUS POLICE DEPARTMENTS

The birth of public policing in the United States (1844) was the product of the tension between increasing crime rates flowing from urbanization, industrialization, and immigration, and the residue of a strong distrust of centralized government authority existing in the colonies since America declared its independence from Great Brittan (1783). Borrowing selectively from the English model of public policing proposed by Sir Robert Peel (1829), Americans were careful to distinguish police from the military as a means of securing public support. In recent years, however, this distinction has become increasingly "blurred," as police have come to more closely resemble the military in both thought and appearance, a phenomenon that in large part can be traced to the Cold War, emergence of community-oriented policing, and reliance on the "war" metaphor in policy discourse. The implications for this intensification of military culture among public and campus police forces are numerous, including the potential for increased risk to officers and citizens, strained police community relations, the potential erosion of democratic freedoms, and reduced institutional effectiveness.

Origins and Functions of Public Police

The birth of public policing began in England with Sir Robert Peel, who introduced a bill in Parliament, *An Act for Improving the Police in and Near the Metropolis* (1829). This bill replaced military troops and local militia with a national "professional" police force, which emphasized ruling by consent, rather than by force. To this end, British Bobbies (named after Sir Robert Peel) were modestly paid (so as not to acquire an air of superiority) and wore blue uniforms to distinguish them from the military services, which wore red. What is more, Peel appointed an unarmed police force (equipped only with a bludgeon) to avoid criticism and secure public support, while elevating the order of the maintenance role of police (i.e., lighting lamplights, calling out time, and watching for fires) over that of crime fighting.

Across the Atlantic, the urbanization, immigration, and economic stratification that accompanied the Industrial Revolution (1760–1830) in the United States rendered existing *citizen* forms of policing ineffective, similar to England. As a result, states and local communities began to adopt public police forces by selectively borrowing from the British model. To this end, they sought to establish a professional and decentralized police force, taking care to distinguish public police from the military not only in appearance, but also in thought. Consequently, early police forces elevated order maintenance over crime fighting by emphasizing the provision of public services to new and arriving immigrants.

Beginning in the early 1900s, however, the police mandate changed from that of providing services and maintaining order to crime control, as reformers sought to increase the efficiency and effectiveness of government more broadly and of police specifically. Thus, police were no longer appointed by political machines but instead selected and promoted based on a system of merit. Technology and science also began to significantly alter police practices as the "beat" was replaced by random motor patrols—resulting from the intersection of the automobile, two-way radio, telephone, and deterrence theory—and an increased reliance on bureaucratic organization in an attempt to ensure accountability and enhance operational efficiency and effectiveness.

This professional policing model, which emphasizes crime control and the use of science and technology, dominated policing during the 20th century and largely persists today. Subtle changes to the character of public policing began to appear, however, in the 1970s in response to the conclusion of the Cold War and reliance on the "war" metaphor in policy discourse. Metaphors are implied comparison in which one word is used to denote or describe another. As such, not only are metaphors important devices for creating strategic representations in policy discourse, but in a more subtle way they are used to prescribe action. For example, to describe America's infrastructure as "crumbling" implies reconstruction is necessary. From this vantage, the use of metaphors in policy discourse is advantageous in that they not only allow comparisons to be made, but they also allow for prescriptions or remedies in the form of policy or action.

Rise and Normalization of Police Paramilitary Units

Politicians, the media, and police personnel have leveraged the war metaphor (i.e., the War on Terror and the War on Drugs) for political advantage and promise in prescribing action. The use of the "war" metaphor implies a sense of urgency, that our survival is at stake, and that the enemy is foreign. In doing so, it not only allows for the costs of a particular policy to be ignored (allowing for deficit spending) but also for the expansion of police power through the erosion of constitutional rights (e.g., asset forfeiture laws, which allow for the seizure of property obtained or used in connection with a drug offense without a prior criminal conviction). The militarization of American police is, consequently, a logical outgrowth of the war metaphor, which suggests the use of domination and force is adequate for solving social problems. At the same time, there is a glorification of the tools necessary to accomplish this: military power, technology, and hardware.

Contributing to this transformation was the rise and conclusion of the Cold War (1947–1991). During this period American politics was characterized by a need to combat the communist threat posed by the Soviet Union. The corollary was a significant and persistent investment in military preparedness and spending for a longer period than any other in U.S. history. The end of the Cold War brought the freeing of substantial economic resources and military hardware that both the president and congress directed to America's law enforcement apparatus. To be sure, in an attempt to make America's military more "socially useful," all branches of the military had become involved in both domestic and international drug law enforcement. What is more, congress and the Clinton administration broadened the military/police connection by requiring the departments of Justice and Defense form a partnership to "engage the crime war with the same resolve they fought the Cold War" (National Institute of Justice 1995). The result has been training partnerships with elite "special operations" (e.g., Navy Seals and Army Rangers) and a fundamental change to the character of public—and to a lesser extent school—police agencies.

Police Paramilitary Units (PPUs) are distinguished by their heavy reliance on military equipment and technology. In fact, these units are sometimes referred to as "heavy weapons" units and are often revered by other officers who view them as "elite." The most popular weapon utilized by these PPUs is the Heckler and Koch MP5 submachine gun for its futuristic style, direct connection with elite military teams, and contentious training and marketing programs conducted by the Heckler and Koch Corporation. Complementing the MP5 in police agency arsenals include semi-automatic shotguns, sniper rifles, M16s, and automatic shotguns (also called "street sweepers"). Police also employ a wide selection of "less than lethal" technologies for organizing "dynamic entries" (e.g., executing search warrants), including gas grenades (tear gas), stinger grenades (containing rubber pellets), percussion grenades (explosive devices designed to disorient residents), shotgun-launched bean-bag systems, hydraulic battering rams for gaining entry, C4 explosives, and military-armored personnel carriers. This unmistakable military culture that pervades American police is further reinforced by a military command structure, discipline, and military fatigues, including black or urban camouflage, full-body armor, goggles, lace-up combat boots, Kevlar helmets, and "ninja" style hoods (Kraska and Kappeler 1997).

Operationally, these units have also morphed over time. During the 1960s and 1970s the units were utilized *reactively*, typically responding to hostage situations, terrorism, civil riots, and barricaded suspects. What is more, at least initially, these units were present only in the nation's largest police departments. Today, PPUs are widely distributed across agencies of all sizes and have been utilized more *proactively* in their deployments. In fact, initially PPUs were confined to large, urban departments that served populations of at least 50,000 people, with activities narrowly directed at reactive forms of policing. Ethnographic studies during the 1990s, however, reveal that PPUs have become a common fixture in both large- and medium-size U.S. police departments. In fact, although early PPUs were established in the 1970s and almost exclusively confined to large urban departments, by 1996, 89 percent of police departments that served both large- and medium-sized (25,000 people or more) populations had police paramilitary units, which is almost double what existed in 1980. Also between 1985 and 1995, the rise of PPUs in small jurisdictions (25,000 to 50,000) witnessed a 157 percent increase in the number of units. By 2001, more than 65 percent of small-town police departments had a PPU, and an average of two out of every ten police officers (20 percent) in these departments served on police paramilitary units (Kraska 2001, 142).

Accompanying the increased distribution of PPUs in U.S. police agencies of all sizes has been a marked change in frequency and manner in which they are deployed. Police departments serving all sizes of jurisdictions reported approximately 3,000 deployments of their PPUs in 1980, but by the end of 1995 that number grew to almost 30,000. The bulk of work carried out by these units in 1980 was limited mostly to *reactive* deployments—barricaded suspect, rare hostage, or civil disturbance situations—but by 2001, most of these activities had become proactive in nature. Indeed, these units were mainly being used as search warrants for private residences that had "dynamic entry," or no-knock tactics. Also, the units have increasingly been utilized for routine patrol. In fact, where the initial use of PPUs for proactive patrol was virtually nonexistent, by 1997 more than 20 percent of all departments utilized them in this manner, which represents a 257 percent increase since 1989.

School districts have not been immune to these secular trends in police militarization. Police officers were introduced into public schools in the 1950s as School Resource Officers (SRO) whose initial role was that of a collaborative educator in the areas of conflict resolution and law. National incidents such as that which occurred at Columbine High School (1999) led to calls for increased security at schools, which the public largely applauded for its promise in creating safe learning environments. Similar to state and local police, school districts began applying for surplus military equipment on the grounds that they are necessary for counter-terrorism or counter-drug efforts within America's schools. As a result, grenade launchers, M16s, and Mine-Resistant Ambush Protected (MRAP) vehicles have been awarded to at least 26 school districts (Peak 2015, 213).

Social and Political Consequences of Police Militarization

The rise and normalization of PPUs has precipitated in several unintended consequences that threaten not only their civilian nature—which has largely been taken for granted—but also come with several attendant consequences that have been further exacerbated by their proactive deployment and the simultaneous rise and expansion of community-oriented policing. The proactive use of PPUs for routine police work (e.g., execution of search warrants using dynamic entry, or no-knock methods) may appear benign and insignificant. Unfortunately, reliance on PPUs in this manner may actually increase risk to both officers and citizens by manufacturing risk. Such use is rationalized on the grounds that lives may be endangered, or evidence (typically narcotics) may be destroyed if police were to take the time to obtain a warrant or announce their presence. The 1990s witnessed a precipitous rise in the use of PPUs in this manner, despite the fact that they may actually increase risk. Thus, disoriented residents (who may be innocent, startled, or guilty and bent on protecting their criminal enterprise and freedom) may respond with gunfire. And the sheer number of weapons, in conjunction with their relative power, means that when a shoot-out does occur, innocent bystanders may be injured, as stray bullets often easily pierce most construction materials.

> "We did a crack-raid and got in a massive shoot-out in an apartment building. Shots were fired, and we riddled a wall with bullets. An MP5 round will go through walls. When we went in the next apartment where the bullets were penetrating, we found a baby crib full of holes; thank god those people weren't home."
> —Anonymous quote from a captain in a large southwestern police department (Kraska and Kappeler 1997, 9)

The proactive use of PPUs for routine patrol may also strain police-community relations. In fact, studies conducted in the 1990s revealed that some police agencies allow these units to patrol in full tactical gear for the purpose of intimidation. This is particularly problematic in that police resources are often disproportionately deployed to high crime and disorderly neighborhoods. Unfortunately, it is often these areas that are occupied by first-generation immigrants and other minorities who are usually poor. The routine use of officers in this manner not only likely offends the sensibilities of those living in such communities, but also further strains police-community relationships, as they come to be viewed as an "occupying army" whose appearance and military culture work to discourage genuine police-citizen interaction and communication.

Contributing to strained police-community relations and the erosion of democratic freedoms has been the simultaneous rise of community-oriented policing. Community-oriented policing (COP) emerged during the 1980s and was in part a response to increased recognition among police administrators and public officials of the link between community disorganization and more serious and violent offenses. The core of the COP model is the recognition that minor quality-of-life issues (e.g., loitering), if left unattended, invite more serious violent offenses (e.g., robbery) by signaling a lack of community control. Initially what emerged was a "velvet glove" approach to policing aimed at improving police-community relations and agency effectiveness through the adoption of democratic and open police-citizen processes (i.e., regular COP meetings with community members to allow for citizen input into police priorities). Today, COP is viewed by some as an "iron fist" or "zero tolerance" form of bifurcated policing congruent with the "war" metaphor, which emphasizes police using domination and force for the sole purpose of controlling and displacing disreputable behaviors and people (e.g., vagrancy, loitering, public drunkenness, addicts, mentally ill individuals, etc.) by the dominant group (i.e., the middle and upper classes).

Militarization of School Resource Officers (SROs) has largely been traced to, and justified by, the perceived increase in public school violence following sensationalized incidents gaining national attention. Unfortunately, militarization of SROs may be an overreaction not supported by existing realities. In fact, data suggest that not only are schools safer today than in previous decades, but that the majority of SRO work is in fact directed at addressing behavioral problems rather than responding to violent offenses (Peak, 2015). What is more, the intensification of military culture in public schools can be seen as a symbolic declaration of war that serves to inhibit institutional effectiveness by breeding distrust of school officials and cultivating fear among students—both of which are necessary for effective learning.

Steven J. Ellwanger

See also: Bow Street Runners; Civil Asset Forfeiture as a Source of Department Funding; Community Policing Today; RICO Act; Sir Robert Peel and Principles of Modern Policing

Further Reading

Brown, Cynthia A. "Divided Loyalties: Ethical Challenges for America's Law Enforcement in Post 9/11 America." *Case Western Reserve Journal of International Law* 43 (2011): 651–675.

Kraska, P. *Militarizing the American Criminal Justice System: The Changing Roles of the Armed Forces and the Police*. Boston, MA: Northeastern University Press, 2001.

Kraska, Peter, and Victor E. Kappeler. "Militarizing American Police: The Rise and Normalization of Paramilitary Units." *Social Problems* 44 (1997): 1–18.

National Institute of Justice. "Technology Transfer from Defense: Concealed Weapon Detection." *National Institute of Justice Journal* 1 (1995): 229.

Peak, Bethany J. "Militarization of School Police: One Route on the School-to-Prison Pipeline." *Arkansas Law Review* 68 (2015): 195–229.

CIVIL ASSET FORFEITURE AS A SOURCE OF DEPARTMENT FUNDING

Asset forfeiture is the process in which the government seizes private property involved in a crime or derived from a crime. The property is forfeited to the government, which means that the government takes over ownership of the property without compensating the former owner. Property subject to asset forfeiture includes houses, businesses, motor vehicles, cash, jewelry, stocks, and any other type of real estate or personal property. Under federal law, property is subject to forfeiture when it is traceable to or represents the proceeds obtained, directly or indirectly, from many federal crimes including money laundering, terrorism, drug laws, and even

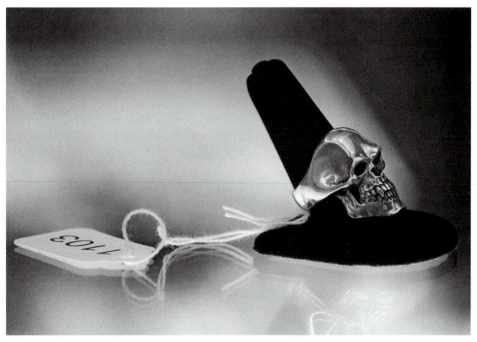

A skull ring belonging to notorious Boston mobster James "Whitey" Bulger is displayed during a press preview before an asset-forfeiture auction in Boston, Massachusetts, 2016. The U.S. Marshals Service auctioned off items seized in 2011 from the Santa Monica hideout of Bulger and his girlfriend. (Scott Eisen/Bloomberg via Getty Images)

removing or altering motor vehicle identification numbers. The states also have asset forfeiture laws, although these may vary somewhat from the federal laws and each other. Every year, local, state, and federal law enforcement agencies seize more than $1 billion in assets, and in some cases the owner is not even charged with a crime. When assets are forfeited over to the government, much of the revenue is provided to police departments, while some goes to compensate victims of crimes and to cover the forfeiture program expenses.

The major goals of asset forfeiture are to take the profit out of crime, provide restitution and other services for victims of crime, and fund law enforcement agencies. For instance, if a drug dealer uses a boat to smuggle drugs, the police may seize the boat without waiting for a criminal trial and conviction of the drug dealer. In fact, they do not even need to arrest the drug dealer. If the drug dealer does not contest the seizure within a specified time, the boat is forfeited to the government. Depending upon the jurisdiction of the police agency, the police may receive up to 100 percent of the proceeds from the forfeiture of the boat. This appears to be a "win-win" situation: a boat used in the commission of criminal activity is taken out of commission, and the police department receives much-needed revenue from the sale of the boat. However, civil asset forfeiture laws are controversial, and there has been much public outcry against them. For instance, in the above situation, suppose the boat did not belong to the drug dealer. Instead, the drug dealer borrowed the boat for one day from his cousin who reasonably believed the drug dealer was using the boat for pleasure rather than criminal activity. Should the cousin, who was not involved in the crime, lose his boat?

Those who support civil asset forfeiture argue that it deters crime by taking away profit, and that it provides funds to help the victims of crimes. Another argument in favor of civil asset forfeiture is that it provides much needed revenue to police agencies without burdening the taxpayers any further, and provides more funds for police to fight crime. Finally those in favor of civil asset forfeiture point out that police and other law enforcement agencies, whether on the local, state, or federal level, are more likely to cooperate with each other due to civil asset forfeiture laws.

Opponents of civil asset forfeiture argue, among other things, that it violates the constitutional rights of property owners, that it can deprive innocent property owners of their assets, and that it encourages police agencies to engage in questionable behavior. Critics also argue that civil asset forfeiture leads to "policing for profit" in order to supplement police department budgets.

Asset forfeiture falls into two categories: criminal asset forfeiture and civil asset forfeiture. The less controversial is criminal asset forfeiture, also known as *in personam* (against a person) asset forfeiture, which requires that the property owner be convicted of a crime and that the property is somehow linked to the crime. The prosecutor, on behalf of the government, charges or indicts the defendant who is accused of committing a crime. The defendant will lose the property in addition to incurring any other punishments such as incarceration and/or fines as long as the defendant is found guilty beyond a reasonable doubt and the property itself is a forfeitable asset. A defendant who takes a plea bargain and pleads guilty will agree to the forfeiture as well. Such cases have captions (names) such as *United States v. John Smith* or *Delaware v. Jim Brown*. The government is the plaintiff (person bringing the lawsuit) in the case and the accused is the defendant in the case. Throughout the process, the defendant's constitutional rights (under both the federal and state constitutions) are protected.

On the other hand, civil asset forfeiture does not involve a criminal prosecution against the property owner; the process is very different. Although the property owner may be tried in a separate criminal case, this is not part of the civil asset forfeiture process. A property owner can lose his or her property under civil asset forfeiture without ever being convicted in a court of law. In fact, civil asset forfeiture can occur even when the property owner is never charged with a crime or even arrested. Civil asset forfeiture occurs in two ways: judicial forfeiture or administrative forfeiture. In judicial forfeiture cases, the legal action is not filed against the property owner, but rather against the property itself, and the case goes before a judge. Such a legal action against property is known as an *in rem* (against a thing) legal action. In an *in rem* action, the property itself is the defendant, not the owner of the property. Such cases have captions such as *United States v. $116,850 in U.S. Currency* or *In the Matter of 2004 Harley DAVIDSON, VIN# 1VF9FV31A84R116374.* The owner of the property is not the defendant in the case, but rather a third party claimant who may try to reclaim his or her property. Unlike criminal asset forfeiture cases, the property owner does not have the same constitutional rights, and the burden of proof (the evidence that the government must bring forth to win its case) is much lower than in a criminal case. The burden of proof in federal cases is a preponderance of the evidence, which means that it is at least 51 percent certain that the property was connected to a crime and is therefore forfeitable. In criminal cases, the burden of proof is beyond a reasonable doubt, which is a much higher standard of proof than a preponderance of the evidence. The states vary as to their burden of proof requirements: many use the same preponderance of the evidence standard as the federal government, whereas some use a higher clear and convincing evidence standard, and others use a lower probable cause standard.

In administrative forfeiture cases, the courts are not involved unless the property owner takes action. In administrative cases, the government agency that seized the property starts the forfeiture action by giving legally required notice to the property owner, any co-owners, and other interested parties. The owner or other interested party has a certain number of days to make a claim to contest the seizure of his or her property. If the property seizure is contested, there will be a judicial proceeding. However, if the owner does not contest, the property is automatically forfeited to the government after the deadline has passed. Real estate cannot be administratively forfeited, but any personal property under $500,000 is subject to the process under federal law.

In the early 2000s, the annual revenue from federal asset forfeitures increased tremendously. In 2012, the U.S. Government Accountability Office (GAO) prepared a "Report to Congressional Requesters" about the Assets Forfeiture Fund (AFF). In the report, the GAO stated, "In the 9-year period from fiscal years 2003 through 2011, AFF revenues totaled $11 billion, growing from $500 million in fiscal year 2003 to $1.8 billion in fiscal year 2011. Since 2006, an increase in the prosecution of fraud and financial crime cases has led to substantial increases in AFF revenue" (U.S. GAO 2012). The GAO also attributed the increase to "an overall increase in the number of forfeiture cases together with higher-value forfeitures." Furthermore, according to the GAO report, "equitable sharing payments to state and local law enforcement agencies have generally increased since fiscal year 2003; in fiscal year 2003, equitable sharing payments totaled $218 million, and in fiscal year 2011, equitable sharing totaled $445 million." According to the report, the equitable sharing program between federal and other law enforcement agencies is vital because it supplements local and state police department budgets that largely go to pay salaries and other personnel costs. It is only through equitable sharing that police departments are able to purchase equipment as well as pay for training and other programs (U.S. GAO 2012).

Asset forfeiture laws have been used by governments for centuries. In medieval England, for instance, if property was used to kill a person, the government could seize the property to help pay for the funeral of the deceased. The earliest civil asset forfeiture laws in the United States were based upon British Navigation Acts of the 17th century. If the Act was violated, such as a crew member smuggling something without the ship owner's knowledge, the ship and cargo could be seized by the government, even if the owner was not guilty. Early asset forfeiture laws in the United States mainly involved the customs and admiralty (shipping) law and involved shipping, and the importing, and exporting of goods. One of the rationales for early civil asset forfeiture laws was that in admiralty or customs cases, the government could not obtain jurisdiction over the owners of property (who often lived in other countries), therefore there could be no criminal prosecution resulting in criminal asset forfeiture. Without the ability to obtain *in personam* jurisdiction over the property owner, the government was left to "prosecute" the property through *in rem* jurisdiction.

As part of its efforts to fight illegal drug use, the federal government enacted the Comprehensive Drug Abuse Prevention and Control Act of 1970, which, among other things, expanded civil asset forfeiture in drug-related crimes. Assets seized under this law, as well as under earlier forfeiture laws, did not go directly to police agencies but instead to a general government fund. The federal Comprehensive Crime Control Act (CCCA) of 1984 changed the process significantly. Under the CCCA, police agencies were allowed to keep much of the proceeds from the assets that they seized. While one purpose of the CCCA was to take the profit out of crime by seizing assets from criminals, another purpose was to increase police budgets and make more money available to fight crime. The Act also allowed state and local law enforcement agencies to take assets from suspects and to transfer the assets to federal agencies. In a process known as equitable sharing, the federal government would then share the proceeds of the forfeited property with these state and local police agencies.

Prior to 2000, innocent property owners had very few rights in federal civil asset forfeiture cases. For instance, if a husband and wife allowed their adult son to live in their home, and the son was dealing drugs without his parents' knowledge, the parents could lose their home without being able to argue their innocence. In fact, the United States Supreme Court looked at such an issue in 1996 in the case *Bennis v. Michigan*. In the *Bennis* case, a man was found in his vehicle with a prostitute, and the police seized the vehicle. However, the vehicle was also owned by the man's wife, Tina Bennis, who did not know about her husband's criminal activity. Ms. Bennis tried to argue that she had a right to prove that she was innocent, and therefore her vehicle should not have been seized by the police. However, the Supreme Court held that innocent owners such as Ms. Bennis did not have a right to present an "innocent owner" defense. After the Bennis case, Congress passed the Civil Asset Forfeiture Reform Act of 2000 (CAFRA), and the act provides property owners with an "innocent owner" defense. However, the burden is on the innocent owner to prove that he or she did not have knowledge of the criminal activity rather than on the government to prove that he or she did have such knowledge. In addition to providing for an innocent owner defense, CAFRA expanded the scope of civil asset forfeiture so that money laundering and the Racketeer Influenced and Corrupt Organizations (RICO) Act then fell under the civil asset forfeiture laws.

There are many federal laws that provide for civil asset forfeiture in a wide variety of areas such as drug crimes, white collar crime, organized crime, and terrorism. Government departments that participate in civil asset forfeiture include the Department of Justice, the Secretary of the Treasury, and the Postal Service. Federal law enforcement agencies that participate include, among others, the Federal Bureau of Investigation (FBI), the Drug Enforcement Administration (DEA), the Bureau of Alcohol, Tobacco, Firearms and Explosives (ATF), and the United States Marshalls Service. State and local agencies also participate with the federal government under the equitable sharing program.

State civil asset forfeiture laws vary a greatly, and the outcome for property owners under state law can be very different depending on the state in which the property was seized. As previously stated, the burden of proof differs from state to state, with many using the same burden, preponderance of the evidence, as the federal government. However, several states have a lower burden of proof called probable cause, which means the government need only prove that the police had a reasonable belief that the asset was used in or derived from a crime when it was seized. A few states require a criminal conviction for asset forfeiture to take place. Another area in which states differ is for proceeds that police agencies may keep. Some states permit police agencies to keep 100 percent of the forfeited assets, whereas other states require police agencies to turn over all proceeds to a general government fund. As stated above, equitable sharing provides a means for state and local policing agencies to work with federal agencies. In some states, equitable sharing results in state and local police agencies being able to retain more revenue than they would under their state laws.

Elizabeth W. Marchioni

See also: Constitutional Mandates; Corruption; Fleeing Felon Legislation; RICO Act

Further Reading

Block, Walter E. "Don't Steal; the Government Hates Competition: The Problem with Civil Asset Forfeiture." *Journal of Private Enterprise* 31, no. 1 (2016): 45–56.

Jones, Tyler K. "Will Eric Holder's Memo Have a Substantial Effect on Civil Asset Forfeiture Practices?" *Journal of Drug Policy Analysis* 8, no. 1 (2013): 37–46.

Osler, Mark. "Asset Forfeiture in a New Market-Reality Narcotics Policy." *Harvard Journal on Legislation* 52 (2015): 221.

Sheth, Darpana, M. "Policing for Profit: The Abuse of Forfeiture Laws." *Engage: The Journal of the Federalist Society Practice Groups* 14 (2013): 24.

U.S. Department of Justice. "Asset Forfeiture Program." 2016. https://www.justice.gov/afp.

U.S. Government Accountability Office (GAO). "Justice Assets Forfeiture Fund: Transparency of Balances and Controls over Equitable Sharing Should Be Improved." Office Report to Congressional Requesters. July 12, 2012. http://www.gao.gov/products/GAO-12-736.

DEATHS IN THE LINE OF DUTY

Peaceable or not, the United States has a history of both revolutionary and reactionary behavior. Some of the country's greatest political leaders and social activists have thrown down the gauntlet, asking the country to preserve its civil liberties through the spirit of resistance. The figurative message of their words was calling people to action versus inaction and challenging the status quo, overturning it when it yielded unjust responses. Embracing that spirit leads to civil disobedience and the right to dissent under the First Amendment of the U.S. Constitution. There is a divide, however, in how best to force a government to assume its constitutional role—especially when a society does not know how to be obedient in the first place. U.S. law enforcement is currently caught in a crossfire as it strives to protect citizens against growing violence between each other while also taking on a hailstorm of violence against *themselves*.

Failed institutions and organizations are at the root of a dysfunctional society and not just cops who are largely seen as carrying out marching orders from a totalitarian government intent on oppressing its citizens. Even with a few bad apples on both sides of the law, firing, suing, or killing any cop might offer some measure of symbolic justice for those who believe they have been wronged or wish to use them as a poster for deterrence, but it actually leaves unchanged the *conditions* that fostered or tolerated the failed institutions to begin with.

According to statistics published by the Federal Bureau of Investigation (FBI) and National Law Enforcement Officers Memorial Fund (NLEOMF), which are the two largest, statistical reporting bodies on police officers assaulted and killed in America, an average of 151 officers are killed each year. From 2000 to 2010, at least 57,000 officers were assaulted, annually, and more than 15,000 of those assaults led to an injury to the officer. Since 1791, when the first police death was recorded, more than 20,000 police officers have died in the line of duty with nearly 1,500 deaths between 2005 and 2015. Of these, 55 percent were wearing body armor at the time of their deaths. The 1920s was the deadliest decade with 2,437 deaths, and the deadliest day was September 11, 2001, when 72 officers died as a result of terrorist attacks. There are just under 900,000 sworn law enforcement officers-to-date and, according to the FBI's Uniform Crime Report (UCR), nearly 1 million violent crimes are committed from our growing population each year.

Law enforcement deaths in the line of duty cover a wide range of circumstances. Over the past decade, gunfire leads with 539 deaths, followed by automobile and motorcycle accidents at 482. A total of 193 have died from job-related illnesses while 134 were killed having been struck by vehicles. Of significant concern is the increase in firearms-related deaths, which includes nearly all states in the country.

Looking at the problem, police agencies, police benevolent groups, and researchers are examining how firearm-related deaths are different than in years past. Shootings that escalate from investigations and arrests have always been commonplace and expected; however, the incidences of people *assassinating* police officers today are astounding, leading to what is considered a "war on cops." That is, officers are now being ambushed while stopped at a traffic light, filling their police cruisers at a gas station, or eating breakfast or lunch at a public restaurant. They are being hit by snipers who dial fake 9-1-1 calls and shoot as the officers respond to the location or walk toward the structure.

Before coming to the job, most police officers are not aware that shootings are a rare occurrence. Their perceptions are similarly shaped by the same media forces that frame the concept of shootings for the rest of the public. Therefore, unless they are aware from family or friends in the business, they may likely share the misperception that law enforcement officers shoot others regularly. Our American systems of law and morality stress the sanctity of human life and condemn the taking of it. Even so, officers are permitted to use deadly force (which is a powerful human aversion anyway), and now that they are being targeted by ways and reasons never seen before, officers are able to mitigate the risk of being stabbed, beaten, or shot in the course of trying to control a suspect—and the consequences mean more police shootings. Moreover, the climate has created a trepid police force that, instead of doing the job it has always been doing and doing it correctly, now fears legitimate litigation due to "legislation from the bench," weakening support at all levels of the judicial system, a failure of their own agency or government to back them, an increasingly violent society, anti-police rhetoric, and a litany of expectations on how to handle criminals, those with mental illnesses, or placing handcuffs on a senior citizen. Unfortunately, violent crime is rising, especially in large U.S. cities. Compared to 2015, 2016 has a higher number of homicides, rapes, robberts, assualts and shootings. Violent crime rising in U.S. cities, study finds (Bruer 2016). How rising violence in just 10 cities drove up the U.S. murder rate (Beckett and Aufrichtig 2016).

The legal and policy features that factor into watchdog groups or even criminal justice agencies attempting to force the swing of the pendulum in the other direction regarding police practices calls into question one of the most visible and controversial aspects of duty: the use of force. The judicious use of police force is a potent display of authority and control, and application of that force is dependent upon many factors that include split-second decisions against legal requirements as well as individual agency policies and the politics that drive those policies. The goal of force presents a dichotomy of control and self-defense, which makes its use and application difficult for the public at large to understand.

Law enforcement officers are often not provided the resources to effectively handle all of the calls for service they are required to respond to. As a result, officers resort to common sense and experience when policies, training, and equipment are poor or nonexistent. The caveat to suiting up for another shift on the streets without proper and appropriate support by their department and administration is an increased threat of injury and death. The landmark U.S. Supreme Court cases of *Graham v. Connor* (1989) and *Tennessee v. Garner* (1985) have long-provided law enforcement with logical, legal, but most importantly, a reasonable response to danger that, if applied properly, decreases the potential for behavior that is deemed unconstitutional. It also reduces hesitation and confusion given the lack of policies and training that are benchmarks of risk management in the policing profession.

The trepidation that trickles down, however, from sound, legal practices are from events such as the Police Executive Research Forum's *30 Guiding Principles* (PERF 2016) that have made suggestions for cops to "soften up" their tactics and, in doing so, portrays them as bad cops, with poor tactics and training. Furthermore, President Barack Obama's federal scope into Ferguson, Missouri (which led to suing the city in federal district court for failing to agree to terms regarding law enforcement reform) strategically moved the city to finally approve a consent decree to agree to the federal government's terms. Agencies across the United States are feeling similar pressures, as they continue to "arm" their officers with body cameras in the name of community relations while the government systematically takes away their equipment and weapons (Gambino 2015).

In 2016, the U.S. Supreme Court voted 4–3 to abolish the long withstanding *public duty doctrine*, which now makes officers more susceptible to civil litigation under tort laws for failure to respond to victims or crimes in a manner appropriate to the public. Couple this decision with conflicts that arise when mental health professionals withhold information on potentially dangerous patients and politicians who ask officers to respond to crises (including suicide by cop) with lesser force than what is allowed by law, and it further agitates an otherwise "thin blue line."

Other deaths in the line of duty that often go unnoticed are job-related illnesses such as heart attacks, suicide, and mental illnesses. Like our soldiers who return home from war physically and psychologically battered, our law enforcement officers come home every single day from war-like trenches (*if* they come home at all). Still wounded, they wake up each day, put on a bandage, and assume their post on the front line. This pattern continues for years.

Police studies indicate that three to five years is the general cutoff for many officers in the field. By year five, no matter the size of the agency, a cop will have experienced all domains of human suffering, convoluted and twisted within competing cultures in society. Burnout, divorce, suicide, and other symptoms of stress have, by then, crept up on many, forcing some to leave and others yet to endure while suffering.

Law enforcement officers must constantly reaffirm their own values and morals while working within a paradoxical line of business. Their frontline assault against evil, most often illustrated by the badge, the car, the gun, and uniform, is woven into their own personal feelings about crime and victimization, and we typically see their behaviors as the larger manifestation of right and wrong.

A depiction of the predatory social dynamic that places line-of-duty deaths at the center of the good-versus-evil campaign was an essay on "Sheep, Wolves, and Sheepdogs" (Grossman 2009, 24). In this essay, our general society are *sheep*. They are kind, productive, gentle creatures who can only hurt one another by accident. Cared for by the shepherd, they live in a world of perceived security afforded to them by a locked gate, a cozy loft, and the communion of other sheep. Next are the *wolves*. Violent beasts, they are the sociopaths and psychopaths in our society, and they prey and feed on the sheep. Finally, there is the *sheepdog*. The sheepdog lurks around at night, checking the perimeter and howling at the moon. They would never turn their teeth on the flock, but they yearn for a righteous battle. The sheep are leery of the sheepdog until the wolf arrives—at which time the entire flock tries desperately to hide behind one lonely sheepdog.

Extraordinary tales of selflessness have long brought a sense of security and justice from the swells of evil that plague our social fabric. In light of this human toll, there is a continued need to protect and preserve the mission of law enforcement officers so that they may never wander far from the flock.

Brian Kinnaird

See also: Community Policing Today; Deadly Force; Increase in Violent Crime Rate and Risk to Law Enforcement; Perceptions of Police Today; "Thin Blue Line": Police as a Guard against Anarchy; Uniform Crime Reports

Further Reading

Barlow, D., and M. Barlow. *Police in a Multicultural Society: An American Story*. Long Grove, IL: Waveland Press, 2000.

Beckett, L, and Aufrichtig, A. "1500 More People Murdered in 2015 Than in 2014." *The Guardian*, VDARE September 26, 2016. https://www.theguardian.com/us-news/2016/sep/30/us-murder-rate-chicago-fbi-data-police.

Bruer, W. "Violent Crime Rising in U.S. Cities, Study Finds. 2016." CNNPolitics.com, July 25, 2016. http://edition.cnn.com/2016/07/25/politics/violent-crime-report-us-cities-homicides-rapes/.

Federal Bureau of Investigation (FBI). "Officers Assaulted and Killed." UCR Publications. 2016. https://www.fbi.gov/about-us/cjis/ucr/ucr-publications.

Gambino, L. "Obama to ban police military gear that can 'alienate and intimidate'." *The Guardian*. May 28, 2015. https://www.theguardian.com/us-news/2015/may/18/president-obama-limits-supply-military-style-equipment-police.

Grossman, D. *On Combat: The Psychology of Physiology of Deadly Conflict in War and Peace*. Mascoutah, IL: Warrior Science Publications, 2009.

Klinger, D. *In the Kill Zone*. San Francisco, CA: Wiley Books, 2004.

"Officer Fatality Data." National Law Enforcement Officers Memorial Fund. 2016. http://www.nleomf.org/facts/officer-fatalities-data/daifacts.html.

"30 Guiding Principles." Police Executive Research Forum (PERF). 2016. http://www.policeforum.org/assets/30%20guiding%20principles.pdf.

Walker, S. *Police Accountability: The Role of Citizen Oversight*. Belmont, CA: Wadsworth Press, 2001.

Whitehead, J. *A Government of Wolves: The Emerging American Police State*. New York: Select-Books, 2013.

SEAN BELL SHOOTING

Sean Bell, an African American male who, on November 25, 2006, was celebrating his bachelor party with his friends, Trent Benefield and Joseph Guzman, when he was fatally shot by officers from the New York Police Department (NYPD). The circumstances surrounding the shooting were controversial due to the fact that the three male victims, two African American and one Latino, were all unarmed. The shooting fueled concerns whether the NYPD were policing in a racially biased manner, even though three of the officers involved were African American or Hispanic.

The NYPD is no stranger to debatable police encounters with members of the minority community. However, this shooting sparked several protests, led by Reverend Al Sharpton and the National Action Network, an African American civil rights leader, who over the years has led several contentious demonstrations against police brutality. Sharpton demanded that (then) police commissioner Ray Kelly be fired and cried out for the end to police terror. Michael Bloomberg (then) mayor of New York City called for citizens to demonstrate patience and not to draw conclusions but ultimately deemed the actions of the detectives as excessive force.

The greatest concern for politicians, at the time, was to avoid a similar scenario as the February 4, 1999, police-involved shooting of Amadou Diallo, a 23-year-old street peddler, who had emigrated from Guinea, West Africa. In a case of mistaken identity, four NYPD officers fired 41 shots at Diallo after he reached for his wallet while standing in a dimly lit stairwell of his apartment building. Diallo was struck by 19 of the 41 bullets and killed. The officers who were assigned to a plain-clothes street crime unit had been searching for a serial rapist and claimed that Diallo fit the description. This shooting also caused widespread dissension in the African American community because the four officers were ultimately acquitted of second-degree murder charges. In the aftermath of the acquittals, many New Yorkers marched down Fifth Avenue in Manhattan and protested in front of City Hall. Several of the interracial protestors were arrested for disorderly conduct and inciting violence.

Bell, who had been scheduled to marry his fiancée, Nicole Paultre, later that evening, was at Kalua Cabaret, a strip club in Jamaica, Queens, with Guzman and Benefield. At the same time, while under the supervision of Lieutenant Gary Napoli, undercover detectives Gescard Isnora, Michael Oliver, Marc Cooper, Paul Headley, and uniformed officer Michael Carey—all assigned to a special vice unit—conducted surveillance for possible prostitution and drug activity. One of the detectives observed Bell and his friends getting into a verbal confrontation with other patrons at the club. The detective then radioed his observations to the remaining detectives who were outside waiting in a minivan and Toyota Camry. It was also alleged that the detective claimed that he observed a gun tucked in Guzman's waistband.

According to an eyewitness, threats were made between both groups, but it was Bell who made the decision to de-escalate the situation and depart with his friends. It was at this point that the detectives allegedly believed that Bell, who was walking toward his vehicle, went to retrieve a weapon. After Bell got into the car, Isnora claimed he identified himself as a police officer; however, Benefield, Guzman, and several eyewitnesses refuted this statement. Amid the confusion, Isnora also claimed that Guzman, while sitting in the front passenger seat in the car, made a suspicious movement, which led him to believe that Guzman had a gun tucked in his waistband. Bell then attempted to flee the scene and was alleged to have jerked his car forward, striking the undercover detective. He then drove his car in reverse, hitting an iron gate, lurched his car forward again, and rammed into the undercover minivan. Isnora then opened fire and was immediately assisted in the shooting by the other undercover detectives and uniformed officers. Isnora shot at the car 11 times, Detective Oliver fired 31 shots, and Detective Cooper shot 4 times at the car. Bell was struck 4 times and killed. Guzman, who was in the front passenger seat, was struck 11 times. The bullet entry points spanned the right side of his body, hitting him in his face, shoulder, thigh, buttocks, and ankle. Benefield, who had been positioned in the rear passenger seat, was struck 3 times in the leg and buttocks, but his injuries were not critical. After the shooting, the NYPD was criticized for handcuffing Benefield, even though it was standing operating procedure to do so. While all the bullets didn't strike the victims or their vehicle, despite the officers being in close proximity, some struck nearby cars and buildings, which indicates how chaotic the scene was at the time of the shooting.

In 2007, Bell's fiancée, along with Guzman and Benefield, filed a federal lawsuit accusing the NYPD of civil rights violations, wrongful death, and negligent assault.

Detectives Michael Oliver, Marc Cooper, and Gescard Isnora were indicted in 2007 on state charges. Detectives Isnora and Oliver, who fired most of the shots, were charged with the most serious crimes, first-degree and second-degree manslaughter. Detective Cooper was charged with reckless endangerment. However, on April 25, 2008, following a seven-week trial, in which the detectives waived their right to a jury trial, Judge Arthur J. Cooperman, who presided over the proceedings, acquitted the detectives of all charges stemming from the shooting. Moreover, citing insufficient evidence, the federal government also declined to pursue civil rights violations against the officers.

In 2010, the City of New York settled the federal civil lawsuit for more than $7 million. Although Nicole Paultre was never married to Bell, under the terms of an agreement, their children, Jada and Jordyn, received more than $3 million. Guzman, who has undergone numerous surgeries due to his injuries, received $3 million. And Benefield, the least injured, received $900,000. None of the officers involved in the shooting was held financially responsible for reimbursing the City of New York.

Brian L. Royster

See also: Amadou Diallo Case; Deadly Force; Police Brutality; Racial Profiling

Further Reading

Belur, J. *Permission to Shoot? Police Use of Deadly Force in Democracies*. London: Springer, 2010.

Browne-Marshall, G. J. *Race, Law, and American Society: 1607 to Present*. New York: Routledge, Taylor & Francis Group, 2007.

Calloway, J. *Black America, Not in this America*. Bloomington, IN: Xlibris, 2011.

Jones, D. M. *Fear of a Hip-Hop Planet: America's New Dilemma*. Santa Barbara, CA: Praeger, 2013.

PTSD AND FAMILY ISSUES AMONG OFFICERS

Discussions about work-related stress are not new, yet little research has explored the impact of post-traumatic stress disorder (PTSD) on families of law enforcement officers. Although most occupations carry varying degrees of stress, police work inherently exposes officers to a greater likelihood of being involved in a variety of traumatic events such as serious accidents, violent attacks, fatal shootings, natural disasters, and more. This frequent exposure to life's challenging and traumatic events can take a toll on the officer's well-being, perspective, and family. In many cases, the demands of the job can lead to emotional exhaustion, work-family conflict, and overall fatigue. In some cases, this stress can also spill over from work into the home and negatively affect the officer's relationships. In the most challenging of situations, officers are expected to respond in a crisis as minimal information reveals itself throughout the event. Additionally, negative public attention and antagonistic hostility toward the police, such as the sniper attacks that killed and injured multiple officers in Dallas in July 2016, adds to the stress that officers experience while at work.

For an officer's family life, rotating shifts, long hours, overtime, and shiftwork can often add to the challenges of the officer participating in important family events, children's school activities, or family vacations. Additionally, for the spouses of officers, "the unpredictability of off duty requirements can be particularly frustrating" (Karaffa et al. 2015, 121). Even under the best circumstances, officers may feel torn between work and family responsibilities when they are unable to meet the challenges of balancing both realms of their lives. In some cases, the challenges of the work-life balance can add to the stress level of the officer in addition to the work stress. On these occasions, officers may feel as if they have failed and disappointed the family.

In extreme cases, officers may experience PTSD. According to the National Institute of Mental Health, PTSD represents a response to extreme or persistent stress resulting from a single traumatic event or the ongoing stress of witnessing human tragedy. Despite the fact that the experience of PTSD can date back to World War II, in the 1980s the American Psychiatric Association first classified PTSD in the *Diagnostic and Statistical Manual of Mental Disorders* (DSM III) (Trimble 1985). While PTSD was first categorized as an anxiety disorder, the most recent revision of the DSM IV in 2015 has shifted its classification to a category identified as "trauma and stressor-related disorders" (APA 2013).

Initially, research conducted on PTSD focused on military veterans who had endured trauma during combat, yet slowly mainstream society began to identify PTSD symptoms in others who suffered trauma, including law enforcement officers as well as disaster aid workers, emergency personnel, medical staff, or first responders. Although much of police work involves report writing, routine patrols, and community interactions, officers remain acutely aware that with each day, they are risking their lives. Generally, an officer's work setting is not a combat zone; however, the situations in which officers are involved are fraught with traumatic elements such as being the first point of contact for orphaned children after a serious automobile accident or violent murder.

Depending on the incident, law enforcement officers may experience a loss of sleep or appetite, nightmares, anxiety, depression, and a host of other symptoms. No one can imagine what law enforcement and the first responders of the September 11, 2001, attacks endured, as they had to respond quickly to secure areas, protect individuals, and soothe those who had lost loved ones. Witnessing and experiencing such tragedy not only affects the officer, but also how she or he handles the stress and interacts at home with family and friends. The stress from being involved in these critical incidents has the potential to leave officers feeling confused, guilty, withdrawn or depressed (Scoville 2013), yet it is important to understand that not all law enforcement officers develop PTSD because of their occupation. Even after witnessing or being involved in the most serious critical incidents, a small percentage of officers exposed to a traumatic event develop PTSD while the majority will develop symptoms that are short-lived (Inslicht et al. 2010).

Resiliency and the Protective Factors That Mitigate PTSD

Researchers have attempted to examine some of the protective factors that officers may utilize to cope with traumatic events without negative impacts (McCanlies et al. 2014). They found that an officer's level of resilience, life satisfaction, and gratitude can all mitigate the developing of symptoms of PTSD. In the case of officers involved in the September 11th attacks, those who experienced or felt greater levels of gratitude experienced lower levels of psychological anguish (Fredrickson et al. 2003; McCanlies et al. 2014). Findings suggest that "while practically 50 percent of the general population has been exposed to a traumatic event, approximately 5 to 6 percent of those will develop PTSD (McCanlies et al. 2014, 405). Officers who are part of specialized units (i.e., child victim units) or frequently find themselves involved in traumatic incidents are more likely to develop PTSD, yet researchers have not conclusively identified rates of PTSD among officers. While there can be a great deal of variability of PTSD among officers, researchers estimate the rates of PTSD for officers to be in the range of 7 to 19 percent (McCanlies et al. 2014):

> [For officers] the severity of symptoms and risk of PTSD is associated with a number of different factors including the severity of the disaster, degree of exposure, personal losses . . . [and] increased work obligations while concurrently trying to meet the needs of their family. (McCanlies et al. 2014, 407)

Although policing is significantly different from being in combat, an officer's exposure to traumatic incidents over a career of over 20 years can take its toll. In her research on war veterans, Solomon and associates (1987) found that repeated trauma experienced by war veterans resulted in longer-lasting symptoms, which were more severe and debilitating. Even after the physical effects of PTSD had subsided, the psycho-emotional impacts were more difficult to eliminate. In the case of police officers, the possible continuous experience of traumatic events in the course of a career could leave an officer vulnerable to enduring PTSD symptoms (Violanti 1996).

Literature and the media often refer to the use of alcohol among officers to address stress, but studies also indicate that "resilience characteristics can mitigate both substance abuse and alcohol usage" (McCanlies et al. 2014, 412). Repeatedly, the research indicates that not all officers exposed to traumatic incidents will develop symptoms of PTSD, yet those who did utilize alcohol as a coping technique experienced greater psychological effects as a result of the alcohol use (Ballenger et al. 2011).

Burke (1993) claims that the work of law enforcement officers suffers from variety of work-family issues, including a "police culture that interferes with satisfying marital relationships." While there is some debate as to whether police offices have higher divorce rates than married people with other occupations, Karaffa and associates (2015) point to the fact that:

> . . . police officers occasionally develop new personality characteristics after joining the force, which may contribute to the marital problems . . . [as] the officer's working personality can inadvertently set into family life, the complaint about authoritative demands, overprotectiveness, or cynicism. (121)

Because police work largely involves having "officers spend much of their careers preparing for the worst" (Violanti 1996), some officers consequently adapt by approaching each interaction with suspicion, which makes it challenging for family and friends. Some of the challenges of reducing the lasting impact of PTSD on officers is the traditional culture of law enforcement, which views the role of police as one of displaying toughness and strength (Karaffa et al. 2015). In the early 2000s, officers were expected to "be tough" and get through the day since trauma and violence were perceived as ordinary aspects of law enforcement (Evans 2013).

Research among military personnel, as well as law enforcement officers, has shown that traumatic experiences can cause greater rates of PTSD among married individuals as a result of the added partnership responsibilities such as companionship, support, and so on (Solomon, Mikulineer, and Wosner 1987; Violanti 1996). Officers whose spouse or partner was also involved in the policing profession reported fewer concerns (Mikkelsen and Burke 2004). Additionally, Meffert and associates (2014) found in military personnel that individuals suffering from PTSD are more likely to have violent marriages than those without PTSD.

High-Profile Traumatic Events

Large incidents such as the attacks of September 11th and natural disasters such as Hurricane Katrina intensify the level of trauma faced by law enforcement because officers are expected to respond quickly and intelligently with minimal information. While the world was in shock after watching airplanes destroy the Twin Towers in Manhattan, police personnel continued to respond as they absorbed the impact of the tragedy. Similarly, during Hurricane Katrina, the officers' tasks included "crowd control, rescuing individuals from flooded areas as well as retrieval and removal of bodies" (McCanlies et al. 2014, 407). Additionally, during Hurricane Katrina some officers experienced antagonism, hostility, attacks, and assaults from the residents they were attempting to assist. In most emergencies, officers work with limited resources, poor communication, and make-shift headquarters. Additionally, neither of the police departments in New York City or New Orleans were equipped with specialized units to address the specific needs of working with traumatized families during crisis and disasters. On September 11th, initially "five police officers from the Community Affairs Division (CAD) were dispatched to the city morgue to assist victims' families" (Piotrkowski and Telesco 2011, 42); as the need for more officers grew, 200 officers were assigned to assist families at the service centers.

Little research has explored the impact on the officers who worked extremely long hours accompanying families through Ground Zero; reviewing lists of missing, injured, hospitalized, or deceased individuals; dispensing death certificates and urns; and gathering DNA and evidence (Piotrkowski and Telesco 2011). Two months after the hurricane, 19 percent of the officers showed signs of PTSD with even higher rates of PTSD experienced by officers who had been assaulted, had family victimized, or were directly involved in the retrieval of bodies and crowd control (McCanlies et al. 2014). In more recent terrorist attacks and mass shootings, police are constantly adapting to the changing situations such as the San Bernardino mass shooting (2015) of a holiday party at a regional center or the Orlando mass shooting of Latin Night at a gay nightclub (2016). For officers, responding to these types of calls for service can also turn deadly as witnessed in the shots aimed at police that killed five officers in Dallas, Texas, and three officers in Baton Rouge, Louisiana (July 2016).

Vicarious Trauma and Fatigue

Police work not only involves the stress that the officers experience themselves, but also the vicarious trauma experienced as they witness and assist victims enduring various levels of human suffering. Large-scale traumatic incidents such as the terrorist attacks, mass shootings, the on-duty death of a fellow officer, natural disasters, and other major critical events expose officers to trauma that emotionally takes a toll. For officers, the amount of tragedy and long work hours may continue well beyond one's shift. As stated by Vila and Kenny (2002), other professions such as airline pilots and truck drivers have regulations that standardize the amount of hours an individual may work yet "no such structure exists for police officers" (17). Officers who experienced greater levels of exhaustion carry home greater levels of cynicism and experience higher levels of work-family conflict, physical health concerns, and increased rates of suicide contemplation (Mikkelsen and Burke 2004). According to Vila and Kenny (2002):

> Weary from overtime assignments, shiftwork, and school, endless hours spent waiting to testify, and the emotional and physical demands of the job—not to mention trying to patch together a family and social life during your regular breaks of off-duty time—police officer fend off fatigue with coffee and hard-bitten humor (17).

During these extreme circumstances, officers are also susceptible to the impacts of vicarious trauma (referred to as "secondary traumatization"). For these officers, the trauma endured by those they assist also has an impact on their own psyche and well-being. Piotrkowski and Telesco (2011) found 22 percent of the officers who had assisted in the September 11th attacks experienced symptoms of PTSD according to the post-traumatic symptom checklist.

Marriage, Family, and the Home Environment

For police families, no one can comprehend the fears of first hearing over the radio about an officer being injured, having public anti-police outcries, and having the frequent sacrifices of the officer working on holidays, graduations, and other special events because police work never stops. Despite the best planning among officers for time off, no one can predict when an emergency may delay that officer from going home (Karaffa et al. 2015). Despite the fact that research has not conclusively identified police work as any more stressful than any other profession (Mikkelsen and Burke 2004), changing work schedules, odd hours, work-related stress, and possible personality changes that can occur in police work can all contribute to challenges within police-family relationships (Karaffa et al. 2015). Alexander and Walker (1996) identified that 38 percent of officers handle their stress by keeping it to themselves without discussing it with others. Additionally, "roughly one-third of [police] spouses reported that their significant other tended to displace work frustrations unto family members" (Karaffa et al. 2015, 128).

For the families of officers who have been involved in critical incidents, it is also possible for the family to suffer certain elements of secondary distress from exposure to the officer's stress (Figley 1985). Just as police officers can suffer the effects of PTSD from having continuous contact with traumatized individuals, the families of officers can also develop and experience signs of secondary trauma from their exposure to the officer's PTSD (Meffert et al. 2014, 1). Post-traumatic stress disorder "can have far-reaching effects to an officer's family and friends, coworkers and the public they serve" (Scoville 2013).

Support, Treatment, and Resources

Officers involved in a shooting, chase, or death may re-live the day's events and question their decisions, especially when faced with public criticism or if receiving personal threats through social media (Carson 2015). In the case of police involved shootings, Carson describes that:

> The pain behind the badge is real and if not treated, can end marriages and lives. . . . Police departments must offer counseling and peer support for police officers involved in shooting incidents for extended periods, counseling for co-workers directly involved in the shooting, and for family members. Often, spouses and children are left to pick up the pieces when the police officer becomes over burdened by the shooting. Police officers tend to turn towards other police officers and cut off the family from the situation. (8)

Whereas professionals prefer to address PTSD through the integration of psychotherapy and medication, historically the police culture has stigmatized seeking assistance and mental health services (Karaffa et al. 2015). Despite the emotional stressors prevalent in police work, law enforcement has traditionally perpetuated an image of strength, toughness, and masculinity (Violanti 1996) without any regard for the impact of the human suffering witnessed by officers in the course of a 20-year career. Police who witness or are involved in traumatic incidents have been expected to simply "move on." Even in police units in which mental health services are available, officers are often reluctant to enroll due to fear of non-guaranteed confidentiality or fear of being stigmatized as weak and unable to perform the duties of the job. From the perspectives of police spouses and families, "only approximately 11 percent agreed that the department provides adequate sources of stress relief for officers and 7 percent agree that the department provides ways for spouses or family members to deal with stress" (Karaffa et al. 2015, 127).

September 11th changed some of the stigma regarding seeking support for grief and trauma and led to the creation of psychological support systems to aid both the officer and the families. A confidential 24-hour crisis hotline for officers was developed called the *Safe Call Now* to provide a forum for officers to discuss, share, and process their experiences with other officers in a nonjudgmental manner

(Scoville 2013). Through these sites, officers and their families can speak confidentially with peers who can empathize with the specific challenges of police work and provide appropriate referrals (such as a mental health professional, chaplains, or other services) in a nonjudgmental manner.

Critical Incident Stress Management (CISM) was also integrated into the world of law enforcement with the intention of uniting those experiencing similar trauma. CISM consists of a confidential and structured intervention developed to assist individuals in sharing, processing, and healing from traumatic events. It was originally utilized in aiding veterans returning from combat but was quickly expanded to other arenas where trauma is a frequent occurrence, such as with disaster rescue personnel, emergency workers, first responders, and medical staff. CISM provides strategies such as debriefing, which can assist after a traumatic event as well as with pre-crisis education to better prepare those most likely to encounter a traumatic event (Everly, Flannery, and Eyler 2002). Scoville (2013) found that "pre-incident education in combination with after-action methods reduces not only PTSD, [but also] a divorce, alcoholism, and suicide rates among emergency responders."

For some officers though, the impact of the trauma endured can feel too overwhelming. Approximately one officer commits suicide every 17 hours (Perin 2007) and women involved in "protective service" professions such as law enforcement have the highest rates of suicide among women of any occupation (McIntosh et al. 2016). According to Evans, who served as the chaplain that supported officers during the Virginia Tech shootings of 2007, "communities, churches, and pastors can work closely and carefully with police departments to make available empathy, support, and care" (Evans 2011). As departments have begun acknowledging the "need to have peer support and psychological counseling helping officers cope with what they witnessed and what they had to do in the performance of their job" (Perin 2007), Peer Support Units (PSUs) have been implemented throughout that nation. Departments have integrated debriefings for officers who experienced trauma or critical incidents that involve the police chaplain, mental health professionals, and trained officers who facilitate discussions about the feelings, impact, and outcome of having been involved in a critical incident (Evans 2011). Additionally, the West Coast Post Trauma Retreat (WCPR) was established for first responders needing residential treatment and educational programs specifically created to assist first responders in identifying the signs and symptoms of PTSD. Similarly, the First Responder Support Network also provides educational treatment and recovery programs for first responders and their families (http://www.frsn.org). Families of officers also have resources available through support groups such as the LAPD Wives Association which provides support for women who are the partners, spouses, or widows of LADP police officers (http://lapdwives.org).

The events of the past two decades have resulted in numerous changes in policing strategies and police management. The attacks of September 11th left the nation, and law enforcement, with a much greater awareness of addressing safety differently in the wake of multiple terrorist attacks around the world. Additionally, mass shootings at schools, places of worship, and more recently in an Orlando nightclub, have begun a dialogue about the state of violence in the United States. Police work is inherently dangerous and exposes officers to suffering and tragedies on a much more frequent basis than most other professions. These work-related stressors not only affect the well-being of the officer, but also of his or her family. Greater awareness about the impact of PTSD on law enforcement personnel has led to an array of resources that may provide a platform for traumatic incidents to lead to positive outcomes resulting in post-traumatic growth rather than perpetuating continuing symptoms of post-traumatic stress (Tedeschi and Calhoun 1996; McCanlies et al. 2014). More importantly, greater awareness has demonstrated that services must be made available not just for the officer, but also for his or her family.

Silvina Ituarte

See also: Community Policing Today; Deadly Force; Deaths in the Line of Duty; Increase in Violent Crime Rate and Risk to Law Enforcement; Perceptions of Police Today

Further Reading

American Psychiatric Association (APA). *Diagnostic and Statistical Manual of Mental Disorders*, 5th ed. Washington, DC: American Psychiatric Publishing, 2013.

Andersen, J. P., K. Papazoglou, M. Koskelainen, M. Nyman, H. Gustafsberg, and B. B. Arnetz. "Applying Resilience Promotion Training among Special Forces Police Officers." *SAGE open* 5, no. 2 (2015): 1–8.

Ballenger, J. F., S. R. Best, T. J. Metzler, D. A. Wasserman, D. C. Mohr, A. Liberman, A., and C. R. Marmar. "Patterns and Predictors of Alcohol Use in Male and Female Urban Police Officers." *American Journal on Addictions / American Academy of Psychiatrists in Alcoholism and Addictions* 20, no. 1 (2011): 21–29. doi:10.1111/j.1521-0391.2010 .00092.x.

Burke, R. J. "Work-Family Stress, Conflict, Coping, and Burnout in Police Officers." *Stress and Health* 9, no. 3 (1993): 171–180.

Carson, K. "The Police Side of Shooting Deaths and Other Trauma." *Journal of Law Enforcement* 4, no. 3 (2015): 1–11.

Evans, C. *Law Enforcement Agencies: New York Police Department*. New York: Chelsea House, 2011.

Evans, A. "Pastoral Leadership for Police in Crisis." *Journal of Religious Leadership* 12, no. 1 (2013): 1–33.

Evans, R., N. Pistrang, and J. Billings. "Police Officers' Experiences of Supportive and Unsupportive Social Interactions Following Traumatic Incidents." *European Journal of Psychotraumatology* 4 (2013): 1–9.

Everly Jr., G. S., R. B. Flannery, Jr, and V. A. Eyler. "Critical Incident Stress Management (CISM): A Statistical Review of the Literature." *Psychiatric Quarterly* 73, no. 3 (2002): 171–182.

Figley, C. R. "The Family as Victim: Mental Health Implications." *Psychiatry* 6 (1985): 283–291.

Fredrickson, B. L., M. M. Tugade, C. E. Waugh, and G. R. Larkin. "What good are positive emotions in crises? A prospective study of resilience and emotions following the terrorist attacks on the United States on September 11th, 2001." *Journal of Personality and Social Psychology* 84, no. 2 (2003): 365–376.

Friedman, M. J. "Finalizing PTSD in DSM-5: Getting Here from Three and Where to Go Next." *Journal of Traumatic Stress* 26 (2013): 548–556. doi:10.1002/jts.21840, PILOTS ID: 87751.

Inslicht, S. S., S. E. McCaslin, T. J. Metzler, C. Henn-Haase, S. L. Hart, S. Maguen, and C. R. Marmar. "Family Psychiatric History, Peritraumatic Reactivity, and Posttraumatic Stress Symptoms: A Prospective Study of Police." *Journal of Psychiatric Research* 44, no. 1 (2010): 22–31.

Johnson, L., M. Todd, and G. Subramanian. "Violence in Police Families: Work-Family Spillover." *Journal of Family Violence* 20 (2005): 3–12.

Karaffa, K., L. Openshaw, J. Koch, H. Clark, C. Harr, and C. Stewart. "Perceived Impact of Police Work on Marital Relationships." *The Family Journal: Counseling and Therapy for Couples and Families* 23, no. 2 (2015): 120–131.

McCanlies, E. C., A. Mnatsakanova, M. E. Andrew, C. M. Burchfiel, and J. M. Violanti. "Positive Psychological Factors Are Associated with Lower PTSD Symptoms among Police Officers: Post Hurricane Katrina." *Stress and Health* 30, no. 5 (2014): 405–415.

McIntosh, W., E. Spies, D. M. Stone, C. N. Lokey, A. T. Trudeau, and B. Bartholow. "Suicide Rates by Occupational Group—17 States, 2012." *Morbidity and Mortality Weekly Report* 65 (2016): 641–645.

Meffert, S. M., C. Henn-Haase, T. J. Metzler, M. Qian, S. Best, A. Hirschfeld, and C. R. Marmar. "Prospective Study of Police Officer Spouse/Partners: A New Pathway to Secondary Trauma and Relationship Violence?" *PLoS one* 9, no. 7 (2014): e100663.

Mikkelsen, A., and R. J. Burke. "Work-Family Concerns of Norwegian Police Officers: Antecedents and Consequences." *International Journal of Stress Management* 11, no. 4 (2004): 429–444.

Perin, M. "Police Suicide." *Law Enforcement Technology* 34, no. 9 (2007): 8.

Phillips, S. W., J. J. Sobol, and S. P. Varano. "Work Attitudes of Police Recruits: Is There a Family Connection?" *International Journal of Police Science & Management* 12, no. 3 (2010): 460–479.

Piotrkowski, C. S., and G. A. Telesco. "Officers in Crisis: New York City Police Officers Who Assisted the Families of Victims of the World Trade Center Terrorist Attack." *Journal of Police Crisis Negotiations* 11, no. 1 (2011): 40–56.

Powers, M. F. "Critical Incident Stress Management: The Whole Team." *Journal of Emergency Nursing* 41, no. 1 (2015): 1–2.

Scoville, D. "Police and PTSD." *Police Magazine*, February 22, 2013. http://www.policemag.com/channel/careers-training/articles/2013/02/police-and-ptsd.aspx.

Solomon, Z., M. Mikulincer, B. Fried, Y. Wosner. "Family Characteristics and Posttraumatic Stress Disorder: A Follow-Up of Israeli Combat Stress Reaction Casualties." *Family Process* 26 (1987): 383–394.

Tedeschi, R. G., and L. G. Calhoun. "The Posttraumatic Growth Inventory: Measuring the Positive Legacy of Trauma." *Journal of Traumatic Stress* 9, no. 3 (1996): 455–471.

Trimble, M. D. "Posttraumatic Stress Disorder: History of a Concept." *Trauma and Its Wake: The Study and Treatment of Post-Traumatic Stress Disorder*. Revised from *Encyclopedia of Psychology,* edited by R. Corsini. New York: Wiley, 1994.

Vila, B., and D. J. Kenney. "Tired Cops: The Prevalence and Potential Consequences of Police Fatigue." *National Institute of Justice Journal* 248 (2002): 16–21.

Violanti, J. M. "Residuals of Police Occupational Trauma: Separation from Police Duties." *Traumatic Stress in Critical Occupations: Recognition, Consequences, and Treatment*. Edited by D. Patton and J. M. Violanti. Springfield, IL: Charles C. Thomas, 1996.

TRAYVON MARTIN SHOOTING

Trayvon Martin was a 17-year-old African American male who was shot to death on February 26, 2012, in Sanford, Florida, by a neighborhood watch guardian, George Zimmerman. Martin was walking back from a convenience store that was close to the home of his father's girlfriend. The shooting and following legal case brought national attention to the issues of racial biases by community guardians and police departments monitoring these guardians against young African American males, the limitations and negative consequences of communities policing themselves, use of deadly force for self-defense purposes in stand-your-ground laws, and the reluctance of police and prosecutors to challenge citizen use of deadly force due to these new laws including overreliance on community policing.

The shooting historically preceded the Black Lives Matter movement, protesting police shootings and targeting of younger minority males with use of lethal force but was a key event in precipitating intense focus on gun violence and disproportionate concentration in minority groups and communities. Unlike the police shooting deaths of Tamir Rice in Cleveland, Michael Brown in Ferguson, and Sean Bell in New York, Martin was killed by a civilian, which triggered memories of popular justice in earlier periods of racial injustice in American history. The death of Trayvon Martin highlighted the ongoing and polarizing debate about the causes and consequences of racial profiling. One side sees intentional discrimination and targeting as the biggest contributor to lethal violence, while the other side sees violence as a product of real threats, not intentional profiling, posed by violent criminals. The ultimate significance of the case lies in America's challenge to stop and prevent escalation of gun-related violence. Escalation of deadly force and the greater likelihood of its use have expanded

A memorial to Trayvon Martin stands outside The Retreat at Twin Lakes community where Trayvon was shot and killed by George Michael Zimmerman on April 12, 2012, in Sanford, Florida. Second-degree murder charges were brought against Zimmerman who was not charged with any crime initially due to Florida's "Stand Your Ground" self-defense law. (Getty Images)

beyond the police to the rest of society due to legal protections from these laws, their preventive aspects being viewed as good policing, and for the benefit of communities to protect themselves from predatory criminals. Given that the police cannot have a presence everywhere and at all times, citizen involvement in policing could expand even further.

Zimmerman was the neighborhood watch coordinator for a gated community. He had called the police several times for suspicious persons and activities. Claiming he used his weapon as Martin was beating him during an altercation in which he feared for his life, Zimmerman ignored a police dispatcher's advice to wait for the police and not confront Martin. Zimmerman was initially not arrested nor charged until public outcry and a special prosecutor assigned by the Florida governor charged him with second-degree murder. Florida was the first state to pass a "stand your ground" law in 2005 that allowed citizens to be immune from prosecution when using deadly force for self-defense in public places. Although self-defense laws have existed for centuries, and deadly force can be used in the sanctity of one's home (known as the Castle Doctrine), these laws required those facing imminent threats to their lives to retreat outside their homes ("duty to retreat" and avoid use of deadly force when possible). Proponents argued that, as duty to retreat was no longer a requirement with the "stand your ground" law, citizens were allowed to assert their rights to protect themselves without being found responsible for justifiable self-defense. Prior to the passing of this law, some Florida police chiefs and prosecutors opposed to the legislation had publicly argued that justifiable use of deadly force by criminals and aggressors would increase. Allegations exist that violent criminals use deadly force and deflect convictions for homicide by using these laws.

The Sanford Police Department, like the practice common to most police departments in Florida and other stand-your-ground states, did not arrest Zimmerman due the lack of evidence contradicting his self-defense claim and inability to establish probable cause for an arrest. While the absence of witness testimony and physical evidence is problematic in many criminal cases, overcoming self-defense as an excuse becomes especially challenging in such a situation. The immunity claims at a pretrial hearing under the stand-your-ground law were never pursued by Zimmerman and his lawyers so that the law was not part of the legal case. A subsequent one-month trial concluded in July 2013 resulting in Zimmerman's acquittal. Like the police, prosecutors did not challenge self-defense as a legitimate and substantive right as part of their case due to the case receiving extensive media coverage and going to trial only after public outcry. These laws were brought under scrutiny due to Martin's shooting and Zimmerman's claims that deadly force was justified. The low threshold in using deadly force and the lack of holding citizens accountable were particularly worrisome for some critics. Proponents argue that deadly force was needed to prevent victimization by violent criminals and to protect citizens from real dangers.

Concerns surfaced about biased criminal justice systems and expansion of discrimination by citizens shielded by these laws. Racial profiling has become an issue in American policing and argued by some to reflect the poor relations between police and minority communities. Reflective of over-policing, profiling resulting in disproportionate deaths, injuries, and convictions for young African American males under the umbrella of the wars on crime, drugs, terrorism, and gangs, according to some scholars and activists. A solution that was offered for the police to improve relations and increase trust emerged in community policing. Law enforcement was to consult and work as partners with these communities and populations. Martin's death demonstrated the difficulties of improving relations when the involvement of some community members prone to profile themselves and mete out justice on their own resulted in deadly consequences. Community policing also would be less likely to work if the police and the courts were perceived as not reining in profiling and pitting community members against each other. The prospects of vigilante justice being promoted are considered as real and dangerous as the combination of community policing and citizen-friendly deadly force laws.

Prosecutors and the police were against such laws, but they publicly supported community policing and Second Amendment rights. The lack of training and the inability to hold citizens accountable are in direct opposition to the case for police training and judicial mechanisms that require proportional and necessary deadly force. Police powers are being given to citizens, as Martin's shooting death confirmed for some parties. With statutory immunity and real rights, some argued that police became reluctant to arrest and prosecutors reluctant to charge. Some went further to argue that the law did not address any problem given that self-defense protections are already strong. From this point of view, the law was not a solution to a problem (as there was no problem or need for the law) but actually created more problems.

The Trayvon Martin shooting put suspicion of Black criminality on the map in American criminal justice systems and society. Concerns grew in African American communities about young males being stereotyped and labeled. The fact that Trayvon Martin had been unarmed, was wearing a hoodie, and brought back candy and a drink from the store from seemed to point to the double victimization of minority youth. The high rates of Black-on-Black violence (victimization from their own) and perceived increase in deadly shootings from the police and now from citizens (victimization from others) plagued these communities. Stories of African American parents and older relatives, siblings, and friends teaching their younger male family members and friends how to handle altercations with police surfaced and spoke to the different realities of these populations from other ethnicities. Anxieties grew that ordinary activities and actions by these individuals and groups would lead to deadly outcomes. The police and prosecutors assisted little in changing perceptions due to their actions in Martin's shooting death. Police and the courts were considered as largely ignoring or tacitly supporting injustices against minority communities. Laws and justice were unfair and unequal in terms of treatment and outcomes as seen from these perspectives.

An important lesson from Martin's shooting was how political and policy solutions worked against police and prosecutors. Police felt severely restricted and helpless to make arrests and pursue investigators. Prosecutors were equally hampered in pursuing convictions in the face of substantive rights providing immunity. Legal systems, as demonstrated in Zimmerman's case, emphasize intentionality and establishing proof beyond a reasonable doubt. With the stand-your-ground law behind defendants, the decisions of police and prosecutors are carefully calculated. In the end, the perceived necessity of gun rights and citizen use of deadly force are sustaining the expansion of lethal force in American society. Trayvon Martin's death is a symbol of popular justice and the complications in obtaining justice through popular means and methods. The police, many times, are merely bystanders.

Proposed modifications to the legal basis of gun rights and use of deadly force by citizens seem to emphasize the necessity (only where deadly force is the last resort) element of deadly force versus the appropriateness (deadly force is warranted). Police use of deadly force is also governed by necessity with the addition of proportionality. (Deadly force is proportional to the threat of severe injury or death.) Some scholars and analysts point to the focus on requiring that citizen deadly force be evaluated on whether deadly force is necessary evaluated objectively and not subjectively defended. In the case of police deadly force, legal doctrines allow police to subjectively defend their lethal actions. Citizens being allowed to have the same subjective defense of deadly force can lead to tragic outcomes such as in Trayvon Martin's death. As a decision, preventative action is difficult to avoid in some cases but increasing citizens' rights to use deadly force increases the likelihood of avoidable gun violence.

Gun violence in the United States has been difficult to address with the now substantial individual right to bear arms (a landmark 2009 Supreme Court ruling), easy access and low cost of deadly weapons, and huge black markets. Police cannot prevent gun violence if such conditions continue. Trayvon Martin's tragic and preventable death required citizens to show restraint in policing, which Zimmerman failed to follow. Communities can perpetuate suspicion and are even less likely to show restraint than the police. The trend of a societal arms race and gun violence becoming even more deadly leaves police with lessened abilities to keep guns from being used by citizens when not necessary and appropriate.

Sanjay Marwah

See also: Community Policing Today; Deadly Force; Michael Brown Shooting and the Aftermath in Ferguson; Racial Profiling

Further Reading

American Bar Association National Task Force on Stand Your Ground Laws. *Final Report and Recommendations.* Chicago: ABA, September 2015.

Bloom, Lisa. *Suspicion Nation: The Inside Story of the Trayvon Martin Injustice and Why We Continue to Repeat It.* Berkeley, CA: Counterpoint Press, 2015.

Brewer, Russell, and Peter Grabosky. "The Unraveling of Public Security in the United States: The Dark Side of Police-Community Co-Production." *American Journal of Criminal Justice* 39 (2014): 139–154.

Fair, Madison. "Dare Defend: Standing for Stand Your Ground Law." *Law & Psychology Review* 38 (2013): 153–176.

Lawson, Tamara. "A Fresh Cut in an Old Wound—A Critical Analysis of the Trayvon Martin Killing: The Public Outcry, The Prosecutor's Decision, and the Stand Your Ground Law." *University of Florida Journal of Law and Public Policy* 23 (2012): 371–318.

Megale, Elizabeth. "Disaster Unaverted: Reconciling the Desire for a Safe and Secure State with the Grim Realities of Stand Your Ground." *American Journal of Trial Advocacy* 37 (2013): 255–314.

MICHAEL BROWN SHOOTING AND THE AFTERMATH IN FERGUSON

In the early 21st century, the death of Michael Brown captured the nation's attention and focused it squarely on police use of force, particularly in minority communities. Brown was an unarmed, 18-year-old African American. What transpired in the moments before his death in Ferguson, Missouri, is widely contested, and questions about the need for deadly force remain. Nevertheless, several events are undisputed: on the morning of August 9, 2014, at 11:51 a.m., the Ferguson Police received a call regarding a convenience store "strong arm robbery." After that call, and within just minutes of police officer Darren Wilson coming upon Michael Brown and a friend, Brown was fatally shot by Wilson. The response to his death was deeply and widely felt: for many, it came to epitomize the problems between police and minority communities. For others, his death demonstrated the danger that police officers face in some communities.

The Incident: August 9, 2014

Video footage from the Ferguson convenience store (later released) appears to show Michael Brown grabbing a box of cigarillos valued at approximately $50; he then pushes the store employee out of the way, as he heads out the door. The police were contacted and given a description of the suspect, which the dispatcher then relayed over the police radio: an African American male wearing a hoodie and carrying a box of cigars. Just a few minutes later, at approximately 12:01 p.m., Officer Wilson, who had been a police officer since 2009, encountered Brown and his friend Dorian Johnson, walking away from the store that had been robbed. On Wilson's way to get lunch, it does not appear that he initially made the connection between the robbery and Brown as a suspect until after Wilson began a conversation with him; Wilson stopped Brown primarily because Brown and Johnson were walking in the middle of the road. At that time, Wilson stated, he asked them to walk to the side of the road, to which Brown's response was aggressive, demanding, "What the f—are you going to do about it?" Officer Wilson then put his car in reverse and parked on the street in such a way that blocked the road so that the men could not get past. Wilson claims that while he tried to exit the car, Brown slammed the door shut and began to punch Wilson on the side of the face. When Wilson reached for Brown's forearm to stop the "barrage," Wilson commented on how overpowered he was. "It was like a five-year-old trying to grab onto Hulk Hogan." The encounter devolved from this point, with Wilson claiming to fight for his life.

Fearing for his safety, Officer Wilson attempted to draw his weapon. Seeing this, Wilson explained, Brown reached into the vehicle through the open window and the two began to struggle for the weapon. Two shots were then fired, one of which grazed Michael Brown's right thumb. At that time, Wilson claimed both men began to run away from the cruiser. That is when Officer Wilson exited his vehicle and called after Brown and Johnson to stop running and get down on the ground. Wilson's testimony outlined that Brown did not comply with the order and that Brown turned and began to advance toward Wilson. Wilson said he believed he saw Brown "reaching for something under his shirt between his waistline." Fearing for his safety, Wilson fired the remaining 10 rounds from his magazine. Seven of these bullets made contact, killing Michael Brown.

A closer look at the forensic evidence of the crime scene shows blood trails from where Brown was initially shot to where his dead body would lay in the street for several hours before being removed. These blood trails may indicate that Brown continued to advance toward Officer Wilson, even after he had already been shot.

Dorian Johnson, Brown's companion that day, presented a very different sequence of events, regarding how Brown was killed. Johnson said Officer Wilson approached the men and, after a short conversation, reached out of his cruiser and grabbed Brown by the throat. From there, this confrontation turned into a shirt-grabbing match between the two men, culminating in two shots being fired from inside the vehicle. In contrast to the account by Wilson, Johnson asserted that Brown never attempted to attack the officer, nor did he try to reach for the officer's weapon at any time during this struggle. Fearing for their lives, Johnson said the men began to leave the scene on foot. According to Johnson, after Office Wilson got out of his vehicle he ordered the men to stop running and to turn around. Johnson said that Brown, who was unarmed, raised his arms in a peaceful manner and never attempted to charge toward Officer Wilson. Later, other witnesses would provide a variety of conflicting accounts of what happened in those final few minutes.

The Aftermath

Regardless of what happened in those critical few minutes leading to Brown's death, leaving his body in the middle of the street in the summer heat, uncovered, further fueled the community's tension with the police. Multiple YouTube videos of Brown's lifeless body in the street, with neighbors narrating their disgust at the treatment of Brown's body, went viral.

The following evening a candlelight vigil was held, but what began as a peaceful protest soon turned sections of the town into chaos: riots erupted, looting ensued, and officers were taunted by the crowds. The next night more rioting took place and the police responded by trying to disperse the crowd, firing rubber bullets and using tear gas. After four days of riots, the Missouri State Highway Patrol took over. Heavily outfitted in armored tanks and military gear, they rolled down the streets in an effort to restore order. The governor declared a state of emergency. It was several days before the city quieted down again, but this would prove to be nowhere near the end of the protests. Large-scale protests, attracting thousands from across the country, took place again in October and in November. Protesters coalesced around signs that said "Black Lives Matter" and "Hands Up—Don't Shoot." The November riots, which took place after the grand jury failed to indict Officer Wilson, proved to be even more disastrous; at least 12 buildings and cars were burned. Officers were under attack with various objects.

Pressured by public demands for transparency, the prosecutor released thousands of pages of transcripts from the months-long grand jury investigation—information that would typically be secret. Because grand juries are one-sided inquiry (only the prosecutor presents evidence, no defense) meant to evaluate whether a case should go on to trial, it's fairly easy for a prosecutor to obtain an indictment—that is, if he or she wants one. The transcripts revealed, however, that much about the proceedings in this case was unusual.

Rather than subduing any public fears of prejudice, these transcripts may have stoked the fires: the prosecutor often aggressively cross-examined witnesses who provided testimony that indicated Michael Brown was not a threat to Wilson, or those who were critical of Darren Wilson's actions. Despite being the subject of the investigation, some said that Wilson, who testified for four hours, did not appear to be subject to the same type of vigorous cross-examination.

Moreover, the prosecutor's instructions to the jury at the start of the proceedings were both incorrect and gravely misleading. The assistant district attorney misstated the presiding law on police use of deadly force, citing a Missouri law that had essentially been ruled unconstitutional by the Supreme Court's 1985 *Tennessee v. Garner* decision. The misstatement was hardly unimportant: the inaccuracy led the jury to believe (for some time) that it was legal to use fatal force to stop a fleeing suspect—and that the officer need not be in fear of his or her life in order to use such force. In other words, under that legal assumption, it wouldn't matter whether Michael Brown presented a threat to Wilson or not—under those circumstances he could use lethal force with or without mortal fear for his life. Although the record reflects that the district attorney attempted to correct this mistake to the jury a few weeks later, her new instructions were shockingly unclear. She told them that jurors should "fold in half" the earlier statute she gave them because, "Just so that you know, don't necessarily rely on that [statute] because there is a portion of that that doesn't comply with the law." Without specifically pointing out the error in the first instruction, this confusing and ambiguous correction may have been too little, too late. Even worse, the correction didn't happen until *after* Darren Wilson testified.

In the grand jury proceedings, witnesses presented very different accounts of what happened. Several witnesses stated that Michael Brown's hands were in the air when Officer Wilson fired outside the car. Wilson, however, asserted that Brown reached for his gun, and after he wrestled it back and fired at him, Brown looked at him "like a demon." Muddying the waters even more, one of the key witnesses supporting Wilson's account, Sandra McElroy—who stated that Brown went after

Wilson like a "football player" with his head down—was later found to have a history of bipolar disorder and had (at least once before) injected herself into a police investigation and lied about her testimony.

One anonymous grand juror, after having concluded jury service, filed (with the help of the American Civil Liberties Union) to sue to prosecutor for the right to speak publicly about the case, stating that he/she believed the prosecutor was biased throughout the proceedings, and that the prosecutor "insinuated" that Brown, not Wilson, was at fault. Further, the prosecutor was criticized for not instructing the jury on a potential charge, leaving the instructions open ended.

In all, despite months of testimony, many were left with the feeling that the demands for justice for Michael Brown's death may have gone unfulfilled. Others see the jury's refusal to indict as a vindication for Wilson, who left the Ferguson Police Department (FPD) after the incident. Still other analysts have found a middle ground in asserting that any criminal case against Wilson was never on solid legal ground because the constitutional standards on police use of force (*Graham v. Connor*, 1989) weigh the subjective feelings of the officer very heavily. Ultimately, analysts found that Brown's death may fall into the "lawful but awful" category: the force may technically have been *legal*, but some criticize whether a more experienced officer would have been able to de-escalate the situation other ways.

DOJ Investigation and Potential for Reform

The U.S. Department of Justice (DOJ) Civil Rights Division began a comprehensive investigation into the FPD in 2014. Although the DOJ declined to pursue federal civil rights charges against Wilson, the report issued in March was scathing in its criticism of the FPD. Citing structural problems with the department and city management as fueling unconstitutional and racially biased police and court practices, the DOJ found longstanding significant problems between the police, the city government, and the community.

One of the primary findings of the investigation was that the FPD had made revenue generation for the city too high a priority. The city's finance director had issued a directive to the police chief, stating, "Unless ticket writing ramps up significantly before the end of the year," the city would face a significant budget shortfall. As a result, many of the citations written by police were often for vague, questionable charges, such as "Manner of Walking in the Roadway" or "Making a False Declaration." Moreover, these citations disproportionately fell onto African Americans— fully 85 percent of vehicle stops, 90 percent of citations, and 93 percent of arrests were of African Americans. And in many of these stops, community members received multiple citations, adding to additional fines to be paid. Moreover, this emphasis on writing tickets was deeply structural within the department—patrol shifts were scheduled around what would be the most aggressive time to write tickets, and officer evaluations were focused on "productivity" of how many tickets that individual officers issued. Worse still, the investigation concluded that FPD's use of force was significantly disproportionate against African Americans. Ninety percent of use-of-force incidents involved an African American; every use of a police canine was against an African American suspect.

All of these factors created the perfect recipe for civil unrest: a community that viewed police as unfair, racially biased, and uninterested in community safety, and a police force that viewed the community as its adversary. This all added up to deep mistrust between the community and the police. For many, this report vindicated why the community was so outraged at the FPD's operating procedures.

A separate DOJ investigation, this time by the Office of Community Oriented Policing, found the St. Louis County law enforcement to be "lacking in the training, leadership, and culture necessary to truly engender community policing and to build and sustain trusting relationships with the community."

A subsequent *New Yorker* interview with Darren Wilson further explored the police/community tensions in Ferguson, with Wilson admitting that he felt unprepared to work in the nearly all-Black neighborhood, stating that he took a mentor who sounded "like a Black guy." He told the mentor, "Mike, I don't know what I'm doing. This is a culture shock. Would you help me? Because you obviously have that connection, and you can relate to them. You may be White, but they still respect you. So why can they respect you and not me?"

The findings from the first report prompted the DOJ to push for a consent decree with the City of Ferguson. The agreement was designed to address longstanding issues: totally revamp the citation system, improve community relations, and re-establish trust with the community.

The impact of the changes for Ferguson remains to be seen. Despite the scathing report by the DOJ, not everyone agreed that policing procedures needed to change. In early 2016, the city of Ferguson bucked the consent decree, which the DOJ had proposed, citing the changes it required would cost too much. The local paper, the *St. Louis Dispatch*, investigated the reasons for the refusal, finding that city officials had inflated the costs of the proposed reforms, adding in raises for firefighters (and other city employees) at a rate of 25 percent, using inappropriate sites for compensation comparisons, and failing to implement a staged implementation plan for the raises. The city claimed that litigation against the DOJ would cost less than the actual proposed reforms. In turn, the DOJ promptly filed to sue the city. The legal battle is now underway, with one analyst noting that such a pursuit on the part of Ferguson is like a "kamikaze" mission with "zero chance of success."

Critics of the backlash against police cited a "Ferguson Effect" which infected policing across the country—asserting that police, due to the strain they are under, are backing off in doing their jobs, for fear of retaliation or criticism. They assert that the consequence of this has been an escalation in crime. The data on this, however, does not support this assumption. In one study of 81 of the largest cities in country, researchers found no increase in violent crime since the Michael Brown case happened. With that said, it is without question that police-community relations have been severely strained—all around the country. Whether or not that has led to more lax policing and higher crime, however, is less clear. Reformers have argued for better training and education for officers, particularly in the area of community policing, for better data collection on the use of force, for less "militarization" of local police, and for more widespread use of body cameras for officers as measures that will improve the current tension.

While the Brown case was notable for many reasons (including the extent of protests and riots that followed it), it was one of *many* high-profile, police-involved shootings in 2014 and 2015. In particular, the Eric Garner case roiled New York City, and the protests for Brown and Garner overlapped in the last quarter of 2014. Ultimately, these police-involved killings highlighted what many minority communities had complained about for decades (but had received little sustained national attention in the media): disparate and unfair treatment by police with all too frequent fatal encounters involving unarmed minorities. For their part, police reported that it became increasingly difficult for them to do their jobs—with many in communities across the country voicing hostility and distrust.

Like the O. J. Simpson trial in the 1990s, the American public watched the events following Michael Brown's death with polarized interest. Some focused on the injustice of a young, unarmed African American youth being killed and left to die in the street; others zoned in on Brown's alleged criminal activity and what appeared to be senseless crime and rioting in the community. Competing narratives—one of "Black Lives Matter," the other "All Lives Matter"—emerged. At the time of this writing, the American public remains deeply divided by these events. This division can be found regularly in the mainstream media, in ongoing (if less frequent) protests around the country, and in the comments section of nearly any news story on the topic posted online. (Internet trolls on both sides of the issue point to fault on one side or the other.) Even the 2016 presidential candidates weighed in on the Black Lives Matter movement, and on the question of whether wide-ranging criminal justice reforms were necessary to correct inequities. Many compare the events in 2014 and 2015 to the Civil Rights Movement in the 1960s and 1970s, but ultimately, the legacy of these events will be written in the years to come.

Jennifer M. Balboni and Jared Berman

See also: ACLU; Eric Garner Case in New York City and Subsequent Tensions; Police Accountability; Police Brutality; Racial Profiling; Sean Bell Shooting

Further Reading

Brown, E. "Timeline: Michael Brown Shooting in Ferguson, MO." *USA Today*, August 10, 2015. http://www.usatoday.com/story/news/nation/2014/08/14/michael-brown -ferguson-missouri-timeline/14051827.

Comey, James. "Hard Truths: Law Enforcement and Race." FBI.gov, February 12, 2014. https://www.fbi.gov/news/speeches/hard-truths-law-enforcement-and-race.

Deere, Stephen. "Analysis: Did Ferguson Inflate the Cost of Federal Consent Decree?" *St. Louis Post-Dispatch*, February 21, 2016. http://www.stltoday.com/news/local/metro /analysis-did-ferguson-inflate-the-cost-of-federal-consent-decree/article_899ced97 -7a75-59b9-8452-6304d084205e.html.

Fagan, Jeffrey, and Bernard Harcourt. "Professors Hagan and Harcourt Provide Facts on Grand Jury Practice in Light of Ferguson Decision." Columbia Law School, December 2014. https://www.law.columbia.edu/media_inquiries/news_events/2014/november2014/Facts-on-Ferguson-Grand-Jury.

"Ferguson Protests: What We Know about Michael Brown's Last Minutes." BBC News, November 25, 2014. http://www.bbc.com/news/world-us-canada-28841715.

"Ferguson Unrest: From Shooting to Nationwide Protests." BBC News, August 10, 2015. http://www.bbc.com/news/world-us-canada-30193354.

Halpern, Jake. "The Cop." *The New Yorker*, August 10 and 17, 2015. http://www.newyorker.com/magazine/2015/08/10/the-cop.

Norton, Blake, Hamilton, Edwin, Braziel, Rick, Linskey, Daniel, and Jennifer Zeunik. *Collaborative Reform Initiative: An Assessment of the St. Louis County Police Department.* Office of Community Oriented Policing Services. Department of Justice, October 2015. https://www.policefoundation.org/publication/collaborative-reform-initiative-an-assessment-of-the-st-louis-county-police-department.

Pitts, Byron. *Officer Darren Wilson Says He Struggled with Brown, Feared For His Life.* ABC News (YouTube.com), November 25, 2014. https://www.youtube.com/watch?v=YVVmn14NnII.

Startling Cell Phone Video from Michael Brown Shooting Scene. CNN (YouTube.com), August 16, 2014. https://m.youtube.com/watch?v=nvE-1qAs1W4.

TCR Staff. "What Ferguson Effect?" The Crime Report, February 5, 2016. http://thecrimereport.org/2016/02/05/what-ferguson-effect.

U.S. Department of Justice, "Investigation of the Ferguson Police Department." Civil Rights Division, March 4, 2015. https://www.justice.gov/sites/default/files/opa/press-releases/attachments/2015/03/04/ferguson_police_department_report.pdf.

ERIC GARNER CASE IN NEW YORK CITY AND SUBSEQUENT TENSIONS

The fatal events that transpired involving Eric Garner, a resident of Tompkinsville, on Staten Island, on July 17, 2014, pivoted the country's attention to question not only the use of deadly force by the New York Police Department (NYPD), but also police use and abuse of force throughout the country. Coming on the heels of several other well-publicized police-involved shootings, Garner's death, and subsequent lack of legal accountability for the officers involved, sparked a national debate about police-community relations. Although this debate was particularly felt with the African American community, this discussion caught the attention of the world.

Born in 1970, Eric Garner lived in Staten Island, New York, with his wife, Jewell Miller, and their six children. Garner was known as a peacemaker in his neighborhood, and despite his size—6 foot 3 and 350 pounds—community members commented that he was a "gentle giant." Garner had many health issues: he was a severe asthmatic, had diabetes, and suffered from sleep apnea. In part due to these health issues, he quit his job with the New York City Department of Parks and Recreation and was unemployed at the time of the incident with the NYPD.

Garner had longstanding issues with the police, having been arrested many times (generally over minor offenses) as well as having lodged complaints against the police for harassment. Dating back to the 1980s, Garner had been arrested 30 times. His

A demonstrator holds a sign calling for justice during a rally in New York on July 18, 2015, where several hundred people rallied outside the federal courthouse in Brooklyn to demand action in the fatal chokehold death of African American Eric Garner by a White police officer. (AP Photo/Mary Altaffer)

previous arrests were for assault, grand larceny, and most commonly, illegally selling cigarettes. In 2007, Garner filed a federal lawsuit against the NYPD for constantly harassing him and once performing, in public, a cavity search on him. In fact, on the day of the fatal events, Garner was out on bail for misdemeanor offenses that included allegedly selling untaxed cigarettes and driving without a license.

According to several witnesses, on July 17, 2014, Garner was on Bay Street in the Tompkinsville neighborhood of Staten Island when he saw two men fighting outside a beauty salon. Shortly after, police were called because of the commotion. Having recognized Garner from past interactions, officers Daniel Pantaleo and Justin Damico approached Garner, accusing him of selling loose cigarettes. Within a matter of moments, the NYPD tried to arrest him.

Clearly aggravated, Garner said directly to Pantaleo "Why are you trying to arrest me?" Damico responded that he had seen him selling untaxed cigarettes, at which point Garner questioned him repeatedly, asking, "Tell me, who was I selling the cigarettes to?" Garner became upset, stating, "Every time you see me you want to mess with me. I'm tired of it. This stops today. Everybody standing here said I did nothing. I was minding my business, officer. Please, just leave me alone."

Ramsey Orta, who videotaped the entire incident, concurred that Garner had done nothing wrong—he had just been there breaking up a fight. When Pantaleo tried to arrest Garner, Garner put up his hands, passively resisting, asking to be left alone repeatedly. When Pantaleo failed to get Garner's hand behind his back, he immediately put him into a chokehold. Within a matter of moments, five police officers surrounded Garner, forcing him to the ground, pressing his face into the sidewalk. While on the ground with several officers restraining him, Garner stated 11 times through choked speech, "I can't breathe." During these 11 pleas, officers continued to put pressure onto Garner's head and body, until his pleas eventually stopped and his body stopped moving entirely. At this point, the police handcuffed him.

During the time that Eric Garner appeared not to be breathing, not one of the multiple officers on scene gave him rescue breaths or chest compressions. A second video, taken from another angle that begins after Garner was on the ground not moving (lasting more than 7 minutes), captured multiple officers standing idly by Garner's motionless body. During this time, officers emptied Garner's pockets, taking a cell phone and cigarettes, but they did not attempt to clear his airway or administer any rescue breaths. Taisha Allen, who took the second video, narrated these events, stating, "They treated him like an animal."

Even when the emergency medical technicians (EMTs) arrived, they did not give Garner oxygen immediately. It was not until he was in the ambulance that the EMT called into to dispatch, saying he was in cardiac arrest (when the heart stops functioning and is unable to pump blood). After Garner's death, two paramedics and EMTs were suspended without pay because they did not administer oxygen in a timely fashion.

Both of the videos were posted on the Internet and quickly went viral. Official reports from the autopsy would take nearly a month to be released to the public. Regardless, in the court of public opinion, many of those who saw the video were already convinced of the officers' criminal wrongdoing.

The medical examiner released the autopsy report, finding what was already obvious (to many) from the videos: Garner died from neck and chest compressions. The report concluded that the compression of Garner's neck around his windpipe caused the asphyxiation. Perhaps most importantly, the medical examiner ruled Garner's death a homicide, which is a loaded legal term that means another person (or people) intentionally and directly caused his death (as opposed to ruling the death accidental or natural).

In fact, the chokehold maneuver had been banned in 1993 by New York State law due to the high risk involved in the procedure. While some proponents claim the hold is safe if administered correctly, data suggests that when it is used on someone with a pre-existing condition (as Garner had), the risk of serious injury or death becomes much greater. Still, even with the ban, it is widely acknowledged that the maneuver is used by police, and moreover, when it is used, one report, by the New York City Complaint Review Board, indicated that it is done so disproportionately in predominately African American neighborhoods.

Given these facts, many believed it seemed likely that the officers involved would face some type of criminal charges. However, that assumption was wrong. Much to many people's shock and dismay, in December 2014, a Staten Island grand jury refused to indict Officer Pantaleo.

The grand jury's refusal to indict Officer Pantaleo (or any other officer) was widely criticized, primarily because the on-scene videos captured the fatal encounter from start to finish—an encounter in which Garner (who may or may not have been involved in a very minor crime) was put in a chokehold and died. There were immediate calls for the judge from the grand jury to release the records and unseal the transcript from the proceedings. However, grand jury proceedings are, by their nature, secret, and so the judge was under no obligation to release any information at all. Five groups, including New York Civil Liberties Union, the Legal Aid Society (the city's public advocate), the NAACP, and the *New York Post,* argued before the New York Supreme Court to unseal the transcripts. Their requests were denied, with the court citing the "presumption of confidentiality" for grand juries in New York. The Judge did release a few sparse facts: the jury convened for five weeks, heard from 50 witnesses, saw 60 exhibits, and four different videos were introduced into evidence. But these details shed little light on why a jury would "no bill" (refuse to indict) Pantaleo, given the mountain of evidence, and the standard of proof being only to find "probable cause."

Legal scholars frequently comment that a good prosecutor could indict a ham sandwich, and with good reason. Grand juries are notoriously one-sided: only the prosecutor presents witnesses (no defense counsel is usually present), and the rules of evidence are relaxed. Evidence that would ordinarily be inadmissible in trial is frequently used in grand jury proceedings. Further, the standard of proof in the grand jury proceedings is "probable cause." The grand jury is charged with determining whether there is enough evidence for a trial. For these reasons, it is often the case that if a prosecution wants an indictment, they generally get one. Because of this sentiment, many people who followed this particular case felt the prosecutor was not impartial. In fact, there are questions whether Daniel Donovan (the prosecutor) purposefully tanked the Pantaleo case because of his close ties to law enforcement.

Interestingly, one week before this case, a different grand jury failed to indict in a very similar case. The White officer was involved in the death of an unarmed African American man in Ferguson, Missouri. So when two "no bills" from separate grand juries occurred a week apart, this sparked national protests. From Washington, D.C., to Boston, to New York City and California, people took to the streets in mostly peaceful protests. Quoting Eric Garner's final words, many outraged citizens held signs stating, "I can't breathe," and "This stops today." "Black lives matter!" became the main battle cry for the protests. The protesters objected not only to what they characterized as biased police treatment, but also the lack of accountability provided by the court system.

Not all of the protests were peaceful, however. There was widespread looting and violence in the Ferguson protests, in particular. Further, in December 2014, two NYPD officers in Brooklyn were ambushed in their police cruiser by a man who had made statements on social media that he wished to get revenge for the Garner and Brown killings. The police officers' funeral then became the next site for protest, but this time by police: many officers literally turned their back to New York mayor Bill de Blasio, claiming that his lack of support for officers led to the two officers' murders. Even President Barack Obama weighed in after the officers' funeral, stating that the police, "Deserve our respect and gratitude every single day . . . I ask people to reject violence and words that harm, and turn to words that heal—prayer, patient dialogue, and sympathy for the friends and family of the fallen."

In response to the "Black Lives Matter" movement, social media erupted with "All Lives Matter" and "Blue Lives Matter." PoliceOne, a law enforcement Web site, commented on Garner's death: "This guy [Garner] would have died going up a flight of stairs," "He died because of his preexisting medical conditions," and "His family should sue Papa Johns, Dominos, Pizza Hut, Burger King, and McDonalds."

The impact of the deaths of Eric Garner, Michael Brown, and multiple other unarmed African American men in 2014 and 2015 shined a light on different areas in the criminal justice system, sparking discussions across the country about justice reform. For many, these events—the deaths of Eric Garner, Michael Brown, Freddie Gray in Baltimore, and Walter Scott in South Carolina (as well as countless others)—were proof of clear police bias toward African Americans. Others countered that they were isolated, unconnected incidents, overblown by the media, and often situations in which police had to make split-second decisions that shouldn't be Monday morning-quarterbacked by people who didn't understand the danger of police work.

Of the many issues raised in the national dialogue, one important policy issue that came to light was that there is no central database that tracks police shootings of civilians, and so it is difficult to prove whether or not there is a disparity by race. The FBI, which keeps records on the number of police killed as well as major crimes in the United States, surprisingly, does not keep regular records on police involved shootings of civilians. In 2015, the director of the FBI called this omission "embarrassing" and vowed to implement a system to collect this important data. Collecting this information would be a step toward both understanding the problem, and promoting transparency of police procedures.

President Barack Obama on the Grand Jury's Decision in the Eric Garner Case

The following was President Obama's statement on the grand jury's decision in the Eric Garner Case, December 3, 2014:

"Some of you may have heard there was a decision that came out today by a grand jury not to indict police officers who had interacted with Eric Garner in New York City, all of which was caught on videotape and speaks to the larger issues that we've been talking about now for the last week, the last month, the last year, and, sadly, for decades, and that is the concern on the part of too many minority communities that law enforcement is not working with them and dealing with them in a fair way . . .

(continued)

"And as I said when I met with folks both from Ferguson and law enforcement and clergy and civil rights activists, I said this is an issue that we've been dealing with for too long and it's time for us to make more progress than we've made . . . And I am absolutely committed as president of the United States to making sure that we have a country in which everybody believes in the core principle that we are equal under the law . . .

"And I say that as somebody who believes that law enforcement has an incredibly difficult job; that every man or woman in uniform are putting their lives at risk to protect us; that they have the right to come home, just like we do from our jobs; that there's real crime out there that they've got to tackle day in and day out—but that they're only going to be able to do their job effectively if everybody has confidence in the system.

"And right now, unfortunately, we are seeing too many instances where people just do not have confidence that folks are being treated fairly. And in some cases, those may be misperceptions; but in some cases, that's a reality. And it is incumbent upon all of us, as Americans, regardless of race, region, faith, that we recognize this is an American problem, and not just a black problem or a brown problem or a Native American problem . . ."

Source: Remarks by the President at the Tribal Nations Conference. December 3, 2014. Whitehouse.gov. Available at: https://www.whitehouse.gov/the-press-office/2014/12/03/remarks-president-tribal-nations-conference

Further, the protests caused some police agencies to re-think the aggressive "broken windows" policing strategy, questioning whether it did more harm than good. While many believe in the crime-fighting strategies in broken windows theory (long believed to be a way to contain crime in a community by addressing small crimes before they escalate to larger crimes), others maintain that this policy has the unintended consequence of alienating the community, creating hostility between the police and the community it serves. In many ways, Officer Pantaleo was an excellent example of this approach: in his eight-year history with the NYPD, he made hundreds of misdemeanor arrests. In the aftermath of the Eric Garner case, many agencies "re-trained" their officers in positive community policing techniques, backing away from some of the "stop and frisk" aggressive strategies that often come along with broken windows policing. New York City police commissioner William Bratton and Mayor de Blasio have created new police guidelines that went into effect in early 2016. They plan to implement a force incident report, which officers will fill out when they use force on a civilian, noting the person's race. Still, these reforms were hardly nationwide. Many agencies remain resistant to such reforms.

In addition to putting a spotlight on police practices, the Garner case also highlighted the need for court reforms as well. Even if the prosecutor had intentionally thwarted Officer Pantaleo's prosecution during the grand jury proceedings, there is no legal recourse for such actions. In response, New York governor Cuomo called for broad reform of the grand jury system.

With any criminal responsibility for Garner's death foreclosed, the Garner family sued the City for legal responsibility. After months of negotiation, in July of 2015, New York City settled out of court with the Garner family. In what must have been a bittersweet settlement, the City agreed to pay the family $5.9 million, but only under the condition that the City not admit any wrongdoing on their part. A second suit, brought against the hospital who dispatched the first responders, has also been settled, but the details remain confidential. Like other developments in this case, the settlement was controversial. Of the settlement, one Police Union representative stated,

> I think the department is disgusted. The membership, they're totally disgusted . . . This settlement makes it appear as though the NYPD is totally responsible for Eric Garner's death. It's a minor crime and a guy lost his life, that's true, but is that the only responsibility laying on the hands of the police? Our job is to make arrests for both major and minor crimes. To be fair about it, what responsibility do you share because you were committing that minor crime?

Supporters for the family countered that Garner hardly deserved the way police handled him and that no amount of money could bring him back to life.

At the time of this writing, Daniel Pantaleo is now on desk duty, without his firearm or badge, and reportedly has received so many death threats he has needed police watch outside his home. He states he can't wait to get back to his job.

The impact of the events around Eric Garner's death ultimately will be judged by history. Whether or not any of the reform efforts change the nature of policing remains to be seen. As with other social movements before it, such as Civil Rights, the protesters have been heard. It is unclear how this movement will stack up, in terms of progress for disadvantaged populations, and for police reform overall.

Jennifer M. Balboni and Alexa Belvedere

See also: Deadly Force; Freddie Gray Case; Michael Brown Shooting and the Aftermath in Ferguson; Police Mistreatment in Cases of Civil Disobedience; Racial Profiling; Walter Scott Shooting

Further Reading

Anderson, T., E. Allen, N. Ramos, and J. C. Fox. "Thousands Protest Eric Garner Chokehold Case in Downtown Boston." *Boston Globe*, December 4, 2014. https://www.bostonglobe.com/metro/2014/12/04/protest-planned-christmas-tree-lighting-common/875sx4ZA1JcHliKte9UyCJ/story.html.

Anker, J. "Known for His Death, This Was Eric Garner's Life." HLNtv.com, December 5, 2014. http://www.hlntv.com/article/2014/12/04/who-was-eric-garner.

BBC News. "Barack Obama Denounces Killing of NYPD Officers." Dec. 21, 2014. http://www.bbc.com/news/world-us-canada-30567740.

Calabresi, M. "Why a Medical Examiner Called Eric Garner's Death a 'Homicide.'" *Time*, December 4, 2014. http://time.com/3618279/eric-garner-chokehold-crime-staten-island-daniel-pantaleo.

"Eric Garner on Ground." YouTube.com (video). July 19, 2014. https://www.youtube.com /watch?v=vT66U_Ftdng.

Goldstein, J., and N. Schweber. "Man's Death After Chokehold Raises Old Issue for the Police." *The New York Times*, July 18, 2014. http://www.nytimes.com/2014/07/19/nyregion /staten-island-man-dies-after-he-is-put-in-chokehold-during-arrest.html?_r=0.

Horowitz, E. "Understanding Eric Garner's Death and Grand Jury's Decision." *The Boston Globe*, December 4. 2014. https://www.bostonglobe.com/metro/2014/12/04/unders tanding-eric-garner-death-and-grand-jury-decision/s9uQPMvcKPD2mAmFy2ln9J /story.html.

"'I Can't Breathe': Eric Garner Put in Chokehold by NYPD Officer." *The Guardian* (video), December 4, 2014. http://www.theguardian.com/us-news/video/2014/dec/04/i-cant -breathe-eric-garner-chokehold-death-video.

Knafo, Saki. "The Education of Edwin Raymond." *The New York Times*, February 21, 2016.

Mathias, C. "NYPD Says It Will Track Use of Force, Actually Start Disciplining Cops." *Huffington Post*, October 10, 2015. http://www.huffingtonpost.com/entry/nypd-use-of-force -reforms_us_560d48fae4b0dd85030af152.

McDonald, S. N. "Friends: Eric Garner was a 'gentle giant.'" *The Washington Post*, December 4, 2014. https://www.washingtonpost.com/news/morning-mix/wp/2014/12/04 /friends-eric-garner-was-a-gentle-giant/.

Newman, A. "The Death of Eric Garner, and the Events That Followed." *The New York Times*, December 2, 2014. http://www.nytimes.com/interactive/2014/12/04/nyregion/04garner -timeline.html#/#time356_10543.

Somanader, T. "President Obama Delivers a Statement on the Grand Jury Decision in the Death of Eric Garner." Whitehouse.gov (video), December 3, 2014. https://www .whitehouse.gov/blog/2014/12/03/president-obama-delivers-statement-grand-jury -decision-death-eric-garner.

VARIATIONS IN LAW ENFORCEMENT ATTITUDES ABOUT GUN CONTROL LAWS

Gun control is a controversial topic both in the United States and across the globe. In the past 10 years, more than 100,000 people have been killed in our nation due to gun violence, and millions of others have been the victims of crimes involving a gun. Mass shootings such as those at Columbine, Newtown, or Aurora spark intense feelings about gun possession. All of these incidents increase the intensity of this debate and raise awareness about how our nation can reduce these tragedies. After tragedies such as these occur, the government often re-examines existing gun policies, and law enforcement are often asked about how they would reduce gun violence.

In general, gun control refers to the laws and policies that regulate the manufacturing, selling, possession, or transferring of firearms to control gun violence. The majority of countries worldwide allow civilians to possess firearms, provided they abide by certain regulations, but there is variation in these policies across countries. Some countries, such as Japan, Australia, and the United Kingdom, have strict gun laws. Other countries, such as the United States, have more lenient gun laws, but they vary by state. Additionally, in the United States, the right to keep and bear arms is protected by the Second Amendment of the U.S. Constitution. However, people who have been convicted of a felony, people with a mental illness, and juveniles are not allowed to possess a firearm or ammunition in the United States.

High rates of gun violence, including homicides, assaults with a deadly weapon, suicides, and attempted suicides, are the primary rationale for gun control. Advocates of gun control claim that gun ownership increases the prevalence of gun violence. On the other hand, opponents claim that gun control infringes upon people's individual liberties, and it does little to reduce crime. There is widespread debate about whether gun control increases, decreases, or has no effect on levels of gun violence. Some sources indicate that there is a relationship between firearms-related injuries and mortality, but there is little research on the effectiveness of gun control policies.

Because police officers are directly involved with gun violence, they can offer useful insight into this problem. In 2013, PoliceOne, an online source providing police with resources and information to help them protect communities, conducted a comprehensive survey of police perceptions of gun control. More than 15,000 law enforcement professionals from a variety of regions, ranks, and department sizes participated in this survey. Eighty percent of the respondents were current law enforcement officers, whereas the other 20 percent were retired members of law enforcement. Most importantly, approximately 70 percent of the respondents were field-level officers who worked directly in the streets and had first-hand experience with gun violence.

Overall, this survey found that most of the respondents' beliefs were counter to gun control advocates' claims that restrictions on weapons would help to reduce violent crime. Ninety-one percent of respondents believed that a ban at the federal level on the manufacturing and selling of semi-automatic weapons would have either no effect or a negative effect in reducing violent crime. Only 7 percent stated that a ban would have at least a moderate impact in reducing violent crime. The Federal Assault Weapons Ban of 1994 expired in 2004, and attempts to pass another ban, such as the Assault Weapons Ban of 2013 (AWB Summary 2013), have not been successful at controlling federal assault weapons. The AWB 2013 was introduced one month after the Sandy Hook Elementary School shooting, but it failed to pass through Congress. Critics cited that millions of unregistered high capacity magazines were already in circulation, and the ban would not be effective at keeping the magazines away from criminals.

Moreover, nearly 82 percent of the respondents did not believe gun buyback programs effectively reduced gun violence. In this type of program, police typically pay individuals with cash or gift cards for privately owned firearms. The premise is to decrease the number of firearms in the hands of civilians. The problem often cited with these programs is that law abiding citizens are usually the ones bringing their firearms to the police, but people who engage in violence are not participating. Consequently, gun buyback programs are not actually bringing in the guns that law enforcement are seeking.

However, the majority of the respondents in this survey felt that increasing penalties for gun crimes would help to reduce gun violence. For example, almost 59 percent of the respondents felt that increasing the severity of punishments for gun trafficking would reduce gun crimes. In addition, nearly 60 percent of the respondents thought that increasing the punishment for illegal gun sales could help reduce gun violence.

Generally, proactive choices were more widely accepted among the respondents than implementing more stringent gun control policies. Results of this survey indicated that police favor responsible citizens being armed. For example, 91 percent of the respondents supported arming civilians who had never been convicted of a felony or who had never been diagnosed as psychologically or medically incapable of carrying concealed firearms. Additionally, 86 percent of the respondents believed that there would be fewer casualties if there were legally armed citizens present at active shooter incidents. The survey also asked the respondents how important they thought it was to legally arm citizens to reduce crime on a scale of one to five (one being the lowest and five being the highest). Seventy-six percent chose four or five, indicating that they thought arming citizens could considerably help to reduce gun violence. Furthermore, approximately 80 percent of the respondents supported arming qualified and willing teachers and school administrators to carry a firearm at their school.

In addition, when asked what they thought would be most helpful in preventing large-scale public shootings, the number one answer mentioned by the respondents was having more lenient gun policies for citizens (29 percent). This was followed by more aggressively institutionalizing mentally ill individuals (20 percent), enhancing the number of security personnel (16 percent), and improving background screening prior to the purchase of firearms (14 percent).

Overall, 45 percent of the respondents felt that requiring mental health background checks on prospective buyers of guns from federally licensed dealers would not reduce instances of mass shootings. The majority of Americans experience at least one mental illness in their lifetime, including anxiety and depression, and only a small percentage of them actually poses a threat to society. Therefore, it is likely that the respondents felt that increased mental health screenings could create privacy issues and have the potential to stigmatize harmless people suffering from common mental illnesses.

Finally, when asked about the largest contributor to gun violence in the United States, the number one answer mentioned by the respondents was a decline in parenting and family values (38 percent). This answer was followed by the early release of violent offenders (15 percent) and exposure to violent movies and video games (14 percent).

Based on the results of the PoliceOne survey, law enforcement has varying views on gun control. One of the factors that could explain these differences is a divide between chiefs of police and sheriffs on issues related to gun control. The International Association of Chiefs of Police supports banning assault weapons, as well as limiting ammunition capacity. However, the Constitutional Sheriffs and Peace Officers Association opposes the same measures. These differing opinions could be the result of differences in how police departments and sheriff's departments operate. Police chiefs operate primarily in cities where most of the gun violence occurs. On the other hand, sheriff's departments operate at the county level. Counties are often rural areas where sport shooting is more prevalent, and hunting is often equated with family bonding. Consequently, although guns in cities are often associated with crime, guns in rural areas are more widely accepted as part of American culture.

As noted earlier, there is variation in gun control legislation by country, and Australia has more stringent gun policies than the United States. For instance, Gun Control Australia (GCA) is a lobbyist group that promotes stricter gun control policies in Australia. In 1996, a massacre in which a gunman with a semi-automatic rifle killed 35 people at Port Arthur, a popular tourist site in Australia, led to more stringent gun legislation. After this incident, policies were introduced that promoted stricter regulation of firearm ownership, a national registration program, and a ban on semi-automatic rifles. To date, there has been evidence that these policies have reduced gun violence throughout Australia. Consequently, it is important to see if police in a country with strict gun control have different views than they do in the United States.

Abigail Kohn interviewed 40 sworn police officers in Australia from 2002 to 2003 (Kohn 2005). Of the 40 officers, 15 generally held positive views toward gun control, 15 held positive/neutral views, and 10 held negative views. Kohn found that most of the officers she interviewed thought that "gun control" referred to controlling legal access to firearms, yet preventing it for other people. That is, gun control pertains primarily to legal access to firearms, such as licensing and registration, as well as controls on legal reasons for owning a firearm.

These officers felt that gun control did not affect the illegal firearms market. The overwhelming consensus was that gun control laws were aimed at people who abide by the law. The majority of the officers thought that gun control legislation cannot prevent criminals from obtaining guns, but it was still important to ensure that legal access was controlled to help make society safer. Generally, the respondents felt that firearms were a dangerous commodity and that it was important to control the public's access to them. Interestingly, some of these officers also felt that the United States had a lack of gun control, contributing to high rates of gun violence.

Officers in the positive/neutral category had positive views of gun control, but felt that it had limitations and could be made more effective. These officers felt that gun control has the intention of reducing gun crimes, but gun control legislation cannot reduce crime on its own. Specifically, if the laws are not enforced, they do nothing to reduce crime. Furthermore, the officers felt that gun control needed to be coordinated across states. They noted that it was challenging when gun legislation was lenient in one state, but stringent in a bordering state.

The group of police who had negative views about gun control laws felt most strongly that gun control was effective only for law abiding citizens. They felt it was impossible for gun control policies to affect the illegal gun trade. One officer suggested that rather than have *gun control*, society needed to focus on the illegal gun trade. This group stressed how there would always be a black market for illegal firearms, and it is impossible to control it. However, note that the group with negative views about gun control still believed in controls, such as licensing and registration, because they regulate law abiding citizens.

Similar to the survey conducted in the United States, some of the Australian officers mentioned that gun buyback programs did little to control gun violence. They felt that all these programs did was obtain guns from legitimate owners, but did nothing to reduce the number of guns in the illegal firearms market.

Overall, the police interviewed in this study felt that particular groups of civilians, such as hunters, should be able to own guns. But these individuals should be licensed and own only registered firearms. However, they also felt that gun ownership by the public should be restricted. They thought that if guns were removed from homes, there would be fewer incidents of gun violence. For example, some of the officers felt that gun control could be helpful in reducing firearm-related deaths in domestic violence cases and could prevent non-criminals from harming someone in their own home.

In sum, it is essential to gain the perspective of law enforcement on gun control because they are the ones who deal directly with gun violence in the streets. There is variation in police officers' attitudes about gun control, which can be attributed to many factors, including the country in which they reside, size of their department, personal views regarding gun control, and experiences on the job. Gun control is a topic that creates a large divide in the United States, so it is important to have information on both sides of the debate to create effective gun policy.

Francesca Spina

See also: Constitutional Mandates; Crime Prevention Techniques; Increase in Violent Crime Rate and Risk to Law Enforcement; National Firearms Act

Further Reading

"Armed Violence and Gun Laws, Country by Country." GunPolicy.org. 2016. http://www.gunpolicy.org.

Assault Weapons Ban (AWB) Summary. Senator Diane Feinstein Web Site. 2013. http://www.feinstein.senate.gov/public/index.cfm/assault-weapons-ban-summary.

"Fact Sheet: New Executive Actions to Reduce Gun Violence and Make Our Communities Safer." WhiteHouse.gov, January 4, 2016. https://www.whitehouse.gov/the-press-office/2016/01/04/fact-sheet-new-executive-actions-reduce-gun-violence-and-make-our.

"Gun Policy & Law Enforcement: Survey Results." PoliceOne.com, March 2016. http://police-praetorian.netdna-ssl.com/p1_gunsurveysummary_2013.pdf.

"How Did He Get a Gun?" Gun Control Australia. 2015. http://www.guncontrolaustralia.org.

Irons, Meghan E. "Success of Gun Buyback Program Is Debated." *Boston Globe*, February 13, 2014. https://www.bostonglobe.com/metro/2014/02/12/success-gun-buyback-program-debated/PsITjPCyPkrG9C7fFr979O/story.html.

Johnson, M. Alex. "Police Chiefs, Sheriffs Divided over Gun Control Measures." *NBC News*, January 28, 2013. http://usnews.nbcnews.com/_news/2013/01/28/16740488-police-chiefs-sheriffs-divided-over-gun-control-measures?lite.

Kohn, Abigail. "Police Beliefs and Attitudes about Gun Control." *Current Issues in Criminal Justice* 17, no. 2 (2005): 269–283.

UNDERSTANDING PROBABLE CAUSE

Police officers need to understand the probable cause legal concept because their police powers depend heavily upon it. Probable cause is defined as a cause that rests on sufficient and reliable information or evidence that indicates a crime has happened, is in process, or is about to occur. Therefore, probable cause in law enforcement is a standard tool that is part of the Fourth Amendment to the U.S. Constitution. Based on the Fourth Amendment, we know that police officers must have probable cause to make an arrest, as well as to conduct a search of one's person or property. In addition, they need probable cause to obtain a warrant from a judge.

The Fourth Amendment prohibits unreasonable searches and seizures and states that "no Warrants shall issue, but upon probable cause, supported by Oath or affirmation, and particularly describing the place to be searched, and the persons or things to be seized." In the constitutional context, these specific elements must be fulfilled in order for a magistrate to issue a warrant. If these four elements are not fulfilled, the accused person can challenge the validity of the warrant. First, it is pivotal that probable cause exist before police intervention. Second, the facts of the case must be presented by the police by "oath and affirmation" to a judge, which means that the police swear under oath that the information pertaining to the case is true to the best of his or her knowledge. Third, the warrant must describe the specific location of the area to be searched for the evidence; and fourth, if a warrant is issued for a person who is suspected of a murder, the police officers should not search areas that a person could not be found, such as small cabinets or dresser drawers.

In essence, the Fourth Amendment jurisprudence requires that judicial officers, especially judges, have oversight authority over the operations of police officers. The major ingredient of the Fourth Amendment is the protection of individuals' personal privacy. Therefore, police officers must obtain warrants before executing a search. However, there are some situations in which exigency prevents police officers from obtaining a search warrant from a judge (see *Katz v. United States* [1967]). In such cases, there are exceptions to the requirements of a search warrant under the Fourth Amendment. For example, there are some cases where law enforcement officers may have probable cause to search a person or a piece of property and may have to respond immediately to situations before securing a warrant when an individual may be in imminent harm, where there is suspicion that the relevant evidence may be immediately destroyed or that a suspect may be trying to flee. In pursuance of safeguarding the privacy of the individual, states have the burden of proof of establishing that the warrantless search was conducted pursuant to an exception. In such cases, judges must evaluate if the police established sufficient probable cause while keeping in mind that the search was successful.

For many years, the U.S. Supreme Court has made strides in guiding officers of the court in the identification of the existence of probable cause. A police officer's mere suspicion of an individual alone does not constitute probable cause. Yet, the level of evidence to establish probable cause does not need to meet the same high level of proof required in a criminal trial to convict an individual suspected of criminal offense. Therefore, probable cause demonstrates only that there is evidence that a reasonable person believes that the incriminating object exists in a location that the law enforcement agent is requesting access. An arrest is warranted when there is sufficient evidence that reasonably shows that the individual under arrest is liable given the available evidence and deserves to be prosecuted.

There is no universal definition of probable cause that magistrates can apply in each police-citizen encounter; and there is not a single method used to dictate the amount of evidence required to establish probable cause. Probable cause is purposely designed to be a flexible, legal concept to enable judicial officers to apply it to different real-life situations.

There are leading Supreme Court cases that shed light on the principle of law in relation to probable cause and law enforcement practices, which include *Draper v. United States* (1959), *Spinelli v. United States* (1969), *Illinois v. Gates* (1983), *United States v. Sokolow* (1989), and *Devenpeck v. Alford* (2004).

In 1959, *Draper v. United States* mandated that information received by a confidential informant and corroborated by a law enforcement officer may be adequate for establishing probable cause for an individual's arrest, even though such information would be hearsay and would be inadmissible in a criminal trial. In short, the court decided the agent had probable cause based on the known facts, including the tips provided by the informant, and the circumstances that surrounded the case. This sufficient and reliable information would have caused a reasonable person to believe that an offense had been, or is being, committed. The decision of this case is important because information provided by informants constitutes hearsay information, which is the basis of police action; however, police may act on such information as long as the information is valid, thus, establishing probable cause.

About 10 years after the ruling of *Draper v. United States*, *Spinelli v. United States* (1969) ruled that to establish probable cause, an affidavit that is based on hearsay information that has been provided by an informant must meet the two-pronged test requirement that was handed down in *Aguilar v. Texas* (1964). This states that the informant must be reliable, and the informant's hearsay information must be reliable. Both of these conditions have to be met in order to establish probable cause. The Supreme Court's decision remains valid to date; however, the case has been modified by *Illinois v. Gates* (1983).

To establish probable cause, *Illinois v. Gates* mandated that the Aguilar test is superseded by the "totality of circumstances test." This is a more balanced approach compared to the Aguilar test, which has "encouraged an excessively technical dissection of informants' tips, with undue attention being focused on isolated issues that cannot sensibly be divorced from the other facts presented to the magistrate." The "totality of circumstances test," which is more flexible, enables judges to make a generalized decision concerning whether probable cause or evidence is both sufficient and reliable before they issue a warrant upon request of police officers to conduct a search. Therefore, considering all the circumstances has made it easier for police officers to establish probable cause due to their discretionary power. Subsequently, this may even contribute to magistrates signing more affidavits and issuing more warrants.

As decided in *Terry v. Ohio* and *United States v. Cortez*, the totality of circumstances must be assessed to determine if police officers do, indeed, have reasonable suspicion to stop and detain someone who they believe may have engaged in criminal activity for investigative purposes briefly without a warrant. Subsequently, the decision in the *United States v. Sokolow* (1989) showed the use of "drug courier profile" is lawful under the Fourth Amendment. The Court ruled that, based upon the facts of the case in total, sufficient reasonable suspicion could be established that criminal behavior was occurring; therefore, police officers' action to conduct a search was valid under the Fourth Amendment. Although the Court specified that the totality of the relevant evidence points to a suspicion that a crime is imminent or may have occurred rather than basing it strictly on an individual's profile. Therefore, recognizing that basing a request for a search warrant, for example, on a drug courier's profile might present useful evidence required for conviction, it is more important that the totality of the circumstances leads to the execution of a search warrant and the ensuing search.

Devenpeck v. Alford (2004) ruled that in order for an arrest to be lawful, there is no requirement under the Fourth Amendment for a person to be charged with a crime that established probable cause for an arrest to be "closely related" to and based on the same conduct as the criminal act identified by the officer." Based upon three principles, the court reached such a decision. The principles included the following: (1) because of the complexity of the law, which prescribed what behavior is illegal, officers do not need to know exactly what behavior matches the violation of the law that an individual is engaged in to make an arrest. Thus, an officer may arrest an individual under one aspect of the law, then after further investigation conclude that the actions of the individual that he or she stopped and searched constitute a more fitting violation of the law. (2) The court relied on *Whren v. United States* (1996), which ruled "the officer's state of mind is not a factor in establishing probable cause. The court held that the "closely related rule" violated this precedent because it would make the arrest rely on the motivation of the officer." And (3) the court recognized that it is a good practice for the police to simply inform an individual what and why he or she is being charged with at the time he or she is taken into custody. However, this is not a constitutional requirement.

As the foregoing shows, under the totality of circumstances test, judges are authorized to make general decisions concerning whether evidence is both sufficient and reliable enough for them to issue a search warrant. However, it is not a requirement for judges to prove the "specific reliability of the source of the evidence." For example, this was illustrated in *Riley v. California* (2014). This case involved new technologies used to detect criminal behavior. The use of this technology allowed police officers to follow or examine individuals, vehicles, buildings, and other personal properties they view as being suspicious. These police practices have fueled controversy about police engaging in "unreasonable" searches of individuals and their property. This has resulted in many individuals believing police officers must produce a warrant before they conduct a search.

Over the years, laws have tended to emerge and evolve in our society. Technological developments have also added new challenges to the operations of law enforcement, including mobile phones and their capabilities that compel Americans to "adapt legal principles to new circumstances and social norms" (Vorenberg 2012). There have been Supreme Court rulings about the use of technologies to detect criminal behavior of individuals where the police are believed to have violated the Fourth Amendment. (See *United States v. Jones* and *Kyllo v. United States*.)

Understanding the idea of probable cause and its intent in protecting people's privacy is important to both police operations and the public. Police officers must make decisions either to arrest or not to arrest citizens they encounter. Such decisions may have great impact on some citizens' lives. Therefore, it is important for the law enforcement agencies and the police to agree on what constitutes probable cause. Familiarizing oneself with the decided cases that address the application of probable cause in law enforcement is also important. Police need to obtain search warrants before embarking on a search, even if they are faced with exigent circumstances.

Rochelle McGee-Cobbs, Sherill Morris-Francis, and O. Oko Elechi

See also: Fourth Amendment; *Terry v. Ohio*

Further Reading

Cole, George F., Christopher E. Smith, and Christina Dejong. *The American System of Criminal Justice*, 15th ed. Boston, MA: Cengage Learning, 2017.

del Carmen, Rolando, V. Walker, and T. Jeffery. *Briefs of Leading Cases in Law Enforcement*, 8th ed. Waltham, MA: Anderson Publishing, 2012.

Kerr, Orin. "Why Courts Should Not Quantify Probable Cause." In *The Political Heart of Criminal Procedure: Essays on Themes of William J. Stuntz*. Edited by Michael Klarman, David Skeel, and Carol Steiker. Cambridge, UK: Cambridge University Press, 2014.

Rachlinski, Jeffery J., Chris Guthrie, and Andrew J. Wistrich. "Probable Cause, Probability, and Hindsight." *Journal of Empirical Legal Studies* 8, S1 (2011): 72–98.

Vorenberg, A. "Indecent Exposure: Do Warrantless Searches of a Student's Cell Phone Violate the Fourth Amendment?" *Berkeley Journal of Criminal Law* 17 (2012): 62–96.

BOARDWALK EMPIRE

Boardwalk Empire: The Birth, High Times, and Corruption of Atlantic City (2002), by Nelson Johnson, was a novel describing a relationship of governance to policing and crime. It is a story of corruption as well as a story of efforts to reform and redeem the famous New Jersey resort. Policing in its most basic sense is the maintenance of a regulatory environment—tight enough to enforce laws against violation, and purposeful enough to deter actors from future offenses. The story of Atlantic City, however, is the history of an opportunistic criminal environment maintained through political and criminal leadership, the transformation of a mosquito-infested seaside community into an efficiently corrupt machine. *Boardwalk Empire* is populated with characters so engaging and colorful that the entertainment value of one of Atlantic City's most brazen eras of criminality was adapted into a highly successful television series of the same name. Full of gangsters and bosses and molls, the series ran from 2009 through 2014, mixing fictionalized characters with real-life

Boardwalk Empire is a term that is referred to as a representation of Atlantic City during the time of Prohibition. Atlantic City was run by Enoch "Nucky" Johnson, who controlled the smuggling and distribution of alcohol, as well as prostitution. He had political power, close relationships with politicians, organized crime families, and businessmen. He controlled local law enforcement in order to violate Prohibition laws. (Library of Congress)

counterparts to follow a plot line more suited for dramatic development than a strictly factual narrative. Nelson Johnson is native to the immediate area, a lawyer and judge who spent the better part of two decades of research and interviews, living in its deep past and recent troubles. Johnson even served as attorney for the city's planning commission—a perspective that was both the press box and the locker room of why a place such as Atlantic City simply is what it is—in order to adequately relate what he knew already and later learned. Despite the depth of purpose and execution in *Boardwalk Empire*, Johnson had more to say, so he followed with *The Northside: African Americans and the Creation of Atlantic City* (2010). Johnson's work was initially due diligence: when he began working for the planning commission in the 1980s, he said in a 2010 interview, he realized that he needed to understand how a corrupt and dysfunctional institution became that way in order to do his legal job. "I didn't set out to write a book. I just wanted a better understanding" (Wallace 2012).

What Johnson came to understand was that the Atlantic City of *Boardwalk Empire*, essentially a planned community for vice and graft, was originally envisioned as a health resort for rich people. The land owner, a 19th-century country doctor named

Jonathan Pitney, desperately wanted his quiet beach village on Absecon Island to be a "city by the sea" with a classy reputation. In fact, the famous boardwalks were originally built to keep patrons from tracking sand onto the fancy carpets of the luxury hotels. Despite the mosquitos, the setting was nature's perfection, but early on not even the well-to-do could get there. Thus Pitney became the first in a long line of Atlantic City visionaries who rationalized his grubby deals with the powerful as a necessary step to keep the dream alive. Pitney's pitch was to New Jersey legislators, the pols who would have to approve the railroad infrastructure to transport his wealthy guests. Initially rejected, Pitney realized he would need industrial barons and entrepreneurs to buy in first, for they were the players who had the financial capacity to grease the system in his favor. After the tracks were built and the trains began to arrive, the island was renamed Atlantic City and the rest is a history of pleasure-oriented services honoring clear priorities of development—build and operate for astonishing daily profit, and give the guests what they want for the short time they are staying. "If the people who came to town had wanted Bible readings," one voice in this history observed, "we'd have given them that. They wanted booze, broads and gambling, so that's what we gave them" (Johnson 2002). Yet instead of attracting the wealthy elites according to Pitney's original vision, Atlantic City came to be known as "the World's Playground," drawing hordes of middle and working class families who came for just a few days in the sea and sand and sun. They enjoyed the distractions, legal and illicit, that may have been envisioned for the wealthy but which had been increasingly priced to their own budgets.

Another truth about Atlantic City, hiding in plain sight, is the counter-intuitive notion that a city famous for its corruption could function according to its organizing principles so openly. But such is the charm of a rogue and likewise the nature of corruption; it works because everybody knows how it works. Once operational, machine politics is used to build and grow the "empire" that rises openly against the skyline of civil society. Corruption is a cooperative enterprise, coerced or not, an interest-driven relationship linking service providers, regulators (policymakers or law enforcement), and bosses, all aligned in more or less open deceit of systemic checks. Johnson's history of Atlantic City describes both the architecture and the interior design of his case study. *Boardwalk Empire* exemplifies the transparent functionality of a vice fiefdom that works, not *around* its illegalities, but *because* of them. Yet for all its mechanistic design elements, Johnson's history of corruption in Atlantic City is also organic. It is an evolutionary process where those with a genius for adaptation and survival find their place in a self-contained world unbound by conventional morality but governed by principles of purpose and loyalty nonetheless. There is an almost Biblical succession story embedded: Louis Kuehnle begat Nucky Johnson, Nucky Johnson begat Hap Farley, and so on. It was a world of their own making with everything necessary to sustain it indefinitely.

The Golden Age of corruption for Atlantic City emerged under the skilled attentions of Enoch "Nucky" Johnson (no apparent relation to the author). Nucky was both an organized crime boss and an elected Republican Party official who operated through both camps with a brazen, synergized authority. Nucky's rise pre-dated

Prohibition, but he already understood how to provide middle-class vacationers the good times they desired at reasonable prices. Federal laws against alcohol simply provided a new black market for his network of illicit goods and services, at a higher profit margin. As the author explains, it was all one operation. "Without a flourishing vice industry, Atlantic City would lose an important competitive edge for attracting visitors, and the local Republican Party would lose the money needed to continue its dominance" (Johnson 2002). Law enforcement was under strict guidelines to look the other way from illegality that operated within the closed system, and to enforce the system against enterprise that was outside it. Further strengthening the bonds of political loyalty, Nucky himself was a generous man with constituents, especially those enduring hardship; his ward leaders were often more like social workers, according to Nelson Johnson. The corrupt system of Atlantic City in Nucky's era of glory was inherited from "Commodore" Louis Kuehnle, and passed on after Nucky's imprisonment in 1941 for tax evasion to Francis "Hap" Farley, who ran things until he was dumped by voters in 1971. Nelson Johnson's history of Atlantic City is more than a history of a "boardwalk empire." Much happened even after "Hap" Farley's death in 1977, including the legalization of gambling and the efforts of a New York developer named Donald Trump. His attempt to establish and maintain casino real estate and holdings in Atlantic City, like much of his own business empire, came under heightened scrutiny with his 2016 campaign for the White House. But the Golden Era of corruption for the likes of Nucky Johnson had ended decades earlier.

Nelson Johnson's history of Atlantic City continued for as many pages after the end of Nucky's reign as it had used to develop and finish his story. But even the author himself understood that Nucky and his *Boardwalk Empire* was perhaps the most fascinating part of the story. By the mid-1990s another empire had been established, the entertainment "boardwalk" of programming offered by Home Box Office (HBO). HBO approached producer Terence Winter, whose earlier HBO series—*The Sopranos*—had been a juggernaut of critical success and audience obsession, to develop a series based upon Johnson's book. Out of all the eras captured in *Boardwalk Empire*, Winter's creativity was attracted the most to Nucky's 1920s era. "Atlantic City at that time was a place of excess, glamour, and most of all, opportunity," Winter explained in the Foreword to a new edition of the book released after the television show gained its own following. "Loud, brash, colorful, full of hope and promise—it was a microcosm of America. A place of spectacle, shady politics, fast women, and backroom deals, as well as a real community with real people, not only on its boardwalk but also in its churches, schools, and neighborhoods. It was a place of real Americans, a melting pot of ideas and cultures" (Johnson 2002). Just as Nelson Johnson had wanted to explain, at least to himself, how Atlantic City became a *Boardwalk Empire*, producer Terence Winter hoped to use Johnson's book to entertain the HBO audience with a thin slice of how America became America. Because Winter was proven in his ability to deliver a strong, captivating product in their market, HBO spent extravagantly on his period-set homage to corruption. Academy Award winner Martin Scorsese was already attached to the project, and he directed the first episode; HBO spent millions just creating the *Boardwalk* set in Brooklyn. Even though Johnson's sprawling history was scaled to focus on the episodic events around a fictionalized characterization of Nucky, portrayed by Steve Buscemi, the HBO format allowed for a long-form story arc that could account for characters and historic context taking place over an extended period.

HBO was not required to insert or interpret characters from the book—or outside it—with historic accuracy, but the connection between characters on the series and counterparts from history was a source of intrigue and imagination for the audience and the critical community. Nucky Johnson became Nucky Thompson, and his screen character is presented though Buscemi's wiry physical presence and brooding intensity. The real Nucky was a *bon vivant*, bald, with eyeglasses on a six foot frame, well over 225 pounds. In addition to Nucky's butler, his sheriff brother, and the "Commodore," other historic characters include Arnold Rothstein, Al Capone, and "Lucky" Luciano. These characters actually existed during the era, but the series fictionalizes their encounters with Nucky Thompson to fit the needs of the developing storyline. "They are doing their best to do historically accurate fiction," is how Nelson Johnson explained it (Greene and Robison-Greene 2013). With characters such as Al Capone or Lucky Luciano, the audience could assume that details of events in a dramatized life do not change the way they died in real life. Nucky Johnson, however, died an old man in 1968, and Winter wasn't sure Nucky Thompson was going to get out of his show alive to succumb to a natural death decades later. That was Winter's Google problem: he did not want viewers to read actual history on his main character and believe they knew what was going to happen to Nucky in the show. Changing the character's name seemed to resolve the issue. But it may not be so simple to explain it away as mixing dramatic license with best efforts for accuracy. "Winter is trying to have it both ways—to have the liberty to tell stories that will ensure continued viewership while at the same time claiming the drama is 'realistic,'" Rod Carveth argues. "Research shows that viewers don't always know the difference. Giving viewers a false re-telling of history is unethical" (Greene and Robison-Greene 2013). In other words, such narrative choices represent a kind of open corruption of truth in order serve the ends of ratings. Winter seemed not to care about viewers who will never know the real story, or even that they may be disappointed with the way his version compares, when the fate of his Nucky became known in some future finale event. What really seemed to bother the producer was that his audience might stop watching if they thought they knew what happened to his main character. Perhaps more striking is that the series character of Nucky resorts to violence, even murder, to achieve his ends; Nelson Johnson has stated that he does not believe that is true of the real Nucky, whose machine was organized to respond to challenge with more systemic pressures and without such desperate expressions of authority. Carveth points out that job security was the real threat. "Instead of physical violence, the people who crossed Nucky and his organization lost their government jobs, they were ostracized, their businesses not patronized, their operating licenses were pulled, or they were raided and shut down by complicit police who were a part of the organization" (Greene and Robison-Greene 2013). Economic violence is a long shot to keep viewers tuning in, even if it was extremely effective in real life. But Winter's business decisions are those of a television producer. No one would know better that when a good earner suddenly becomes unreliable on weekly delivery, the show gets whacked.

As with *The Sopranos*, *Boardwalk Empire* became an immediate audience favorite, and during its five seasons on the air developed a following in popular culture strong enough to support a platform of interpretive approaches in other media, such as *The Boardwalk Empire A-Z* background guide (2012), and even a collection of academic essays called *Boardwalk Empire and Philosophy* (2013). The latter volume, for example, offered Freudian interpretation, a Machiavellian reading, even the consideration of whether Nucky or any of the other characters can be seen as a Nietzschean Superman. For his part, Terence Winter indicated his own philosophic perspective to the public as the series finished its run. "It was the flip side of what I had been doing on *The Sopranos* for eight years or so," he said in one interview. "*The Sopranos* was sort of an exploration of the end of organized crime, or the waning days of organized crime. Prohibition was the beginning of that same thing" (*Fresh Air* 2014). For good or for ill, the success of *The Sopranos* and *Boardwalk Empire* is related to a sexy formula that is driven by corruption and violence and a sense that the characters, like the worlds they inhabit, are doomed—a fate they all seem to accept with resigned awareness. It is a successful formula, so HBO has no cause to regret delivering shows the audience wants to consume. The real Nucky Johnson would probably agree, having once said, "We have whiskey, wine, women, song, and slot machines. I won't deny it and I won't apologize for it" (Johnson 2002).

Darrell A. Hamlin

See also: Corruption; Gangsters of the 1900s

Further Reading

Di Ionno, Mark. "Author of 'Boardwalk Empire' Helped Historical Book Transition into Dramatized Crime Series." *The Star-Ledger*, September 19, 2010. http://blog.nj.com/njv _mark_diionno/2010/09/author_of_boardwalk_empire_boo.html.

Ferry, Frank J. *Nucky: The Real Story of the Atlantic City Boardwalk Boss.* Margate, NJ: ComteQ Publishing, 2013.

Fresh Air. "As 'Boardwalk Empire' Comes to a Close, Creator Reminisces About Its Start." National Public Radio, September 11, 2014. http://www.npr.org/2014/09/11.

Greene, Richard, and Rachel Robison-Greene. *Boardwalk Empire and Philosophy: Bootleg This Book.* Peru, IL: Open Court Publishing, 2013.

Johnson, Nelson. *Boardwalk Empire: The Birth, High Times, and Corruption of Atlantic City.* Medford, NJ: Plexus Publishing, 2002.

Wallace, John. *The Boardwalk Empire A–Z: A Totally Unofficial Guide to Accompany the Hit HBO Series.* London: John Blake Publishing, 2012.

DASHCAM VIDEOS

Dash cameras are video cameras mounted to the dashboards of law enforcement vehicles with the intent of recording the activities of law enforcement personnel and citizens during traffic stops. Implemented to improve accountability and provide dependable video evidence of incidents involving law enforcement personnel, the mere presence of a continuously recording dash camera has likely prevented misconduct and has shown the actions of citizens during traffic stops. However, dash cameras have also unfortunately failed to deter and instead have recorded incidents of misconduct that have been publicized by the mainstream media. They also have recorded negative actions of citizens toward law enforcement officers, thus making this technology particularly pertinent to law enforcement personnel.

Although dash cameras have become commonplace in modern policing, the use of them dates back to the 1960s and 1970s. While the system was imperfect, these early dash cameras provided the only means of objectively documenting the activities of traffic stops. However, dash cameras were new, untested, and costly, causing many law enforcement agencies to forgo their implementation—at least, until a spate of civil rights violations during the mid-1990s triggered a wider adoption of dash cameras.

By the mid-1990s, the number of citizens filing lawsuits and alleging race-based mistreatment during traffic stops had grown at an alarming rate. Although some judges ruled that there was sufficient evidence that these traffic stops had been initiated because of the ethnicity of the driver, something needed to be done to regain trust in law enforcement. As a result, law enforcement personnel and citizens reasoned that the lack of an objective means of documenting traffic stops had become a costly liability and that installation of dash cameras in law enforcement vehicles would benefit both law enforcement personnel and the citizens they were tasked with protecting. With the increased use of dash cameras that followed, law enforcement leaders were able to deter police misconduct, gain the public's trust, exempt law enforcement officers from wrong doing, and change the dynamic between law enforcement personnel and citizens. In addition, with infallible video evidence of the traffic stop, dash cams have achieved the following:

- law enforcement leaders have been able to review incidents and take corrective action more quickly,
- law enforcement personnel have spent less time in court defending their actions,
- government attorneys have been able to more effectively litigate their cases,
- judges and jurors have been able to witness the video recording of events before deciding a case, and
- defendants have spent less time in the legal system.

These benefits have led to numerous tangible and intangible social surpluses for the citizens of the communities that have implemented dash cameras.

The Office of Community Oriented Policing Services (COPS Office) is the largest contributor of dash cameras, providing millions of dollars to local, county, and state law enforcement agencies for the purchase of dash cameras. COPS Office does not, however, stipulate which dash camera should be purchased or how the dash camera should be implemented. Therefore, the recording mechanism of the dash camera varies by the type of camera and law enforcement agency. Typically, the dash camera automatically and continuously records the activities of law enforcement personnel and citizens outside the vehicle, once the emergency lights are activated. In order for the recording to be used as a reliable source of video evidence, law enforcement leaders should ensure that the dash camera records continuously, is wired directly to a recording mechanism in a locked box, and is secured in the trunk of the law enforcement vehicle. Furthermore, to prevent interference from law enforcement personnel or citizens, law enforcement leaders should allow only predetermined, authorized personnel to access the locked box and video recordings. By following these protocols, law enforcement leaders can ensure that there is an unbroken video record of any incident that occurred.

Researchers have found that by implementing dash cameras, law enforcement leaders have improved the safety of law enforcement personnel, improved the accountability of law enforcement personnel and citizens, and provided trainers with a simpler means of reviewing an incident by using an incident as a training tool. For these reasons, researchers have also found that most law enforcement personnel are in favor of using dash cameras. Although there is not a consensus on how or when dash cameras should be used, most law enforcement personnel believe that they should be used in some capacity. While some law enforcement personnel have stated that citizens tend to work to de-escalate a situation when they become aware of a dash camera, other law enforcement personnel are distracted by the dash camera and find themselves performing for the dash camera rather than concentrating on the situation. Dash cameras can also help vindicate law enforcement officers: when there is a citizen complaint during a motor vehicle stop, a video recording shows an unbiased viewpoint of the incident so a determination can be made without prejudice.

The dash camera is a powerful tool for law enforcement personnel and is vital to establishing accountability and providing reliable video evidence of incidents involving law enforcement personnel and citizens. As a tool used to ensure accountability, the mere presence of a continuously recording, properly secured dash camera can build confidence and trust in law enforcement and provide a sense of safety for law enforcement. As a policing tool, the continuously recording, properly secured dash camera can provide sound and unbroken video documentation of an incident or a crime, ensuring that judges and jurors have an unbiased record of the incident before making a determination of guilt or innocence. Dash cameras are cost effective: by providing video evidence, the use of dash camera recordings saves money that would have otherwise been used to pay for a longer, less certain litigation or criminal prosecution. Finally, most law enforcement personnel are in favor of the implementation of dash cameras, though there is not a consensus of how or when the dash cameras should be used. Dash cameras provide law enforcement leaders and communities with an objective means of documenting incidents, and the installation of dash cameras in law enforcement vehicles benefits both law enforcement personnel and the citizens they are tasked with protecting.

Anthony M. Aceste

See also: Body Cameras; Fourth Amendment; Police Accountability

Further Reading

Lieberman, Samuel. "Chicago Police Have Been Sabotaging Their Dash Cams." *New York*, January 27, 2016. http://nymag.com/daily/intelligencer/2016/01.

Newkirk, Van. R. "Dash Cameras Help Convict Officers Who Brutalized a Man and Lied about It." *Daily Kos*, November 6, 2015. http://www.dailykos.com/stories/2015/11/6/1445755/-Dash-cameras-help-convict-officers-who-brutalized-a-man-and-lied-about-it.

Westphal, Lonnie J. "The In-Car Camera: Value and Impact." *Police Chief*. 2015. http://iacpmag.wp.matrixdev.net/the-in-car-camera-value-and-impact/.

BODY CAMERAS

As technology has advanced, there are many new devices being used in the field of criminal justice. One such advancement has resulted in police officers using body-worn cameras. This use of technology has caused numerous debates related to the benefits of the cameras versus the threat to privacy rights of the members of the public.

In recent years, there have been numerous videos collected by members of the public, which provide unedited views of police actions. These videos often surface

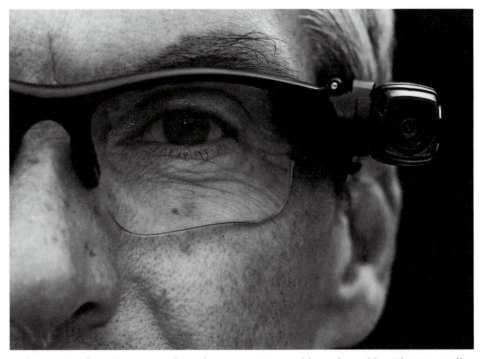

Body cameras for police can make police more accountable to the public. The West Valley City Police Department in Utah has issued 190 Taser Axon Flex body cameras for all its sworn officers to wear starting March 2015. (George Frey/Getty Images)

through social media and several have been shown on the national news. Many such videos are examples of poor police behavior and they are often used to demonstrate the improper use of force by the officers. Negative public opinion has resulted and in some cases riots have occurred in response to these videos.

In an attempt to eliminate the perceived negative police behavior, police have been increasing their use of body-worn cameras. Many people believe that the cameras will make the officers' behavior more visible and cause them to follow approved procedures more carefully. The use of these cameras allows for the collection of video throughout the officers work day. These videos can record all police contact with the public but there are advantages and disadvantages to using this technique for collecting information.

The benefits of body-worn cameras often include a reduction in the use of force by police officers, increased visibility with regard to police interactions with the public, better behavior on the part of the public, and improved collection of evidence for prosecution. These benefits must be weighed against the privacy rights of the public.

In response to people posting their videos online—videos that often show officers appearing to abuse their power—police seem to control their behavior more, which is the most beneficial outcome of using body-worn cameras. The public called for increased supervision and oversight of police officers to stop this apparent abuse of power.

Research on the how body-worn cameras have improved police behavior has found that the number of citizens' complaints against police officers has decreased among those officers wearing cameras (White 2014). Unfortunately the research has presented inconsistent findings. A study conducted in Rialto, California, did show some support for the theory that there would be less use of force by officers using cameras. However, more research needs to be conducted on this aspect of body-worn cameras.

A related benefit of body-worn cameras is that a reduction in assaults on police officers has been found (White 2014). The awareness that police departments are using body-worn cameras may improve behavior among the public as well as among the officers. If people know their behavior is being recorded, they may be more polite and demonstrate appropriate behavior when in contact with an officer.

The Fourth Amendment provides the citizens of the United States a protection against unreasonable search and seizure. Body-worn cameras, though, have caused many debates regarding the rights to privacy of the public. Federal and most state laws prohibit the collection of photos or videos without a warrant, particularly where the public has an expectation of privacy. The cameras will record all activity and sound in the area the officers are working. Therefore, the recordings will show activities of people who are not suspects and are not being arrested. As the videos collected by police-worn cameras immediately become public record, a person's right to privacy is quickly limited.

At least one author has suggested that body-worn cameras may actually increase compliance with the Fourth Amendment privacy rights. Harris (2010) argued that as the officers' actions are being recorded, they will be more likely to follow proper procedure for evidence collection and interviews of suspects. As the videos will be allowed in court, judges can easily identify evidence that was collected improperly and not allow its use.

Overall there has been mixed support for body-worn cameras. Police unions are often opposed as they believe the videos may be used to look for poor work performance of the officers. The unions often believe that supervisors will examine videos to get an officer in trouble (White 2013).

Some police officers support the use of the cameras, as they believe it will protect them from unwarranted citizen complaints. Other officers do not want to use them as they are uncomfortable with the increase in electronic supervision of their work. Many police departments have allowed officers to decide if they will use the cameras or not.

Although some research has been conducted, there has not been enough as of yet to test the claims regarding the benefits of camera use. Additional studies will need to be conducted and strict policies put in place to establish the rights of the public with regard to privacy.

Paige H. Gordier

See also: Dashcam Videos; Fourth Amendment; Police Accountability; Police Ethics

Further Reading

Dillon, Nancy. "Police Body-Worn Cameras Stop-and-Frisk Judge Suggested Have Helped Rialto Police Department." *New York Daily News*, August 13, 2013. http://www.nydailynews.com/news/national/cameras-proposed-stop-frisk-judge-ca-police-article-1.1426025.

Farrar, William. *Self-Awareness to Being Watched and Socially-Desirable Behavior: A Field Experiment on the Effect of Body-Worn Cameras and Police Use-of-Force.* Washington, DC: Police Foundation, 2013.

Harris, David A. "Picture This: Body Worn Video Devices ('Head Cams') as Tools for Ensuring Fourth Amendment Compliance by Police." Legal Studies Research Paper Series. Pittsburgh, PA: University of Pittsburgh School of Law, 2010.

White, Michael. Personal interview with Commander Michael Kurtenbach of the Phoenix (Arizona) Police Department and Professor Charles Katz of Arizona State University about the Phoenix body-worn camera project. September 5, 2013.

White, Michael. "Police Officer Body-Worn Cameras: Assessing the Evidence." Washington, DC: Office of Community Oriented Policing Services, 2014. https://www.ojpdiagnosticcenter.org/sites/default/files/spotlight/download/Police%20Officer%20Body-Worn%20Cameras.pdf.

COMMUNITY POLICING TODAY

Community policing is any effort on the part of the police to get closer to the community. It takes a variety of forms, but, ultimately, its goal is to create a bond with the community so that its law enforcement and other aims might be achieved. What follows are the many facets of community policing.

First, though, it is helpful to delve into the history of community policing in order to appreciate how embedded the concept itself is within police work, even though its practices have not always been labeled in terms of "community policing":

One of the earliest forms of law enforcement was the "mutual pledge" system, involving family groupings being responsible for the acts of their members. This system existed in the ninth century. Obviously, as society became more complex, this form of "law enforcement" simply was not practical, but its connections with the concept of community policing were obvious.

And, later, even with the growth of big city police departments, the connection between the community and the police was obvious. Because the police were the only 24-hour-a-day agency, it fell on them to handle various social service functions, such as caring for the homeless, operating soup kitchens, and dealing with the disenfranchised population in general. In 2016, police departments were still dealing with the homeless population extensively.

Why, then, have we not always called police officers "community police officers," or the like?

It has to do with image. Being able to make arrests and solve serious crimes make headlines, whereas caring for the homeless, seemingly, is more the job of the social worker. In addition, the media, with television programs emphasizing high-speed chases and the police dealing with dangerous criminals, adds "fuel to the fire" as to what serious police work ought to be about. To a certain extent, the public does have the right to expect its officers to put crime control first. In 2015, when the two dangerous convicts escaped from a prison in upstate New York, communities neighboring the prison were in an uproar. A relevant question to ask, however, is how frequent incidents such as these are in relation to other facets of the police officers' job? Also, policing has traditionally been a male-dominated occupation, with "toughness," not "people skills," being emphasized. This, of course, has begun to change as more women have entered law enforcement.

What are these aims of the police? Law enforcement, in the sense of arresting dangerous criminals, is certainly one. Studies continually tell us, however, that not nearly all crimes are cleared by arrest, and this has been a long-standing trend. It seems an aspect of our democracy, in fact, that this relative lack of solving crimes will always be the case: We do not torture suspects to gain confessions, and we do not permit our police to search suspects without "probable cause," to illustrate. So, what are some of the other aims?

In sociology there is a distinction made between a "manifest" and a "latent" function. Insofar as the police are concerned, one obvious "manifest" function is to arrest dangerous criminals. But what are some of the less obvious functions?

Our society today is plagued by a host of problems, including not only crime but, poverty, racism, breakdown of the family unit, and increased incivility in general. Considering all of these problems, could it be that the police, as the only 24-hour-a-day service agency readily accessible by all, serve to deal with all of these problems, in a manner of speaking? To illustrate, they do take many calls for family disputes.

They are involved, as previously indicated, in dealing with the homeless population, as an example of poverty. Insofar as society's problems in race relations are concerned, the police represent the "front line" of the "establishment." They are responsible for keeping society's racial problems from spinning out of control. So, in a manner of speaking, might it be said that the police act in a more general social control role, in addition to their law enforcement duties? This more general social control function is sometimes referred to as their "order maintenance" function.

"Order maintenance" leaves open a wide variety of possibilities, insofar as the police officer's interactions with the community are concerned, thus making the execution of the concept of "community policing" more feasible. "Order maintenance" does not imply making an arrest, but rather "keeping the peace," and that can be done in any number of ways.

First, on the community level, and in its most general sense, "foot patrol" is far preferable to automobile patrol, in that there is considerably more interaction with the community, and the potential to de-escalate a situation before arrest is necessary. A re-emphasis upon foot patrol has taken place in many communities.

Also, on the community level, there are various neighborhood projects that the police have been involved in. One of these has been the Chicago Alternative Policing Strategy (CAPS). In this program, in order for officers to enhance their knowledge of their community, they are assigned to particular neighborhoods, which allows the officers and the residents to personally get to know each other. In this program, officers are required to meet regularly with the community, discuss problems, and then develop strategies to solve them (Walker and Katz 2005, 15). The Charlotte-Mecklenburg Police Department has taken initiatives to assist the Hispanic population, who have been frequently victimized by robberies. Among the steps taken include working with the banking community to educate newly arrived Hispanic immigrants about how to use banking services in general. (These Hispanic residents had been accustomed to carrying cash [Dempsey and Forst 2011, 171–172].)

On the community level, also, one of the most prominent recent trends has been the growth of the residential police officer concept. In Elgin, Illinois, as one illustration, police officers live in subsidized or donated housing, work an eight-hour day, but are on 24-hour-a-day call, in effect. In Macon, Georgia, residential police officers live in rent-free, city-owned housing, in exchange for working with at-risk youth for 24 hours a month (Dempsey and Forst 2011, 173). In Richmond, Virginia, one residential police officer developed such a relationship with a youth that the youth indicated his goal was to one day become a police officer himself.

The use of the school resource officer has been another notable effort in the direction of the police relating to the community. Although school resource officers are in the schools primarily to maintain order, they are also able to develop a significant relationship with students and be a mentor, of sorts. In turn, these students are inclined to have a more favorable view of at least certain police officers.

Community policing has also been implemented on a more micro level. Officers have become involved with both sports and study hall programs with youth and, in turn, have bonded with them as a result. Foot patrol within certain neighborhoods of the city has led to some trust between the community and the police, whereby the latter have been more willing to approach the police about specific problems. In some parts of the country, police have set up mini-stations, including within business establishments, in order to create more bonding between the police and the community.

In short, there is no limit to the potential of community policing. As stated, community policing represents any effort on the part of the police to get closer to the community. And, at no time in our history has this been more important, with the range of social problems in our society today and the police being the one organization consistently in the forefront.

Harry Toder

See also: Perceptions of Police Today; Police Accountability; PTSD and Family Issues among Officers; "Thin Blue Line": Police as a Guard against Anarchy

Further Reading

Dempsey, John, and Linda Forst. *Police*. Clifton Park, NY: Delmar Cengage Learning, 2011.
Walker, Samuel, and Charles Katz. *Police in America*. New York: McGraw Hill, 2005.

EZELL FORD SHOOTING

Ezell Ford was an unarmed African American male who was shot multiple times and killed by Los Angeles Police Department (LAPD) officers. He was 25. Family and outspoken community members deemed the events surrounding his death suspicious because Ford suffered from mental health issues.

According to the LAPD, on August 11, 2014, Ford had been observed walking alone in the vicinity of 65th Street, an area known for alleged gang activity that was blocks away from his home in Florence, Los Angeles, which has one of the highest violent crime rates in the county. Also in the area were members of the LAPD's Newton Division gang enforcement: Officer Sharlton Wampler, an Asian American and 12-year veteran on the force; and Officer Antonio Villegas, a Latino American and 8-year veteran. While on patrol, Officer Wampler spotted Ford, whom Wampler claimed he knew; however, at the time, Wampler didn't immediately recognize him. Both officers subsequently exited their vehicle and challenged Ford to what they deemed an "investigative stop." Ford was reported to have walked away and ducked into a driveway, as both officers followed him.

The officers then observed Ford, squatting down between some bushes and a vehicle. Officer Villegas, believing that Ford may have possessed a weapon because of known gang activity in the area, initially pulled out his service weapon. However, Villegas put it away and took a backup position to keep a watchful eye, which allowed Officer Wampler to take the lead and accost Ford. At this point, it is alleged that Ford made several suspicious movements and tried to conceal his hands possibly to discard drugs that he may have possessed. Then, as described by Officer Wampler, they got into a life-and-death struggle to maintain his weapon. Wampler claimed that they fought and fell to the ground. As they wrestled, it was alleged that Ford mounted Officer Wampler and tried to remove his service weapon from his holster. Wampler screamed out to his partner to advise him that Ford had been attempting to grab his gun. Officer Villegas shot Ford twice. Officer Wampler, who claimed he feared for his life, then retrieved his backup gun, a five-shot revolver, from his uniform and shot Ford in the back. Ford died later at the hospital.

The timing of this police-involved shooting came days after two sergeants of the same Newton Division stopped Omar Abrego, an unarmed 37-year-old Hispanic male, for allegedly driving erratically. An altercation ensued, and Abrego suffered a laceration. Witnesses alleged that the two sergeants repeatedly beat him with their fists and a baton. Abrego died shortly after that, but a subsequent autopsy report determined Abrego died from physical and emotional distress from the altercation and the effects of narcotics in his system. These deaths also coincided with the fatal shooting of Michael Brown in Ferguson, Missouri. Brown was an unarmed 19-year-old Black male who was shot and killed by police two days earlier than the Ford shooting. It also followed two other contentious incidents.

Eric Garner, a 43-year-old unarmed Black male suspect was killed while being arrested by New York Police Department (NYPD) detectives. Garner, alleged to have been selling loose cigarettes, was seen on national television pleading for his life. He yelled out to the arresting detectives that he couldn't breathe on 11 separate occasions as an NYPD detective attempted to subdue him with an unauthorized choking technique. Within this same timeframe, John Crawford, a 22-year-old Black male, was killed by a police officer in Beavercreek, Ohio, while holding a toy BB gun in a Wal-Mart store. In 2004, Ohio became an open carry state, which allows individuals who legally possess the firearm to carry their weapon in public.

The LAPD is the third-largest police department in the United States and has a history of negative interaction with members of minority communities. In 1992, Rodney King, a passenger in a motor vehicle that had been in a high-speed chase, was Tasered and beaten severely with side-handled batons by five White LAPD officers. Unbeknownst to the officers, their actions were covertly video-recorded and released to the media and publicly aired. Four of the five officers were charged with assault and use of excessive force but later acquitted by a jury of nine White and three minority jurors. The acquittals sparked the Los Angeles riots that were concentrated in South Central Los Angeles. Of the 55 people who died during the unrest, 8 were killed by police officers, and Army National Guardsmen killed 2. Although estimates vary, it has been suggested that the damage caused by the riots total more than $1 billion.

After Ford's shooting, hundreds of protestors took to the streets in the downtown Los Angeles area. Several demonstrators carried signs and chanted slogans, including, "Justice for Ezell Ford" and "Hands up, don't shoot." The latter has been the call-and-response cry after the general public became aware that several unarmed Black males had been shot or killed by the police. Members of the Black Lives Matters activist movement participated in the protests. This group has been at the forefront of controversial police shootings of minorities since the 2013 acquittal of George

Zimmerman, who had shot and killed Trayvon Martin, an unarmed, 17-year-old African American male.

A follow-up investigation into the Ford shooting uncovered several revelations. Ashanti Harris, who claimed he had witnessed the encounter, contradicted the LAPD's account and advised that Ford had his hands in the air when initially stopped by the officers. He said that the police officer tackled Ford to the ground and then shot him in the back while he was lying down. Family members and friends argued that Ford had no affiliation with any gang. However, Ford had a prior criminal record for possession of a loaded firearm, trespassing, and possession of marijuana with the intent to sell.

Ford's parents claimed that their son suffered from depression, schizophrenia, and bipolar disorder, which had been known by the police officers who patrolled the area where they lived. Neighborhood friends recall Ford being somewhat of an introvert as a teenager possibly because of the medication he took for his mental health condition.

An autopsy was performed to ascertain the cause of death. The Ford family requested that the Los Angeles County coroner's release a copy of their son's autopsy report to find out what happened. Initially, the coroner's office denied their request, citing it was an ongoing investigation. However, after 134 days, Los Angeles mayor Eric Garcetti ordered the LAPD to release the report. The results concluded that Ford had marijuana in his system, but no drugs were found at the scene of the shooting. The attorney, Steven Lerman, representing the Ford family, speculated that they withheld the report due to political reasons. He described Ford's shooting as an execution. Afterward, he advised that the family had filed a $75 million federal wrongful death lawsuit, accusing the LAPD, Officer Wampler, and Officer Villegas of using excessive force and racial profiling.

The autopsy report revealed that the two officers shot Ford three times. One nonfatal shot hit Ford in his right arm. The remaining two shots fatally struck him in the lower right side and right back. The shot in the back left a "muzzle imprint," which meant one of them fired it at close range. Concerning speculation that the LAPD Newton Division had previously known Ford, in 2008, Officer Wampler had arrested him for possession of marijuana. Moreover, Officer Wampler had also been accused of assault in 2009, and they settled the case without disclosure of court records.

The investigation into the Ford shooting resulted in LAPD chief Charlie Beck finding that the police officers had been justified in using deadly force because of evidence that a struggle had ensued between Ford and the police officer. However, the Los Angeles Police Commission, an independent oversight board, declared that only Officer Wampler's actions, that is, tactics, of drawing of the weapon, use of force, and non-lethal use of force were outside the scope of the LAPD official policy. The commission cleared Officer Villegas of any wrongdoing because they decided that he was justified in shooting Ford to protect Officer Wampler. Nevertheless, they found that his initial drawing of the weapon on Ford was outside of the LAPD official policy.

Since the August 2014 shooting of Ezell Ford, the LAPD issued a mixed ruling (finding that Wampler's use of deadly force was a violation of policy). However, the other officer, Beck, was cleared in the fatal shooting. The crime of murder has no statute of limitations and charges can ultimately be filed against the police officers. Despite that, there is a three-year statute of limitations for potentially charging the police officers with any other criminal charge. Jackie Lacey, the first African American Los Angeles County district attorney, has yet to file charges against either police officer. Ford's killing has connected him to the wider conversation of deaths of unarmed Black men by police officers. The Ford family's $75 million federal lawsuit is still pending.

Brian L. Royster

See also: Corruption; Deadly Force; Eric Garner Case in New York City and Subsequent Tensions; Michael Brown Shooting and the Aftermath in Ferguson; Police Accountability; Police Brutality; Rodney King Beating and Riots; Trayvon Martin Shooting

Further Reading

Bultema, J. A. *Guardian Angels: A History of the Los Angeles Police Department*. Cohshohocken, PA: Infinity Publishing, 2014.
King, R. *The Riot Within: My Journey from Rebellion to Redemption*. New York: Harper Collins, 2012.
Salters, J. *Deadly Force: Fatal Confrontations With Police*. New York: AP Editions, 2015.

TAMIR RICE SHOOTING IN CLEVELAND

The case of Tamir Rice raises various liabilities for police misconduct regarding lethal force. When police officers use lethal force, they are subject to criminal and civil liabilities, administrative review, as well as U.S. Department of Justice (DOJ) oversight of possible civil rights violations for patterns, practices, and policies of the police department regarding excessive use of force.

On November 22, 2014, a dispatcher received an anonymous 911 call that a Black male, probably a juvenile, had a gun, probably fake, in the recreational park, Cudell Park, in the city of Cleveland, Ohio. The dispatcher relayed the information from the anonymous call with the exception that he was probably a juvenile and probably a fake gun. A surveillance video revealed that quickly after arrival on the scene, the White rookie police officer, Timothy L. Loehmann, 26, fatally shot the African American male, Rice. Police Officer Frank Garmback, 46, was the driver. After the shooting, the police officers realized Rice was merely an African American youth who had a black pellet gun that they perceived as a real gun. His black pellet gun did not contain the orange tip that distinguished it from a real gun. Rice, 12, died at the hospital on November 23, 2014. The Cuyahoga County Medical Examiner's Office determined Rice's death was a homicide.

Police officers are subject to both criminal and civil liability for the use of lethal force in violation of the U.S. Constitution. The Fourth Amendment provides certain protections for individuals against the abusive exercise of force by law enforcement.

Demonstrators protest the police shooting of Tamir Rice as they block Public Square in Cleveland, November 2014. Tamir Rice was a 12-year-old African American boy who was shot by Cleveland police officer, Timothy Loehmann, at a gazebo outside the recreation center on November 22, 2014. (AP Photo/Tony Dejak)

When police officers employ deadly force, the court analyzes whether they had probable cause to believe a suspect is an immediate threat to the police, or to others.

The Fifth Amendment protects the police officers against an alleged unconstitutional use of lethal force. Under the Fifth Amendment, the prosecution presents the case to the grand jury, which determines whether there should be an indictment for lethal force exercised by the police officers. State law determines the procedure for grand jury proceedings. A judge, the defendants, and their attorneys are not present at these secret proceedings. Some argue that grand jury proceedings should be open to the public. Historically, grand jury proceedings are closed to avoid damaging an individual's reputation such as if there is a decision by the grand jury not to indict or a "no bill." The grand jury usually consists of up to 23 citizens. The grand jury or the prosecutor may call witnesses. In this specific case, the police officers read statements before the grand jury. If the grand jury decides to indict, it is called a true bill. The judge accepts the indictment and then, the charge is made public (Samaha 2015, 481–483). On December 28, 2015, the Cuyahoga County grand jury returned a "no-bill," which is a decision that there was not sufficient evidence for probable cause of a crime to indict the police officers.

Special prosecutors may be assigned to certain police lethal use of force cases. In various criminal cases, some assert that there may be bias expressed by the prosecutors in favor of police officers. In some instances a special prosecutor is requested if the victim's family has a concern with a conflict of interest or appearance of bias of the prosecutor toward the police officers. The prosecutors work closely with the police officers with many cases and sometimes there is the fear that the prosecutors will not be objective in their presentation of the case to the grand jury. In this instance, the family of Rice requested a special prosecutor. However, the request for a special prosecutor was not granted.

In addition to criminal liability, the court may determine civil liability exists when police use excessive force. When there is a case that involves lethal force, the victim's family has a legal right to sue civilly against the municipality and appropriate law enforcement officers. This civil lawsuit may be filed regardless of any criminal proceedings. Rice's family filed a federal wrongful death lawsuit under Ohio statutes, the Fourth and Fourteenth Amendments and 42 U.S. Code Sections 83 and 88 Civil Rights Action in January of 2015 against the municipality and the officers involved as well as the dispatchers. In this action, the family of Rice sought damages (money) for his wrongful death. On April 25, 2016, the federal lawsuit was settled for $6 million and the City of Cleveland acknowledged no fault.

Along with the criminal and civil liability, there are several levels of administrative review when lethal force is an issue. One is an internal review within the police department. The Internal Affairs Unit (IAU) conducts the internal review. IAU accepts complaints of excessive force, investigates, deliberates, and then decides whether there has been police misconduct. If it is determined there has been police misconduct, discipline can be recommended, including the most severe: dismissal. Both the Cleveland Police Department and the County Sheriff's Office investigated the Rice case. External review of police misconduct is also available by individuals who are not police. Because of independent investigations, different review boards may suggest punishment for police misconduct to appropriate law enforcement authorities.

An additional accountability mechanism is the federal government oversight. The DOJ Civil Rights Division intervenes in some cases involving alleged civil rights violation at the state level by police officers. In this case, Rice's family requested that the DOJ intervene. The DOJ had already found the City of Cleveland Police Department in violation of Fourth Amendment constitutional use of force according to a prior review. The DOJ will continue provide oversight of the City of Cleveland Police Department.

Moreover there is an educational aspect to police use of lethal force. As preventive measures, some have insisted upon comprehensive training for police officers regarding the use of lethal force. Simultaneously, others have urged education for the youth, parents, and the community through faith-based organizations, nonprofit organizations, and police departments with regard to the dangers of use of pellet guns and certain responses to police officers. In this instance, Rice was only a perceived threat to pertinent officers, and the latter were not in actual danger. Everyone agreed that it was in the best interest of society to prevent future tragic incidents of this sort.

Finally, there is a perception of disproportionate misconduct of police officers within the racial minority community. A distrust of police officers exists among the racial minority communities. People in these communities complain more about inappropriate use of force than in White communities. Acknowledging that police officers are needed in racial minority communities, some assert that "community policing" is perhaps a preventive measure. Community policing exercised by the police department involves a methodology that tries to prevent crime by developing proactive strategies, accountability of police officers, and greater community involvement (Swanson 2012, 50–51). It is argued that community policing would develop greater trust of the police officers among the racial minority community.

Theresa Andrews

See also: Deadly Force; Fifth Amendment; Fourth Amendment

Further Reading

Almasy, Steve. "Tamir Rice Shooting Was 'Reasonable,' Two Experts Conclude." CNN, October 12, 2015. http://www.cnn.com/2015/10/10/us/tamir-rice-shooting-reports.

Banks, Cyndi. *Criminal Justice Ethics*. Los Angeles, CA: Sage Publications, 2016.

Chapman, Christopher. "Use of Force in Minority Communities Is Related to Police Education, Age, Experience, and Ethnicity." *Police Practice & Research* 13, no. 5 (2012): 421–436.

Crimesider Staff. "Autopsy Calls Tamir Rice Shooting Death a Homicide." *Crimesider*, December 12, 2014. http://www.cbsnews.com/news/medical-examiner-rules-tamir-rices-death-a-homicide.

Jefferis, Eric, Fredrick Butcher, and Dena Hanley. "Measuring Perceptions of Police Use of Force." *Police Practice & Research* 12, no. 1 (2011): 81–96.

Katz, Walter. "Enhancing Accountability and Trust with Independent Investigations of Police Lethal Force." *Harvard Law Review* 128, no. 6 (2015): 235–245.

Lee, H., H. Jang, I. Yun, H. Lim, H., and D. W. Tushaus. "An Examination of Police Use of Force Utilizing Police Training and Neighborhood Contextual Factors." *Policing* 33, no. 4 (2010): 681–702. doi:10.1108/13639511011085088.

Ly, Laura, and Jason Hanna. "Cleveland Police's Fatal Shooting of Tamir Rice Ruled a Homicide." CNN, December 12, 2014. http://www.cnn.com/2014/12/12/justice/cleveland-tamir-rice.

Pinizzotto, Anthony J., Edward F. Davis, Shannon B. Bohrer, and Benjamin J. Infanti. "Law Enforcement Restraint in the Use of Deadly Force within the Context of 'The Deadly Mix.'" *International Journal of Police Science & Management* 14, no. 4 (2012): 285–289.

Roberson, Cliff. *Constitutional Law and Criminal Justice*. Boca Raton, FL: CRC Press, 2009.

Samaha, Joel. *Criminal Procedure*. Stamford, CT: Cengage Learning, 2015.

Swanson, Charles R., Leonard Territo, and Robert W. Taylor. *Police Administration Structures, Processes, and Behaviors*. Upper Saddle River, NJ: Pearson Education, 2012.

FREDDIE GRAY CASE

Freddie Gray, born Freddie Carlos Gray Jr. (1989–2015), was a Baltimore, Maryland, resident who died following an arrest made by members of the Baltimore Police Department (BPD). Gray's death resulted in criminal charges against six police officers and led to riots and protests nationwide.

Gray was born prematurely in Baltimore on August 16, 1989, to a heroin-addicted mother. As an infant and toddler, both he and his twin sister, Fredericka, were exposed to extremely high levels of lead-based paint, and blood tests conducted during the first two years of their life indicated that the lead level in his blood was two to six times the normal levels (McCoy 2015). From an early age, Gray exhibited behavior issues, including poor academic performance and truancy. By the time of his death, Gray had been arrested at least 12 times for drug and other minor offenses, and there were 5 pending criminal cases against him.

Arrest and Death

On April 12, 2015, the Baltimore police arrested Freddie Gray. According to police reports, officers Garrett E. Miller and Edward Nero, as well as Lieutenant Brian W. Rice, were on bicycle patrol in the Gilmor Homes neighborhood. The officers encountered Gray and made eye contact with him. But then Gray fled. A foot chase ensued, and Gray was apprehended by Nero and Miller. In his report, Officer Miller stated that Gray was apprehended "without force or incident" (Golgowski 2015). According to court documents, however, Gray was placed in a position that rendered him unable to breathe. Gray informed the officers that he suffered from asthma and was subsequently denied his inhaler. Officers Miller and Nero found a knife in Gray's possession that they claimed was illegal under Baltimore law. Upon locating the knife, Officer Miller placed Gray in a leg lace—a restraining position in which an individual is placed face down on the ground and has both legs restrained and lifted up. Officer Nero held Gray down. A witness to the event stated that Officer Nero placed his knee on Gray's neck (Rector 2015). The events following the restraint were filmed by two bystanders.

A Baltimore Police Department transport van driven by Officer Caesar R. Goodson, Jr., a 16-year veteran of the police force, arrived on the scene several minutes after Gray was apprehended. The video of Gray's arrest shows the three officers dragging him to the transport van. Witnesses can be heard in the background, stating that Gray was unable to use his legs and that his legs appeared broken (Cooper 2015). Officers placed Gray in the back of the transport van but failed to secure him with a seatbelt as mandated by department policies put in place three days prior to Gray's arrest.

The transport van made four stops en route to the police station. According to police documents, Gray acted irate while in the van and, in response, officers removed Gray from the van and placed him in leg irons. A resident recorded Gray's shackling on a cell phone. According to court documents, officers placed Gray back in the transport van head first, laying him on his stomach and not securing him with a seatbelt.

Officer Goodson radioed dispatch and requested an officer to check on Gray's condition. Officer William G. Porter and Sergeant Alicia D. White met with the transport van at its second stop. Gray requested medical attention, but neither Officer Porter nor Sergeant White called for medical assistance. Several minutes later the van stopped a third time while officers made a second arrest and placed that individual in the van with Gray. At 9:24 a.m., 30 minutes following Gray's initial arrest, the van arrived at the West District police station. At this time, the officers called emergency services and requested paramedics. Paramedics arrived and treated Gray for 21 minutes. Gray was then taken to the University of Maryland R. Adams Cowley Shock Trauma Center where he fell into a coma. According to relatives, Gray had suffered a spinal injury and a crushed voice box. On April 19, 2015, seven days after his arrest, Gray died.

Public Outcry

Gray's arrest and death sparked nationwide protests. The first notable protest occurred in Baltimore on April 18, 2015. Protests occurred there daily for nine days. Protests also occurred in other major cities, including Chicago; Denver; Miami; Seattle; Philadelphia; Washington, DC; and New York City.

On April 25, 2015, several hundred people gathered in downtown Baltimore to peacefully protest Gray's death. These protests were attended by members of a variety of organizations including the NAACP, Black Lives Matter, and the Southern Christian Leadership Conference. Although initially peaceful, these protests quickly devolved into violence. Stephanie Rawlings-Blake, the mayor of Baltimore, and the Baltimore Police Department indicated that a small group of individuals in the crowd became violent toward the police. As a result, 15 officers were injured and 34 people were arrested (Wenger and Campbell 2015).

On April 27, 2015, following Gray's funeral, protestors in Baltimore began rioting. Rioters looted and caused property damage, including setting fire to a local CVS pharmacy and destroying two Baltimore Police Department patrol cars (Yan and Ford 2015). The Maryland governor Larry Hogan declared a state of emergency in response to the riots. He also ordered the National Guard in Maryland, as well as 500 state troopers and 5,000 officers from surrounding jurisdictions into Baltimore to regain control of the city (Stolberg April 27, 2015). The mayor followed with a citywide curfew order, between the hours of 10 p.m. and 5 a.m. Additionally, the schools in the city and the downtown campus of the University of Maryland were closed. The citywide curfew and the National Guard presence remained in place until May 3, 2015.

Investigations and Settlement

In response to the events, each officer who was involved in the arrest of Gray was suspended without pay, pending an investigation. A press conference was held on April 24, 2015, in which Baltimore police commissioner Anthony Batts acknowledged that officers did not follow department protocol that mandated officers to secure arrestees with seatbelts (Payne, Almasy, and Pearson 2015). This protocol was put into place to address an informal police policy known as "rough rides." A rough ride is a form of police brutality where handcuffed individuals are placed in transport vans without being secured by a seatbelt while an officer drives erratically. Rough rides in the Baltimore Police Department have resulted in severe injuries, including paralysis (Donovan and Puente 2015).

A medical examiner completed an autopsy of Gray's body and concluded that his death was a homicide. On May 1, 2015, the officers involved in the arrest and aftermath were charged with second-degree assault by attorney Marilyn Mosby. In addition, all six were charged with involuntary manslaughter, and misconduct in office. Officers were also charged with false imprisonment because they placed Gray under arrest, although he had not committed a crime. Although officers claimed they arrested Gray for illegally possessing a knife, the knife in Gray's possession was not illegal under Baltimore law, and officers were not aware of the knife until after they placed Gray under arrest. The most serious charge, second-degree depraved heart murder—an act in which a defendant is aware that his or her actions could result in death—was filed against Officer Goodson, the driver of the van. The perpetrator is said to have acted with little or no concern for human life. Prosecutors in the case argue that Officer Goodson was implementing a "rough ride" and was aware of the potential harm caused by his actions and should be held responsible for Gray's death. Goodson, Porter, Rice, and White were also charged with involuntary manslaughter.

On May 21, 2015, the officers were indicted by a grand jury—on all charges except the false imprisonment charge. The grand jury also added a reckless endangerment charge to the indictment. Reckless endangerment means that an individual committed an act that had a substantial risk for causing serious physical harm to an individual. On September 2, 2015, a judge decided that each officer would be prosecuted in separate trials. Officer Porter was the first officer brought to trial. His trial began on November 30, 2015. On December 16, 2015, the case resulted in a mistrial because the jury was unable to agree on a verdict. Following the mistrial, a temporary halt was placed on the remaining five trials as courts deliberated on whether compelling Porter to testify against the remaining officers violated his Fifth Amendment right against self-incrimination. In March 2016 the Maryland Court of Appeals ruled that Porter could be compelled to testify so long as his testimony was not used at his subsequent retrial. The six defendants elected to waive their right to a jury trial. A judge found Officer Goodson, Officer Nero, and Lieutenant Rice not guilty of all charges. On July 27, 2016, prosecutors announced they were dismissing charges against the remaining three defendants. In addition to the state investigation into Gray's death, U.S. Attorney General Loretta Lynch claimed the U.S. Department of Justice (DOJ) had begun an investigation into the Baltimore Police Department's unlawful practices that had included illegal searches and seizures and the use of excessive and deadly force. The DOJ was also investigating whether Gray's civil rights had been violated. Gray's family filed a civil lawsuit against the City of Baltimore. The lawsuit was settled for $6.4 million (Stolberg September 8, 2015).

Jennifer M. Ortiz

See also: Deadly Force; Michael Brown Shooting and the Aftermath in Ferguson; Police Brutality; Police Ethics; Tamir Rice Shooting in Cleveland

Further Reading

Cooper, Anderson. "Eyewitness Describes Freddie Gray's Arrest." Anderson Cooper 360, CNN.com. 2015. http://edition.cnn.com/videos/tv/2015/04/23/ac-freddie-gray-witness -speaks-to-anderson-cooper.cnn.

Donovan, Doug, and Mark Puente. "Freddie Gray Not the First to Come Out of Baltimore Police Van with Serious Injuries." *Baltimore Sun*, April 23, 2015. http://www.baltimoresun .com/news/maryland/baltimore-city/bs-md-gray-rough-rides-20150423-story .html#page=1.

Golgowski, Nina. "Freddie Gray Was Arrested 'Without Force' Before Fatal Spine Injury: Baltimore Police." *New York Daily News*, April 21, 2015. http://www.nydailynews.com /news/national/baltimore-man-arrested-force-death-cops-article-1.2192233.

McCoy, Terrence. "Freddie Gray's Life a Study on the Effects of Lead Paint on Poor Blacks." *The Washington Post*, April 29, 2015. https://www.washingtonpost.com/local/freddie -grays-life-a-study-in-the-sad-effects-of-lead-paint-on-poor-blacks/2015/04/29 /0be898e6-eea8-11e4-8abc-d6aa3bad79dd_story.html.

Payne, Ed, Steve Almasy, and Michael Pearson. "Police: We Failed to Get Freddie Gray Timely Medical Care after Arrest." CNN.com, April 24, 2015. http://www.cnn.com/2015/04 /24/us/baltimore-freddie-gray-death.

Rector, Kevin. "The 45-Minute Mystery of Freddie Gray's Death." *Baltimore Sun*, April 25, 2015. http://www.baltimoresun.com/news/maryland/freddie-gray/bs-md-gray-ticker -20150425-story.html.

Stolberg, Sheryl Gay. "Baltimore Enlists National Guard and a Curfew to Fight Riots and Looting." *The New York Times*, April 27, 2015. http://www.nytimes.com/2015/04/28/us /baltimore-freddie-gray.html?_r=0.

Stolberg, Sheryl Gay. "Baltimore Announces $6.4 Million Settlement in the Death of Freddie Gray." *The New York Times*, September 8, 2015. http://www.nytimes.com/2015/09 /09/us/freddie-gray-baltimore-police-death.html.

Wenger, Yvonne, and Colin Campbell. "Baltimore Police Arrest 35, 6 Officers Injured in Protest." *Baltimore Sun*, April 25, 2015. http://www.baltimoresun.com/news/maryland /baltimore-city/bs-md-ci-protest-arrests-20150426-story.html.

Yan, Holly, and Dana Ford. "Baltimore Riots: Looting, Fires Engulf City after Freddie Gray's Funeral." CNN.com, April 28, 2015. http://www.cnn.com/2015/04/27/us/baltimore -unrest.

WALTER SCOTT SHOOTING

On Saturday, April 4, 2015, Walter Scott was driving his Mercedes-Benz sedan when Officer Michael Slager stopped him for a broken tail light (Martinez 2015). The time-line of events caused controversy, as the North Charleston police reports submitted by Officer Slager and backup Officer Habersham differed greatly from eyewitness and video evidence. Officer Slager reported that the encounter occurred around 9:30 a.m. on April 4th. Officer Slager asked Scott for his driver's license, registration, and proof of insurance and proceeded back to his vehicle. As Officer Slager walked back to his police vehicle, Scott exited his vehicle and began to run into a grassy lot. Officer Slager then reported that he pursued Scott, on foot, into a vacant lot behind a pawnshop at 5654 Rivers Avenue (Knapp 2015). It was at this point that the two men engaged in a physical altercation. According to Officer Slager's report, he unsuccessfully tried to deploy his Taser. Scott allegedly grabbed the stun gun in an attempt to use it against Officer Slager. This action caused Officer Slager to feel threatened and led him to reach for his firearm and fire eight shots. Five shots hit and killed Walter Scott. Upon arrival, backup officer Habersham falsely reported that he performed lifesaving measures, but it was too late for Scott.

After Officer Slager's version of the event was released, a witness's cell phone video footage was released that contradicted Officer Slager's explanation of what happened during his encounter with Scott. The dashcam video recording from Officer Slager's vehicle showed him asking Scott for his driving and vehicle documentation and returning to his vehicle (Fantz and Yan 2015). At this moment Scott can be seen running away from his Mercedes. However, an eyewitness, Feidin Santana, was on his way to work when he witnessed Scott and Officer Slager in an intense situation. Santana pulled out his cell phone and started to record the event. This action provided visual clarity of what led up to the actual shooting. Santana took out his phone in time to record Officer Slager and Scott on the ground, with Officer Slager on top of Scott. Santana reported that it did not look like Officer Slager was in fear for his safety, stating that it appeared as if Officer Slager "had control of Scott" (Fantz and Yan 2015). Santana also reported hearing the Taser go off and that it seemed as if Scott was trying to escape to avoid being electrocuted a second time.

As the case unfolded, news reporters claimed that, without the evidence, Officer Slager's account of the event would have probably gone unquestioned. Officer Slager reported that fear was what led to him to fire his weapon. However, the infamous video shows otherwise. The video footage shows that at the moment that Officer Slager fired his weapon, he was in no danger and could not have been in fear for his life. Instead, Officer Slager fired upon a fleeing unarmed man, shooting him in the back.

Shooting an unarmed, fleeing suspect was declared illegal by the U.S. Supreme Court in 1985 (*Tennessee v. Garner*). North Charleston police chief Eddie Driggers publicly declared that he was sickened by what he saw. Santana reported that he did not want to release the video initially out of fear for his life but later changed his mind, deciding it was the right thing to do (Fantz and Yan 2015). Santana's video led not only to the firing of Slager by the North Charleston Police Department but to his arrest and subsequent murder charge.

On June 8, 2015, a South Carolina grand jury indicted Slager on charges of murder (*Los Angeles Times* 2015). On January 4, 2016, Slager was released on a $500,000 bond after being jailed for nine months without bail. Slager's trial was scheduled for October 31, 2016 (Schoichet and Friedman 2016). On December 5, 2016, a mistrial was declared. The prosecution plans to seek a new trial. Police records indicate Slager was no stranger to problems; during his tenure as an officer he was involved in 19 uses-of-force incidents. Of the 19 incidents, 14 involved the use of a Taser (Blinder and Williams 2015). However, Slager never fired his handgun while on patrol, until the Scott case.

The police shooting of Scott sparked several conversations. The first was the local conversation protesting the North Charleston Police Department. Protestors called for the resignation of Chief Driggers, and the National Bar Association called for the firing and indictment of Officer Habersham for filing a false report (Blinder and Fernandez 2015). Peaceful protestors were also seen wearing t-shirts declaring "Black Lives Matter" and "Stop Killing Us." Police nationwide linked this to the second conversation regarding the oppression of African American males. Walter Scott's murder occurred in the wake of the Eric Garner and Michael Brown killings. On July 17, 2014, Garner was killed by New York City police officer Daniel Pantaleo in Staten Island, New York, because of an illegal chokehold. Garner was arrested on charges of illegally selling cigarettes, but he resisted arrest. On August 9, 2014, Police Officer Darren Wilson, from Ferguson, Missouri, shot and killed unarmed Michael Brown. Eyewitnesses claimed that Brown was holding his hands high in the air in surrender. Brown was apprehended as a robbery suspect and was also resisting arrest.

Although all of these cases involved resistance on the part of the victim, public outcry from North Charleston and around the country claimed that police systematically use excess force and racially biased tactics against African American males. The public outcry sparked taking the Black Lives Matter Movement to the streets. This movement began in response to the civilian killing of 17-year-old Trayvon Martin by 29-year-old George Zimmerman on February 12, 2012 (Shor 2015). Although the shooter was not a police officer, initially the Sanford, Florida, police did not make an arrest because there was no evidence to refute Zimmerman's self-defense claim under Florida's stand your ground law. However, mass media scrutiny and public outcry pressured the police to arrest Zimmerman. Public protest centered on the racial profiling allowed by and practiced by the police in this case. The Black Lives Matter Movement was borne out of massive protesting and advocacy to treat African Americans with equity and respect. It was in response to the police killings of unarmed African American males that the Black Lives Matters Movement refocused more directly on police tactics.

The Black Lives Matters movement calls for police transparency. Had it not been for the video recording of the killing of Walter Scott, many speculated that Officer Slager would have gotten away with his crime. This speaks to the third conversation of police accountability and surveillance. Since the recording of the Los Angeles police beating of Rodney King and the increased use of cell phone technology and social media, the public has recorded and distributed many police interactions with civilians. However, research has found that police tend to become frustrated and discontent with citizens who engage in this practice, and the more bothered they are with the idea of recording the police, the more likely the police are to side with the recorded officer who is being accused of abuse (Kopak 2014).

Abuses by police have incited activists to call for greater surveillance of law enforcement in the form of body cameras. In response to the death of Walter Scott, the South Carolina legislature passed a bill requiring police departments to equip themselves with body cameras. Research has revealed that police question the effectiveness of body cameras to successfully aid prosecution and claim that they encroach on police discretion (Young and Ready 2015). Regardless of the reasons for resistance, officers who are not wearing body cameras often adopt the negative perceptions of those who are wearing the camera. These negative perceptions tend to have an adverse effect on police-public relations.

The fourth conversation that was sparked in the wake of the Walter Scott murder, as well as the Brown and Garner killings, was whether this would increase police-public conflict and ultimately decrease police presence. This is known as the "Ferguson effect" (Wolfe and Nix 2016). The Ferguson effect states that police will be reluctant to interact with the public for fear of being recorded and of being accused of racial profiling and abuse. This reluctance results in de-policing, which subsequently increases crime within their jurisdiction. Although the media and some scholars have claimed that the Ferguson effect has occurred, to date, there is no empirical evidence to support these claims. Furthermore, Wolfe and Nix (2016) found that while police are reluctant to partner with the community, this is tempered when supervisors ensure fair treatment. Regardless of police perceptions of the use of cameras and their willingness to interact with the communities under their jurisdiction, one cannot argue that the legitimacy of the police organization is being questioned.

Venessa Garcia and M'Balu Bangura

See also: Body Cameras; Dashcam Videos; Deadly Force; Eric Garner Case in New York City and Subsequent Tensions; Fleeing Felon Legislation; Michael Brown Shooting and the Aftermath in Ferguson; Perceptions of Police Today; Police Accountability; Police Brutality; Racial Profiling; Rodney King Beating and Riots; Trayvon Martin Shooting; Use of Tasers

Further Reading

Blinder, Alan, and Manny Fernandez. "North Charleston Prepares for Mourning and Protest in Walter Scott Shooting." *The New York Times*, April 11, 2015. http://www.nytimes.com/2015/04/11/us/north-charleston-prepares-for-weekend-of-mourning-and-protest-in-walter-scott-shooting.html.

Blinder, Alan, and Timothy Williams. "Ex-South Carolina Officer Is Indicted in Shooting Death of Black Man." CNN.com, June 2015. https://www.google.com/amp/s/amp.cnn.com/cnn/2016/05/11/us/north-charleston-police-michael-slager-indicted-walter-scott-shooting/index.html.

Fantz, Ashley, and Holly Yan. "Dash Cam Video Shows the Moments Before South Carolina Police Shooting." CNN.com, April 9, 2015. http://www.cnn.com/2015/04/09/us/south-carolina-police-shooting.

Knapp, Andrew. "Attorney: North Charleston Police Officer Felt Threatened Before Fatal Shooting." *Post and Courier*, April 2015. http://postandcourier.com/archives/lawyer-officer-reacted-to-threat/article_9ab8b977-23de-569e-99db-bb74ff1e7df0.html.

Kopak, A. "Lights, Cameras, Action: A Mixed Methods Analysis of Police Perceptions of Citizens Who Video Record Officers in the Line of Duty in the United States." *International Journal of Criminal Justice Sciences* 9 (2014): 225–240.

Los Angeles Times. "Indictment Against Michael Thomas Slager." June 8, 2015. http://documents.latimes.com/indictment-against-michael-thomas-slager.

Martinez, Michael. "South Carolina Cop Shoots Unarmed Man: A Timeline." CNN.com, April 9, 2015. http://www.cnn.com/2015/04/08/us/south-carolina-cop-shoots-black-man-timeline.

Shoichet, Catherine E., and Chandler Friedman. "Walther Scott Case: Michael Slager Released from Jail after Posting Bond." CNN.com, January 5, 2016. http://www.cnn.com/2016/01/04/us/south-carolina-michael-slager-bail.

Shor, Francis. "'Black Lives Matter': Constructing a New Civil Rights and Black Freedom Movement." *New Politics* 15 (215): 28–32.

Tennessee v Garner, 471 U.S. 1, 3. (1985).

Wolfe, Scott E., and Justin Nix. "The Alleged 'Ferguson Effect' and Police Willingness to Engage in Community Partnership." *Law and Human Behavior* 40 (2016): 1–10.

Young, Jacob T. N., and Justin T. Ready. "Diffusion of Ideas and Technology: The Role of Networks in Influencing the Endorsement and Use of On-Officers Video Cameras." *Journal of Contemporary Criminal Justice* 31 (2015): 243–261.

SANDRA BLAND DEATH IN TEXAS

Sandra Annette Bland was born February 7, 1987, to Geneva Real-Veal of Chicago, Illinois. On July 10, 2015, Bland was pulled over in Prairie View, Texas, by Texas State Trooper Brian Encinia for failure to signal while changing lanes. Upon initiating the traffic stop, Encinia asked Bland to "put out her cigarette." When she refused to comply with this directive, he instructed her to exit the vehicle. After she refused to get out of her vehicle, Encinia attempted to physically remove her from the vehicle. Then, after his inability to remove her from the vehicle, he drew his Taser and threatened to use the device on her if she did not get out of the vehicle. Once she exited the vehicle, there was some exchange of words between the two, which ultimately resulted in Bland being handcuffed and eventually arrested. Three days following her arrest, Bland was found dead in her Waller County jail cell with a garbage bag over her head.

Focusing on the elements of police procedures, many have questioned if the initial traffic stop was necessary. Or was it an act of police harassment based on racial profiling? Another questionable element of police behavior that emerged from the traffic stop is that of Encinia's "use of force." Many speculate about the amount of force (verbal and physical) Encinia used to get Bland to comply with his directives. A final element in question was the justification of the arrest.

Bland had recently returned to Prairie View, Texas, to start a new job at Prairie View A&M University from which she had previously graduated. Prior to starting her new job, she was pulled over on FM 1098 by a Texas state trooper for failure

On July 10, 2015, Sandra Bland was pulled over by a Texas state trooper. Three days later she was found hanged in her jail cell. Her death was ruled a suicide. About one thousand activists rallied in Brooklyn, honoring the life of Sandra Bland exactly one year after the African American woman died in police custody at the age of 28. (Erik Mcgregor/Pacific Press/LightRocket via Getty Images)

to signal while changing lanes. Texas State Trooper Encinia approached Bland's vehicle on the passenger side and stated the reason for the traffic stop. She provided him with the necessary documentation allowed to operate a motor vehicle in the state of Texas, and he returned to his patrol car. While in his patrol car, Encinia verified Bland's identity, issued her a warning, and then returned to his vehicle. The traffic stop was valid.

Law enforcement officers are given a considerable amount of discretion. However, the public opposition to the traffic stop based on racial profiling as an act of police harassment has not been validated. Early detection, intervention, and training strategies for problematic officers has been found to be an effective way for dealing with officers who are suspected of misconduct. This early detection, intervention, and training would have been useful in this incident only if Trooper Encinia had had a record of disproportionately detaining people of color for moving violations that warranted an intervention or other types of ethical issues.

In returning to Bland's vehicle, Encinia began to ask her about her demeanor before providing her with a warning. This unrelated line of questioning is known as a detention tactic to prolong the traffic stop. Encinia commented on Bland's agitation level, and then exploited her response to prolong the stop. This detention tactic proved to be effective for Encinia when Bland responded to the trooper's line of questioning in an unfavorable position against the officer. Bland explained her frustration with the traffic stop and with the trooper. Encinia was then able to determine that Bland was agitated, and he was able to continue the detention tactic through the inquiry of more unrelated questioning. Or he may have ended the detention tactic and moved on to direct command or requested to elicit more negative responses from Bland.

Trooper Encinia opted to move toward making a direct request, and he requested Bland to put out her cigarette. She, in turn, refused to put out her cigarette, and when she provided Encinia with the reason as to why she was not going to put her cigarette, the nature of the traffic stop changed. Encinia asked her to step out of the vehicle, and Bland refused. Then, Encinia called for female cover because he decided Bland was noncompliant, and he was going to remove her from her vehicle.

He later was indicted on perjury charges for making false statements in his arrest report. In the report, Trooper Encinia had claimed that he "had Bland exit the vehicle to further conduct a safe traffic investigation," as opposed to documenting the interaction consistent with police procedures and the video footage taken from the Trooper's dashboard camera. Once this video was released to the public, his behavior had planted a seed of deception for the public as well as the police department. Trooper Encinia was placed on administrative leave for failing to follow proper traffic stop procedures.

The manner in which Encinia removed Bland has been scrutinized. Encinia was accused of using excessive force. Improper use of force occurs when officers use force that is disproportionate to the situation at hand. It is also governed by the "use of force continuum," which links the level of police force with the resistance of the victim. According to this criterion, the dashboard camera, footage and the voice recording of the encounter, it was evident that Trooper Encinia used unnecessary force in trying to control this situation. The gender and size differences were grounds for the public agreement.

The interaction between Bland and Encinia outside of her vehicle was provided as the basis for her arrest. Trooper Encinia stated in his report that Bland had kicked him in his shin. Parts of the interaction between the two individuals were recorded through the trooper's dashboard camera. Bland was thus arrested for assaulting a public servant. Three days later on July 13, 2015, she was found hanging in her cell with a plastic bag around her neck. Her death was ruled a suicide.

Georgen Guerrero and Doshie Piper

See also: Police Accountability; Police Brutality; Racial Profiling; Use of Tasers

Further Reading

Barnum, C., J. Miller, and G. Miller. "An Evaluation of an Observational Benchmark Used in Assessing Disproportionality in Police Traffic Stops: A Research Note." *Policing* 9, no. 4 (2015): 405–417.

Crockett, Stephen A., Jr. "Sandra Bland Drove to Texas to Start a New Job, so How Did She End Up Dead in Jail?" The Root, July 16, 2015. http://www.theroot.com/articles/news

/2015/07/sandra_bland_drove_to_texas_to_start_a_new_job_so_how_did_she_end
up_dead.html.

Giroux, Henry. "Taking Notes 48," America's New Brutalism: The Death of Sandra Bland."
Philosophers for Change, July 28, 2015. https://philosophersforchange.org/2015/07/28
/taking-notes-48-americas-new-brutalism-the-death-of-sandra-bland.

Ridgeway, G. "Assessing the Effect of Race Bias in Post-traffic Stop Outcomes Using Pro-
pensity Scores." *Journal of Quantitative Criminology* 22, no. 1 (2006): 1–29.

Solomon, Dan. "Brian Encinia Charged with Perjury in Sandra Bland's Case." *Texas Monthly*,
January 8, 2016. http://www.texasmonthly.com/the-daily-post/why-a-perjury-charge
-for-the-officer-who-arrested-sandra-bland-falls-short-of-justice.

Walker, S. "Searching for the Denominator: Problems with Police Traffic Stop Data and an
Early Warning System Solution." *Justice Research and Policy* 3, no. 1 (2001): 63–96.

USE OF TASERS

The use of Tasers has been adopted by law enforcement and other defense markets
as an effective and less-lethal form of technology to neutralize unlawful and potentially dangerous situations. A type of electronic control weapon (ECW) or conducted
energy device (CED) that is in the same category as stun guns and stun belts, the Taser
disrupts normal bodily functions by triggering involuntary muscle contractions,
thereby causing the target to fall to the ground. Once subdued, the threatening
situation is neutralized and the target may be more easily apprehended by law
enforcement.

The name "Taser," which is actually an acronym for Thomas A. Swift Electric
Rifle, was adapted from the 1911 novel of a similar name, *Tom Swift and His Electric
Rifle*, by Victor Appleton. The Taser was originally developed by an aerospace scientist and professor named John Higson Cover, Jr., and was later modified in collaboration with inventor and entrepreneur Rick Smith. The original device created by
John (more commonly known as "Jack") used gunpowder as a propellant. The
central modification to the device was the replacement of gunpowder with nitrogen, which removed it from the firearm category.

Prior to the advent of widespread firearm use, police readily adopted less-lethal
weaponry such as batons. In the 1990s through the 2010s, however, there was been
a resurgence in the interest and ultimate use of this form of response to alleged
criminal activity. Most notably are devices that restrict physical movement or interrupt the senses and effectively diffuse an otherwise volatile situation. This form of
technology includes devices that propel objects such as bean bags or rubber bullets,
or gasses such as pepper spray. It also includes those that use the force of water or
viscosity of foamy substances to restrict freedom of movement. Finally, there are
also devices that temporarily challenge the senses and emit objectionable odors,
bright or otherwise visually disruptive lighting, and sounds that are uncomfortable
to the ears.

The overriding interest in of this type of technology has been generated by a concern for the use of excessive force to apprehend individuals suspected of criminal
activity. Ranging from the least extreme of minimal force to the most extreme of

deadly force, the Taser has been hailed as a safer and more humane method by law enforcement. Although the level of force associated with this form of technology may not be considered by some to be minimal or even non-lethal, it is generally viewed as effective and less-lethal, as it lies more at the "minimal" end of the force continuum. The need for safer, yet effective, methods of enforcing the law is paramount, not only on a humanitarian basis but also as a legal mandate. In basic terms, the U.S. Supreme Court held in *Tennessee v. Garner* (1985) that lethal force may be used against a suspect only in situations where that individual poses an immediate threat to public safety. Over the years, further evolutions and limitations of this holding followed, as subsequent court interpretations of the Fourth Amendment considered the development of associated technologies and continued legal challenges.

CEDs work by emitting large amounts of electrical volts designed to stun the recipient and cause involuntary muscle contractions that lead to unsteadiness. The individual will typically and inevitably collapse to the ground and be subject to easier apprehension. The two basic modes of Taser operation are through drive stun and dart. In drive stun mode, the officer must place the device directly against the body of the individual. The contacting part of the device has two exposed electrodes that permit the passage of an electrical current through the body. Although substantial, the current is isolated to the general area of the precise place of contact. The officer controls the frequency of electrical discharges as well as when it will cease. Although the discharge emanated through this mode may arguably be less distressing to the subject than its projective alternative, the effective operation is limited only to situations where the officer may be in direct contact with the suspect. In dart mode, the Taser delivers the electrical current through a dart-like object propelled by highly compressed nitrogen that is aimed at the subject. Although there are currently wireless versions of this technology, the most widely used varieties have the projectile connected to the Taser by very thin wires that carry the electrical current to be delivered.

In order for the dart mode device to be most effective, it must be deployed properly. A proper deployment of the projected device requires that the contacts be separated when they connect to the body. The separation enables the passing of the electrical current through the body. Many Tasers are equipped with laser guides that facilitate a more accurate aim. Those that are equipped with one laser, will focus the primary aim on one of the conductors while the other is designed to automatically project a standardized and effective distance from the other. Those that are equipped with two lasers will permit the officer to individually gauge the distance between each dart.

The usual contact lasts approximately 5 to 15 seconds in duration and is typically not associated with any contraindications other than momentary extreme physical pain and increased heart rate to the average healthy person. However, this technology is not without potential risks, namely the risks associated with an involuntary fall. Such an unguarded collapse may result in head or other injury, or even potential death. Furthermore, as the general health of the subject may be unknown at the time of the event, a less healthy individual could experience a heightened risk of injuries such as cardiac arrest. In such a situation, although highly dependent upon the attending circumstances and other related matters, the force could be potentially lethal.

Many factors influence the effective use of Tasers. Specifically, efficiency may be subject to the training of the officer who employs its use, the personal characteristics of the individual subject to the forceful action, and the officer's evaluation of attending circumstances. The evaluation may include an assessment of the immediate danger, level of resistance, and any applicable regulations or policies. Consistent with established legal interpretation, the level of force associated with the use of a Taser must be reasonable in light of the presented level of danger. Simply put, if the level of danger dictates a degree of force less than the level of the Taser, the Taser may not be lawfully discharged. The operator may only use a less forceful means to subdue the subject. Furthermore, should the resistance level of the suspect not elevate to where the use of a Taser would be justified, its use would be considered unreasonable. In sum, although highly dependent upon the facts associated with the particular situation, there needs to be an increased level of resistance in order to justify the use of a Taser.

Various administrative policies have been established that dictate permissible usage by an authorized operator. For example, the Federal Law Enforcement Training Center has developed a use-of-force model that specifies when one may employ the use of a Taser. According to the model, technology such as a Taser may be considered only when the officer is confronted with a minimum of active resistance on the part of the subject. Although this and other such models and policies may be adopted, each situation is unique and must comply with the reasonableness standard established through the U.S. Supreme Court's constitutional interpretations.

In general, the Taser has been so widely adopted by law enforcement because it is deemed effective. Although any such level of force is not without issue, its use has been associated with an overall decrease in injuries to both officer and subject. In addition, it is also not readily subject to collateral or unintended effect to others (including the operator). Pepper spray, for example, may be subject to an inadvertent overspray, or it may blow back toward the user during operation.

Regardless of the touted efficiency, its use is not foolproof and its intended outcome in a given situation is not guaranteed. For example, the officer is prevented from using the drive stun mode unless within a close proximity to the suspect where the necessary contact may be achieved. Hence, under circumstances where the individual maintains a distance from the officer, its application may be much less effective. Also, the effectiveness may be compromised in situations where the suspect is offering an active resistance or other physical impediment to submission. In dart mode, the operator may miss the intended target or be effectively disarmed by the suspect. If the targeted area of contact for either dart is restricted by an obstruction, surrounded by very loose fitting clothing, or if the darts are not adequately spaced apart, the effectiveness may be compromised. Furthermore, unlike its more recent wireless counterpart, a wired dart mode unit requires the discharge to take place at a relatively short distance from the target. Finally, regardless of the mode (as with any technological device), its effectiveness is always subject to the actions of the operator, mechanical defect, or failure in proper operation.

The use of Tasers is widely criticized by many, including public advocacy groups such as the American Civil Liberties Union, NAACP, Amnesty International, and the National Lawyers Guild. Its critics suggest an undue reliance by departments and subsequent overuse by operators when less forceful means may be alternatively available. These groups contend that repeated use on a given subject also carries an increased risk of resulting injuries such as cardiac conditions that could include a dangerously elevated heart rate, heart attack, or even death. They also allege overuse by citing instances in which Tasers have been used on restrained persons, pregnant women, children, and the elderly. Conversely, however, criticism has also been generated by those who insist that an event may have ultimately benefited from the use of a less lethal level of force. Such critics contend that the availability and use of a Taser or similar device may prove to be a much-preferred alternative to what may ultimately result in a lethal outcome.

In general, the parameters of the lawful use of Tasers remain somewhat inconsistent and uncertain, as there are no uniform laws that delineate applicable guidelines for law enforcement. Some contend that such uniformity is unrealistic, as each situation is unique in its surrounding circumstances, including the officer, alleged criminal activity, assessment of the potential threat, as well as the known and unknown attributes of the suspect, and so on. Others suggest that despite any such actual or perceived limitations, uniformity is necessary in order to ensure proper use. In the absence of applicable unifying laws, there has been a reliance on court rulings, legislative mandates, and departmental policies.

The court rulings regarding Taser use stemmed from *Graham v. Connor* (1989), in which the U.S. Supreme Court set forth criteria for balancing the authority of the officer with the rights of the suspect. In sum, proper and lawful use requires a balance of suspect resistance, criminal activity alleged, and threat to the officer. When practicable in assessing the situation, the officer should use the least force necessary to control the situation. Therefore, the level of force associated with CEDs may be excessive when the level of resistance dictates that verbal commands, control techniques such as wrestling the suspect to the ground, or similar methods may likely be effective. Conversely, CED use may be reasonable and appropriate where such less-forceful methods would objectively seem futile. Furthermore, the threat associated with the altercation must be immediate and substantial enough to justify the level of force associated with the Taser. Since the *Graham* decision, courts have further explored this issue and increasingly enlarged the scope of considerations. Regardless, the overall concern remains to match (as closely as practical) the level of force associated with the confrontation to the level of force needed to defuse and control it under the particular circumstances.

Guidelines for Taser use have also been sought on the state level. However, for a multitude of reasons, states largely remain silent on the issue. The lack of legislative mandates may stem from the inevitable complexity associated with each unique situation, the vast range of considerations potentially involved, and the overall lack of specificity and subsequent generalizability of the existing court rulings on the subject. Most notably, Florida and Georgia reign among the few states that have legislatively provided any form of statutory guidance on this issue. New Jersey, on the other hand, stands alone in its complete ban on any such use by both law enforcement and members of the public.

Over the years, some police departments have developed their own policies for the proper and effective use of Tasers. The protocols may be formal as in a written policy or informal through departmental practices and procedures. However, these protocols are typically individualized and lack any universal homogeneity.

In sum, the existing guidelines for the proper use of CEDs such as Tasers lack uniformity and specificity. As a result, there is no clear or definitive consensus as to the acceptable use and proper application of this popular device. Members of law enforcement, public advocacy groups, and the public remain divided by the use and suspected misuse of this form of technology. Some suggest that as long as the ultimate determination of constitutionality lies with the Judiciary, in the circumstances surrounding each event, and the discretion of the officer involved, the uncertainty and lack of universal guidelines will likely persist.

Taser use by police has been popularized by the need for a safer and more effective means of law enforcement. Although it has its staunch critics, its use has been attributed to an overall reduction in injuries for both police and subjects. Recently, a new design of Tasers has been developed. It is equipped with cameras that automatically record the details of each event. The results provided by this update expect to potentially aid both law enforcement and public advocates in a viable discussion and debate on the lawfulness of its continued use. Nonetheless, for the near future, Tasers are believed to remain a popular tool for law enforcement. As the related technology continues to evolve consistent with the needs of those involved in its application, the devices are likely to remain in widespread use. Otherwise or because of a more appropriate and viable alternative, police will employ the use of a different device or tactic in order to achieve its law enforcement goals.

Thomas Lateano

See also: Deadly Force; Fourth Amendment; Police Ethics

Further Reading

Appleton, Victor. *Tom Swift and His Electric Rifle (Or Daring Adventures in Elephant Land)*. New York: Grosset & Dunlap, 1911; reprinted by Kesinger Publishing, 2007.

Cronin, James M., and Joshua A. Ederheimer. "Conducted Energy Devices: Development of Standards for Consistency and Guidance." Washington, DC: U.S. Department of Justice, Office of Community Oriented Policing Services and Police Executive Research Forum, 2006.

Ready, Justin, Michael D. White, and Christopher Fisher. "Shock Value: A Comparative Analysis of News Reports and Official Police Records on TASER Deployments." *Policing: An International Journal of Police Strategies & Management* 31, no. 1 (2008): 148–170.

Smith, Michael R., Matthew Petrocelli, and Charlie Scheer. "Excessive Force, Civil Liability, and the Taser in the Nation's Courts: Implications for Law Enforcement Policy and Practice." *Policing: An International Journal of Police Strategies & Management* 30, no. 3 (2007): 398–422.

Sousa, William, Justin Ready, and Michael Ault. "The Impact of TASERs on Police Use-of-Force Decisions: Findings from a Randomized Field-Training Experiment." *Journal of Experimental Criminology* 6, no. 1 (2010): 35–55.

Thomas, Kyle J., Peter A. Collins, and Nicholas P. Lovrich. "Conducted Energy Device Use in Municipal Policing: Results of a National Survey on Policy and Effectiveness Assessments." *Police Quarterly* 13, no. 3 (2010): 290–315.

White, Michael D., and Justin Ready. "The TASER as a less Lethal Force Alternative Findings on Use and Effectiveness in a Large Metropolitan Police Agency." *Police Quarterly* 10, no. 2 (2007): 170–191.

POLICE ETHICS

Ethics refer to the unwritten rules that govern behavior in different situations and circumstances. Ethical behavior is influenced by many things, such as the characteristics of the people involved and the context of the situation. This produces a wide range of standards, and it is a complex undertaking to try to make sense of it all. In policing, ethical concerns arise in many areas, including racial profiling, police use of force, recruitment practices, and the sheer stress associated with police work.

Ethics are important at two levels—organizational and individual. At the individual level, officers are constantly considering different ways of responding to situations, as no two situations are the same. Even when situations appear to be similar, the characteristics of the individuals involved might be different. And if the individuals have similarities, differences may occur in the location of the incident, time of the day, type of bystanders and their expectations, and so forth. At the organizational level, departmental policies may specify ethical behavior, yet officers have the discretion to choose what to do when there is no express policy statement.

Whether on or off duty, an officer has to be conscious of the decisions that may have ethical implications. For example, officers are offered goodies and freebies by businesses from time to time. They may be offered free lunch at a restaurant, free tickets to a movie theater, or coupons for merchandise at discounted prices. Although there is nothing inherently wrong with accepting such offers, the offers have a potential to turn into corruption in advance. For example, a restaurant owner who gives an officer the favor of a free lunch might expect the officer to remember the favor and not issue a speeding citation to the restaurant owner later on. If the department is silent on whether to accept such offers or not, officers are left to make the decision about whether acceptance of the offer is ethical or not. Some people argue that offering donations to police officers is justified by the importance of the services they provide to the community. However, other people argue that the donations are not genuine as they are based on expectations of future reciprocation by the officer. They argue that absence of such expectation from other professions is the reason that similar offers are not extended to those professions.

Police Discretion

The term "discretion" means the freedom to decide what to do when there are multiple alternatives. Police officers and other law enforcement officials have a wide range of discretion when dealing with criminal suspects. They can choose to turn the other way and ignore the suspect, issue only a verbal warning, frisk and let go, arrest, or even shoot, depending on the circumstances and the seriousness of the alleged offense. Because of the many choices police have, they are compelled to exercise a great deal of ethical standards. For instance, suppose an officer stops a motorist suspected to be driving while intoxicated. Suppose also that, as the officer draws nearer, it turns out that the motorist is a family member of the officer. Should the officer give a citation or let the driver go? Or suppose one of the officers responding to a road accident observes another officer pickpocketing the accident victim. Should the officer report the observation or cover up the pickpocketing officer and hope to receive a reciprocal favor in the future? These are some of the ethical dilemmas that police officers often face.

Police Brutality

One of the biggest complaints against the police is the use of excessive force—brutality—against criminal suspects. Police brutality occurs when officers use more force than is required to successfully arrest a suspect. When there is no threat to life or property, the normal practice for the officer is to begin at the lowest level of force including benign acts such as issuing verbal commands. The officer is to escalate force according to the resistance of the suspect. If necessary, the officer is to apply physical force including pepper spraying or a hit with a baton in order to subdue the suspect. If the suspect gives spirited resistance, the officer should escalate the amount of force to non-lethal, which may include the use of electroshocking weapons such as stun guns and Tasers. Only when the suspect poses a real threat would the officer use lethal force (firearms). Even then, the desirable outcome is to arrest the suspect alive. Ethical questions revolve around the legality of using more force than necessary, especially because it is incumbent upon the officer to correctly judge the nature and amount of the force to use.

Media and Police Use of Force

It is difficult to ignore the media's response when police use of force is questioned. When an officer uses the right amount of force, it is not as newsworthy, especially if there is no lethal force. However, if the officer opens fire, the attention of the media is called upon and public sensitization of use of lethal force is enhanced. This is when legality and ethical bases begin to be questioned. The ethical concerns in police use of excessive force gains even more currency partly due to the role police embody as custodians of authority and the fact that the public's focus on police activities is stronger than the attention given to most other professions.

The police are legally entitled to use force, in the first place. The proper exercise of this legal entitlement requires high moral principles and the likelihood of its abuse is high. Brutality and violent activities, whether by the police or civilians, attracts more media attention than the mundane day-to-day happenings. The media focus on a single act of brutality by a single officer opens the entire police organization to questions about their integrity, akin to the old adage that a single rotten apple spoils the entire basket. There are many aspects of police misconduct associated with use of force. They include false arrest (putting a person into custody without probable cause), sexual abuse, corruption, racial profiling, and "Peeping Tom" acts (illegal surveillance for personal pleasure), among others. The ethical concerns of these forms of behavior arise from the fact that the police have more opportunities than the civilian population to engage in such vices, and that many of these acts are performed as part of law enforcement.

Racial Profiling

Quite often, the process of law enforcement dictates that the police must stop individuals they have probable cause to believe been involved in a crime. The police also stop individuals who are on the police watch list for other reasons, such as prior escape from custody, previous evasion of arrest, or fitting the description of a wanted suspect. In stopping individuals in these categories, police officers are to avoid a pattern of stopping only individuals with predictable social demographic characteristics such as race, ethnicity, religion, or even social economic status. Officers have been blamed for stopping and frisking members of racial minority groups, especially African American males, preponderantly more than other racial and gender groups. This has been particularly true of minority drivers. Racial profiling occurs when the police stop members of certain racial groups more than their fair share in relation to the composition of the population.

A controversy occurs in relation to why minorities are disproportionately stopped by the police. Here is some background data to consider: a car that has dysfunctional features, such as broken tail lights, is eligible for a police stop. Older cars are more likely to have dysfunctional features than newer cars. People who drive older cars generally tend to fall into the lower social economic category. This category is composed of people with lower educational attainments and lower-paying jobs. Historical facts suggest that members of minority groups have generally lower educational attainment than the mainstream Caucasian population, have lower-paying jobs, and are therefore more likely to drive older and less-functional vehicles.

Two main ethical concerns arise regarding the disproportional police stop of members of ethnic minority and racial groups. The first is if minority groups are economically disadvantaged and therefore drive vehicles that are more eligible for police stops, should the police not consider the double disadvantage of the minority groups? If the police should treat everyone equally as the law mandates, is the stop of a driver of the dysfunctional vehicle not based or on the economic status of the driver? The second ethical concern is whether the officer stops a dysfunctional vehicle and finds later that the driver is a racial minority person, or whether the officer notices the race of the driver and then decides to initiate the stop. Those who support the police in this controversy argue that the officer notices the dysfunctional vehicle first and later learns that the driver is a racial or ethnic minority person. Those who think that police officers seize the opportunity to disproportionately stop racial and ethnic minority groups argue that the police must first notice the driver before making the decision to initiate the stop, citing the fact that there are many Caucasian drivers with equally dysfunctional vehicles on the roads.

Overall, the ethics involved in racial profiling are more important than whether the officer sees the condition of the vehicle before the driver. The question is, why would the totality of circumstances invariably produce a disproportionate number of stops for ethnic and racial minority groups? Research has suggested that hiring of more minority officers may help to alleviate the disproportionate stop and even arrest of members of ethnic and racial minorities. However, there is also research that demonstrates that police are more likely to stop and arrest members of their own racial groups than they are to stop and arrest members of other racial groups. This practice is used by officers who hope to stay away from complaints of racial discrimination. Regardless of the ethnic or racial background of the arresting officer, the ethical question of why there are disproportionate numbers of ethnic and racial minority stops still remains relevant.

Affirmative Action in Police Recruitment

Affirmative action describes policies that remedy underrepresentation of groups of people especially in employment and educational opportunities. Under these policies, underrepresented groups are allocated a specified number of places free of competition from the mainstream society. Affirmative action represents reverse discrimination. Policing in America has been a preserve of White men since time immemorial. Minorities and women are yet to reach equal representation to White men. Even with affirmative action, eligible members of minority communities are often reluctant to join policing. After years of race-sensitive policing, minorities may feel that joining policing amounts to betraying their own racial and ethnic groups. This has hindered the efforts to diversify police departments and justified the use of affirmative action even more.

There are many ethical questions about the use of affirmative action when many qualified and interested candidates happen to be White men. The main question is, why should a department continue to keep an open position for applicants with specific characteristics while there are ready candidates to take up the position? This question places police recruiters between a rock and a hard place. If they drop affirmative action and focus only on basic eligibility, they risk continued wrath of the community for fair representation. If they maintain the quota system, they risk complaints of reverse discrimination by qualified candidates for whom quotas have already been filled.

Stress in Policing and Associated Ethics

Police work is one of the most demanding careers. Although police officers command considerable amounts of authority, what is least known about policing is that it generates tremendous amounts of strain and causes untold amounts of stress. Stress in police work comes from many sources. The most common of these is the fear of the unknown. Consider that most people begin their daily routines with little or no concern that they might not return home, alive, at the end of the day. For police officers, though, the fear of not returning at the end of their shift and what would happen to their loved ones if they don't is real. This is amplified by the fact that many officers have witnessed their colleagues die in the line of duty or know a former colleague who did not survive what may have started off as an ordinary day. Others have survived major attacks in which they cheated death by a whisker. Living with these fears is not only stressful, but can cause post-traumatic stress disorder (PTSD) with symptoms such as distressing flashbacks, nightmares, sleeplessness, detachment, and loss of interest in ordinary activities.

In addition, police work involves witnessing and seeing human beings at their worst vulnerability. The police are first responders at horrifying scenes including scenes of aggravated criminal behavior, grisly road accidents, and other dreadful emergencies—both natural and human-induced. The police therefore witness victims who have critical and fatal injuries and see human beings as they breathe their last. Moreover, police work itself involves using deadly force sometimes and ending human life, and then handling the bodies of the victims. For many people, witnessing excessive human suffering is both horrifying and stress-inducing. Exposing police officers to these experiences on an ongoing basis is even more horrifying and has a higher likelihood of causing PTSD and its long-lasting effects.

Another common source of police stress is the feeling that they are not making the difference in society that they hoped to make when they entered the profession. This is exacerbated by a parallel feeling that their efforts are not appreciated by the society and even when they are appreciated, they get only lukewarm support. These feelings become even more pronounced because by virtue of being the custodians of authority, officers attract more public attention than most other professions. As a result, when one participates in misconduct, the misconduct easily reverberates through the society and the public attitude toward the entire police force plummets.

Understanding the nature and extent of police stress is important, as it helps us understand in a deeper sense why some officers may sometimes engage in unethical or even irrational behavior. This may also help us approach unethical conduct by officers with restrained criticism and sometimes with compassion. It is likely that the mention of public compassion toward the police will introduce another dimension of ethics and raise fresh questions of whether the public should indeed sympathize with the police. Many supporters of public sympathy toward the police argue that police officers are human beings before they are officers and need to be shown compassion that any other person deserves. Others argue that police service is so important and yet so risky that public support toward the police must be cultivated. Many also argue that the police risk their lives to keep us safe and are therefore deserving of the public support.

Opponents of public support toward the police argue that policing is a job like any other, and that people who do not have the stamina to stand the demands of the job should simply quit. They also argue that the choice to join policing is voluntary, as are most other jobs. People who maintain this position question why police officers should expect preferential treatment by the public while nurses, teachers, lawyers, clergy, and so forth, do not expect any special attention from the public.

Jospeter Mbuba

See also: Corruption; Deadly Force; Police Brutality; PTSD and Family Issues among Officers; Racial Profiling; Use of Tasers

Further Reading

Culhane, S. E., J. H. Boman, and K. Schweitzer. "Public Perceptions of the Justifiability of Police Shootings: The Role of Body Cameras in a Pre- and Post-Ferguson Experiment." *Police Quarterly* 19, no. 3: 251–274.

Jackson, R. "If They Gunned Me Down and Criming While White." *Cultural Studies/ Critical Methodologies* 16, no. 3 (2016): 313–319.

Lott Jr., J. R. "Does a Helping Hand Put Others at Risk? Affirmative Action, Police Departments, and Crime." *Economic Inquiry* 38, no. 2 (2000): 239.

Maran, D. A., A. Varetto, M. Zedda, and V. Ieraci. "Occupational stress, anxiety and coping strategies in police officers." *Occupational Medicine* 65, no. 6 (2015): 466–473.

Mbuba, J. M. "Do Members of Racial Minority Groups Have an Affinity With Serious Crimes? An Empirical Analysis." *Journal of Ethnicity in Criminal Justice* 7, no. 2 (2009): 121–134.

Mbuba, J. M. "Attitudes toward the Police: The Significance of Race and Other Factors among College Students." *Journal of Ethnicity in Criminal Justice* 8, no. 3 (2010): 201–215.

Moniuszko, Ł. "Police Ethics in Theory and Practice." *Professional Education in the Modern World* 6, no. 1 (2016): 121–124.

Ryberg, J. "Racial Profiling and Criminal Justice." *Journal of Ethics* 15, no. 1–2 (2011): 79–88.

RACIAL PROFILING

The modern-day issue of racial profiling began in the mid-1970s when the U.S. Drug Enforcement Administration (DEA) developed profiles of drug couriers that were designed to assist police officers in identifying individuals engaged in drug trafficking to prohibit the distribution of illegal drugs. Racial profiling has become a highly charged issue because of the increasing number of complaints that ethnic minority drivers are being stopped and searched by the police in disproportionate numbers. Racial profiling has been an issue of concern and discussion in the U.S. Congress, at state, county, and city levels, as well as among civil rights and professional police organizations. Media coverage has illustrated the cost of racial profiling, both socially and individually, and national surveys have confirmed the belief that this issue is a serious social problem and is pervasive throughout the nation.

A rally protesting against racial profiling at the state Capitol in Sacramento, California, April 2000. Hundreds were there to show support for SB1389, the so-called "Driving While Black/Brown Bill." Racial Profiling is the targeting of individuals based on their race or ethnicity. (AP Photo/Steve Yeater)

Law enforcement has long used "profiles," "criminal profiling," or other profiling techniques to aid in their search for individuals suspected of being involved in criminal activities. Profiles include certain characteristics of individuals and situations as indicative of criminal behavior, and these could include the individual's dress and demeanor, age, gender, and race. Using these visual cues and inferred personality traits to arrest, are accepted police practices when targeting individuals suspected of criminal activities. Racial profiling arises out of this practice and results in individuals being profiled based mainly on their race, ethnicity, or national origin. Historically, this occurs predominately in three different contexts. First, the "War on Drugs," where police officers target African Americans or Hispanics in the beliefs that they are likely to be involved in drug trafficking. The profiles of drug couriers developed by the DEA were designed to assist police officer's in identifying individuals who they believed were distributing illegal drugs.

Secondly, when individuals are stopped because they appear to be out of place, for example, an African American in an exclusively White neighborhood or a White person in what is considered a Black neighborhood. This leads to the assumption that a person does not "belong" in an area because of his or her race and therefore is suspected of engaging in some criminal activity (Rights Working Group 2010). The third context involves a crackdown on crime, where police departments, through their stop, question, and frisk policies, decide to get tough on street crime. These aggressive measures are likely to focus on high-crime neighborhoods, which in most cases are African American or Hispanic communities (Meehan and Ponder 2002). In these instances, racial profiles use various demographic and behavioral clues to identify the individual's potential for violating the law.

Racial profiling can be defined either conceptually or operationally based on how it is measured. Defined conceptually, racial profiling is "any police-initiated action that relies on the race, ethnicity, or national origin rather than the behavior of an individual or information that leads the police to a particular individual who has been identified as being, or having been, engaged in criminal activity" (Ramirez, McDevitt, and Farrell 2000, 3). Defined operationally, racial profiling occurs "when minorities are stopped at disproportionately higher rates than they are represented" within a particular situation (Lamberth 1994). Racial profiling in this instance is used to describe the actions of law enforcement personnel who target particular individuals to stop, detain, question, or subject to other law enforcement activities, based not on their behavior, but on their personal characteristics such as race, ethnicity, national origin or religion.

Racial profiling is considered a violation of the constitutional rights granted to individuals by the Fourth, Fifth, and Fourteenth amendments. The Fourth Amendment protects against unreasonable searches and seizures and, with the exceptions to the warrant rule, namely the consent search, makes this very relevant to the racial-profiling debate. The Fifth Amendment protects against discrimination by federal law enforcement officers based on biases of racial, ethnic, or national origin. The Fourteenth Amendment guarantees equal protection of the laws. Criminal proceedings involving traffic stops are usually based on some aspects of the Fourth, Fifth, and the Fourteenth Amendments; civil cases are filed under the pattern and practice statutes, on Section 42, U. S. C., Section 14141, and could possibly be filed on Section 42, U. S. C., Section 1983. Today, many states in America have instituted state-level statutes making racial profiling in all forms, illegal.

Six unrelated points have been identified as contributing to or intensifying the racial profiling debate. The first two have been controversial for many years and precipitated the current debate. The other four occurred in the mid-1990s. The six factors as described by Withrow are:

1. The long-term conflict between police and the minority community—many examples of these are documented in the history of American policing with many incidents occurring in the Civil Rights era.
2. The power dynamics of the traffic stop and the benefit of the consent search. Traffic stops form a great part of police work, and officers may use the pretextual (before the facts are known) traffic stop, which occurs when an officer, based on the suspicion of a vehicle or driver, but does not have probable cause, follows that vehicle until the driver is involved in some minor traffic violation. The officer now has probable cause for initiating the stop, but may ignore the initial violation and ask the driver to consent to a search.
3. Law enforcement's overreliance on profiles that are designed to help officers in identifying and apprehending a criminal suspect. Police officers enjoy a tremendous amount of discretionary authority throughout all areas of their daily routine. However, they have no formal written standards to follow in using this discretion. Within the area of traffic-stops, for example, the officer must use his judgment as to which of the many cars, in violation of the law, should he or she stop. Because police departments often use traffic stops as a means of apprehending persons with illegal drugs and weapon, the decision to stop must be made on the spot. In this regard, many officers will routinely stop certain cars and individuals. The use or the alleged misuse of discretionary

authority is an important issue within the racial profiling debate. The accusation is that the police are inconsistent in their approach, particularly with respect to the minority population. They are often accused of vigorously enforcing minor violations of the law when a minority suspect is involved, while ignoring serious violations committed by non-minorities.

4. Increased media attention on victims of racial profiling. Stories on racial profiling get the public's attention when the alleged victim is seen as honorable and the police officer's explanation seems contrary to the facts. Stories about minority professionals and others being stopped for various reasons suggest that they were stopped because of their race. Examples of widely publicized cases include: the 1991 case of Rodney King, an African American driving in Los Angeles; the Johnny Gammage case in Pittsburgh, another African American pulled over by officer in 1995; and the high profile arrest of Professor Henry Louis Gates, Jr., in 2009, along with the "beer summit" held at the White House with President Obama and the arresting officer. Since then, there have been numerous stories of racial profiling in the news.

5. The validation of the pretextual stop by *Whren v. United States*. The decision in this case did not establish the pretextual stop that is seen to be the context in which most racial profiling incidents occur, but has validated this practice.

6. The New Jersey Turnpike Racial Profiling study. During the 1980s, minority drivers using the New Jersey Turnpike claimed that they were targeted by state troopers as suspected drug couriers. This intensified the racial profiling debate in the mid-1990s. A number of lawsuits were filed alleging the violation of the Equal Protection Clause in New Jersey and Maryland. These cases against the states were seen as instrumental in bringing the issue of racial profiling to the forefront and have continued to fuel the racial profiling debate. These cases resulted in the respective police departments accepting comprehensive consent decrees that until recently have impacted their overall operations. (Withrow 2011, 3210)

Although the racial profiling debate began in the context of street and traffic stops, it is seen in many other contexts, including education, shopping, traveling, working, immigration, and terrorism, but profiling motorists have received the most public attention. The term "racial profiling" first came to the public's attention in a newspaper story on October 8, 1987 (San Diego Union Tribune 1987), describing a major drug find in Utah. By the late 1990s, many stories appeared in the media about this issue, prompting derisive terms such as, "driving while Black," "driving while Brown," "flying while Arab," and "shopping while Black," all describing the alleged pattern of behavior where law enforcement directs its activities on individuals because of their race or ethnicity.

Research evidence and personal accounts confirm perceptions about the prevalence of racial profiling in immigration, in traffic and street stops, and in the fight against terrorism. Over the years, minorities complained that they received unjustified attention from police officers while driving or just walking on the street. A 1999 report by David Harris described police and minorities' encounters at the state and local levels. Harris's report describes police stopping drivers for three main reasons: because they or their passengers do not "match" the type of car that they are driving; because they are traveling through areas considered to be "predominately

White areas" and might only be there to engage in criminal activities; and for very minor traffic violations, such as not signaling before changing lanes, driving faster than the posted speed limit, driving with underinflated tires, and having a license plate that is not easily seen or read.

National data also confirm this evidence. Data from the Bureau of Justice Statistics showed that in 2008, rates of police stops were very similar for White, Black, and Hispanic drivers (8.4 percent; 8.8 percent and 9.1 percent respectively). However, Black drivers were more likely to be searched at three times the rate of White drivers (12.3 percent versus 3.9 percent) and two times the rate of Hispanic drivers (12.3 percent versus 5.8 percent) at these stops. More Black and Hispanic drivers received traffic tickets (58 percent and 63 percent, respectively) than White drivers (53 percent). The arrest rate for Black drivers (4.7 percent) was also higher than White (2.4 percent) and Hispanic (2.6 percent) drivers (BJS 2011).

In 2011, the situation was the same. While persons walking on the streets were stopped at similar rates, this was not the case for drivers. Thirteen percent of Black drivers were stopped compared to 10 percent each for White and Hispanic drivers. Black drivers (7 percent) also received more traffic tickets than White drivers (6 percent) and 5 percent of Hispanic drivers (BJS 2013).

Experts on police stop and search practices and its relationship to individual drivers have reaffirmed that racial profiling is prevalent in our society. These individuals have also served as expert witnesses in many lawsuits against the police. For example, *Wilkins v. Maryland State Police* (1993) was a notable case that used scientific research evidence to underscore the police extensive use of racial profiling practices.

With respect to immigration, in 2010, Arizona and several other states passed laws giving the local police the authority to stop and question the immigration status of motorists that fit a certain profile, propelling immigration as a major national controversy in the racial profiling debate (see Arizona Bill 1070). The Arizona Bill 1070 received major criticism on the grounds that it would lead officers to racially profile certain individuals. It was noted that the police process of questioning and confirming ones' immigration status may take many hours. These individuals would be deprived of their liberty for no reason, other than for who they were. Also, law enforcement, in cooperation with the federal government and agencies, has conducted raids on immigrant communities and workplaces, targeting the Hispanic communities in particular. These policies have expanded the scope of local law enforcement work, damaging the relationship with these communities, and creating an atmosphere of fear and mistrust.

Formal agreements between federal immigration authorities and local and state jurisdictions as it concerns immigration enforcement were charted. For example, the Department of Homeland Security's (DHS) 287(g) program established formal agreements with some local and state law enforcement agencies, empowering them to act as immigration officers, after receiving training, and are supervised by the Immigration and Customs Enforcement (ICE) agency. Another notable program is the Criminal Alien Program (CAP), which screens and processes immigrants detained in jails or prisons following pretextual arrests. These individuals are detained and placed on immigration holds and are processed for removal. The Secure Communities Initiatives, initiated in 2008 and implemented through jails, submits the fingerprints of persons booked to be checked against immigration databases even before any decision on guilt is made. The National Security Entry-Exit Registration System (NSEERS), initiated by the government after September 11, 2001, used immigration laws as a counterterrorism measure, requiring all males between 16 and 45 years old from selected countries to register with the federal government, be fingerprinted, photographed, and subjected to intense interrogation.

Three decades ago, terrorism commonly took the form of persons hijacking planes, holding the passengers as hostages, flying the plane to a different destination, and waiting for their demands to be met. Today, terrorism has taken on a new face. The United States developed a list of traits that hijackers of planes usually exhibit in order to easily identify these individuals, but these profiles have changed since the number of terrorist attacks on the United States, including the one on September 11, 2001. These attacks have spurred the development of new policies and programs to protect the citizens of the United States, but these have also impinged on the individual rights and liberties of citizens. The most affected individuals are those of the Muslim faith and others from the Middle East and South Asia, as well as those who are mistaken as members of these groups, who face many forms of racial and religious profiling and are subject to increased scrutiny at airports and other borders, and for investigations of their financial records, their homes, jobs, schools, places of worship and social networks (see also the USA PATRIOT Act). New Transportation Security Policy (TSA) guidelines (2007) target persons with Sikh turbans and Muslim head dress, and bulky clothing for additional screening. "Operation Frontline" operated by DHS, designed to identify, prevent, and interrupt terrorist operations, use the NSEERS database to identify targets. The majority of individuals targeted through this program were from Muslim countries. Due to the prospects of future terrorists attack, concerns about racial profiling have expanded, and public opinions shifted in favor of racial profiling toward these groups.

Racial profiling is seen as an important civil rights issue. This issue is discussed at the highest levels of government, by academics, by civil rights groups, by law enforcement administrations, and by members of the public. Steps that have been taken to address this issue over the years include: an executive order from President Clinton in 1999 directing federal agencies to document their stop and frisk activities, clearly identifying the race and gender of individuals they encounter; states passing laws requiring data collection, and some departments beginning this practice voluntarily (Harris 2002); through directives from President Bush in 2001, "Racial Profiling and Data Collection" was placed as a top Department of Justice (DOJ) priority; the reiteration of traditional strategies combining exhortation and training, issuing statements that race discrimination is prohibited and offering specific training on the proper use of race in traffic stops; law enforcement agencies adopting policies and procedures governing how officers conduct traffic stops; the consent decree in the DOJ suit against New Jersey State Police, and subsequently many other police departments, adopted similar policies that officers would be held accountable for their actions when conducting traffic stops. Officers were required to document each stop, and many departments have begun videotaping these encounters. (See DOJ Web site for states' consent decrees.) A final strategy involves litigation by suing police departments for race discrimination.

The American Civil Liberties Union (ACLU), through its nationwide network of offices in every state, has made many strides in this area. The ACLU's focus on racial profiling includes its work in the area of public education, advocacy, and litigation. They are also vigorously lobbying for the passage of data collection and anti-profiling legislation and filing lawsuits on behalf of victims of racial profiling. Because it is of top national concern, the End Racial Profiling Act (H.R. 1933/ S. 1056) was introduced in 2015 in Congress and in the Senate. This act specifically addressed the issue of racial profiling by law enforcement on five levels: It gives a clear definition of practices perceived as discriminatory by law enforcement; it creates a federal prohibition against profiling; it mandates data collection; it provides resources for retraining law enforcement personnel on how to prevent racial profiling; and it holds agencies accountable for their actions.

In the United States, racial profiling is a well-established and highly debated problem that is evident in all areas of society. This occurs daily during the course of law enforcement operations. Minorities going about their daily activities are detained, interrogated, and searched without evidence of criminal activity, all because of their appearances. As a result, many minority communities are viewed suspiciously; individuals therefore live in fear and are alienated from law enforcement, which in turn impedes community policing efforts and results in citizens losing confidence and trust in law enforcement. Based on the foregoing, minority communities tend to be unwilling to confide in these officers, will not report crimes, will not act as witnesses or serve on juries, and will not be willing to participate in any problem-solving activities.

Sherill Morris-Francis, Rochelle McGee-Cobbs, and O. Oko Elechi

See also: ACLU; Fourth Amendment; Fifth Amendment; Impact of the War on Drugs; Police Accountability

Further Reading

Bureau of Justice Statistics (BJS). https://www.bjs.gov

Eith, Christine, and Matthew R. Durose. "Contacts between Police and the Public, 2008. U.S. Department of Justice, Office of Justice Programs, Washington, DC, 2011.

Harcourt, B. E. Guns, Crime and Punishment in America. "Utah Troopers Seize Couriers in Cocaine Lane Crackdown" *San Diego Union Tribune*, Oct 8, 1987, A32.

Harris, David A. "Driving While Black." American Civil Liberties Union (ACLU) Special Report. June 1999. https://www.aclu.org/report/driving-while-black-racial-profiling-our-nations-highways.

Harris, David A. *Profiles in Injustice: Why Racial Profiling Doesn't Work*. New York: New Press, 2002.

Lamberth, J. "Revised Statistical Analysis of the Incidence of Police Stops and Arrests of Black Drivers/Travelers on the New Jersey Turnpike between Exits or Interchangers 1 and 3 from years 1988 through 1991 West Chester, PA." 1994. www.lamberthconsulting.com/research_articles/asp.

Langton, Lynn, and Matthew Durose. "Police Behavior during Traffic and Street Stops, 2011." U.S. Department of Justice, Office of Justice Programs, Washington, DC, 2013.

Meehan, Albert. J., and Michael C. Ponder. "Race and Place: The Ecology of Racial Profiling African American Motorists." *Justice Quarterly* 19 (2002): 399.

New Jersey Consent Decree and others are available on the U. S. Department of Justice Web Site. 2016. https:www.justice.gov/crt/us-v-new-jersey-joint-application-entry-consent-decree-and-consent-decree.

Ramirez, Deborah, Jack McDevitt, and Amy Farrell. "A Resource Guide on Racial Profiling Data Collection Systems: Promising Practices and Lessons Learned." Washington, DC: United States Department of Justice, Bureau of Justice Assistance, 2000.

Rights Working Group. "Faces of Racial Profiling: A Report from Communities across America." Washington, DC: Rights Working Group, 2010. https://www.prisonlegalnews.org/media/publications/rights_working_group_racial_profiling_report_2010.pdf.

Withrow, Brian L. *The Racial Profiling Controversy: What Every Police Leader Should Know.* Flushing, NY: Looseleaf Law Publications, 2011.

RECIDIVISM

The term "recidivism" refers to the rate of re-offending by a criminal. A well-organized and functional police force is an important aspect of society's preservation of law and order. Police efficacy in maintaining order in society has a lot to do with perception of their authenticity and trust from the public. It is therefore important that the police force uphold the rule of law in discharging their duties by enforcing the law equally without treating anyone or group preferentially. In the United States, law enforcement officers enjoy wide discretion in the cause of discharging of their duties, which, while essential and necessary for their efficiency, may also be subjected to discriminatory and arbitrary abuse by some officers. To those who are at the receiving end of such discriminatory and arbitrary enforcement of the law, nothing can be more destructive. This could easily result in resentment and distrust of the very people whose lives, rights and property the police are obliged to protect (Chapman 2012).

Police perception in the United States varies based on race, class, and ethnic backgrounds. Caucasian Americans have a more favorable or positive view of police officers. The Caucasian communities (Whites) view police officers as a necessary entity that protects lives, rights and property in a democratic setting. On the other hand, minority groups (Blacks and Latinos) who live in disadvantaged neighborhoods do not have a favorable opinion of the police. The effects in many cases of such negative perception are resentment, distrust, fear, and ill feelings toward police officers, which turns to impede their efficiency in these neighborhoods (Chapman 2012).

"Perception" as is often stated is reality; the minority communities believe there is a bias effect in policing. They view racial profiling as a systematic, historic, and calculated measure by law enforcement and the system to tame, control and punish minorities. Research has shown that Whites are treated with more reverence by the police force than other members of the minority groups (Chapman 2012). According to racial threat theory, the bias effect in the criminal justice system is simply a

Recidivism refers to the rate of reoffending by offenders. It has been on the rise in the United States for decades. Issues such as education and criminal history can create barriers for re-entry into society, which can lead to relapsing into a life of crime. (Flynt/Dreamstime.com)

case of the White population reacting out of fear as the minority population increases by applying greater amount of social control on the minority group (Siegel and Welsh 2014). Reportedly, African Americans among the minority population are maltreated consistently during encounters with the police force (Holmes 2000; Jacobs and O'Brien 1998). Blalock (1967) explained this phenomenon by using the group threat theory. According to Blalock (1967), the fear of crime and threat of the potential loss of supremacy and dominance by Whites as the African American and immigrant population increases is the rationale behind the development of punitive approaches towards crime. In response to the social threat, police officers, prisons, or a mental asylum are utilized as mechanism to enforce formal social control. Due to the perception of social threat, large sums of monies are being dedicated to policing minority neighborhoods instead of channeling the same resources toward preventive activities (Perry 2003).

The social threat theory, however, does not explain police maltreatment of minorities; the multiplier effect of the population alone does not justify brutality. McElvain and Kposowa (2008) reported police officers, regardless of race, are generally more likely to treat suspects who are belligerent, disrespectful, physically resistant, and uncooperative with force. The likelihood of the police employing excessive force on a suspect is higher when the suspect displays uncooperative attitudes. Most police officer duties in maintaining law and order do not always require force and officers attempt to resolve several cases with a nonviolence approach; however, this does not take away from the fact that they are confronted with the impending probability of death or injury. Police training legitimately permits them to use force as needed when there is an imminent threat to public safety. Such threat is a judgment call an officer must make, based on training, prior experiences, experiences of colleagues, and wisdom developed on the street over time. The amount of force used is also elevated by the neighborhood context (Lee, Jang, Yun, Lim, and Tushaus 2010).

Disparity within the System

In comparison to the Western world, incarceration rates in the United States are very high. Imprisoning citizens has become such a lucrative business venture that distressed counties in some states rally to have prisons built in their states with the hope of job creation and aiding local businesses. Some states have gone as far as outsourcing their prisoners to private prisons, resulting in enough profit to be listed on the stock exchange (Staples 2012). With more prisons and the lucrative nature of the business, politicians campaign with a promise to keep society safe by getting tough on crime. New laws are created, and stiffer punishment is handed down for the already existing offenses, resulting in an increase in the prison population. Interestingly, the new laws and stiffer punishments are not targeted at those whose actions pose the greater threat to society, as common sense would suggest, but rather target the poor and powerless, who for the most part are citizens of the minority communities. In this present dispensation, it is not the severity of the crime that determines punishment but rather the color or social status of the offender. For example, white collar crime has a more devastating long-term effect on society at large, but because culprits of white collar crimes are the rich, powerful, and mostly White who have considerable influence in the law-making process, these crimes are not viewed as worthy of stiffer punishment. However, many of the prison population are in prison for offenses such as writing bad checks, substance abuse, vagrancy, and quality of life offenses associated with the poor (Staples 2012).

The over-representation of young African Americans in the juvenile justice system is concerning. Data on cumulative prevalence arrest indicates that Black juvenile males are 50 percent more likely than White juvenile males to have been arrested before their 18th birthday (Brame, Bushway, Paternoster, and Turner 2014). Differential treatment between Whites and Blacks starts early in the juvenile justice system and persists throughout the criminal justice system. For the same offense, a minority juvenile is more likely to be subjected to prosecution and referral than a White juvenile. Similarly, the probability that for the same offense, a minority will receive harsher punishment is higher, and minority juveniles are also less likely to have their cases dismissed. They are also more likely to be sent to secured confinement and be transferred to adult facilities than Whites. Judges tend to view offenses committed by minorities as more serious, be they juveniles or adults (Siegel and Welsh 2014; Barrett, Katsiyannis, and Zhang 2010).

Incarceration rate indicates the most glaring disparity in criminal justice system. Minorities are disproportionally confined in prison given their number in society.

The disparity is overwhelmingly present with respect to drug offenses. Research indicates that there is a higher probability for minorities to be arrested for drug-related offenses because police selectively target their communities for the sale and use of drugs (Staples 2012). By all accounts, the affluent White population uses refined/pure cocaine as opposed to crack cocaine favored by the poor minority communities. But until 2010, the punishment for crack cocaine was a hundred times greater than that of refined cocaine. This explains why the percentage of minorities' drug users may not be that high (15 percent among Blacks) but they constitute 75 percent of the prison population incarcerated for drug-related offenses. This also explains the disproportionate overrepresentation of the minority group in the prison system. The rich and the powerful have used their influence to enact mandatory sentences for drug-related crimes with an unfair balance, with the weight tilting more toward the drugs that are commonly used by the poor (Staples 2012). Criminal laws seem to protect mainstream Americans over minorities.

The death sentence is another area in which disparity is apparent. Minorities receive the death penalty more often than Whites. Prior to the eradication of the death penalty for rape cases, the South was notorious for executing Blacks for rape cases, especially where the victim was White; however, this was not the case where the victimized party was a member of a minority group. Even with the elimination of rape as a capital punishment, minorities are still executed at a disproportionate rate in comparison to Whites. Blacks are subjected to stiffer punishments when their offense is perpetrated against a White person rather than another minority. This is not the reality with White offenders. The outcome of Trayvon Martin's case might possibly have been different if Trayvon had been White and his assailant Black (*The Washington Post*). One reason for the disparity in sentencing is because most minority defendants are usually indigent and have to rely on court-appointed attorneys. Many of these attorneys are overwhelmed with cases and do not put forth a valid defense or possibly do not believe in the innocence of the defendant.

Police Abuse of Power and Its Consequences

The broad discretion the police force enjoys in the line of duty when faced with imminent threat often leads to a chain of negative consequences. The high incarceration rate in the United States in comparison to other countries in the Western world is blamed upon police officers' selective enforcement, which is mainly directed toward Latinos and Blacks. Research by the Center for Constitutional Rights indicated that more than half of the people who are stopped and frisked in New York are minorities; however, Whites are 70 times more likely to be in possession of a weapon (Staples 2012). Selective application generates a cycle of hostility as members of the minority group view their encounter with the police as unfair and degrading, and thereby approach subsequent encounters with pre-existing hostility even when the need does not arise. In response to such hostility, police officers sometimes react with excessive force or harsher treatment and often deadly force, as they perceive the minority community as dangerous (Chapman 2012). Because of selective enforcement, one in three Black males is likely to have a prison record before the age of 30. Once a person has a record, he or she is prejudged and the likelihood of subsequent incarceration is almost certain (Staples 2012).

Police officers' abuse of power toward minorities has received very little attention in the past. However, recent cases of police brutality against Blacks, such as the cases of Tamir Rice, Eric Garner, and Freddie Gray, have awakened the conversation regarding alleged cases of police brutality that has led to a nationwide protest with the Black Lives Matter movement. In spite of recent incidences regarding alleged police brutality, the courts are reluctant to indict these officers for the killing of minorities; it has, however, sparked a renewal of the conversation.

Police abuse of power can leave long-lasting effects. Imprisonment presents a major challenge to minorities. For instance, a growing problem among the incarceration of minorities is the absence of a father figure in households, especially among Blacks. A huge number of children are growing up in minority communities absent a father figure. Because of recidivism, young males are in and out of the system and their children's lives, and this is a cycle that continues to repeat itself. With the frequency of incarceration within these communities, children grow up assuming that the cycle of "in and out of prison" is the norm. This stigma often results in low self-esteem. The system continues to victimize minority males by closing up avenues to make amends. Most employers are not receptive to the idea of hiring Black males who have a record. In some states, they are even deprived of the right to vote. With little or no choice, they become resentful and end up offending and returning to prison, a place that many offenders consider a safe haven (Staples 2012).

Reoffending

The United States started witnessing increments in incarceration rate beginning in the 1970s and it has persisted to date. At present, more than 2 million inmates are confined in either federal or state prisons (Glaze and Kaeble 2014). When theses prisoners are released, they face a number of challenges, which include difficulty in securing housing, abstaining from substance abuse, reconnecting with family members, and finding employment. It is difficult to secure a decent job post-release, as most ex-convicts are hampered by discrimination from employers because of their criminal record. A low educational background is usually an obstacle because of the dwindling demand for well-paying low-skilled workers. Poor work history or little work experience and sometimes health issues also pose a challenge in finding steady work (Western 2006; Pager 2007). All these odds increase the possibility of recidivism and because a disproportionate percentage of ex-convicts are minorities, this explains why recidivism is very high among Blacks (Pager 2003).

Other factors that predict recidivism are age, race, seriousness of prior offense, length of sentence, prior record or criminal history, and more. Reportedly, former prisoners who recidivate do so within the first two to three years after they are let out of prison. A study by Liem, Zahn, and Tichavsky (2012) found prior conviction for a financially motivated homicide and race to be strong predictors of criminal recidivism. According to Roberts, Zgoba, and Shahidullah (2007), the significant determining factor between recidivist and non-recidivist is a rap sheet, particularly for violent offenses. Liem and associates (2012) found race to have a strong correlation with recidivism. Their study showed Blacks have a higher recidivism rate than Whites. A number of factors can explain the higher recidivism rates among Blacks, such as a disadvantaged neighborhood, stiffer sentences, police intolerance, perception of police, and so on. Life course theory offers the best explanation for this phenomenon. For the same offense if convicted, Blacks tend to received stiffer punishment than Whites. Because of the longer sentence received, by the time they are released many have "aged out" of the conventional milestones that are usually considered turning points in someone's life. These include marriage, parenthood, and gainful employment (Laub and Sampson 2003). According to Sampson and Laub (2003), these factors are considered turning points in a person's life that serve as informal social control, and when achieved, it can cause an offender to conform to societal expectations and deviate from a criminal lifestyle. However, for Black offenders, after several years of incarceration, they return back to society to realize they have missed out on the critical periods that serve as informal social control. Feeling despair, they return to what they feel they know best—crime.

Scholars have found securing steady employment to be an integral part of reintegration back into society. The lack of steady employment is a predictor of recidivism. According to research, when an ex-convict secures employment, the employment serves as a turning point and helps the ex- convict to deviate from a criminal lifestyle (Sampson and Laub 2003). With a secure job, bonds are formed with colleagues that serve as an informal form of social control; the job also provides a source of livelihood that takes away the incentive of criminality. More so, employment does not only keep a person productive; it also provides a positive support system that can help an ex-convict desist from criminal activity (Valentine and Redcross 2015).

Another explanation lies with a disadvantaged neighborhood. Alexander (2012), among other studies, show long incarceration periods and the disadvantaged neighborhoods that Black offenders return to are significantly associated with a high recidivism rate. A number of the offenders are involved in the system by virtue of the low-income, structurally disadvantaged, highly impoverished, and segregated neighborhood in which they live. Returning back to the same neighborhood merely increases the odds and potential for reoffending. Anderson (1999), in his book entitled *Code of the Street,* examined similar neighborhoods in Philadelphia and found that Black males living in these neighborhoods adopt a "code of the streets," which is permissive to behaviors such as robbery and the use of violence for economic advantages. Such survival skills conflict with the mainstream society. This is how the journey into the system begins; thus, returning to the same environment after incarceration increases the odds of recidivism among Black males. Structurally disadvantaged, highly segregated, low-income, and impoverished neighborhoods are perceived to have a higher crime rate, and since perception is reality, police officers patrol such communities more often, thereby increasing the probability of the use of force, as they consider these neighborhoods dangerous. The fact that a majority of Black males have a record before their thirties is a hindrance. A prior criminal record usually leads to harsher sentences, resulting in distrust and resentment for police officers. The average Black male from this environment is in a state of despair, lacks hope and any form of informal social control, and is not willing to control his or her desire for instant gratification regardless of the cost involved.

Dorothy Aerga, Ifeoma E. Okoye, and O. Oko Elechi

See also: Deadly Force; Eric Garner Case in New York City and Subsequent Tensions; Freddie Gray Case; Racial Profiling; Tamir Rice Shooting in Cleveland; Trayvon Martin Shooting

Further Reading

Alexander, M. *The New Jim Crow.* New York: New Press, 2012.

Anderson, E. *Code of the Street: Decency, Violence, and the Moral Life of the Inner City.* London, England: W. W. Norton, 1999.

Brame, R., Bushaway, S. D., Pateternoster, R., and M. G. Turner. "Demographic Patterns of Cumulative Arrest Prevalence by Ages 18 and 23." *Crime and Delinquency* 60 (2014): 471–486.

Barrett, D. E., and A. Katsiyannis. "Juvenile Delinquency Recidivism: Are Black and White Youth Vulnerable to the Same Risk Factors?" *Behavioral Disorders* 40, no. 3 (2015): 184–195.

Blalock, H. M. *Towards a Theory of Minority Group Relations.* New York: Wiley, 1967.

Chapman, C. "Use of Force in Minority Communities Is Related to Police Education, Age, Experience, and Ethnicity." *Police Practice & Research* 13, no. 5 (2012): 421–436.

Glaze, L. E., and D. Kaeble. *Correctional Populations in the United States, 2013.* Washington, DC: U.S. Department of Justice, Office of Justice Programs, Bureau of Justice Statistics, 2014.

Holmes, M. D. "Minority Threat and Police Brutality: Determinants of Civil Rights Criminal Complaints in US Municipalities." *Criminology* 38, no. 2 (2000): 343–367.

Jacobs, D., and R. M. O'Brien. "The Determinants of Deadly Force a Structural Analysis of Police Violence." *American Journal of Sociology* 103, no. 6 (1998): 913–925.

Laub, J. H., and R. J. Sampson. *Shared Beginnings, Divergent Lives: Delinquent Boys to Age 70.* Cambridge, MA: Harvard University Press, 2003.

Liem, M. "Homicide Offender Recidivism: A Review of the Literature." *Aggression and Violent Behavior* 18, (2013): 19–25.

Liem, M., M. A. Zahn, and L. Tichavsky. "Criminal Recidivism among Homicide Offenders." *Journal of Interpersonal Violence* 29, no. 14 (2014): 2630–2651.

Lee, H., H. Jang, I. Yun, H. Lim, and D. W. Tushaus. "An Examination of Police Force Utilizing Police Training and Neighborhood Contextual Factors." *Policing: An International Journal of Police Strategies and Management* 33, no. 4 (2010): 681–702. doi:10.1108/1363 9511011085088.

McElvain, J. P., and A. J. Kposowa. "Police Officers Characteristics and the Likelihood of Using Deadly Force." *Criminal Justices and Behavior* 35, no. 4 (2008): 519–552.

Mears, D. P., and J. C. Cochran. *Prisoner Reentry in the Era of Mass Incarceration.* Los Angeles, CA: Sage, 2015.

Pager, D. The Mark of a Criminal Record." *American Journal of Sociology* 108, no. 5 (2003): 937–975.

Pager, D. *Marked: Race, Crime, and Finding Work in an Era of Mass Incarceration.* Chicago, IL: University of Chicago Press, 2007.

Perry, B. "Accounting for Hate Crime." *Controversies in Critical Criminology.* Edited by M. D. Schwartz and S. E. Hatty. Boston, MA: Allyn & Bacon, 2003, 147–160.

Roberts, A. R., K. M. Zgoba, and S. M. Shahidullah. "Recidivism among Four Types of Homicide Offenders: An Exploratory Analysis of 336 Homicide Offenders in New Jersey." *Aggression and Violent Behavior* 12 (2007): 493–507.

Siegel, J. L., and B. C. Welsh. *Juvenile Delinquency: The Core.* Belmont, CA: Wadsworth, 2014.

Staples, R. "White Power, Black Crime, and Racial Politics." *Black Scholar* 41, no. 4 (2011): 31–41.

Valentine, Erin Jacobs, and Cindy Redcross. "Transitional Jobs after Release from Prison: Effects on Employment and Recidivism." *Journal of Labor Policy* 4, no. 16 (August 27, 2015). doi:10.1186/s40173-015-0043-8.

Western, B. *Punishment and Inequality in America.* New York: Russell Sage Foundation, 2006.

CONSTITUTIONAL MANDATES

The incidents covered throughout this book raise several constitutional questions, and this essay outlines the constitutional constraints on use of force by police officers. Constitutions are designed with an aim to regulate and limit the conduct of government actors, to protect the interests of the people in that society. Law enforcement officers in the United States have a duty to adhere to standards found in the U.S. Constitution and in court cases that interpret constitutional provisions. The Fourth Amendment to the U.S. Constitution protects against "unreasonable searches and seizures," and federal courts consider any force used by police to be a *seizure* of a suspect. Whether a seizure is *unreasonable* is key to determining if a police officer acted unlawfully. Additionally, force used must not be excessive. The Fourteenth Amendment is also relevant regarding use of police power, guaranteeing equal protection of the law, for example prohibiting police officers from treating individuals differently because of race or other factors. In a use of force incident, the officer may have violated other laws and internal police policies, but those are not covered here.

But good standards do not always mean good practice: there can be a disjoint between everyday police practice and constitutional rules. Even if police power has been abused and a constitutional claim is made in court, difficulties can arise in substantiating allegations with objective evidence and determining whether a constitutional right was infringed. When a constitutional violation *is* found to have occurred, the practical outcome for victims and their families may be disappointing in relation to the harm done. A judicial decision cannot remedy injuries or bring back someone who died because of police use of force. The police officers involved are not always fired, disciplined, or criminally punished, although in some cases they are. Victims are often, but not always, financially compensated. Despite these imperfect resolutions, individuals and organizations are increasingly seeking to hold police departments accountable for constitutional violations. Law enforcement agencies generally seek to adhere to the U.S. Constitution for moral, practical, and financial reasons, well aware that violations of the Constitution may lead communities to lose faith in the police and may result in financial repercussions.

When Can Force Be Used?

Clear legal rules set out when a police officer can use force against a suspect and the degree of force that is appropriate in given circumstances. Nonetheless, determining whether these standards have been met can be difficult. The Fourth Amendment of the U.S. Constitution reads in part: "The right of the people to be secure in their person, houses, papers, and effects, against unreasonable searches and seizures, shall not be violated . . ." A "seizure" occurs not only when law enforcement takes hold of objects or property (such as drugs), but also when officers take a person into custody or detain them. Using force to effect detention or arrest is also a seizure, which is generally how Fourth Amendment issues arise in use of force cases.

Police officers can use force against a suspect in five circumstances: self-defense; when the officer is defending another person; to ensure the suspect is arrested, if there is probable cause that a crime occurred or will occur; to prevent escape and the destruction of evidence; and when a suspect resists arrest or detention. The amount of force that can be used increases depending on the conduct of the suspect. Known as a "use of force continuum," the main goal of such policies is to diffuse and resolve tense situations (National Institute of Justice 2009). At one end of the continuum is *no* use of force: in response to resistance or a potentially violent situation, the officer uses mere presence of law enforcement to alter circumstances. The officer can then incrementally use more force if required by the situation, including verbal commands, bodily force not involving weapons, "less-lethal" force such as batons or Tasers, and—in extreme circumstances—lethal force.

Deadly weapons and lethal force "should only be used if a suspect poses a serious threat to the officer or another individual" that may result in serious bodily injury or loss of life. This last point is significant in light of the many lethal force cases that have been covered in this book. The rule was established in a 1985 U.S. Supreme Court case called *Tennessee v. Garner*, which found the use of deadly force by a police officer "constituted an unreasonable seizure in violation of the Fourth Amendment" (para. 25) after a 15-year-old boy was shot in the back of the head while attempting to flee from the police. The boy was apparently unarmed and the police officer was reasonably sure he was not dangerous. In contrast, in cases where law enforcement officers have probable cause to believe that the suspect is dangerous, lethal force may be constitutionally acceptable, even if the suspect is fleeing. In these cases the officers should warn the suspect, if feasible, that lethal force will be used. Deadly force can even be used to stop a motorist who is putting innocent lives at risk (*Scott v. Harris* 2007).

More generally, fleeing from the police may amount to reasonable suspicion that a suspect was involved in criminality if there is additional information that leads to that conclusion, warranting some level of force to stop the suspect. Law enforcement officers consider the totality of the circumstances to determine whether reasonable suspicion of wrongful conduct exists. If they so determine, officers are justified to stop and question the person and use some force (if necessary) to do so.

How Is Reasonable Force Determined?

In each of the use of force scenarios discussed here and throughout the book, the Fourth Amendment specifies that only "unreasonable" seizures are problematic. Reasonableness refers to the decision to use force at all and also the level of force relied on in a particular situation.

Law enforcement officers are provided significant discretion in deciding how to respond to ongoing situations in carrying out their duties, and decision-making in use of force cases is no different. According to the Supreme Court, a court's decision *after the fact* about whether the use of force by officers was reasonable should take into account that officers "are often forced to make split-second judgments—in circumstances that are tense, uncertain, and rapidly evolving—about the amount of force that is necessary in a particular situation" (*Graham v. Connor* 1989). The *Graham* case made clear that, when a court is evaluating the conduct of officers in a use of force case, "The reasonableness of a particular use of force must be judged from the perspective of a reasonable officer on the scene, rather than with the 20/20 vision of hindsight" (396). With this perspective in mind, courts will assess the severity of the crime that occurred or might have taken place if the officers had not acted, whether there was an imminent threat to any individual, and whether the suspect was resisting arrest or attempting to elude arrest. These inquiries allow courts to assess whether the police interest in seizing a suspect justified "the intrusion on the individual's Fourth Amendment interests" based on the circumstances of each case (396). Force cannot be used without reason or for insufficient or unlawful reasons. In addition, the *level* of force should not go beyond what is reasonable in the circumstance. Thus, "reasonable" in this context means fair, suitable, and not arbitrary or excessive.

If it is determined that use of force in a specific situation was reasonable, courts do not demand that the officer used the least amount of force possible or that the officer had no other option. Even so, in reviewing a constitutional claim, a judge may take into account whether a less-intrusive option was considered by officers. Courts also do not prohibit particular forms of force. Police departments in a number of major cities have banned certain tactics such as the use of chokeholds. (Chokeholds involve placing pressure on the throat or windpipe, which may prevent or obstruct breathing.) Nonetheless the Eric Garner case in New York demonstrates that department policy does not necessarily prevent the use of a specific technique. In 2015 U.S. Congress Member Hakeem Jeffries (D-NY) introduced a bill that would criminalize the use of chokeholds at the federal level, but the bill has not progressed in Congress.

Use of Force in Practice

High quality police training is essential. Effective training helps officers learn how to adapt to ongoing circumstances and ensures officers are fully informed of lawful conduct and the rights of suspects. Such training can not only aid in keeping officers, suspects, and bystanders safe, but it also helps to avert constitutional violations.

Applying Fourth Amendment rules in specific real-life situations is what matters, and errors in the use of force can be made for a variety of reasons. Violent incidents can occur when a police officer is mentally unstable or lacks appropriate self-control. In other circumstances an officer may simply misperceive the need for the use of force or the threat posed by a suspect. That misperception might be reasonable or unreasonable. Or the officer may have adequately understood the initial situation but then, as the incident unfolded, perceived the suspect's reaction as requiring stronger force. The culture of the police force and policies that officers work under may influence their conduct, and an officer may be more prone to use force in neighborhoods or settings in which the officer has had to use force previously. Another factor, which many experts consider significant in various police departments, is biases held by police officers about individuals, groups, or communities that impact on officers acting impartially.

A constitutional issue arises when a police force or government agency focuses on one racial, religious, or ethnic group as a target of law enforcement. Racial profiling or religious profiling takes place when race or religion is used to trigger a law enforcement intervention or as representative of criminality. Such practices, considered by experts to be commonplace, violate the Fourteenth Amendment of the U.S. Constitution, which provides in part that no state shall "deny to any person within its jurisdiction the equal protection of the laws." How might racial profiling influence the use of force? According to numerous studies, restraint and force is applied disproportionately to members of certain racial, ethnic, or religious groups, particularly African Americans and Latinos, in specific cities, towns, and neighborhoods. "The rate at which [African American] individuals are killed by law enforcement is three times higher than that of white people" (Sibley 2014). Subjecting an individual to force based on race, ethnicity, or religion is prohibited by the Fourteenth Amendments and considered unreasonable under the Fourth Amendment.

Some argue that law enforcement motivation is geographical rather than racial: Terrill and Reisig found that higher degrees of force used by law enforcement are associated with neighborhoods that have increased levels of economic deprivation. "Minority suspects are more likely to be recipients of higher levels of police force because they are disproportionately encountered in disadvantaged and high-crime neighborhoods" (2003, 306).

Consequences of Constitutional Violations

Several potential consequences can result from use of force that violates the Fourth Amendment or the Fourteenth Amendment. Use of force in an unlawful manner may result in, for example:

- Evidence being excluded in the suspect's criminal trial. If a suspect is prosecuted for an offense, an officer's unlawful use of force to detain or arrest the suspect in relation to that offense may result in evidence against the suspect being excluded at trial.

- Disciplinary consequences for the officer or officers involved. Officers may be fired, suspended, or transferred.
- Initiation of a criminal case against the officer(s).
- Civil claims by private individuals against the department and officers involved.
- The U.S. Department of Justice (DOJ) may initiate a civil rights investigation into conduct related to a particular incident or general practices of a police department.

The DOJ has investigated dozens of police departments throughout the United States. Several major police departments such as those in Albuquerque, New Mexico, and Cleveland, Ohio, engage in patterns or practices of use of excessive force that contravenes the Fourth Amendment. Investigations into the Newark Police Department and the Ferguson Police Department, among others, found unconstitutional policing and racial disparities in stops, searches, and the use of force in a way that violates the Fourth and Fourteenth amendments. Once the DOJ makes such a finding, it attempts to work with city officials and representatives of the wider community to agree to a process for reforming the police department based on DOJ recommendations. The DOJ can also investigate individual incidents, as it did the killing of Michael Brown by Officer Darren Wilson of the Ferguson Police Department. The DOJ determined, concerning that incident, that federal civil rights charges against the officer were not merited. Some law enforcement agencies have been the subject of class action lawsuits challenging stop-and-frisk practices and use of racial profiling. In *Floyd v. City of New York* (2013), a federal judge determined the New York Police Department had conducted racial profiling and stop-and-frisk encounters in violation of the Fourth Amendment and the Equal Protection Clause of the Fourteenth Amendment. The City of New York subsequently dropped its appeal in the case, and a process of reform was initiated involving all stakeholders. Civil rights claims against a police department for such constitutional violations can be difficult to sustain and generally require extensive data on police practices. In contrast to broad cases related to investigatory stops, use of force cases in the courts—civil or criminal—tend to involve the conduct of individual officers in a specific incident.

As you consider the constitutional rules set out in this essay that apply to the use of force by the police, keep in mind the difficulties faced by prosecutors, judges, and juries in determining *after the fact* whether constitutional standards were met *at the time an incident took place*. Was the officer aware of significant information about the suspect and the case? What did the officer see and hear? A prosecutor or court may determine that a police officer acted reasonably based on what was known at the time, even if it is clear in hindsight that force (or a certain degree of force) was not necessary. If the officer acted lawfully because of appropriate information, the officer cannot fairly be prosecuted or sanctioned. The public may be justifiably frustrated, believing that the outcome was wrong. After all, in such a scenario, the officer's actions have been deemed acceptable despite the use of force being unnecessary.

The high standard required for convictions to be successful—proof of criminal conduct *beyond reasonable doubt*—is one reason why law enforcement officers are not commonly prosecuted or convicted in incidents involving the use of force. A study by *The Washington Post* found that in the decade through 2015, only 11 of 65 officers charged in fatal shootings were convicted (Kindy, Fisher, Tate, and Jenkins 2015). (The same report found that police officers had shot and killed close to 1,000 civilians in 2015.) Several other reasons contribute to these statistical outcomes. First, officers are given latitude to determine the correct course of action in high-pressure situations. Second, in some cases courts may not have sufficient evidence to determine whether use of force was reasonable. Recently, cases have succeeded when there is video evidence of the incident, such as when a bystander has recorded the event. But such evidence is not always available, and the testimony of witnesses may be contradictory. Third, many experts believe that prosecutors and judges value the evidence of police officers over victims and witnesses, in some cases thwarting indictment and conviction of officers. For this reason, community members have rejected the outcomes of several recent use of force cases as illegitimate.

A successful constitutional claim in an individual case may not lead to significant practical changes. But if that same police force has demonstrated a pattern of excessive force in other cases, department-wide reform may be necessary. Such remedies might include new policy guidelines, changes in management, further training, or modification of local or state law.

Marny Requa

See also: Crime Control versus Due Process; Deadly Force; Fifth Amendment; Police Accountability; Racial Profiling

Further Reading

Graham v. Connor, 490 U.S. 386 (1989).

Harr, J. Scott, Karen M. Hess, Christine Orthmann, and Jonathon Kingsbury. *Constitutional Law and the Criminal Justice System*, 6th ed. Stamford, CT: Cengage Learning, 2015.

Kindy, Kimberly, Marc Fisher, Julie Tate, and Jennifer Jenkins. "A Year of Reckoning: Police Fatally Shoot Nearly 1,000." *The Washington Post*, December 26, 2015. http://www.washingtonpost.com/sf/investigative/2015/12/26/a-year-of-reckoning-police-fatally-shoot-nearly-1000.

National Institute of Justice. "The Use-of-Force Continuum." August 4, 2009. http://nij.gov/topics/law-enforcement/officer-safety/use-of-force/Pages/continuum.aspx.

Scott v. Harris, 550 U.S. 372 (2007).

Sibley, Ryan. "Death by Law Enforcement: What the Data Tells Us—and What It Doesn't." Sunlight Foundation. August 25, 2014. http://sunlightfoundation.com/blog/2014/08/25/cdc-data-tells-us-black-people-are-at-higher-risk-than-white-people-to-be-killed-police/#fbgplus.

Terrill, William, and Michael D. Reisig. "Neighborhood Context and Police Use of Force." *Journal of Research in Crime and Delinquency* 40 (2003): 291–321.

CRIME PREVENTION TECHNIQUES

Crime prevention techniques refer to the establishment of mechanisms to inhibit, or at a minimum, reduce unlawful behavior within society. Many present-day crime prevention techniques tend to focus on the enactment of criminal laws created by elected officials, which impose sanctions to the offender because of their illegal act. Law enforcement, the courts, and corrections each play an integral role in the reinforcement of criminal law sanctions. However, many recommendations by policymakers for preventative policies neglect to address the source of the criminal behavior.

Throughout history, many sentencing techniques have been used as an attempt to prevent crime, such as deterrence, incapacitation, retribution, rehabilitation, and restitution. Deterrence, a popular goal of sentencing with a lengthy history, has the objective of convincing either the offender (specific deterrence) or society (general deterrence) to either not violate criminal laws, or reoffend (e.g., recidivate), due to the severity and certainty of the punishment that outweighs the benefits of committing the criminal act. However, research shows little support for incarceration reducing future criminal offending. In fact, many offenders will recidivate. Consequently, this has resulted in the demand for policy reform by many researchers, who emphasize the need to evaluate the cause for criminal behavior, whether due to lack of education or job skills, drug addiction, psychological or physical abuse, mental health concerns, and other social problems.

While the United States is one of only a few countries that continue to implement capital punishment, research has shown the death penalty is an ineffective deterrent in criminal behavior, especially because most murders are categorized as crimes of passion. Throughout history, this method of crime prevention has transformed from being a public spectacle for deterrent purposes (hanging), to occurring behind prison walls via such methods as electrocution, firing squad, and lethal injection. Some researchers have proposed a brutalization effect occurring immediately after an execution, in which homicide rates increase. Although, it appears to be ineffective as a crime prevention technique, it is still influential in policy making decisions. It has been proposed that the most prevalent form of capital punishment within the United States, lethal injection, constitutes a form of cruel and unusual punishment. However, the U.S. Supreme Court has not concurred with this argument.

Another sentencing technique utilized is incapacitation, which also serves as a crime prevention technique. Under this ideology, offenders will not have the opportunity to reoffend while they are incarcerated. It is intended for dangerous criminals, with the belief that if they are behind bars, they will not be permitted to engage in criminal activities. Currently, the United States has nearly 1.6 million offenders incarcerated. Both prisons and jails are immensely overcrowded, due to policy recommendations and stringent laws, as with drug laws, three strikes laws, mandatory-minimum sentencing, and sentencing guidelines. Diminished returns have been found using incapacitation as a means to reduce, or prevent crime. In many instances, offenders, once released, experience much adversity, such as lack of legal employment opportunities, psychological concerns, few if any job skills, and substandard educational backgrounds.

Retribution, as a sentencing technique to prevent crime, is designed to punish offenders both fairly and justly. With this type of sentencing, the punishment is proportional to the severity of the crime, or blameworthiness. This technique is not used as a deterrent effect, but rather to punish offender's illegal actions, which is characterized by the concept of just desert.

Rehabilitation, in comparison to the previously discussed sentencing techniques, incorporates contemporary ideology. Rehabilitation is an attempt to stop future crime from happening by treating the particular needs of the offender. Thus, by treating the criminal etiology, the offender will no longer be a threat to society; the objective is to treat the offender. Thus, rehabilitation is opposed to the belief of punishment and incarceration. Rehabilitation was not always a prominent approach in tackling drug use and abuse, and in the past it was not always as humane, compared to today.

Historically, rehabilitation was originally implemented within Pennsylvania at Eastern State Penitentiary. It was proposed that inmates could reform themselves through penance. Offenders would remain in complete isolation within a single cell. It was believed by immersing oneself in daily Bible reading, repenting, and working within one's cell, that an inmate could reform himself or herself and become a productive member of society upon release. Unfortunately, partly due to the isolation, in addition to the brutality experienced by inmates with harsh punishments, Eastern State experienced a high rate of suicides among its inmates.

The "War on Drugs," becoming most prevalent during the 1980s with the presidency of Ronald Reagan, resulted in the enactment of many punitive, even draconian, forms of punishment as a means to prevent drug use and abuse. Harsher drug laws were enacted in an attempt to prevent, or reduce, drug use. New laws resulted in harsher penalties for possession of drugs, increasing penalties for selling illicit drugs to minors, and the reinstatement of the death penalty for offenders convicted as a "drug kingpin" or anyone convicted of a drug-related murder. Consequently, the number of drug offenders escalated to the highest level ever. Tough penalties were also enacted for drunk driving. Drug testing was instituted within schools and the workplace. Therefore, the courts became backlogged and prison overcrowding universal. Numerous commercials were developed to created fear within the public. While the War on Drugs policy was unsuccessful in preventing illicit drug use, present-day efforts focus on decriminalizing certain drugs (marijuana), and providing greater access to drug courts for offenders, in an attempt to prevent future criminal behavior.

Drug courts are perhaps one of the most recognized form of rehabilitation. Based on the recommendation of the drug court workgroup, consisting of the judge, probation officer, prosecutor, and defense, offenders are provided with drug treatment, in addition to a number of court requirements (e.g., passing a General Educational Development [GED] test, maintaining employment, attending status hearings, meeting with probation officer, submitting to urinalysis testing, performing community services, and paying court fees). Overall, drug courts have shown much success; however, results vary depending upon the actual court. While drug courts appear to have many benefits, some argue drug court participants are pressured, or coerced, to enroll. For those drug court participants who successfully graduate from the program, the drug offense that originally resulted in assignment to drug court is eliminated from their record. As a result, this can provide drug court graduates with employment opportunities, and a reduction in recidivating. Economically, drug courts and providing rehabilitation have been found to be cost efficient, when compared to incarceration.

Restitution is a sentencing technique utilized to prevent future crime by requiring offenders to reimburse their victims, or society, for the impact of their crimes. As a result, offenders do not benefit from their unlawful behavior, and victims are compensated for their losses. The ideology of restitution focuses on the concept of equity, in which offenders reimburse, or pay back, the damage to their victims, the justice system, and society. There are two forms of restitution: monetary and community service. Restitution permits the offender to avoid incarceration, or a lengthier probation sentence, while maintaining connections with society and being provided a second chance. Research has found this alternative sanction to be beneficial in reducing future crime.

All offenders do not engage in criminality for the same justifications. There are a number of explanations for various crimes, as different offenders commit different crimes for a number of different reasons, such as impulse, emotion, intoxication, and individuals socialized into crime. Thus, crime prevention techniques must consider this when developing policy and prevention recommendations.

Three main areas for crime prevention are developmental, community, and situational. Developmental prevention specialists, or developmentalists, conduct research in the areas of psychology, psychiatry, education, medicine, and public health settings by analyzing developmental and criminological concerns linking developmental processes to later delinquency. They have proposed poor school performance, hyperactivity, and impulsivity to have a correlation with an increased probability of delinquency. Developmentalists have proposed interventions for children who may be at risk for engaging in criminal behavior to improve their life chances.

Community crime prevention analyzes why crime occurs within particular neighborhoods. Criminological theories within this paradigm focus on community and ecological explanations for crime, proposing that a transformation within the community may alter the behavior of the residents. Community crime prevention strategies emphasize community organization as a means to reduce crime, as shown with the Chicago Area Project, New York's Mobilization for Youth, and Neighborhood Watch programs. However, the effectiveness of community prevention programs is challenging to estimate due to concerns regarding the evaluation quality of these strategies.

Another community crime prevention technique involves community-oriented policing. As opposed to law enforcement officers responding to a crime in progress, also referred to as reactive policing, community policing is proactive. Officers, oftentimes on foot patrol, work alongside residents within a particular neighborhood, as a means to stop crimes before they occur. This crime prevention technique emphasizes a cooperative partnership and sharing power between the community and law enforcement, permitting officers to form a bond with residents. Community-oriented policing (COP) programs have been put in place in a number of diverse neighborhoods, not merely metropolitan areas, but also suburban and rural communities. The federal government has not only encouraged the development of COP programs, but also has provided billions of dollars in financial assistance since its onset.

Situational crime prevention attempts to eliminate, or diminish, the opportunities to engage in criminal behavior. It is believed that by increasing the perceived risks of engaging in criminal behavior, the rational criminal will not be motivated to engage in the illegal act. One of the classical criminological perspectives, proposed by Lawrence Cohen and Marcus Felson (1979), argues that if a motivated offender, a suitable target, and a lack of capable guardians were brought together at the same place but at a different time, most likely the same criminal behavior would take place. By eliminating one of the three factors, crime is less likely to occur. Modern examples and applications of such situational crime prevention include investing in a home security system and posting such signs in visible locations around the residence, increasing lighting at bus stops, installing security cameras, purchasing a dog, locking doors and windows, and walking with a group of people at night, as opposed to being alone.

Rational choice theory, proposed by Cornish and Clarke (1986) is also associated with the classical school of criminology, contending the criminal offender is one who is rational and engaging in free will, consistently making decisions as to engage in a crime or not. This theory is unique in that it analyzes the decision-making processes of the offender. Under the assumption the criminal is rational when weighing the benefits and costs of engaging in illegal behavior, a number of crime prevention techniques have been suggested.

Three strikes laws were enacted by legislatures as a means to prevent offenders (e.g., rational offenders) from committing future felony offenses. Offenders convicted of a third felony offense could potentially be in prison for life, specifically 25 years to life. Research has found little support in the three strikes laws in reducing felony recidivism, but has resulted in increasing the overcrowded prison population. Extralegal factors have been found to be more beneficial in reducing crime or recidivism, when compared to formal sanctions. For example, the effects of shame, loss of self-esteem, peer influence, and perceived social disapproval, especially by family and loved ones, have been found to be influential in deterring criminal activity.

While punitive laws have had little success in reducing crime, a number of intermediate sanctions have been developed, which result in being less costly than incarceration, and permit the offender to maintain their connections to family and society. Other sanctions to prevent crime involve shock probation, house arrest, intensive probation supervision, residential community corrections, and electronic monitoring. Shock probation requires offenders to serve a brief prison term prior to beginning probation. The intention behind this sanction is to shock offenders into being law-abiding citizens from their short incarceration. Intensive probation supervision (IPS) involves probation officers with small caseloads, in order to closely monitor offenders. IPS has the primary goals of decarceration, control, and reintegration.

House arrest also provides an alternative to incarceration. As opposed to being incarcerated, offenders are required to spend extensive periods of time within their home. Some offenders are sentenced to 24-hour home confinement, whereas others are permitted to leave their home to attend work or school. Many house arrests are monitored through the probation department. Arrestees are required to be at their residence at assigned times, with random calls and visits required in order to check on compliance. Electronic monitoring (EM), unlike house arrest, requires offenders to wear a monitoring device as part of their sentence. The EM transmits a radio signal at least two times per minute. It is also battery powered. These are secured with a tamper-resistant strap on the offender's ankle or wrist. It must be worn at all times. Newer EM devices limit offenders' movements to court approved areas, while others rely on global positioning satellite (GPS) technology, permitting authorities to monitor the offender's geographic locale. Residential community corrections (RCC) is another technique utilized to reduce crime, consisting of a nonsecure facility, not affiliated with a jail or prison, housing probationers who need a more secure environment. RCC provides offenders with an alternative to incarceration. Residents are permitted to leave the RCC for work, school, treatment, and other programs. As a result of intermediate sanctions, incarceration rates, although still exceedingly high, have assisted in decreasing the warehousing of inmates.

Criminological theories have proposed a number of arguments as to why individuals engage in criminal behavior. From these various theoretical propositions, sentencing goals and policy proposals have been implemented, revised, and in some cases eliminated. As a result of tough-on-crime laws, jails and prisons quickly became overcrowded. And, rarely were offenders receiving the treatment, education, and employment skills needed to prepare them for a life back in society once released. Contemporary crime prevention techniques are focusing more so on rehabilitation and intermediate sanctions, as opposed to simply incarceration. Without treating the cause of the individual's criminal behavior, it is challenging to prevent recidivism.

Stephanie L. Albertson

See also: Community Policing Today; Impact of the War on Drugs; Recidivism; Wilson and Kelling's Broken Windows Theory; Zero Tolerance Policy

Further Reading

Adams, Kenneth. "The Effectiveness of Juvenile Curfews at Crime Prevention." *Annals of the American Academy of Political and Social Science* 587 (2003): 136–159.

Beccaria, Cesare. *On Crimes and Punishments.* Indianapolis, IN: Hackett Publishing, 2013.

Cohen, Lawrence, and Marcus Felson. "Social Change and Crime Rates: A Routine Activities Approach." *American Sociological Review* 44 (1979): 214–241.

Cornish, Derek, and Ron Clarke. *The Reasoning Criminal: Rational Choice Perspectives on Offending.* New York: Springer-Verlag, 1986.

Grasmick, Harold, Robert Bursik, and Bruce Arneklev. "Reduction in Drunk Driving as a Response to Increased Threats of Shame, Embarrassment, and Legal Sanctions." *Criminology* 31 (1993): 41–67.

Mears, Daniel, Joshua Cochran, and William Bales. "Gender Differences in the Effects of Prison on Recidivism." *Journal of Criminal Justice* 50 (2012): 370–378.

Morris, Norval, and Michael Tonry. *Between Prison and Probation: Intermediate Punishments in a Rational Sentencing System.* New York: Oxford University Press, 1990.

Olson, David, Arthur Lurigio, and Stephanie Albertson. "Implementing the Key Components of Specialized Drug Treatment Courts: Practice and Policy Considerations." *Law and Policy* 23 (2001): 171–196.

Petrosino, Anthony. "Standards for Evidence and Evidence for Standards: The Case of School-Based Drug Prevention." *Annals of the American Academy of Political and Social Science* 587 (2003): 180–207.

Reisig, Michael D. "Community and Problem-Oriented Policing." *Crime and Justice* 39 (2010): 1–53.

Sherman, Lawrence W., Denise C. Gottfredson, Doris Layton MacKenzie, John E. Eck, Peter Reuter, and Shawn D. Bushway. "Preventing Crime: What Works, What Doesn't, What's Promising." Washington, DC: U.S. Department of Justice, National Institute of Justice, 1997.

Siegel, Larry J., and John L. Worrall. *The Essentials of Criminal Justice*, 9th ed. Stamford, CT: Cengage, 2015.

Spohn, Cassia, and David Holleran. "The Effect of Imprisonment on Recidivism Rates of Felony Offenders: A Focus on Drug Offenders." *Criminology* 40 (2002): 329–359.

Tiger, Rebecca. *Judging Addicts: Drug Courts and Coercion in the Justice System.* New York: New York University Press, 2012.

Tonry, Michael, and David P. Farrington. "Strategic Approaches to Crime Prevention." *Crime & Justice* 19 (1995): 1–20.

Walsh, Brandon C., and David P. Farrington. "Toward an Evidence-Based Approach to Preventing Crime." *Annals of the American Academy of Political and Social Science* 578 (2001): 158–173.

Walsh, Brandon C., and David P. Farrington. "Monetary Costs and Benefits of Crime Prevention Programs." *Crime & Justice* 27 (2000): 305–361.

PERCEPTIONS OF POLICE TODAY

Community relations between the police and minorities can sometimes be extremely negative. The events of Ferguson, Missouri, and Baltimore, Maryland, as well as video footage on phones and via media outlets have led to heavy scrutiny by the people the police are supposed to protect. These views and depictions have led to a movement/campaign to address some of the frustration experienced by the community.

The goal of serving and protecting can be a challenging and risky endeavor. In the past, the general public has not wanted the police to become involved in their personal lives and felt they could take matters into their own hands. As was seen during the 17th century and the English roots of policing, many citizens thought justice would be best served by community members working together to protect their own community. The Frankpledge and the Tithing systems are good examples of this perspective.

However, problems developed with this technique, as did the notion of vigilante justice. When the first official police departments were formed, they were fraught

Thousands of protestors, including members of the Black Lives Matter social movement (formed on July 13, 2013), converge on Manhattan's Washington Square Park to march through Manhattan to protest police violence on December 13, 2014. (Mustafa Caglayan/ Anadolu Agency/Getty Images)

with corruption, and political problems were commonplace. It took decades for policing to become professional and "fair."

Justice for All

What defines "fair"? Is the focus of police response supposed to be based on law enforcement, order maintenance, or service? Are officers supposed to focus on crime control, protecting due process rights, or social work? How compatible are each of these goals? And where do all of these questions lead us? Unfortunately, incidents in the past sometimes cause the public to develop negative attitudes toward the police. Whether socially constructed or based on legitimate factors, there are often communication problems between communities and police.

One of the themes we as a society have noticed is that the police mandate to control crime often causes dissention among the communities they serve. Over the years, the police have been accused of using too much force and of being too quick to pull the trigger (literally and figuratively). That has led to negative perceptions of the police, and maybe even an expectation that the police are going to abuse their position of power. That perception has been taken a step further (according to the statistics and anecdotal evidence). In particular, there has been the assumption that not only are the police overly aggressive to the point they may be violating due process rights in order to control crime), but also that they are acting in this manner more so with minorities and those of lower socioeconomic status. Research has demonstrated that many police departments use excessive force with minorities.

In the 1980s, one particular case brought to light this exact sentiment. A Black man named Rodney King was severely beaten and Tased by the police. A bystander video-recorded the incident, which led to widespread disrespect for the Los Angeles Police Department. Many other incidents have become public relations nightmares because of improvements in technology and the ability for people to record encounters on their cameras and cell phones.

Based on these too-public displays, agencies began to thoroughly examine incidents, and once statistics were tabulated, experts and officials began to realize that minorities were being approached, pulled over, arrested, and brutalized by the police more often than non-minorities.

Statistics demonstrate that racial bias may be worse in 2016 than it was in January 2015. Following the killing of Michael Brown in Ferguson, Missouri, the use of deadly force increased (465 to 491). There was a 6-percent increase in fatal shootings by police after January 2015, and Blacks are shot at two and a half times the rate of Whites. That year, nearly 1,000 people were fatally shot by the police, and many incidents were caught on video. However, most of these shootings involved armed assailants firing at the police.

Black Lives Matter

When the Black Lives Matter (BLM) movement developed after the Trayvon Martin shooting in 2012, the goal was to increase awareness and decrease the amount of negative treatment of racial minorities. However, this movement may have made matters worse (at least regarding perceptions). Especially disheartening are the publicized cases since 2012 (Michael Brown, Freddie Gray, Ezell Ford, etc.), to the shootings of police in Dallas in July 2016. Obviously, perceptions of the police have become more negative than ever. In fact, some assessments show that the entire BLM movement has led to increased negative perceptions of law enforcement. Although the intention may have been peaceful protests, some have established anti-police sentiment, leading to a greater racial divide (some within the group and some between groups).

Officers have been affected by the movement negatively, perhaps due to the media portrayal of them. They may have become frustrated and demoralized because they feel the community is judging them harshly. Thus, police began to become more conservative, enforcing the law less frequently. In fact one study found a 5.3-percent increase in violent crime after the Michael Brown shooting (called the Ferguson effect), suggesting that either the crime rate increased or that the police were not as aggressive with their law enforcement tactics (for fear of being judged for their decision-making). The media may have contributed to some of these views, and the statistics can be manipulated. But some studies have found that the Black Lives Matter movement and the Ferguson effect have actually led to increased crime because of the lack of police response. Pro-police sources show that the BLM movement by some extremists has actually hampered their ability to serve the community. Some of the attitudes of members of BLM have created a culture of inflammatory rhetoric and negative perceptions that can adversely affect the safety of officers.

On the other hand, the movement has been met with increasing support from the public. Young White adults are more and more concerned about police accountability. At the University of Chicago, the Black Youth Project paid for a survey conducted on 18- to 30-year-olds in August of 2016. It found that just over half (51 percent) of young White adults supported BLM. Interestingly, 85 percent of African Americans, 67 percent of Asians, and 62 percent of Hispanics supported it as well.

Changing Views

What can be done to mend this divide? There needs to be a way to establish police legitimacy—a way to build trust between the public and police regardless of race, religion, ethnicity, or other demographic factors. This is two-sided; the police need to learn to respect and trust those different from them, and the public needs to do the same.

One goal is to train officers to de-escalate confrontations—so that the community will gain respect for them and not see them as the enemy. Another goal is for the community to comply when police officers do approach them. This means when someone is approached by police, that person needs to have their hands where the police can see them, have a positive demeanor, speak when spoken to, stay in the car, wear their seat belt, and have papers in order and up to date (license, insurance, and registration). Additionally, compliance means not drinking and driving, not using drugs while driving, and not making sudden movements when pulled over. Protests against police misconduct may make sense, but the protests should not just be anti-police.

Police do not know what type of situation they are going to come across when they walk into an encounter or pull over a car. Many of these officers have seen the worst in people. If they have ever pulled someone over who was drunk, belligerent, violent, or carrying a gun or other weapon, they know how volatile a situation might become. They also want to be prepared and keep themselves safe. Due to their experience (and sometimes just a gut level suspicion), officers must be hyperaware. They have tried to pull over suspects with arrest warrants against them, and others who will do anything not to get caught.

Police believe that if the public could place themselves in the police officers' shoes, they might be better able to understand split-second decisions and perceived prejudgments. But the general public believes the police need to understand the perspectives of community members who might be doing nothing wrong, and feel offended and abused when the police approach or pull them over for what seems to them to be "no reason."

Findings

Research shows that lower-income groups and minorities are more negative about the police. In general, the police are more likely to approach, question, detain, arrest, and hassle minorities. For many years, citizens (and police administration) tended to believe that this statistic was because minorities commit more crime. However, self-report data, which is collected by the U.S. Census Bureau that asks residents to report crimes that occurred against them, shows that young, White males do commit crime. Yet, they are less likely to be detained or arrested. Without an arrest, they probably won't be sent through the criminal justice system. Hence, there is the assumption that male minorities are more likely to be involved in criminal behavior. Thus, police may approach a minority with a bias not seen with non-minorities.

Unfortunately, the cycle continues when minority parents and siblings pass on the word to their children and younger siblings that the police are not friends. Then it becomes the perpetual argument of which comes first: Are police biased against minorities and then minorities react in a negative way toward them? Or are minorities so suspicious and critical of the police that they start out the encounter in a negative fashion? Which comes first? And how do we end that cycle, regardless of how it started?

Former professional basketball player Michael Jordan recently made the decision to donate money ($1 million each), to two different groups (the NAACP and the Institute for Community-Police Relations) to combat these negative perceptions and improve police-community relations. Giving equal attention to both groups may be part of the solution, as each does not exist in a bubble, and maybe they can work together to change perceptions.

The media can also play a role that affects perceptions of the police. By focusing on the bad seeds, society tends to lump all officers into one category (as biased or racist). This is the same as the media portraying all minorities (or those of low socio-economic status) as violent criminals.

The real issue affecting police-community relations might have more to do with socio-economic status than race. Most research indicates that people in poor neighborhoods are the most likely to become involved in violent behavior (that includes victimization and offending). Thus, most crime is not only intra-racial but also intra-socio-economic status. Anger and frustration among Black and White citizens, lower- and upper-income individuals, has resulted.

Education

Other research has examined whether there is a correlation between police officers' education and the probability of them using force. According to the Bureau of Justice Statistics, only 8 percent of police departments require a four-year degree. In 2010, a study was conducted to suggest officers with even a little college education will be less likely to use force (56 percent), in comparison to those with no education (68 percent). Research does show that educated officers are more creative with problem solving, improved critical thinking, and have more tools to evaluate whether to use force nor not. They may be able to come up with multiple avenues to solve problems based on their experiences in college.

The University of Chicago has a research team analyzing data to attempt to determine in advance whether a police officer will have an adverse interaction with citizens. The Crime Lab Team is working with the Chicago Police Department to create a predictive data program in order for them to improve their Early Intervention System. This system was designed to determine if an officer is likely to engage in improper interactions with citizens, and which officers are more likely to be aggressive. Predicting misconduct sounds like the theme of a movie (i.e., *Minority Report*), where predicting criminality led to law enforcement to take action before the offender could commit a crime. Yet, data crunching has been used in policing since in the late 1970s. In North Carolina, the Charlotte Police Department is launching a similar system as part of the Center for Data Science and Public Policy. But the question remains as to what action to take once the system predicts that an officer is prone to behave inappropriately.

Disparity or Discrimination

African Americans comprise almost one-quarter of those shot and killed by the police (yet they represent only 13 percent of the population). Thus, Black Americans are two and a half times more likely than White Americans to be shot and killed by police (MacDonald 2016). However almost all Black homicide victims are intra-racial. This means that most violent crime is Black on Black, and occurs within the same race.

As a society, we must question whether the perceptions of the police are based on fact. Research has demonstrated that some of the differences in treatment of Black and White citizens may be based on actual behavior. One explanation for the difference in treatment is that Black and White individuals actually commit crime at different rates. Thus, minorities would be more likely to be arrested and sent though the criminal justice system than White individuals and, therefore, they would have more contact with the police. That contact can be likely to lead to a negative encounter, and a higher likelihood of an altercation.

Another explanation could be that law enforcement treats Blacks and Whites differently due to their preconceived notions about these groups. Unconscious racial bias can be based on training, experience, or simple agreement with what officers grew up around. If that is the case, then regardless of a minority's criminality or his or her chance of getting caught committing a crime, police officers may just be more inclined to arrest and process minorities through the system (even though non-minorities may commit just as much crime). Support for this hypothesis can be found in self-report surveys where youth are asked about their own criminality reporting what they committed whether caught or not. These statistics suggest that male, White youth commit just as much crime as minorities, but they are more likely to be released by the police. That action decreases the chance of a non-minority engaging in a negative confrontation with the police.

In taking this proposition a step further, there is some support that it is not just the police who carry preconceived notions, but that it also might be society in general. Between the media portrayal of minorities and traditional views regarding the differences between Blacks and Whites, White society may be more judgmental against minorities. So if a citizen looks outside his window and sees two White boys out in the courtyard, he or she may think nothing of it. However, place two minority boys outside and the perception may be different. Are they gang members or drug dealers? Therefore, that citizen might be more inclined to notify the police. Once the police arrive, being told there may be gang or drug activity going in in the area, they are on alert. The innocent parties are offended, and may resent and even resist the authority figures. This can lead to a negative confrontation. One can see how a situation can escalate under these circumstances.

So, who is to blame for the negative perceptions of citizens (regarding minorities) or suspects (regarding police), and of police (regarding suspects)? And how can we change them? What has changed about police brutality? What reforms have worked? Getting rid of lifetime terms for police chiefs has been one effort that is similar to removing tenure for teachers. After many years, they get burnt out and don't work as effectively. We as a society want fresh, eager, energetic, well-trained officers working in the field, using the best tactics and techniques to de-escalate a situation so that it ends peacefully. However we must also take into account the perspective of a seasoned professional—those officers who have been on the force for a long time, develop a "gut" level suspicion. Sometimes a suspect is in an area known for drug activity, or is giving officers evasive answers or strange body language. Officers know to look for the location of a suspect's hands or that if they are giving them "furtive glances," they might be doing something illegal. Learning what the correct response to that level of suspicion, or altering the "typical" aggressive response, can be a step in the right direction. However, an officer cannot be expected to put his or her life in danger to please the community. It is clear that there is a dilemma when presented with street encounters, but better training in less-lethal force and dealing with those on drugs (or even those who are mentally challenged), is a good idea.

Community Policing

How has community-policing impacted the perceptions of police today? This effort was created as an attempt to improve police-citizen relations, but the effort to have the police rely on other stakeholders (citizens and residents) for successful law enforcement has not led to the panacea that was intended. One such new effort has been the practice of police taking kids to church instead of the police station when they violate the curfew ordinance. In Trenton, New Jersey, for example, if minors are on the street after midnight, police officers give them the option of having their parents pick them up at headquarters, or getting dropped off at a safe haven (church or faith-based organization). The curfew ordinance has been on the books since 1967, but is rarely enforced. However, if a police officer can show that it is dangerous for kids to be on the streets late at night, and that they are acting to protect their safety, youth might understand the ramifications of staying out late, as well as gain respect for the police who are trying to help them.

The suggestion of using a "buddy system" has been proposed as well. Two-officer patrol cars may help protect the safety of officers, but as research has shown, it can also lead to a lower ability cover a wide geographic area, and leads to a slower response time. Another interesting effort has been instituted recently in Augusta, South Carolina (and other cities in the past). Cop Cards are handed out to local youth, so they can trade them like baseball cards. The goal is to get them to interact with the local police, and forge a positive relationship with them. The media can both help and hinder this effort. By focusing on negative altercations and "spinning" stories, police become caricatures of themselves. Ill-informed or misinformed members of the community also need to be educated as to the role of the police and the difficulty with which they have to carry out their duties, and often react in a split second. It appears that improved dialogue between the police and the public is a good suggestion as well as increased education for community members (about what the police do). Increased education for law enforcement officers, as well as proper training to respond in a way that protects their safety, while they protect the community they serve, is the ultimate goal.

Modernizing Police

These attitudes have created perceptions (on all sides) of unfair treatment by all parties. It is clear that the militarization of police has actually led to more animosity. When police respond to peaceful protests in SWAT gear, the situation often escalates. Instead there needs to be a response that attempts to treat all parties with respect. What modern techniques may work to improve perceptions of police? Policymakers need to be mindful of the needs of the community—with respect to establishing positive relationships and cooperation. However, the police need to feel respected, safe, and supported, too.

Regardless of the recent tragedies and media and public outcry, protests should be against police misconduct, not the police. There is definitely a need for police reform in a number of areas. Teaching officers the skills needed to de-escalate violent encounters, increased use of body cameras to improve accountability, and better data collection are some goals.

Our nation has become too divided by race, and the police are sometimes asked to do too much. Any failure on the part of society cannot be blamed on the police. On the other hand, police reform is necessary. The criminal justice system cannot protect the bad seeds or dismiss their actions. Detecting at-risk officers (those who use significant force), and isolating those officers against whom complaints are being filed is a good idea. Instead of blame, the focus needs to be on prevention and improving the community for all.

Gina Robertiello

See also: Body Cameras; Colonial Night Watches; Community Policing Today; Deadly Force; Racial Profiling; Rodney King Beating and Riots; Trayvon Martin Shooting

Further Reading

Antrobus, Emma, Ben Brandford, Kristina Murphy, and Elisa Sargeant. "Community Norms, Procedural Justice, and the Public's Perceptions of Police Legitimacy." *Journal of Contemporary Criminal Justice* 31, no. 2 (2015): 151–170.

Holmes, Malcolm D., Matthew A. Painter, and Brad W. Smith. "Citizens' Perceptions of Police in Rural U.S. Communities: A Multilevel Analysis of Contextual, Organizational and Individual Predictors." *Policing & Society* (April 2015): 1–21.

MacDonald, H. "Police Shootings and Race." *The Washington Post.* July 18, 2016. https://www.washingtonpost.com/amphtml/news/volokh-consipracy/wp/2016/07/18/police-shootings-and-race/.

Matusiak, Matthew C., William R. King, and Edward R. Maguire. "How Perceptions of Institutional Environment Shape Organization Priorities: Findings from Survey of Police Chiefs." *Journal of Crime and Justice* (2016): 1–15.

Mazzerolle, Lorraine, Emma Antrobus, Sarah Bennett, and Tom R. Tyler. "Shaping Citizen Perceptions of Police Legitimacy: A Randomized Field Trial of Procedural Justice." *Criminology* 51, no. 1 (2013): 33–63

About the Editor and Contributors

Editor

Gina Robertiello, Ph.D., is a full professor in the Department of Criminal Justice at Felician University in Lodi, New Jersey. She is the author of more than 30 publications in the areas of policing, domestic violence, restorative justice, and crisis intervention. Her first book, *Police and Citizen Perceptions of Police Power*, was published in 2004 (Edwin Mellen Press). It focused on developing a definitive picture of how police and citizens viewed the typical street encounter and determining how contextual variables such as demographic and situational characteristics were expected to influence the outcomes of encounters. She continues to work in this area and examine perceptions of the police by the public.

Dr. Robertiello received her B.S. in Administration of Justice from Rutgers University (New Brunswick, New Jersey), and her M.A. and Ph.D. from Rutgers University (School of Criminal Justice, Newark, New Jersey). She teaches courses in research methods, victimology, criminology, juvenile delinquency, and deviance, and is a First Year Experience (FYE) instructor. She is a textbook reviewer, a manuscript reviewer, a member of a number of advisory boards, and a volunteer for many organizations, especially those that support her Italian heritage. She resides in New Jersey and enjoys participating in activities with her husband and three children, as well as reading at the beach, jogging, and Zumba.

Contributors

Anthony M. Aceste, Caldwell University, Caldwell, New Jersey, has been in law enforcement for 15 years in both the federal and county governments. He earned a Ph.D. from Creighton University, is a prominent lecturer in the criminal justice system, and is a scholar in college campus safety and police regionalization.

Dorothy Aerga is an associate professor of criminal justice in the Department of Social and Behavioral Sciences at Elizabeth City State University, North Carolina. She holds a J.D. from Ahmadu Bello University, Nigeria, and an M.A. and Ph.D. in Juvenile Justice from Prairie View A & M University, in Texas.

Stephanie L. Albertson, Ph.D., is an assistant professor of criminology and criminal justice at Indiana University Southeast. Her primary area of research focuses on jury decision-making and reform, with secondary research on the drug courts and community policing.

Marco Aliano is an adjunct faculty member in Justice Studies at Montclair State University, New Jersey. He is a graduate of Seton Hall University where he obtained his B.A. in Criminal Justice and his M.A. in Human Resources Training and Development. He has more than 17 years of law enforcement experience where he is currently assigned as a supervisor in the Major Crimes Unit, and is an adjunct professor at a state university where he has lectured on criminal justice for more than 11 years.

Theresa Andrews Saint Peter's University, has been a licensed lawyer in New Jersey since 1983. She is an adjunct Criminal Justice Professor at Saint Peter's University with both J.D. and M.Div. degrees.

Jennifer M. Balboni is an associate professor and co-director of the Master of Arts program at Curry College in Milton, Massachusetts. Her primary areas of expertise include criminal justice policy reform, prosecutorial accountability, and the impact of the War on Drugs.

M'Balu Bangura received her master's from New Jersey City University and has focused her studies in program evaluation and police brutality.

Alexa Belvedere is a senior at Curry College, Milton, Massachusetts, and secretary of the CJ Honors Society. She plans to attend law school to study criminal law.

Jared Berman is a senior at Curry College, Milton, Massachusetts, and president of the senior class. After graduation, he plans to pursue a master's degree in higher education to work in the field of student affairs.

Steven Block, Ph.D., is an assistant professor in the Department of Criminology and Criminal Justice at Central Connecticut State University, in New Britain, Connecticut. He has published peer-reviewed articles in *Western Criminology Review, The Prison Journal,* and *Journal of Research in Crime and Delinquency.* His teaching and research interests relate to crime data and victimless crimes.

Sriram Chintakrindi is an assistant professor of criminal justice at California State University, Stanislaus. His research interests include offender recidivism and rehabilitation, mental illness, drug addiction, and constitutional rights.

Kaitlyn Clarke received her Ph.D. from the University of Massachusetts. She is a professor at Saint Anselm College, Goffstown, New Hampshire. She considers herself a generalist in criminology, researching a variety of topics related to social inequality and public policy.

Kyle Conklin is a University of Scranton graduate. He studies American Policing and Prison Reform and will be working for the Federal Bureau of Prisons as he continues his graduate work.

David Patrick Connor is an assistant professor of criminal justice at Seattle University, Washington. His research focuses on inmate experiences, sex offender management, and social deviance.

Raymond Elliot Doyle Cowles is a Seattle University graduate, with a master's in Criminal Justice: Research and Evaluation. He currently works as a social science researcher for the U.S. Probation and Pretrial Services office in Western Washington, evaluating programs, policies, and conducting various research in evidence-based practice.

Anne Cross, Center for Homicide Research, St. Paul, Minnesota, and School of Law Enforcement and Criminal Justice at Metropolitan State University, Brooklyn Park, Minnesota.

Emirhan Darcan earned a Ph.D. in criminal justice from Rutgers University and is an independent consultant from Turkey. His academic research interests include risk modeling, counter-violent extremism, and conflict issues.

Oguzhan Omer Demir is an associate professor of sociology at Giresun University. He has been a researcher at the International Center for Terrorism and Transnational Crime.

Deborah A. Eckberg, Ph.D., is an associate professor of criminal justice at Metropolitan State University, St. Paul, Minnesota. Dr. Eckberg's research and teaching interests span a wide range of topics related to criminal courts, special populations in the criminal justice system, and program evaluation.

O. Oko Elechi is a professor of criminology and criminal justice at Mississippi Valley State University. He received his Ph.D. from Simon Fraser University, in Canada. He also holds two degrees from the University of Oslo, Norway. His writings on restorative justice, community policing, and the African indigenous justice systems have been extensively published in international journals, books, and anthologies.

Steve J. Ellwanger is an associate professor of criminal justice at California State University, in Bakersfield. His research interests include the structural and social sources of crime and delinquency as well as police practices and ethics.

Venessa Garcia teaches at New Jersey City University and focuses her research area predominantly on intersectionality in crime and justice. She has published in the areas of police culture, public perceptions of police, and policing minority groups.

Paige H. Gordier is a professor of criminal justice at Lake Superior State University, in Sault Ste. Marie, Michigan. Her research interests include prison gangs, the history of corrections, prison violence, and the death penalty.

Georgen Guerrero is the Criminal Justice department coordinator and an associate professor at the University of the Incarnate Word, in San Antonio, Texas. He earned his Ph.D. in criminal justice with a specialization in criminology from Sam Houston State University and his master's in criminal justice from Texas State University. His areas of expertise include criminology, deviant behavior, penology, and ethics. Dr. Guerrero's research interests focus primarily on incarcerated populations, juvenile populations, and unethical practices by criminal justice practitioners, which have led to several publications in the areas of criminology, penology, and juvenile justice.

Frank Hall, Northwestern State University, Natchitoches, Louisiana, is an assistant professor in the Department of Criminal Justice, History, and Social Sciences at Northwestern State University. Frank is a recently retired military intelligence officer with 28 years of service in the U.S. Army.

Darrell A. Hamlin, Fort Hays State University, Hays, Kansas, is associate professor of criminal justice and a senior fellow at the Center for Civic Leadership at Fort Hays State University. As a writer, educator, consultant, and certified leadership coach, he has focused on expanded narratives of public life, cultural criminology, international criminal justice, and public policy issues related to criminal justice.

Jabril A. Hassen is a graduate student in criminal justice at Seattle University. His research interests are juvenile delinquency, community-based research, and ex-offender re-entry.

Silvina Ituarte is a professor in the Department of Criminal Justice at California State University East Bay. Her teaching and research interests focus on issues related to bias crimes, social justice, youth empowerment, restorative justice, and community-based programs. She earned her Ph.D. from Rutgers University. Before graduate school, she served as a victim specialist for the Victim Witness Program in California and later became an Alternatives to Violence Supervisor in Manhattan.

Michael J. Jenkins, University of Scranton, Pennsylvania, Ph.D., is an associate professor at the University of Scranton. He studies community problem-solving policing and broken windows policing. He's authored two books in these areas and is completing a third on international policing.

Allan Jiao, Rowan University Camden, New Jersey, is a professor of criminal justice and has engaged in research with many police organizations in the United States and abroad. He has published extensively on policing, policy analysis, and comparative criminal justice issues.

Brian Kinnaird, Bethany College, Lindsborg, Kansas, Ph.D., is a former law enforcement officer with the Ellis County Sheriff's Department, in Waxahachie, Texas, and currently serves as professor and department chair of criminal justice at Bethany College in Lindsborg, Kansas.

Jonathan Kremser, Kutztown University, Pennsylvania, is an associate professor at Kutztown University of Pennsylvania. He earned his Ph.D. in criminal justice at Rutgers University and his research focuses on school-related violence and security.

Kari Larsen is an associate professor at Saint Peter's University in Jersey City, New Jersey. She completed a J.D. at Fordham University School of Law, and an LL.M. at Seton Hall University School of Law. She has served as an assistant district attorney in Brooklyn, New York, and a municipal prosecutor in Rutherford, New Jersey.

Thomas Lateano, Kean University, New Jersey, is an associate professor in the Department of Criminal Justice at Kean University. His research has covered many topics including female sex offenders and Good Samaritan laws. His current research is focused on predictors of threats to state-level prosecutors. His research has been published in the *Justice System Journal*, *The Criminal Law Bulletin*, and *Teaching in Higher Education*. He teaches courses in criminal law, criminal procedure, constitutional theory, criminal evidence, and the American legal system.

Robert J. Louden, Georgian Court University, Lakewood, New Jersey, Ph.D. and professor emeritus of criminal justice at Georgian Court University, was a college-educated cop who morphed into a cop-educated academic. Following an active 21-year NYPD career, he retired as their chief hostage negotiator and went on to pursue full-time academic activities at John Jay College, in New York, and Georgian Court University, in Lakewood, New Jersey.

Tamara J. Lynn, Fort Hays State University, in Hays, Kansas, is an assistant professor in the Department of Criminal Justice at Fort Hays State University and holds a Ph.D. from Kansas State University. Dr. Lynn's areas of research include service-learning pedagogies, media framing of political protest, determinate sentencing structures, and perceptions of intimate personal violence.

Emily M. Malterud is a graduate student at Seattle University, in Washington, pursuing a degree in criminal justice research and evaluation, as well as a master's certificate in crime analysis. Her thesis will focus on working-memory capacity and the importance of varied types of testing for police recruits. She is an assistant researcher at the Washington State Criminal Justice Training Commission, measuring the effectiveness of the LEED model of police training, which focuses on the inclusion of Crisis Intervention Training (CIT) and Blue Courage.

Elizabeth W. Marchioni, Wesley College, Delaware, J.D., is an associate professor of law and justice studies at Wesley College in Dover, Delaware.

David A. Marvelli, Federal Bureau of Investigation, Washington, D.C., is a supervisory intelligence analyst for the FBI and an adjunct professor for the University of Mary Washington and the National Intelligence University where he teaches courses on transnational crime and national security policy. He received his Ph.D. from Rutgers University.

Sanjay Marwah, California State University, East Bay, CA, is assistant professor of criminal justice administration at California State University East Bay. With 20-plus years of teaching and research experience in environmental policy, sociology, public policy, and criminology, his current interests include democratization of policing, cultural political economy, and metropolitan crime.

Jospeter Mbuba is an associate professor of criminal justice at Indiana-Purdue University at Fort Wayne. He conducts research on police and law enforcement by reviewing the patterns and trends in arrests, examining the race factor for both the suspect and the police, exploring the attitudes toward the police, and projecting the gender role in crime causation and arrest.

Philip D. McCormack, Fitchburg State University, Massachusetts, is an assistant professor of criminal justice at Fitchburg State University. Dr. McCormack's research spans the spectrum of criminology and sociology, with a focus on utilizing a variety of quantitative applications.

Rochelle McGee-Cobbs, Mississippi Valley State University, Ph.D., is an assistant professor and undergraduate coordinator in the Department of Criminal Justice, Mississippi Valley State University. Dr. McGee-Cobbs's research agenda largely focuses on risk assessment, police and citizen encounters, juvenile justice issues, victimization, and police issues such as use of force, search, and seizure.

Melanie Clark Mogavero is an assistant professor of criminal justice at Georgian Court University. Her research interests include sexual offenders, sex offender policy, autism spectrum disorder, and sexual deviance.

Sherill Morris-Francis, Mississippi Valley State University, received her Ph.D. in Juvenile Justice from the Prairie View A&M University, in Texas, in 2009. She is currently an assistant professor and graduate coordinator in the Department of Criminal Justice at Mississippi Valley State University and former assistant dean of the College of Juvenile Justice and Psychology at Prairie View A&M University. Her research includes program implementation and assessment, minorities and the juvenile justice system, school factors and delinquency, juvenile mental health issues, female juveniles, and restorative and community justice.

Ifeoma E. Okoye is an adjunct professor in the Department of Administration of Justice, Texas Southern University, in Houston. She has interdisciplinary training in law, business administration, social sciences, and administration of justice. Her research interests include homeland security, terrorism and counterterrorism, policing, community policy, restorative justice, research methods, juvenile justice, legal aspects of criminal justice, human rights, and crime.

Brian E. Oliver is an independent researcher and consultant with Brian Oliver Consulting, in Connecticut. His research interests include policing, prisoner re-entry, and crime prevention.

Jennifer M. Ortiz is an assistant professor of criminology at Indiana University Southeast. She earned her doctorate from John Jay College of Criminal Justice.

Bruce Peabody, Fairleigh Dickinson University, Teaneck, New Jersey, is a professor of political science at Fairleigh Dickinson University in Madison, New Jersey. He conducts research on constitutional law and theory and is the editor and author of *The Politics of Judicial Independence: Courts, Politics, and the Public* (Johns Hopkins University Press, 2010) and the co-author of *Where Have All the Heroes Gone: Changing Conceptions of American Valor* (Oxford University Press 2017).

Emmanuel Pierre-Louis, M.S., is an adjunct professor in the Department of Criminal Justice at New Jersey City University and CUNY-Kingsborough Community College. He is pursuing a doctorate of science in civil security, leadership, management and policy. His research interests are theoretical criminology, race and crime, mass incarceration, and national security.

Doshie Piper, Ph.D., is an assistant professor of criminal justice at the University of the Incarnate Word. Her research has primarily focused on gender and violence, and theoretical applications of gendered violence. She has worked with the Nehemiah Community Re-Entry Project, a faith-based collaboration of networks to measure the effectiveness of faith-based re-entry providers, as a recovery support services. Her commitment to the teacher-scholar model has allowed her to build service-learning partnerships and internships with other academic departments, disciplines, and community agencies.

John Raacke is chair and associate professor of criminal justice at Fort Hays State University, in Hays, Kansas.

Marny Requa is an associate professor and director of the graduate program in the Department of Criminal Justice, Anthropology, and Sociology at Georgian Court University.

Donald Roth, Dordt College, Sioux Center, Iowa, is the chair of the Criminal Justice Department at Dordt College in Sioux Center, Iowa. He holds a J.D. and an LL.M. in taxation from Georgetown University Law Center.

Brian L. Royster, Saint Peter's University, Jersey City, New Jersey, is an assistant professor in the Criminal Justice department. He retired from the New Jersey State Police after 25 years of service. He is a graduate of the FBI National Academy 214th Session and former member the FBI Joint Terrorism Task Force (JTTF).

Tim Sandle is a chartered biologist with more than 25 years of experience in microbiological research and biopharmaceutical processing. He is head of microbiology at Bio Products Laboratory and a visiting tutor at the University of Manchester in the United Kingdom.

Miriam D. Sealock is a professor in the Department of Sociology, Anthropology, and Criminal Justice at Towson University in Maryland. Her research focuses primarily on criminology theory and decision-making within the criminal justice system and includes published work on the subjects of police discretion, general strain theory, and the prevention and treatment of juvenile delinquency and drug use.

Cathie Perselay Seidman is a professor of Criminal Justice at Hudson County Community College, Jersey City, New Jersey, and the coordinator of the Criminal Justice Program. She received her M.A. in Criminal Justice from the School of Criminal Justice, Rutgers University, and her J.D. from the Benjamin N. Cardozo School of Law, Yeshiva University.

John Sember is a second-year undergraduate criminal justice student at the University of Scranton Pennsylvania. His hometown is Sparta, New Jersey.

Raj Sethuraju is assistant professor in the School of Law Enforcement and Criminal Justice at Metropolitan State University. He teaches research methods, diversity matters in law enforcement and criminal justice, victimology, citizenship, comparative criminal justice, and community engagement. His research includes race relations, drug courts, restorative justice, and diversion programs. His most recent article is "The Consequences of Teaching Critical Sociology on Course Evaluations: Multiple Perspectives on the Nature of Black and Latino/a Intergroup Relations and Speaking Truth to Power" (in *The Spirit of Service: Exploring Faith, Service, and Social Justice in Higher Education*). He earned his Ph.D. in Sociology at Texas Woman's University and his M.A. in counseling at the University of Monroe, Louisiana.

Matthew J. Sheridan is an instructor of Criminal Justice and the director of the CJ Internship Program at Georgian Court University, Lakewood, New Jersey. He is also the author of *Exploring and Understanding Careers in Criminal Justice* (2016) He retired after a career in corrections and juvenile justice with the State of New Jersey.

Francesca Spina, Ph.D., is an assistant professor in the Social Sciences department and the coordinator of the Criminal Justice Program at Springfield College. Dr. Spina is also an adjunct faculty member in the Division of Online and Continuing

Education at the University of Massachusetts Lowell. She earned a Ph.D. in Criminal Justice and Criminology from the University of Massachusetts Lowell and a B.A. in Economics from Trinity College. Her research interests include race and justice, environmental justice, ex-offender rehabilitation and re-entry, and criminal justice policy reform. She is currently working on a book entitled *Massachusetts's Criminal Justice System*.

Harry Toder is assistant professor of criminal justice and criminology at Lincoln Memorial University, in Harrogate, Tennessee. He takes a broad view of criminal justice, focusing upon how justice professionals can make an impact upon society as a whole. In addition to teaching, he has contributed to the popular media, in the form of numerous newspaper opinion pieces, in addition to doing academic research.

Index